LABOUR MOBILITY, EARNINGS AND UNEMPLOYMENT

Labour Mobility, Earnings and Unemployment

Selected Papers

John Creedy

The Truby Williams Professor of Economics, University of Melbourne, Australia

Edward Elgar

Cheltenham, UK • Northampton, MA, USA

Published by
Edward Elgar Publishing Limited
Glensanda House
Montpellier Parade
Cheltenham
Glos GL50 1UA
UK

Edward Elgar Publishing, Inc.
136 West Street
Suite 202
Northampton
Massachusetts 01060
USA

A catalogue record for this book is available from the British Library

Library of Congress Cataloguing in Publication Data

Creedy, John, 1949–
    Labour mobility, earnings and unemployment : selected papers /
John Creedy.
    Includes bibliographical references.
    1. Labor mobility.   2. Wages — Effect of labor mobility on.
3. Wages — Skilled labor.   4. Trade-unions.   5. Unemployment.
I. Title.
HD5717.C74   1999
331.12′7 — dc21

99–21906
CIP

ISBN 1 84064 137 1
Printed and bound in Great Britain by MPG Books Ltd, Bodmin, Cornwall

Contents

v

PART III   TRADE UNIONS AND WAGES

Acknowledgements

The publishers wish to thank the following who have kindly given permission for the use of copyright material.

Australian Bulletin of Labour for article: 'Migration and Population Ageing in Australia', with J. Alvarado, *Australian Bulletin of Labour*, **21** (1), 1995, 32–47.

Australian Journal of Labour Economics for article: 'The Choice of Early Retirement Age and the Australian Superannuation System', with M.E. Atkinson, *Australian Journal of Labour Economics*, **1** (1), March 1997, 1–23.

Australian National University for articles: 'A Tax Package to Reduce the Marginal Rate of Income Tax and the Wage Demands of Trade Unions', with I.M. McDonald, *Economic Record*, **66**, September 1990, 195–202; 'Models of Trade Union Behaviour: A Synthesis', with I.M. McDonald, *Economic Record*, **67**, December 1991, 346–59.

Blackwell Publishers Ltd for articles: 'Variations in Earnings and Responsibility', *Journal of the Royal Statistical Society (series A)*, **150** (1), 1987, 57–68; 'The Economic Analysis of Internal Labour Markets', with K. Whitfield, *Bulletin of Economic Research*, **40** (4), 1988, 247–69; 'Union Wage Responses to a Shift from Direct to Indirect Taxation', with I.M. McDonald, *Bulletin of Economic Research*, **44** (3), 1992, 221–32.

Economic Analysis and Policy for article: 'Can Tax Cuts Increase Investment in a Unionised Economy?', with I.M. McDonald, *Economic Analysis and Policy*, **23** (2), September 1993, 123–37.

Flinders University of South Australia for article: 'Income Tax Changes and Trade Union Wage Demands', with I.M. McDonald, *Australian Economic Papers*, **31**, June 1992, 47–57.

Institute For Fiscal Studies for article: 'Trade Unions, Wages and Taxation', with I.M. McDonald, *Fiscal Studies*, **10** (3), 1989, 50–59.

Journal of Industrial Relations for articles: 'Job Mobility and Earnings: An Internal Labour Market Analysis', with K. Whitfield, *Journal of Industrial Relations*, **1**, March 1988, 100–117; 'Opening the Black Box: Economic Analyses of Internal Labour Markets', with K. Whitfield, *Journal of Industrial Relations*, **3**, September 1992, 455–71.

Labour Economics and Productivity for article: 'Changes in the Responsibility and Earnings of Professional Scientists', *Labour Economics and Productivity*, **4**, 1992, 114–29.

MCB University Press Ltd for articles: 'Earnings and Job Mobility: Professional Chemists in Britain', with K. Whitfield, *Journal of Economic Studies*, **13** (2), 1989, 23–37; 'Flattening the Tax Rate Structure, Changing the Tax Mix and Unions' Wage Demands', *Journal of Economic Studies*, **17** (1), 1990, 5–15.

Oxford University Press for articles: 'Eligibility for Unemployment Benefits in Great Britain', with R. Disney, *Oxford Economic Papers*, **33** (2), 1981, 256–73; 'A Note on the Analysis of Trade Unions and Relative Wages', *Oxford Bulletin of Economics and Statistics*, **31** (2), 1979, 235–8.

Routledge for article: 'Firm Formation in Manufacturing Industry', with P.S. Johnson, *Applied Economics*, **15** (2), 1983, 177–85.

Scottish Journal of Political Economy for articles: 'Inter-regional Mobility: A Cross-section Analysis', *Scottish Journal of Political Economy*, **21** (1), February 1974, 41–53; 'Changes in Labour Market States in Great Britain', with R. Disney, *Scottish Journal of Political Economy*, **28** (1), February 1981, 76–85.

Preface

This volume reproduces 22 papers in the general area of labour economics, written mainly during the 1980s and early 1990s. They are arranged in chronological order under three main headings. Part I contains a 'mixed bag' of papers relating to labour mobility; Part II contains papers on skilled labour markets which make use of several special surveys of career histories of professional scientists; Part III is concerned with the analysis of trade unions.

I should like to thank the many anonymous journal referees whose comments and suggestions have helped to improve the papers. I should especially like to take this opportunity to acknowledge the colleagues involved in producing these papers. Indeed, two-thirds of the papers were written with joint authors. In particular, just three people were involved with about 55 per cent of the papers; these are (in Part order) Richard Disney, Keith Whitfield and Ian McDonald. I have benefited considerably from these collaborations.

My greatest debt is to Kath, who made too many sacrifices without complaint.

PART I

MOBILITY IN
LABOUR MARKETS

INTER-REGIONAL MOBILITY:
A CROSS-SECTION ANALYSIS

JOHN CREEDY*

I

INTRODUCTION

The purpose of this paper is to consider the extent to which the inter-regional mobility of labour can be explained in terms of economic incentives. A characteristic of much of the recent empirical work on migration is the use of some function of relative unemployment percentages as the independent variable, within the context of linear least squares regression models. The dependent variable is usually taken as gross inward or outward flows between one region and the rest of the country during each year. Although an unemployed person in a ' high employment ' region may in fact move to, and obtain a job in, a high unemployment area (depending on his particular skills, etc.)—such models would seem to imply that movement would be predominantly in only one direction. This will be particularly important when applied to each pair of regions in turn rather than to a gross figure.

Movement from low to high unemployment regions can be explained more easily, however, by incentives provided by higher wages to those who are already employed. Indeed the desirability of information showing whether the employed or the unemployed are the most mobile has often been pointed out (Oliver, 1964; Hart, 1972, p. 154)—though of course this remains unknown because of the lamentable lack of data. The present model, however, takes as its starting point the proposition that the employed and the unemployed have essentially different motives for moving—so that although the available data does not distinguish between the two categories it is important to do so in the model building stage. This is therefore a fairly short run model in the sense that an unemployed person is assumed to be mainly interested in finding a job, while an employed person (who must have a job to move to in the region of destination) is looking for an increase in his income. Within a more general framework (though the job of the econometrician is to test more and more specific and restrictive hypotheses) a person may be assumed to evaluate the prospects of being unemployed in the future along with frequency and duration), as well as the opportunities for increasing his income. Where such probabilities would be used as weights in calculating the present value of future income, the strict dichotomy used

* I would like to thank my colleagues at Durham for very helpful discussions at all stages in the preparation of this paper, and R. A. Hart for comments on an earlier version.

here would of course break down—though it certainly seems useful to
investigate the appropriateness of this simplifying assumption.

Not only does the model presented below provide a simple rationale for
the movement of labour into areas where unemployment is higher than in
the region of origin, but a more detailed specification allows for the effect
of income differentials. In contrast to many previous investigations the following presents very strong support for Hick's argument (1963, p. 76) that
wage differences have a significant influence on labour mobility, while the
process of equalization works very slowly. In this context Jack (1970, p. 15)
has argued forcibly that, '. . . it may be questioned whether regional differences
in earnings can validly explain short term variations in migration', and their
influence, '. . . is best represented by a constant term . . .' in a linear regression model. It is suggested here, however, that the relative neglect of (and
small support for) income differentials arises from a simple and inappropriate comparison between average earnings in two different regions. The
implication that there is such a simple functional relationship between the
volume of migration and differences in average earnings is considered to be
the major reason for the ' poor performance ' of such a variable in regression
models.

The necessity to consider the complete distribution is clear once it is
realised that a person may obtain an increase by moving from a low decile in
the distribution of income in his region of origin to a higher decile in that of
another region—even though mean income in the latter may be lower than
that in the former. This also has implications for current theories of inflation
framed in terms of ' dynamic market interdependence ', and where regions
with high relative earnings are assumed to influence the pace of wage increases in other regions because of the threatened or realised (unidirectional)
migration.

It should be mentioned that the model does not consider the extent to
which regional moves involve a change in industry or the type of occupation,[1]
nor the problem of new entrants into, or exits from, the labour force.[2]
Furthermore it does not explicitly analyse movements as part of an equilibra-
ting process since it is not formulated in terms of labour supply and demand
functions—though the results have important implications for this problem.

II

The Accounting Framework

The relations between the main aggregates can be set out as follows. Let:—

p_i = labour force in region i at the beginning of the period

e_i = proportion of p_i employed at the beginning of the period

[1] Secular change in industrial composition due to different income elasticities of
demand, technological change, etc.

[2] There is a further complication in that some new entrants will come from
migrant families. Evidence shows that many migrants are young people about to enter
the labour force, and therefore at their most mobile.

m_{ij} = number moving from region i to region j during the period
α_{ij} = proportion of employed in i moving to j during the period
β_{ij} = proportion of the unemployed in i moving to j during the period.

It is argued here that any study of regional mobility should take the α_{ij} and β_{ij} as dependent variables, though the appropriate data is not available. Most previous models have, however, considered total ' in ' and ' out ' movements. Using the above definitions these can be expressed as :—

$$\text{Number leaving } i \text{ during the period } = p_i e_i\left(\sum_j \alpha_{ij} + \frac{u_i}{e_i}\sum_j \beta_{ij}\right)$$

$$\text{Number entering } i \text{ during the period } = \sum_j e_j p_j\left(\alpha_{ji} + \frac{u_i}{e_j}\beta_{ji}\right)$$

where $u_i = 1 - e_i$ = the proportion of p_i who are unemployed. A much more convenient expression is obtained using the fact that (m_{ij}/p_i), the proportion of i's labour force moving into j in the period, is a weighted average of the α_{ij} and the β_{ij}. Thus :

$$\frac{m_{ij}}{p_i} = e_i\alpha_{ij} + u_i\beta_{ij} \tag{1}$$

which is the basic equation of the model. The matrix $M = \{m_{ij}\}$ obviously has the property that the sum of the column sums is equal to that of the row sums ($i'Mi = i'M'i$; where i is a vector of the appropriate dimension whose elements are all equal to unity). A more disaggregated analysis would prefer to apply equation (*1*) to homogeneous groups; for example households in the same stage of the life-cycle, those in the same occupation etc., since demographic factors would be expected to play an important part in the decision to move. If a household is comprised of several ' employees ' any movement may, as Pigou (1952, p. 505) has indicated, ' . . . carry with it a large loss by cutting off the wages they have hitherto been able to earn. This loss is really a part of the cost of movement of the member of the family who is tempted by higher wages to move elsewhere.' Children of school age, and the difficulty of finding new accommodation (especially for council house tenants) also impose very strong constraints on mobility. If equation (1) is used for all households (or individuals) then the parameters α_{ij} and β_{ij} should strictly be regarded as resulting from a very complicated process of aggregation over the multivariate distribution of the characteristics mentioned above. This is, of course, a very common problem in applied econometric work, where one must ultimately appeal (with the present data limitations) to the relative stability of these distributions.

The above provide only the accounting identities, to which empirical content must be given by the specification presented below.

III

SPECIFICATION OF THE MODEL

Consider first the determination of the α_{ij}'s. Suppose the probability that an employed person in region i (who could find a job to move to in region j) will migrate to j during the period is given by:

$$\text{prob}\,(x_j/x_i \geqslant k)$$

which is the probability that the ratio x_j/x_i exceeds the 'threshold' level of income increase, k, which is required to induce the person to move. If x_j and x_i denote the prospective incomes which could be earned by moving to j or remaining in i respectively, then the percentage increase required (expressed as $(x_j - x_i)/x_i$) is equal to $k-1$. The values of x_j and x_i are not, of course, directly observable (though one's expectation of x_i may perhaps be held with rather more confidence than that of x_j)—so the approach adopted here is to regard the actual distribution in each region as the basis from which expectations are formed.

A more dynamic approach may regard the potential mover as a utility maximiser who considers discounted net benefits which would accrue as a result of the move. Indeed, as Pigou (1945, p. 35) has again pointed out when discussing the 'actuarial attractiveness' of different regions, 'The elements really relevant to choice are future wage rates and future chances of employment, while the only elements that can be known are past and present wage rates and unemployment percentages.'

Such a long-run approach would, however, require the construction of a more sophisticated 'expectations' model, the testing of which would involve detailed knowledge not only of the demographic characteristics of the migrants but also of age-income profiles for each region, relative frequency of unemployment by age group etc. The suggestion (very popular in many fields) that the simple addition of lagged variables or use of distributed lags (on aggregate values) adds an element of 'dynamism' is rejected here in favour of a more simple specification which can be given a meaningful interpretation.

If k is then assumed to be constant over all individuals,[3] then the proportion of the unemployed in i (who could find jobs in j) who would move to j during the period is given by:

$$\int_k^\infty dF(x_j/x_i) \tag{2}$$

where $F(x_j/x_i)$ denotes the distribution function of the ratio x_j/x_i.

This formulation assumes, of course, that people move in an attempt to increase their income and are not concerned with their position in the distribution. Some people may in fact attach utility to being in the higher

---

[3] It is of course possible to allow for k to be distributed among individuals (as, for example, in probit analysis), but a more simple approach was preferred at this stage.

deciles of their 'local' distribution, and would not be particularly attracted by a move to the lower deciles of another distribution, even though their earnings may actually be increased.

The problem therefore arises of choosing a specific functional form for F. Now the strongest candidate for the distribution of incomes (at any level of aggregation), both from the point of view of its ability to graduate the observed data and its tractability when included in larger models of economic behaviour, is considered to be the lognormal distribution.[4] Thus if income in the ith region is lognormally distributed as

$$\Lambda(x_i|\mu_i, \sigma_i^2), \text{ where } \mu_i \text{ and } \sigma_i^2$$

are the location and variance parameters respectively then:

$$f(x_i) = \frac{1}{\sigma_i x_i \sqrt{2\pi}} \exp\left\{-\frac{1}{2\sigma_i^2}(\log x_i - \mu_i)^2\right\} ; x_i > 0$$

Now $\log(x_j/x_i)$ is distributed as

$$N(\log x_j|\mu_j, \sigma_j^2) - N(\log x_i|\mu_i, \sigma_i^2)$$

so that the ratio (x_j/x_i) is distributed as:

$$\Lambda(x_j/x_i|\mu_j - \mu_i, \sigma_j^2 + \sigma_i^2) \tag{3}$$

where x_j and x_i are uncorrelated. There is a difficulty here in that there is an important sense in which x_j and x_i are correlated, since for any individual they are both 'expected' values. This would require a term $2\rho\sigma_j\sigma_i$ to be subtracted from the variance parameter, where ρ is the correlation coefficient between $\log x_j$ and $\log x_i$; though of course no data is available and experiments using various *a priori* values for ρ did not significantly improve the empirical results. Nevertheless this could be merely a consequence of the high level of aggregation used here (all occupations and age groups are combined), and the fact that the contemporaneous distribution is used as proxy for income prospects over a longer period of time in the future. Making the appropriate substitution for F, equation (2) then becomes:

$$\int_k^\infty d\Lambda\left(\frac{x_j}{x_i}|\mu_j - \mu_i, \sigma_j^2 + \sigma_i^2\right)$$
$$= 1 - \Lambda(k)_{ij} \quad \text{say,} \tag{4}$$

where by definition:

$$\Lambda(k)_{ij} = N\left\{\frac{\log k - \mu_j + \mu_i}{\sqrt{\alpha_j^2 + \alpha_i^2}}|0, 1\right\} \tag{5}$$

A very strict hypothesis, which is not of course necessary to the approach, is that k is constant over all (i, j) as well as over all individuals in each region. Alternatively, k could be assumed to depend on a function of geo-

---

[4] The standard work on this is Aitchison, J. and Brown, J. A. C. (1957). But see also Aitchison & Brown (1954).

graphical distance or the difference between house prices in the two regions
—though the above simplified version is retained for the time being.

To complete the specification of the α_{ij}'s suppose that the proportion of
the employed in region i who could find work in j during the period is
given by:

$$b(v_j/p_i e_i) \qquad (6)$$

where b is constant and v_j is equal to the number of vacancies in j at the
beginning of the period. This implicitly assumes that people in all regions
compete for a job in j on an equal basis, this being absorbed into the
constant b. The chances of finding a job are also assumed to be independent
of income, although there is an obvious difficulty here since income will be
a function of occupation and age—both of which will influence the probability of obtaining employment in another region.

Equations (4) and (6) can be combined to give:

$$\alpha_{ij} = b\{1 - \Lambda(k)_{ij}\}v_j/p_i e_i \qquad (7)$$

A particular problem concerning the income comparisons which may arise
by the combination of all age groups is that some older workers will actually
anticipate a reduction in income whichever region they live in. For some
age groups k may therefore be less than unity—though discounted future
income may still be larger in the region of destination. This may perhaps
be mitigated to some extent because of the fact that the age distribution of
migrants is positively skewed with most people in the younger age groups.

Furthermore, it is considered not too unreasonable to assume that the
income distributions (specifically the characteristics of the dynamics of
income change) remain fairly stable through time, along with industrial
structure and other demographic and socio-economic characteristics of the
regions.

Dynamic considerations may also be thought to apply to the movement
of the unemployed. The length of time a person has been unemployed, the
different rates of change of unemployment; combined with the length of time
a region has been, and is expected to remain, depressed are all factors which
are relevant where the decision to migrate is concerned.

Although an employed person is considered a potential migrant only if
he can move to another job in the region of destination, an unemployed
person may be thought to move only if his estimate of his 'chances' of
finding a job in another region are higher than those of finding one by not
moving. Furthermore one would perhaps be expected to make some kind
of 'estimate' of the time taken to find a job in each region—in order to
evaluate the opportunity costs of 'waiting' in any particular region.

While the framework used here would allow the use of more sophisticated specifications for the β_{ij}, the approach adopted at this stage—based
partly on previous results of other investigators—was simply to regard
unemployment percentages as proxies for the relative 'unemployment prospects'. Thus it is implicitly assumed that people have (more or less imper-

fect) information about present unemployment rates (or factors governing job prospects which are reflected in these rates), on which their expectations are based. So far as the formation of these expectations is concerned, such rates are considered to be the major determining factors. Again this implicitly requires an assumption that such 'relative prospects' remain fairly stable—that the variations across regions are significantly larger than variations over time within the regions. ('Participation' rates do show less inter-regional variation than unemployment rates, of course). Other factors which may influence expectations must also be assumed to exhibit temporal stability.

The problem is therefore one of choosing an appropriate functional form for the β_{ij}, and in this case more attention was paid to the shape of the function rather than the theoretical restrictions (for example, that $0 \leq \beta_{ij} \leq 1$) imposed on it. This was done partly in order to avoid considerably more non-linearities in the model. (The data would probably not discriminate too well anyway.)

Various alternative forms chosen for the β_{ij} are given by:

$$
\begin{aligned}
&\text{(i)} && \beta_{ij} = c \log (u_j/u_i) && c - ve \\
&\text{(ii)} && \beta_{ij} = c \log (u_j) && c - ve \\
&\text{(iii)} && \beta_{ij} = c/u_j && c + ve \\
&\text{(iv)} && \beta_{ij} = c/\log (u_j) && c - ve
\end{aligned}
$$

These are formulations which have been found to give reasonably successful results by previous authors in this field. Equations (ii) to (iv) imply that an unemployed person in i is attracted by low values of u_j irrespective of unemployment in his region of origin (which he contemplates leaving anyway).

IV

ESTIMATION AND RESULTS

With the additional assumption that all parameters are constant over all pairs (i, j)[5] the statistical problem is therefore to estimate k, c and b given cross-section data on the matrix M and the vectors

$$\{p_i\} \{v_i\}, \{e_i\}, \{\mu_i\} \{\sigma_i^2\}$$

Although a 'time series of cross-sections' would be ideal for this situation, so far only the 1965–66 matrix M is available from the sample census

[5] Any difference in the coefficients between regions would be due to differences in the willingness of people to move to, or leave a particular region for reasons which are not included in the specification of the model. Stability of coefficients over (different pairs of) regions is considered to be a desirable property of any model which captures the main aspects of the process.

of 1966[6]—and unfortunately the regional classification used was changed in January 1966. This meant that the p_i, v_i and e_i's could be obtained for the beginning of the appropriate period—though the error involved should not be too drastic since (as argued above) the relative values remain fairly stable. The values of μ_i and σ_i^2 were obtained[7] from the first and ninth deciles and the quartiles of the regional income distributions given in the Family Expenditure Survey (1966). Scotland, Wales and Northern Ireland were excluded from the analysis.

Other data was obtained from the Department of Employment and Productivity Gazette (January 1966) and the Historical Abstract of Labour Statistics (1971).

Now consider the case where $\beta_{ij}=c \log (u_j)$, for example, then substituting for α_{ij} and β_{ij} in equation (*1*) above to form:

$$\frac{m_{ij}}{p_i} = bx_{ij}+cu_i \log (u_j)$$

where x_{ij} is defined by:

$$x_{ij} = (v_j/p_i)\{1-\Lambda(k)_{ij}\}$$

so that with N regions in all there are $N(N-1)$ observations (since the diagonal of M is not defined) which can be re-arranged into the more convenient form:

$$y_t = bz_t+cs_t \qquad (t = 1, \ldots, N(N-1)) \tag{8}$$

where:
$$\left.\begin{array}{l} y_t = m_{ij}/p_i \\[4pt] z_t = x_{ij} \\[4pt] s_t = u_i \log (u_j) \end{array}\right\} \begin{array}{l} \text{for} \quad (i, j = 1, \ldots, N; i \neq j) \\[10pt] (t = 1, \ldots, N(N-1)) \end{array}$$

Thus, by assuming a particular initial value for k the $N(N-1)$ values of z_t could be calculated (using a polynomial approximation for the lognormal integral)—from which b and c could be found using ordinary least squares[8] on equation (*8*). Starting with an initial value for k of unity this procedure was repeated for variations in k—the values chosen being those which gave the best fit (as measured by standard errors and R^2). It should again be stressed that the two parts of the model (specification of α_{ij}'s and β_{ij}'s) cannot be tested independently due to data limitations, though hopefully this may be possible in the future.

---

[6] Regional abstract of statistics 1971, p. 10 tables for males and females. A migrant is defined as one where region of residence at April 1966 was different from that at April 1965. This includes people who move more than once a year. Furthermore, some of these moves will be purely 'statistical' in that they may only have moved a few miles across a regional boundary without changing jobs. The extent of these 'moves' will depend on the length of the boundary connecting two regions.

[7] Using the method of quantiles. See Aitchison & Brown, op. cit., p. 40.

[8] It would, of course, be possible to use a non-linear method of estimation which would allow confidence intervals for k to be obtained.

The above procedure was used with data relating to adult males only and to both males and females. Again, the level of aggregation which is demanded by the available data is unfortunate. Some results for males only (Table I) and both males and females (Table II) are given below; and considering all the problems alluded to above the model does seem to fit surprisingly well and suggests that it does capture some of the main aspects of the process.

Table I

MALES ONLY

Form for β_{ij}	b	c	R^2
(i)	0·100	−0·0039	0·42
	(0·0097)	(0·0289)	
(ii)	0·0812	−0·0183	0·61
	(0·0083)	(0·0035)	
(iii)	0·0799	+0·00084	0·58
	(0.0089)	(0·00018)	
(iv)	0·0838	−0·3440	0·62
	(0·0081)	(0·0657)	

Table II

MALES AND FEMALES

Form for β_{ij}	b	c	R^2
(i)	0·1067	−0·0441	0·45
	(0·0100)	(0·0472)	
(ii)	0·0906	−0·0331	0·66
	(0·0083)	(0·0057)	
(iii)	0·090	+0·0013	0·64
	(0·0087)	(0·00024)	
(iv)	0·0928	−0·6948	0·66
	(0·0082)	(0·1197)	

Note: For all the above equations $k = 1·05$. Standard errors are given in parentheses immediately underneath parameter estimates.

Although the model seems to provide a slightly better fit for males and females combined (at least as measured by R^2) the most notable point is that for every case the value of k which gave the best fit was 1·05. This, of course, implies that a 5 per cent. income increase is required to induce an employed worker to move to another region. Furthermore, the coefficient of x_{ij} is highly significant, and roughly the same, for every case. (About 0·09 for males and females and 0·08 for males only.)

The coefficient c, is also significant in nearly every case (the exception being equation (i))—and always has the correct sign.

On the further assumption that the parameters remain stable over time it would, of course, be possible to obtain predictions for the transition matrix $\{m_{ij}\}$ given suitable values of population, wages and unemployment in each region at any time.

By contrast the extreme case where only employed people move can be examined by setting $\beta_{ij} = 0$ for all (ij). This, in fact, did not change the values of k and b, the latter remaining highly significant and the overall fit (measured by R^2) very good. These results were also compared with those obtained from very simple formulations which excluded the effect of income differentials, and in this case (although the comparison is not entirely fair) the results were very poor.[9]

All these results therefore provide strong support for the proposition that income differences, operating with a threshold effect, are an important factor influencing the inter-regional mobility of labour.

The point (mentioned above) that movement of the unemployed would be expected to be predominantly in one direction (from high to low unemployment areas) was also considered further. Although some moves would of course take place (due to heterogeneity of the labour supply and industrial composition)—the more restrictive hypothesis that β_{ij} is zero if u_j is greater than or equal to u_i can be tested simply by taking this into account when forming the $N(N-1)$ vector $\{s_j\}$ in equation (8). The elements of s for which $u_i > u_j$ are obtained using the appropriate specification, while all others (where $u_j \geqslant u_i$) are set equal to zero.

Results obtained for such one way movement of the unemployed (only the employed migrate to regions with higher unemployment rates) are given in Tables III and IV below.

Table III

MALES ONLY

Form for β_{ij}	b	c	R^2
(i)	0·0940	−0·0575	0·45
	(0·0097)	(0·0315)	
(ii)	0·088	−0·0136	0·50
	(0·0096)	(0·0046)	
(iii)	0·0869	+0·0006	0·49
	(0·0099)	(0·0002)	
(iv)	0·089	−0·271	0·50
	(0·0096)	(0·0920)	

As expected the absolute value of c is slightly reduced in every case, and although they remain significant (except for (i) in males only) the t values also fall. Again the models seem to fit marginally better for males and females combined than for males only—though the important fact remains that the value of b remains unchanged and highly significant. Furthermore the threshold income increase required remains at 5 per cent. for every case.

---

[9] In fact the best result was:

$$y_{ij} = 0·00216 + 0·00098 \, u_i/u_j \qquad R^2 = 0·034$$
$$\phantom{y_{ij} = }(0·00097) \ (0·00071)$$

INTER-REGIONAL MOBILITY: A CROSS-SECTION ANALYSIS 51

Table IV

MALES AND FEMALES

Form for β_{ij}	b	c	R^2
(i)	0·102	−0·123	0·51
	(0·0097)	(0·0497)	
(ii)	0·0958	−0·0266	0·56
	(0·0095)	(0·0073)	
(iii)	0·095	+0·0010	0·56
	(0·0096)	(0·00028)	
(iv)	0·0970	−0·5880	0·56
	(0·0094)	(0·1650)	

Results for 'one-way' movement of unemployed.

Note: The values of k for all the above cases is equal to 1·05. Standard errors are given in parentheses immediately underneath parameter estimates.

V

SOME FURTHER IMPLICATIONS

It may be useful at this stage to indicate an interesting implication of another aspect of the above approach; that of considering the complete transition matrix rather than simply the inward and outward or net movements. This is really a question of aggregation (at a rather different level from that mentioned above)—though it is considered to be an important point to keep in mind when examining previous work on this topic.

Consider, for example, the form $\beta_{ij} = c \log (u_j)$ which gives reasonably good results (Tables I and II above). Substitute for α_{ij} and β_{ij} in the appropriate expressions to obtain the following forms for gross 'in' and 'out' movements from region i.

$$\text{'outs'} = b \sum_{j \neq i} v_j \{1 - \Lambda(k)_{ij}\} + c p_i u_i \sum_{j \neq i} \log (u_j)$$

$$\text{'ins'} = b v_i \sum_{j \neq 1} \{1 - \Lambda(k)_{ji}\} + c \log (u_i) \sum_{j \neq i} p_j u_j$$

Now the geometric mean, G of unemployment rates in all other regions is given by:

$$\log (G) = \frac{1}{N-1} \sum_{j \neq i} \log (u_j)$$

and the unemployment rate in the rest of the country by:

$$U = \sum_{j \neq i} p_j u_j / \sum_{j \neq i} p_j$$

So that 'outs' are a function of the geometric mean of unemployment rates in all other regions; while 'ins' are a function of the unemployment rate in the rest of the country combined. Furthermore these results do not depend on the specific form chosen for β_{ij}, since in this framework the number entering the region will always depend on the unemployment rate in the rest of the country (and the population). The number leaving will depend on (the population of region i and) some function of the unemployment rates in the other regions—in this particular case the geometric mean.

This should be contrasted with other work where both 'in' and 'out' movements are regarded as functions of relative unemployment rates in the particular region and in the rest of the country. Using the same function for migration in both directions the only difference expected is that the regression coefficient should be negative in one, and positive in the other equation; though as the above shows this is clearly inappropriate.

The same kind of argument can also be extended to the case of net migration, since

$$\sum_{j \neq i} (m_{ij} - m_{ji})$$

will not be a simple function of relative unemployment rates. This also indicates that it would not be appropriate merely to add lagged values as extra explanatory variables, and to claim that this would be a 'dynamic' formulation.

It should also be noted that if time series data are used in regressions of total in and out movements for each region (which has often been the case) then the restriction $i'Mi = i'M'i$ (mentioned earlier) should really be imposed on the estimates. This problem does not, of course, arise here.

VI

Conclusions

The empirical results presented above, although obtained using a highly simplified model, are considered to be reasonably encouraging and at least suggestive for future research. In particular it demonstrates the usefulness of an appropriate 'accounting framework' which allows for the simple statement that the employed and the unemployed usually have different motives for moving. Furthermore, by using the complete distribution of income—rather than a simple comparison of average earnings in each region —strong support has been found for the influence of income differences as an incentive to migrate. This incentive is also seen to operate only after a 'threshold' level of increase is attained.

The results are sufficiently good to suggest that the application of the model (with the addition of the various refinements alluded to above) to more homogeneous groups (using the household rather than the individual as the unit of analysis) would prove fruitful once the necessary data becomes available.

University of Durham

REFERENCES

AITCHISON, J. and BROWN, J. A. C. (1957). *The Lognormal Distribution*. C.U.P.

AITCHISON, J. and BROWN, J. A. C. (1954). On Criteria for Descriptions of Income Distribution. *Metroeconomica*.

HART, R. A. (1972). The Economic Influence on Internal Labour Force Migration. *Scottish J.P.E.*, XIX.

HICKS, J. R. (1963). *The Theory of Wages* (2nd edition). London: Macmillan & Co. Ltd.

JACK, A. B. (1970). A Short-run Model of Inter-Regional Migration. *The Manchester School*, XXXVIII.

OLIVER, F. R. (1964). Inter-Regional Migration and Unemployment 1951-1961. *J.R.S.S.*, 127, Part 1

PIGOU, A C. (1945). *Lapses from Full Employment*. Macmillan.

PIGOU, A. C. (1952). *Economics of Welfare*, IVth edition. Macmillan.

[2]

Estimating the Duration of Unemployment*

1 Introduction

The relationship between the distribution of completed durations of unemployment and that which, under stationary conditions, would be observed in a sample (observed at a random point in time) of those currently unemployed, has recently been examined by Salant (1977). The main concern of the paper is population heterogeneity. Salant, using earlier results of Silcock (1954), was able to reconcile the observation that the aggregate probability of re-employment declines with length of unemployment – with the assumption that individuals have constant but differing probabilities. Using the assumption of stationarity Salant then derived the relationship between the distributions of completed and incomplete spell durations.[1]

Salant calculated parameter values using 'computerised groping' in order to maximise the likelihood function. This note presents maximum likelihood estimates using an iterative procedure based on Fisher's 'method of scoring', and therefore also produces estimated standard errors. Comparisons of implied average durations of unemployment are made with Salant's results. The distributions are derived in section 2 and the empirical results are presented in section 3.

2 Distributions of Spell Length

If the probability of re-employment for any individual, α, is constant, then the distribution of the length of unemployment is exponential. Hence the probability

---

*This note was written in 1977.

[1] The same problem has been considered independently by Cripps and Tarling (1974) using a different approach.

that the individual is unemployed for longer than t is given by $1 - e^{\alpha t}$. Denote the distribution of α over individuals by $g(\alpha)$. If g is the gamma density, then:

$$g(\alpha) = \frac{\lambda^\tau \alpha^{\tau-1} e^{-\lambda\alpha}}{\Gamma(\tau)} \tag{1}$$

with $\Gamma(\tau) = \int x^{\tau-1} e^{-x} dx = (\tau-1)\Gamma(\tau-1) = (\tau-1)!$. The aggregate distribution of completed spells of unemployment, $f(t)$, is given by:

$$f(t) = \frac{1}{\Gamma(\tau)} \int \alpha e^{-\alpha t} \lambda^\tau \alpha^{\tau-1} e^{-\lambda\alpha} d\alpha \tag{2}$$

$$= \frac{\tau}{\lambda} \left(\frac{\lambda}{\lambda+t}\right)^{\tau+1} \tag{3}$$

with mean $E(t) = \lambda/(\tau-1)$. This uses the substitution $x = \alpha(\lambda+t)$ and the fact that $\Gamma(\tau) = \Gamma((\tau+1)/\tau)$. This is the result given by Silcock (1954, p.28). Salant (1977, p.41, n.2) notes that under stable conditions, if $b(t)$ is the distribution of incomplete spells, and $f(t)$ is the distribution of complete spells derived above, then:

$$b(t) = \frac{t f(t)}{E(t)} \tag{4}$$

The conditional probability, $h(\alpha|t)$, that a spell in progress, with completed length t, has been started by someone with re-employment rate α is given by:

$$h(\alpha|t) = \frac{\alpha e^{-\alpha t} g(\alpha)}{f(t)} \tag{5}$$

The marginal distribution, $h(\alpha)$, over incomplete spells is by definition:

$$h(\alpha) = \int h(\alpha|t) b(t) dt \tag{6}$$

Substitution of (4) and (5) into (6) gives:

$$h(\alpha) = \int \frac{\alpha e^{-\alpha t} g(\alpha) t f(t)}{f(t) E(t)} dt \tag{7}$$

$$= \frac{\alpha g(\alpha)}{E(t)} \int t e^{-\alpha t} dt \tag{8}$$

Integrating by parts, $\int t e^{-\alpha t} dt = 1/\alpha^2$ and:

$$h(\alpha) = g(\alpha)/\alpha E(t) \tag{9}$$

2

Salant (1977, p.42) states that under stable conditions the distribution of incomplete spell lengths is the same as that of completed spells. The distribution of interrupted spells, $f^*(t)$, is then given by:

$$f^*(t) = \int f(t|\alpha) h(\alpha) d\alpha \tag{10}$$

Substitution for $h(\alpha)$ from (9) and $g(\alpha)$ from (1) gives:

$$f^*(t) = \frac{(\tau - 1)}{\lambda \Gamma(\tau)} \int e^{-\alpha t} \lambda^\tau \alpha^{\tau-1} e^{-\lambda \alpha} d\alpha \tag{11}$$

Again using the substitution $x = \alpha(\lambda + t)$ and simplifying:

$$f^*(t) = (\tau - 1) \lambda^{\tau-1} (\lambda + t)^{-\tau} \tag{12}$$

Which is Salant's result (1977 p. 49, Table 1). The proportion staying longer than t periods is then:

$$1 - F^*(t) = (\tau - 1) \lambda^{\tau-1} \int_t^\alpha (\lambda + s)^{-\tau} ds$$

$$= \left\{ \frac{\lambda}{\lambda + t} \right\}^{\tau-1} \tag{13}$$

Johnson and Kotz (1970, p.233) also derived this distribution as the result of aggregating over an exponential distribution, where the parameter in turn has a gamma distribution, as in Silcock(1954).

3   Estimation and Results

Salant (1977, p.52l) reported that 'the two parameters were estimated from the data ... on interrupted spell lengths. The method of estimation was maximum likelihood, but since the likelihood function was complicated, the function was maximised by computerised groping in parameter space.' Thus no standard errors were obtained although a χ^2 test was performed after each estimation. However, for small samples maximum likelihood is not equivalent to minimum chi squared estimation. Salant did not make it clear whether in the 'computerised groping' the likelihood function was evaluated at each interaction, or whether a χ^2 value was instead minimised.

3

Table 1: Maximum Likelihood Estimates of τ and λ

Group	MLE		Salant	
	τ	λ	τ	λ
New	3.381	6.829	4.18	12.32
	(0.138)	(.847)		
Prof. and tech.	3.597	11.354	3.12	9.05
	(0.469)	(3.695)		
Managers, Proprietors	3.925	18.094	3.52	15.72
	(0.484)	(4.682)		
Sales workers	2.711	5.180	2.78	6.77
	(0.109)	(.786)		
Clerical workers	3.077	6.935	3.21	9.05
	(0.097)	(.688)		
Craftsmen and foremen	5.101	22.422	4.39	18.34
	(0.708)	(5.717)		
Operator and kindred worker	3.860	13.961	3.40	11.71
	(0.438)	(3.607)		
Non farm labourers	4.038	12.670	4.06	14.11
	(0.242)	(1.755)		
Private households	5.466	22.583	3.82	12.51
	(1.427)	(10.642)		
Service excl. pvt. hshld.	2.819	5.860	2.85	7.21
	(0.124)	(.906)		
Farm labourers	2.086	3.068	3.78	11.09
	(0.181)	(1.519)		
All	3.548	10.451		
	(0.249)	(1.884)		

4

Table 2: Average length of Unemployment: Completed and interrupted spells

Group	Completed		Incompleted	
	MLE	Salant	MLE	Salant
New	2.87	4.19	4.94	6.12
Prof. and Tech.	4.37	4.27	7.11	8.09
Managers, Proprietors	6.19	6.24	9.40	10.35
Sales workers	3.03	3.80	7.29	8.66
Clerical workers	3.34	4.09	6.44	7.46
Craftsmen and foremen	5.47	5.41	7.23	7.68
Operators, etc	4.88	4.88	7.51	8.37
Non-farm labourers	4.17	4.61	6.22	6.85
Private households	5.06	4.43	6.52	6.87
Service excl. pvt. hshld.	3.22	3.89	7.15	8.48
Farm labourers	2.82	3.98	35.6	6.22
All	4.10	-	6.75	-

The maximum likelihood estimation of this function has been examined in Creedy (1977) within the context of an analysis of Pareto's studies of income distribution. It is in fact one of the forms suggested by Pareto and as sometimes called a Pareto distribution of type II. It has recently been used in the analysis of the distribution of wealth and of the demand for recreational facilities; on the latter, see Cheshire and Stabler (1976). Salant (1977, p.48) stated that it 'is similar to the Pareto distriution'. Although the maximum likelihood equations are nonlinear they can be conveniently solved using Fisher's 'method of scoring', which is essentially Newton's method but replacing the second derivatives by their negative expectations.[2]

For this purpose the data in Salant (1977, p.50) were transformed to cumulative form, giving the number, N, who experience more than a given number of weeks unemployment. This also avoids the problem of the open-ended class of 27 or more weeks.

Estimates, with standard errors, are given in Table 1, along with Salant's values for comparison. All the parameters are significantly different from zero. Salant's values are usually within two standard errors of the maximum livelihood values, though in some cases the differences are surprising. Table 2 gives the

---

[2]The distribution can also be easily examined by plotting the values of N against $t + \lambda$ on double logarithmic graph paper, since $\log N = A - (\tau - 1) \log (t + \lambda)$ with $A = (\tau - 1) \log \lambda$.

estimated average length of incomplete and completed spell durations implied by the estimates in Table 1. Most of the values are slightly less than those given by Salant, and the case of farm labourers is rather surprising because of the low value of τ.

4 Conclusions

This note has reported maximum likelihood estimates of the distribution of unemployment spell durations and compared the results obtained by Salant (1977). Some differences in the parameters and expected values were found, but these were in most cases relatively minor. Estimated durations were generally less than those reported by Salant. The main argument of Salant was supported by the maximum likelihood estimates. This is the point that population heterogeneity may be an important factor associated with the observed distributions of the length of spells of unemployment and should be taken very seriously. It is, however, important to note that the empirical distributions used are over observed *spells* of unemployment, rather than over individuals. An obvious extension of the assumption of heterogeneity of the probability of obtaining a job, if unemployed, is the assumption that individuals differ in their probabilities of becoming unemployed. This suggests that small proportion of *individuals* may be responsible for a significant proportion of the observed spells of unemployment, so that Satant has not actually identified the distribution of α over individuals.[3] These arguments suggest that the two flows – onto and off the unemployment register – should be jointly analysed, although much more detailed information would be required.

---

[3]The same applies to Cripps and Tarling (1974).

References

[1] Creedy, J. (1977) Pareto and the distribution of income. *Review of Income and Wealth*, 23, pp. 405-411.

[2] Cripps, T.F. and Tarling, R.J. (1974) An analysis of the duration of male unemployment in Great Britain, 1923-73. *Economic Journal*, 84, pp. 289-316.

[3] Johnson, N.I. and Kotz, S. (1970) *Continuous Univariate distributions, Vol I*. Boston: Houghton Mifflin.

[4] Salant, S.W. (1977) Search theory and duration data: a theory of sorts. *Quaterly Journal of Economics*, 91, pp. 39-57.

[5] Silcock, H. (1954) The phenomenon of labour turnover, *Journal of the Royal Statistical Society*, CXVII, pp. 429-440.

[3]

The Analysis of Labour Market Flows Using a Continuous Time Model*

1 Introduction

The study of labour market flows has received considerable impetus, especially in the United States, from the availability of large scale longitudinal survey data. Most of the recent work in this area has used the well known discrete time/discrete state Markov model, although in very few cases has there been any systematic attempt to test the assumptions on which the model is based. Most of the data are, however, still too fragmentary to allow the complete direct testing of those assumptions.[1]

An important feature of the discrete time models is the necessary assumption that all movement between states takes place 'between' accounting periods. For example, the states occupied by individuals at two discrete points in time are observed, and no direct information is usually available about changes in states which are missed by this method of sampling. This may not be crucial for some applications of the models.[2] However, it is suggested that inferences about the average length of time spent within each state may be misleading.

The purpose of this paper is to examine the use of continuous time models in the context of labour market flows between employment and unemployment. Continuous time models are described in section 2. Several applications are

---

*This paper was written in 1978.

[1]These assumptions include time and population homogeneity and the first order (Markov) nature of the changes. For an examination of the discrete time model using British longitudinal data, see Creedy and Disney (1977). There is obviously a close link between job changes and changes in earnings. The assumptions of Markov models in this context are examined in Creedy (1978)

[2]If it is only required to predict the numbers in each state at given future dates, there is no difference between the models.

1

reported in section 3 where is is found that, by allowing for the possibility of more than one move taking place within an accounting period, different results are obtained for estimates of average durations within each state. Population heterogeneity is briefly considered in section 4.

2 Discrete and Continuous Time Models

2.1 Discrete time models

Define α as the proportion of the sample who were employed at time $t - 1$, but who are observed to be unemployed at time t. Similarly β is the proportion of those who are unemployed at time $t - 1$, but who are employed by time t. These proportions are usually interpreted as the probability of becoming unemployed and the probability of becoming employed respectively, over the relevant time period. In equilibrium, where there is no change in the total number of individuals in each state over time, and if the transition proportions remain constant, the unemployment rate is given by $\alpha/(\alpha + \beta)$. Furthermore the average time spent in unemployment is $1/\beta$ and the average time spent between spells of unemployment is $1/\alpha$ time periods. The average frequency of unemployment spells is the ratio of the unemployment rate to the average duration of unemployment; that is, $\alpha\beta/(\alpha + \beta)$.[3] This type of first-order model is popular in the literature on labour market flows.[4]

2.2 Specification of continuous time models

Define the transition matrix $P(t)$, where the i, j th element is the probability of a move from state i to state j over the period $0 - t$. This is obtained as the solution to the following differential equations:

$$\frac{dP(t)}{dt} = QP(t) \tag{1}$$

with the initial condition $P(0) = 1$, the solution is given by:

$$P(t) = e^{Qt} \tag{2}$$

---

[3] See, for example, Prais (1955) and Bartholomew (1973). The distribution of the total time spent in unemployment is given in Creedy and Disney (1978, Appendix D).

[4] Recent examples include Denton (1976), Marston (1976), Schweitzer and Smith (1976), Toika (1976). An earlier example is David and Otsuki (1968).

with:

$$e^{Qt} = \sum_{k=0}^{\infty} (Qt)^k / k! \tag{3}$$

The matrix, Q, is called the intensity matrix and has the following properties:

$$q_{ii} < 0, \quad p_{ij} > 0 \quad i \neq j, \quad \sum_{j} q_{ij} = 0 \tag{4}$$

In addition, the probability that an individual in state i will move to state j, given that a move is made, is equal to $q_{ij}/(-q_{ii})$, and the expected length of stay in state i is $1/ - q_{ii}$.

The application of equation (2) clearly requires the calculation of the logarithm of a matrix, $log P(t) = Qt$, so that given any observed $P(t)$ the corresponding value of Q can be calculated. This computation is not always possible and often involves considerable difficulties; this subject has been treated at length in Singer and Spilerman (1976), following the earlier work of Doob (1953) and Coleman (1964). The conditions necessary for the unique inversion of the equation $P(t) = e^{Qt}$ have been given in Singer and Spilerman (1976, p.41, Table 1). The computational procedure is described in Appendix A below.

The fact that a unique Q exists for any observed P matrix does not necessarily mean that Q can be interpreted as an intensity matrix, and that the observed P can be regarded as having been generated from a continuous time Markov model. The conditions in (4) also have to be satisfied.

3   Empirical Applications

Schweitzer and Smith (1976, p.253, Table 1) reported observed labour market flows between the three categories of 'employed', 'unemployed' and 'not in the labour force' for white male youths (aged 14-24 in 1966) between 1966 and 1967, and between 1966 and 1968. These flows can be transformed into the required $P(t)$ matrices, and are shown in Table 1. The basic time unit is one month, so for the first case $t = 12$, and for the second $t = 24$.

In both cases the necessary and sufficient conditions required for the inversion of (2) to yield a unique Q matrix are satisfied. The resulting matrices are given in Table 2. It can be seen that the conditions (4) are satisfied, so that the Q's may be regarded as estimates of intensity matrices. A comparison of the

3

Table 1: Observed Transition Matrices $P(t)$

1966	1967			1968		
	E	U	N	E	U	N
Employed (E)	0.8600	0.0294	0.1028	0.8774	0.0252	0.0974
Unemployed (U)	0.6062	0.1631	0.2438	0.6909	0.0931	0.2160
Not in labour force (N)	0.3341	0.0787	0.5872	0.5456	0.0535	0.4009

Table 2: Estimates of $Q = log P(t)/t$

$t = 12$			$t = 24$		
-0.017	0.005	0.011	-0.009	0.003	0.006
0.117	-0.170	0.056	0.075	-0.115	0.040
0.031	0.020	-0.052	0.035	0.010	-0.045

elements between the intensity matrix for $t = 12$ and that for $t = 24$ reveals some differences, but it is not clear how significant these are since the sampling properties are not known.

The interpretation of Q can be further extended by using the decomposition suggested by Singer and Spilerman (1974, 1976). They use the factorization $Q = \Lambda (M - I)$ where the diagonal matrix Λ has elements which are the rates of movement out of the appropriate states, and M governs the transitions followed at each move. A reasonable *a priori* assumption to make here is that the diagonals of M are zero (indeed, non zero m_{ii} do not have a sensible interpretation in this framework). For the Q matrix given above for the 1966-7 transitions the above decomposition gives

$$\Lambda = \begin{bmatrix} 0.017 & & \\ & 0.170 & \\ & & 0.052 \end{bmatrix} \quad M = \begin{bmatrix} 0 & 0.29 & 0.65 \\ 0.69 & 0 & 0.33 \\ 0.60 & 0.39 & 0 \end{bmatrix}$$

If it is only required to contain predictions (on the assumption of time homogeneity) then there is no difference between the discrete and continuous time models. In the first case $P(t) = P(1)^t$ and in the second case $P(t) = e^{Qt}$, so that in both models $\log P(t) = t \log P(1)$.

3.1   The average duration of unemployment

There are, however, significant differences in the expected duration of unemployment implied by the discrete model, using $P(t)$, and the continuous time model

4

Table 3: Discrete and Continuous Time Models: Data from Marston (1976)

Demographic Group			P(4)			$Q = \frac{1}{4}\log P(4)$		
			E	U	N	E	U	N
White	Age	E	0.842	0.037	0.120	-0.049	0.015	0.034
males	16-19	U	0.302	0.369	0.329	0.121	-0.265	0.145
		N	0.154	0.063	0.783	0.043	0.028	-0.071
	Age	E	0.937	0.024	0.038	-0.019	0.009	0.010
	20-24	U	0.362	0.459	0.179	0.129	-0.202	0.074
		N	0.195	0.061	0.744	0.053	0.025	-0.078
	Age	E	0.988	0.009	0.004	-0.004	0.003	0.001
	25-59	U	0.355	0.543	0.102	0.118	-0.155	0.036
		N	0.079	0.038	0.882	0.019	0.014	-0.032
Non-white	Age	E	0.785	0.060	0.155	-0.067	0.022	0.045
males	16-19	U	0.225	0.450	0.325	0.087	-0.217	0.129
		N	0.107	0.090	0.803	0.029	0.037	-0.066
	Age	E	0.940	0.027	0.033	-0.017	0.008	0.009
	20-24	U	0.248	0.643	0.109	0.077	-0.114	0.037
		N	0.124	0.089	0.789	0.032	0.031	-0.063
	Age	E	0.975	0.015	0.010	-0.007	0.005	0.003
	25-59	U	0.316	0.558	0.126	0.104	-0.148	0.045
		N	0.109	0.034	0.858	0.028	0.012	-0.039

which uses Q. Using the transition matrix in Table 1 the expected duration of unemployment is about 14 months, while the corresponding estimate using the appropriate elements of Q from Table 2 is about 6 months.

This contrast can also be seen using data reproduced in Marston (1976, p.175, Table 1). The transition matrices for one month intervals are given in Table 3 for six demographic groups, along with the corresponding estimate of the intensity matrix Q. In this case the basic time unit is one week. The alternative estimates of the average duration of spells of unemployment are given in Table 4, where it can be seen that the continuous time model implies much lower average durations. The explanation of this difference is straightforward. The discrete time model does not allow for the fact that people may move between the sampling dates. Individuals may experience several short spells of unemployment, although the method of recording the flows does not show any change in the labour market state occupied between the two dates. The continuous time model does, however,

Table 4: Alternative estimates of the average duration of spells of unemployment

Demographic Group		Average Duration (weeks)	
		Marston(1976) (p.177 Table 2)	Continuous time model $(1/-(q_{ii}))$
white males	16-19	6.81	3.77
	20-24	7.94	4.95
	25-59	9.41	6.45
Non-white males	16-19	7.82	4.61
	20-24	12.04	8.77
	25-59	9.73	6.76

allow for the fact that multiple flows may have taken place between sampling dates.

4   Population Heterogeneity

The previous section used data relating to population sub-groups defined by, for example, age, sex and colour. If data are available which allow suitable decomposition into fairly homogeneous groups then of course no special problems arise. The above analysis can be carried out for each sub-sample, and if each comprises a proportion s_i of the total sample, with intensity matrix Q_i, the aggregate transition matrix $P(t)$ is given by:

$$P(t) = \sum_i s_i e^{tQ_i} \tag{5}$$

Here $P(t)$ would not be expected to display the properties of a first order Markov transition matrix, although each sub-group follows transitions which are 'instantaneously' Markov.[5] Consider, for example, the simple case with two population sub-groups and two states, say employment and unemployment. A basic 'dual labour market' argument would suggest that one group has few, short spells of

---

[5]This illustrates why there has been a variety of reactions to the observation that simple aggregate transition matrices do not seem to have the expected Markov properties. Some researchers argue that the main reason is because moves are not first-order, while others argue that heterogeneity is the main feature which should be considered; see, for example, Coleman (1964).

unemployment, while a second group experiences more frequent spells of unemployment. This would give

$$P(t) \;=\; s_1 e^{Q_1 t} + (1 - s_1) e^{Q_2 t}$$

$$= \; s_1 e^{\Lambda_1 (M-I)t} + (1 - s_1) e^{\Lambda_2 (M-I)t} \tag{6}$$

$$\Lambda_1 = \begin{bmatrix} \alpha_1 & 0 \\ 0 & \beta_1 \end{bmatrix} \qquad \Lambda_2 = \begin{bmatrix} \alpha_2 & 0 \\ 0 & \beta_2 \end{bmatrix} \qquad \text{and } M = \begin{bmatrix} 0 & 1 \\ 1 & 0 \end{bmatrix}$$

In the (unfortunately more usual) case where only the aggregate $P(t)$ is available, then even this simple model cannot be estimated without further strong *a priori* restrictions on the parameters of the model.[6]

The indirect treatment of heterogeneous populations where several states are concerned is therefore unlikely to be very fruitful. This contrasts with the treatment of one flow, for example from unemployment to employment, which is more tractable. This is shown by the recent analyses of Cripps and Tarling (1974) in the UK and Salant (1977) in the US.[7] It is therefore important to obtain longitudinal data which allow particular groups within the population to be identified.

5 Conclusions

This paper has explored the use of continuous time Markov models for the study of labour market flow, in particular those flows between the states of employment and unemployment. An advantage of continuous time models over discrete time models is that they are able to allow for the fact that individuals may experience more than one transition between the sampling dates.

Using US data from several recent studies it was shown that the observed transition matrices could be generated by continuous time stochastic processes whereby the average duration of unemployment was lower than the usual estimates obtained using the discrete time model. The use of continuous time models for the analysis of heterogeneous populations was also briefly considered.

---

[6]Singer and Spilerman (1976) show that the model is quite tractable where $\alpha_1 = \beta_1$ and so on, and has a gamma distribution over the population. But this assumption is clearly inappropriate in this context.

[7]But for further discussion of this problem see Disney (1979).

The sampling methods used in the collection of longitudinal data unfortunately provide data which are usually too fragmentary to allow the assumptions used in alternative models to be tested directly. In view of the different implications of the models, it is hoped that suitable data which record each move made by individuals will become available to researchers in this area.

A   The Formula $P = \exp(Qt)$

It is required to obtain the logarithm of the matrix P, so that $Qt = logP$. In general, the function $f(P)$ of the matrix P can be written as the line integral:

$$f(P) = \frac{1}{2\pi i} \int_{\Gamma} (\xi I - P)^{-1} f(\xi) \, d\xi \tag{7}$$

Where ξ is the closed curve containing the eigenvalues of p, and $i^2 = -1$. The components of $(\xi I - P)^{-1}$ are:

$$(\xi I - P)^{-1}_{ij} = \frac{(-1)^{i+j} \phi_{ji}}{\phi(\xi)} \tag{8}$$

Where $\phi(\xi)$ is the determinant of $(\xi I - P)$ and ϕ_{ij} is the determinant of the matrix obtained by deleting the ith row and the jth column of $\xi I - P$. Thus $\left[(-1)^{i+j} \phi_{ji} \right]$ is the adjoint.

Since $\phi(\xi)$ is zero where ξ is an eigenvalue, the function (7) contains singularities, and must be evaluated using the 'Theorem of Residues'; see Courant (1936, p.553). This states that if the function $f(z)$ is analytic in the interior of a region R and on its boundary C, except at a finite number of poles, the integral of the function taken round C in the positive sense is equal to the sum of the residues of the fiction at the poles enclosed by the boundary. The residue of a function at a pole is $2\pi_i C_{-1}$ where:

$$C_{-1} = \frac{1}{f'(z_0)}$$

and where $q(z) = 1/f(z)$, if $q(z) = r(z)/\phi(z)$ and $\phi(z)$ has a zero at $z = z_0$ while $r(z) = 0$, then $C_{-1} = r(z_0)/\phi'(z_0)$. Thus where ζ_i is the ith root of a square matrix of size n residue evaluation gives:

$$\log P = \sum_{i=1}^{n} \frac{\log \xi_i}{\phi'(\xi_i)} Adj(\xi_j I - P) \tag{9}$$

8

Furthermore $\phi'(\xi_i)$ is conveniently given by $\phi'(\xi_i) = \Pi_{j \neq i}(\xi_i - \xi_j)$.

For example, consider the matrix $P = \begin{bmatrix} a & 1-a \\ 1-b & b \end{bmatrix}$, then $\xi I - P = \begin{bmatrix} \xi-a & 1-a \\ 1-b & \xi-b \end{bmatrix}$ and the adjoint of $\xi I - P = Adj\,(\xi I - P) = \begin{bmatrix} \xi-b & 1-a \\ 1-b & \xi-a \end{bmatrix}$.

Now:

$$\phi(\xi) = \xi^2 - \xi(a+b) + (a+b-1)$$
$$= (\xi-1)\{\xi - (a+b-1)\}$$

and:

$$\frac{d\phi(\xi)}{d\xi} = \phi'(\xi) = 2\xi - (a+b)$$

The eigenvalues of P are thus $\xi_1 = 1$ and $\xi_2 = a+b-1$. Since $\log \xi_1 = 0$, only the second term in (9) is needed, with $\phi'(\xi_2) = a+b-2$ then:

$$\log P = \frac{\log(a+b-1)}{(a+b-2)} \begin{bmatrix} a-1 & 1-a \\ 1-b & b-1 \end{bmatrix}$$

For this to be legitimate Q matrix log $(a+b-1)$ must be real. Thus all characteristic roots must be real and strictly positive. The more general case is considered in detail by Singer and Spilerman (1976a).

References

[1] Bartholomew, D. (1973) *Stochastic models for Social processes*. New York: Wiley.

[2] Coleman, J.S. (1964) *Introduction to mathematical Sociology*. New York: Free Press.

[3] Creedy, J. (1978) The analysis of changes in earnings. *Economic Journal*, 88, pp. 126-133.

[4] Creedy, J. and Disney, R., (1977) Labour market flows in Great Britain, *University of Kent Discussion Papers in Economics*, No. 29.

[5] Cripps T.F. and Tarling, R.J. (1974) An analysis of the duration of male unemployment in Great Britain 1932-73. *Economic Journal*, 84, pp. 289-316.

[6] Courant, R. (1936) *Differential and Integral Calculus*. London: Blackie and Son.

[7] David, M. and Otsuki, T. (1968) Forecasting short run variations in Labour Market activity. *Review of Economics and Statistics,* 50, pp. 68-77.

[8] Denton, F. et al. (1976) *Short run Dynamics of the Canadian Labour Market*. Economic Council of Canada.

[9] Disney, R. (1979) Recurrent spells and the concentration of unemployment in Great Britain. *Economic Journal*, 89, pp. 109-119.

[10] Doob, J.L. (1953) *Stochastic Processes*. New York: Wiley.

[11] Marston, S.T. (1976) Employment instability and high unemployment rates. *Brookings Papers*, No. 1.

[12] Prais, S.J. (1955) Measuring social mobility. *Journal of the Royal Statistical Society*, 118, pp. 56-66.

[13] Schweitzer, S.O. and Smith, R.E. (1976) The persistence of the discouraged worker effect. *Industrial and Labour relations Review*, 27, pp.249.

[14] Salant, W.S. (1977) Search theory and duration data: A theory of sorts. *Quarterly Journal of Economics*, 91, pp. 39-57.

[15] Singer, B. and Spilerman, S. (1974) Social mobility models for heterogeneous populations. In *Sociological Methodology 1973-74* (ed. by H. Costner), pp. 356-401. San Francisco:Jossey-Ban.

[16] Singer, B. and Spilerman, S. (1976) Some methodological issues in the analysis of longitudinal data. *Annals of Economic and Social Measurement*, 5, pp. 447-474.

[17] Singer, B. and Spilerman, S. (1976a) Representation of social processes by Markov Models. *American Journal of Sociology*, 82, pp. 1-54.

[4]

Scottish Journal of Political Economy, Vol. 28, No. 1, February 1981
© 1981 Scottish Economic Society

0036-9292/81/00050076 $02.00

CHANGES IN LABOUR MARKET STATES IN GREAT BRITAIN*

JOHN CREEDY AND RICHARD DISNEY

University of Durham and University of Kent

I

INTRODUCTION

It is of great importance to measure the movement of individuals between various states in the labour market, such as employment, unemployement and sickness. Knowledge of these flows is necessary in order to devise manpower policies, to examine the employment consequences of macroeconomic policies and to devise effective social security programmes. Yet while there has been considerable empirical work concerning this issue in the United States,[1] there is as yet little evidence in Great Britain. Most British research has concentrated on examining one change of state, namely the rate at which individuals leave the unemployment register to rejoin employment,[2] but has been complicated by the statistical problem that most of the available data only give information about the stock of unemployed in a "snapshot" of the register, rather than describing the characteristics of the flow of individuals onto and off the register.[3]

In addition to methodological problems, there is still relatively little information in Britain about other important flows through the labour market. There is a paucity of evidence about how the probability of entering the unemployment register varies among individuals, although this is an important element in determining the extent to which individuals experience recurrent spells of unemployment, and are thus eligible for National Insurance benefits.[4] Furthermore, leaving the unemployment register may take the form of becoming sick or of leaving the labour force completely, while the flow out of employment into sickness may also be susceptible to economic analysis.[5]

* We should like to thank the Department of Health and Social Security for providing the data used in this study, and Michele Foot for computing assistance. The work reported here is related to a project on the "Earnings and Employment Experience of Individuals in Great Britain", which was financed by the DHSS and carried out under the aegis of the National Institute of Economic and Social Research.

[1] See for instance, Barrett and Morgenstern (1974), Garfinkle (1977) and Marston (1976) and also the important recent study by Clark and Summers (1979).
[2] For recent examples, see Bowers and Harkess (1979), Lancaster (1979) and Nickell (1979).
[3] For a discussion of this issue, see Kaitz (1970) and Salant (1977).
[4] Some evidence is given in Disney (1979).
[5] See Doherty (1979), and Thomas (1980).

Date of submission of final manuscript: 19 May 1980.

Now a full analysis of these issues requires a comprehensive set of longitudinal data which records the movements of a large sample of individuals through different labour market states, and the precise timing of each move. Such comprehensive data are not available in Great Britain. The purpose of this paper, however, is to provide some evidence on individual changes in labour market states in Great Britain, using special longitudinal data which were kindly made available by the Department of Health and Social Security (DHSS). The data, and definitions of labour market states used, are discussed in Section II. Section III then presents empirical results and discusses the implications of the results for the construction of models of labour market flows, while Section IV discusses policy implications.

II

THE USE OF DHSS CONTRIBUTIONS DATA

(a) *The data used in this study*

This study uses evidence from DHSS records which were originally collected for the administration of the National Insurance scheme.[6] Samples are available for men, from all occupations, in three age groups: those born in 1923, 1933 and 1943, and subsequently referred to as "Cohort 1923" etc. The information covers the years 1971, 1972 and 1973,[7] where the years actually run from March of the year indicated to February of the succeeding year. The samples provide, for each person in each of the three years, information about the number of National Insurance contributions paid in Class 1 (employment), Class 2 (self-employment) and, where applicable, the number of weeks which are credited as a result of claims arising from registered periods of sickness or unemployment. In addition, a number of individuals have no recorded contributions or credits in some or all of the years. These are treated as non-participants in the labour market.

It is important to stress that complete information about labour market flows *within* each contribution year is not, therefore, available, and that the DHSS samples are not comprehensive longitudinal data in the sense defined above. Only the total number of weeks of employment, self-employment and non-participation, and credited weeks of registered unemployment and sickness in each of the years is known.[8] Thus the order in which the spells in different labour market states take place, when there are more than one in a single year, is unknown. Furthermore the choice of dates is of course arbitrary, so that in some cases a single spell will overlap more than one "contributions" years. An observation showing that someone was

---

[6] Although the data are for individuals, it should be stressed that complete anonymity has been maintained throughout, and it is not possible to identify individuals from the data.

[7] National Insurance stamps were abolished in 1973.

[8] The fact that contributions are credited does not necessarily mean that unemployment or sickness benefit is received.

unemployed for some time in each of two consecutive years does not therefore necessarily indicate that he suffered two separate spells of unemployment,
although of course he may have experienced more than two spells.

It should not be thought, however, that other longitudinal data are free
from disadvantages. Most studies use survey data obtained from repeated
interviews of samples of individuals at discrete points in time. There are two
main drawbacks to this approach. The first occurs where the sample is itself
drawn from the population of individuals in a particular state at a point in
time. For instance, the follow-up surveys of the unemployed which have been
carried out in Great Britain, such as those by the Department of Employment
(1977) and Daniel and Stilgoe (1977), will observe only the subsequent
experience of those who were on the unemployment register at the time of the
survey. Their characteristics may differ systematically from those of the
population as a whole and even from those of the population who experience
unemployment at some time, since there is an above-average probability of
observing the long-duration unemployed on the register at any point in time.[9]

The second drawback arises because multiple movements which take
place between sample dates are not recorded. In general, the longer the
accounting period the greater is the probability that in practice multiple
movements do take place. Models of labour market flows which rely on this
implicit assumption will therefore lead to predictions of flow rates which are
biassed downwards, as shown in section III (b) below.

(b) *The definition of a labour market state*

The characteristics of the DHSS data complicate the choice of an appropriate definition of the "state" occupied by an individual during the year;
clearly no single definition is unequivocably superior to all others.[10] The
definitions used here reflect an attempt to measure an individual's "attachment" to the labour market, so that the states can be unambiguously ordered
in a hierarchy. The categories must necessarily be quite broad, partly because
of the size of samples and partly because of the fact that the period over which
labour market experience is aggregated is to some extent arbitrary. Five
separate states are distinguished as follows:

State 1: Fully employed in Class 1 and/or Class 2.
State 2: Less than fully employed in Class 1 and/or Class 2 but with no
sickness or unemployment credits.
State 3: From 1–8 sickness and/or unemployment credits.
State 4: From 9–52 sickness and/or unemployment credits.
State 5: Not in the labour force (no National Insurance contributions or
credits).

It should be noted that Class 1 and Class 2 National Insurance contribu-

[9] See Kaitz (1970) and Salant (1977).
[10] Results using two alternative definitions to that used here were reported in Creedy and
Disney (1978).

tions are combined in state 1,[11] and sickness and unemployment are combined in states 3 and 4. A separate classification by weeks of sickness only, unemployment only or both combined, would result in too many states with a small number of observations, but some details are given in the Appendix to this paper. The above definitions reflect the "attachment" requirement, however, as those in state 2 are mostly job changers who do not register as unemployed; those in state 3 are the short term registered sick and unemployed; those in state 4 are the long term registered sick and unemployed; while those in state 5 have left the labour market (not necessarily permanently, of course).

III

EMPIRICAL RESULTS

(a) *Mobility over the three years*

Many studies of changes in labour market states use a first order discrete time Markov model, in which the probability of movement from one state to another is constant, is the same for all individuals in that state, and depends only on the current state occupied and not on previous movements. Analysis of the DHSS data immediately suggests, however, that one of the assumptions of the 1st order Markov model is unrealistic; namely that the probability of movement depends only on the current state and not on previous movements. The importance of past history is revealed by decomposing the change between states of the DHSS sample from 1972 to 1973 so that the previous change from 1971 to 1972 may also be distinguished. This may be achieved using a matrix with 35 rows and 5 columns. Combining cohorts, of course, involves a loss of information[12] but is necessary in order to obtain enough entries in each cell of the 35×5 matrix. The resulting "flows" are shown in Table 1.

The first row of the table shows, for example, that of all those remaining fully employed over 1971 and 1972, 1773 (83 per cent) remained fully employed over 1973 while 207 ($9\frac{1}{2}$ per cent) suffered short term sickness and/or unemployment in 1973. For those who were in state 4 (long term sickness and unemployment) in 1971, 52 (44 per cent) remained so in 1972 and 1973. But of those who moved from state 4 in 1971 to state 5 (not in the labour force)

---

[11] Some individuals change their class of employment during the year, and this would obviously be important in any analysis of changes in earnings. In addition Class 2 contributors are not eligible for Unemployment Benefit and this may affect their propensity to register as unemployed.

[12] Some information about year to year changes for each cohort is contained in Creedy and Disney (1978). Using the present definitions, the only proportions which are uniformly and significantly different among the cohorts are contained in the diagonals. The proportion remaining in full time employment from year to year is significantly lower amongst cohort 1943, and that remaining in long term sickness and unemployment is significantly highest amongst cohort 1943 and cohort 1933. Otherwise the overall experience of the three cohorts is similar.

J. CREEDY AND R. DISNEY

TABLE 1

Labour market flows over three years 1971–2–3 all cohorts combined

State occupied in		State occupied in 1973				
1971	1972	1	2	3	4	5
1	1	1773	121	207	27	21
	2	516	48	24	4	16
	3	255	38	83	29	2
	4	25	9	21	11	4
	5	23	7	0	0	14
2	1	159	35	25	6	3
	2	38	65	17	3	13
	3	32	19	26	13	4
	4	1	3	6	3	5
	5	3	16	2	1	26
3	1	259	25	86	8	2
	2	26	30	16	1	8
	3	115	28	149	47	6
	4	16	5	31	38	5
	5	1	5	3	0	18
4	1	42	6	17	6	0
	2	7	8	5	3	2
	3	22	10	48	26	2
	4	15	11	32	52	9
	5	3	5	2	15	14
5	1	8	2	1	1	7
	2	21	17	6	2	11
	3	2	2	4	2	2
	4	2	1	3	7	4
	5	10	27	6	12	184

in 1972, 15 (38 per cent) moved back into state 4 in 1973, whereas of those who moved to Class 1 in 1972, only 6 (8 per cent) moved back into Class 4 in 1973.

In general, the table shows clearly that past history is important. As just mentioned, 83 per cent of those in Class 1 in 1971 and 1972 remained fully employed in 1973. But only 70 per cent of those who moved from state 2 in 1971 to state 1 in 1972 remained in state 1 in 1973; the corresponding values for those in states 3, 4 and 5 in 1971 are 68 per cent, 51 per cent and 42 per cent respectively. Similarly 11 per cent of those who had been in state 1 in 1971 and 1972 moved to states 3 or 4 in 1973. But 26 per cent of those who had been in states 3 or 4 in 1971 before moving to state 1 in 1972 reverted to states 3 and 4 in 1973. Some of the more interesting results of this type are shown in Table 2. The data clearly show, therefore, that previous experience is important: those who were prone, for instance, to lengthy work interruptions in the past are likely to experience further breaks in the future. Conversely those with stable work histories have a greater probability of remaining in full employment in the future.

The lack of independence between successive moves implies that it is not

TABLE 2

Individuals who make a given move 1972–73, expressed as a proportion of those making given move 1971–72

State occupied in 1972		1	1	3 or 4	1 or 2	5
State occupied in 1973		1	3 or 4	1	5	1 or 2
State occupied	1	0·83	0·11	0·59	0·01	0·68
in 1971	2	0·70	0·14	0·29	0·14	0·40
	3	0·68	0·25	0·30	0·02	0·23
	4	0·51	0·32	0·16	0·02	0·21
	5	0·42	0·11	0·14	0·25	0·16

appropriate to construct conventional transition matrices for flows between only two periods.[13] This can be shown rigorously as follows. Define p_{ijk} as the probability of moving from state j to state k from 1972 to 1973, given a previous move from state i to state j between 1971 and 1972. Then a contingency table can be constructed for each state j (occupied in 1972), showing the frequency of $(k-j)$ changes classified against $(j-i)$. After consolidation of some of the cells a standard χ^2 test of independence can be carried out. The resulting χ^2 values for $j = 1, \ldots, 5$ are given in Table 3.

In each case the null hypothesis of independence between successive class changes is rejected.

TABLE 3

Successive changes in labour market state

Class occupied in 1972	Degrees of freedom	Value of χ^2
1	9	154·37
2	12	291·34
3	9	133·45
4	6	26·04
5	4	52·94

(b) *Models of labour market flows*

The previous section examined the movement between states over a three year period, and clearly indicated the need to consider previous experience. Furthermore, as noted above, this is not simply a result of aggregating over the three cohorts. The most obvious implication for models of labour market flows is that the more conventional transition matrices (and the Markov assumption) should not be used at this level of aggregation. However, it is quite possible that the Markov model may apply to homogeneous sub-groups,

---

[13] If this is done, then the diagonals of the product of two year-to-year matrices are significantly lower than those of the matrix for two non-consecutive years. For further details and results concerning this point see Creedy and Disney (1978).

J. CREEDY AND R. DISNEY

TABLE 4

Alternative estimates of the average duration of spells of unemployment

Demographic group		Average duration (weeks)	
		Marston (1976) (p. 177 table 2)	Continuous time model $(1/-(q_{ii}))$
White	16–19	6·81	3·77
males	20–24	7·94	4·95
	25–59	9·41	6·45
Non-white	16–19	7·82	4·61
males	20–24	12·04	8·77
	25–59	9·73	6·76

though much more disaggregated data would be required than are currently available.[14]

It is perhaps useful here to reinforce the point made in section I concerning the need for longitudinal data which show the precise timing of each move, and the implicit assumption of the conventional discrete time models that all individuals move at the same discrete time intervals. A comparison between discrete and continuous time models shows that in practice this implicit assumption may lead to overestimation of the average time spent in a particular state.

In the discrete time models the i, jth element of the transition matrix $P(t)$ denotes the probability of a change from state i to state j over the period $0 - t$ (the changes occur at the end of the period), and the average number of periods in state i is $1/(1 - p_{ii})$. In the continuous time models $P(t) = \exp Qt$ where Q is the "Intensity matrix" and $q_{ij}/(-q_{ii})$ is the probability that an individual in state i will move to state j, given that a move is made, and $1/(-q_{ii})$ is the expected length of stay in the ith state.[15] Using as an example the empirical transition matrices in the well known paper by Marston (1976, p. 175) it is possible to calculate the corresponding Q matrices and thereby to compare the implications for the average duration of unemployment.[16] These comparisons are given in Table 4, where it is clear that the continuous time model implies much lower durations.

The intuitive explanation of this difference is that some individuals may

[14] The issue concerning the distinction between heterogeneous populations and "dependence on the past" has arisen in a number of areas; including industrial mobility, changes in relative earnings over time, and the probability of leaving the unemployment register. A number of well known models, such as the "mover-stayer" model, have been suggested for indirectly examining the possible extent of heterogeneity; but they do not seem to be appropriate in this context.

[15] To qualify as an "Intensity matrix" Q must also satisfy the conditions that $q_{ii} < 0, q_{ij} > 0$ for $i \neq j$, and $\sum_j q_{ij} = 0$. For discussion of such models see Bartholomew (1973) and Singer and Spilerman (1976).

[16] Calculation of Q requires the computation of the logarithm of a matrix, for which see the references cited in fn. 15. In the case of the data from Marston the conditions necessary for the logarithm to be unique are satisfied. See also Creedy and Disney (1978, Appendix B) for further details. None of the matrices from the DHSS data can be regarded as being generated from a continuous time model, however.

experience several short spells of unemployment, although the method of recording the flows in the discrete transition matrix does not show a change in the state occupied over the period. The continuous time model does, however, allow for the fact that flows may have taken place between sampling dates. Of course, the fact that the average duration of separate spells is lower (than implied by discrete models), does not imply that the total length of time spent in unemployment over a given period is lower.

IV

CONCLUSIONS

The main purpose of this paper has been to examine labour market flows in Great Britain using longitudinal data on National Insurance contributions and credits for three cohorts of males over three years. The use of these data required special definitions of labour market states, though the measures were chosen to represent the "degree of attachment" to the labour market in each year. Analysis of the pattern of movements over the three year period, rather than those between only two years, showed that past experience is important. In particular, those individuals who are fully employed in one year are more likely to experience some sickness or unemployment (or to leave the labour market) if they have previously experienced sickness or unemployment, than if they were previously continuously employed. Similarly, individuals are more likely to return to full employment, following a year in which they experienced some unemployment, if they were previously fully employed.

Most of the discussion of unemployment benefits, incentive effects and unemployment duration has, however, concentrated on the case of isolated long spells of unemployment. The National Insurance regulations also seem to be designed on the implicit assumption that unemployment is a random, isolated, event in an individual's working life. In fact repeated experience of unemployment means that those individuals will exhaust their entitlement to National Insurance benefits, since spells must be separated by 13 weeks before they can be regarded as being "separate" from the preceding spell. Such individuals are also unlikely to be eligible for Earnings Related Supplement,[17] and for full pension rates when they retire. Most studies of incentive effects have, however, ignored the extent to which the unemployed are actually eligible for National Insurance benefits, whereas an important feature of recent experience in Great Britain is that less than 40 per cent of the stock of unemployed have been in receipt of National Insurance benefits.

It would be extremely useful to know the extent to which early experience of sickness or unemployment changes an individual's chances of more stable employment experience, or whether particular groups of individuals with

[17] The question of eligibility for National Insurance benefits is examined within the context of a model of a heterogeneous population in Creedy and Disney (1981).

J. CREEDY AND R. DISNEY

certain personal characteristics (including area of residence and occupation) are more prone to sickness and unemployment than others. When population heterogeneity is recognised it then becomes very important to try to isolate groups with special characteristics and problems, who require different kinds of policies. It is hoped that suitable longitudinal data will become available to researchers working in this area.

APPENDIX: SICKNESS AND UNEMPLOYMENT

In Section III sickness and unemployment were combined in the definitions of labour market states 3 and 4. This appendix provides some further details about flows between these categories. Table A–1 shows the proportion of individuals within each cohort who experience some unemployment (at least one week) in 1972, classified according to the number of weeks during which they are sick in 1971.

Table A–1 clearly shows that the probability of becoming unemployed in one year increases according to the number of weeks of sickness in the previous year. Sickness and subsequent unemployment are therefore related, just as sickness and unemployment in the same year are related. Unemployment is experienced by relatively more of the younger cohort than by the older two cohorts.

TABLE A–1

Proportion experiencing unemployment in 1972

Weeks of Sickness 1971	Proportion unemployed in 1972		
	Cohort 1943	Cohort 1933	Cohort 1923
None	0·057	0·037	0·044
≥1	0·124	0·116	0·096
≥3	0·169	0·119	0·119
≥5	0·186	0·141	0·127
≥7	0·207	0·173	0·130
≥9	0·250	0·171	0·130
≥13	0·263	0·227	0·143

REFERENCES

BARRETT, N. S. and MORGENSTERN, R. D. (1974). Why do blacks and women have high unemployment rates? *Journal of Human Resources*, vol. IX, no. 4, pp. 452–464
BARTHOLOMEW, D. (1973). *Stochastic Models for Social Processes*, Wiley.
BOWERS, J. K. and HARKESS, D. (1979). Duration of unemployment by age and sex, *Economica*, vol. 46, (August) pp. 239–260.
CLARK, K. B. and SUMMERS, L. H. (1979). Labour Market Dynamics and Unemployment: A Reconsideration, *Brookings Papers*, no. 1, pp. 13–72.
CREEDY, J. and DISNEY, R. (1978). Labour Market Flows in Great Britain, *University of Kent Discussion Papers in Economics*, no. 27.

CREEDY, J. and DISNEY, R. (1981). Eligibility for Unemployment Benefits in Great Britain, *Oxford Economic Papers* (forthcoming).

DANIEL, W. W. and STILGOE, E. (1977). Where are they now? *P.E.P. Broadsheet*, no. 572, London.

DEPARTMENT OF EMPLOYMENT (1977). Characteristics of the unemployed: sample survey, June 1976, *Gazette*, vol. 85 (June), pp. 559–574.

DISNEY, R. (1979). Recurrent Spells and the Concentration of Unemployment in Great Britain, *Economic Journal*, vol. 89 (March), pp. 109–119.

DOHERTY, N. (1979). National Insurance and absence from work, *Economic Journal*, vol. 89 (March), pp. 50–65.

GARFINKLE, S. H. (1977). The outcome of a spell of unemployment, *Monthly Labour Review*, vol. 100 (January), pp. 54–57.

KAITZ, R. B. (1970). Analysing the length of spells of unemployment, *Monthly Labour Review*, vol. 93 (November), pp. 11–20.

LANCASTER, T. (1979). Econometric methods for the duration of unemployment *Econometrica*, vol. 47, no. 4 (July), pp. 939–956.

MARSTON, S. T. (1976). Employment Instability and High Unemployment Rates, *Brookings Papers*, no. 1, pp. 452–464.

NICKELL, S. J. (1979). Estimating the probability of leaving unemployment, *Econometrica*, vol. 47, no. 5 (September), pp. 1249–1266.

SALANT, W. W. (1977). Search Theory and duration data: A theory of sorts, *Quarterly Journal of Economics*, vol. 91 (February), pp. 39–57.

SINGER, B. and SPILERMAN, S. (1976). The representation of Social Processes by Morkov models, *American Journal of Sociology*, vol. 82, pp. 1–54.

THOMAS, R. B. (1980). Wages, sickness benefits and absenteeism, *Journal of Economic Studies*, vol. 7, no. 1, pp. 51–61.

[5]

ELIGIBILITY FOR UNEMPLOYMENT BENEFITS IN GREAT BRITAIN

By JOHN CREEDY and RICHARD DISNEY*

I. Introduction

THE regime governing the payment of unemployment benefits has been a source of controversy in recent years in Britain and other industrialised countries. Critics have variously pointed to the alleged disincentive effects of current levels of benefit, the administrative complexity of the system, and the equity or otherwise of its provisions. An important problem that has arisen in recent years, which has some bearing on all these issues, is the increasing proportion of the unemployed who are unable to claim benefits under the provisions of the National Insurance scheme. By November 1978, less than 40 per cent of the unemployed were in receipt of National Insurance benefit.[1] The remainder had to fall back on the means-tested Supplementary Benefit sector, although in the planning stages of the National Insurance scheme it was confidently envisaged that Supplementary Benefit would only be necessary for small numbers—the 'residual categories'.[2]

This situation is clearly unsatisfactory. The low and declining eligible proportion raises the question of whether the 'insurance' content of the National Insurance scheme exists any longer for large numbers of unemployed people. Furthermore, from the point of view of administrative efficiency, the cost of administering the Supplementary Benefit Commission is proportionately much higher than is the case with the National Insurance scheme.[3]

The fundamental question raised by this issue concerns the extent to which declining eligibility is caused largely by the high level of unemployment, or whether it is a more basic fault of the unemployment benefit regime (the set of regulations concerning eligibility for, and exhaustion of, benefits). This cannot be answered simply by reference to available statistics, since there are no published data which classify the ineligible unemployed according to the various reasons for their ineligibility.

* We would like to thank our colleagues in Durham and Kent, and a referee of this Journal, for helpful comments on earlier drafts of this paper.

[1] See Department of Employment *Gazette* (September 1979, Table 112, p. 924). For further details see Clark (1978, p. 387), Atkinson and Flemming (1978, p. 8) and various *Reports of the Supplementary Benefit Commission.*

[2] The phrase is Bevan's, quoted in recent annual *Reports* of the S.B. Commission.

[3] According to Atkinson and Flemming (1978, p. 14) the costs are $13\frac{1}{2}\%$ and 4% respectively. However, a study of the figures given by the Department of Health and Social Security in *Hansard* (18 February, 1977) suggests that the proportions may be even higher.

The main purpose of this paper is to examine this question of eligibility in the British context. The regulations governing the operation of the unemployment benefit regime are described briefly in Section II. In Section III a simple model is developed which is capable of reproducing some of the main features of the flows into and out of unemployment in Great Britain. Section IV uses the model to examine eligibility, and the implications for policy are considered in Section V.

II. The benefit regime in Great Britain

The basis of the benefit regime remained largely unchanged from the start of the National Insurance scheme in 1946 until 1975, when the Social Security Act finalised the move towards earnings-related 'insurance'.[4] During this period individuals in employment (Class 1) and self-employment (Class 2) paid weekly contributions, together with a contribution from the employer in the case of Class 1 employees. For administration purposes these were accumulated in 'contribution years', each individual having been assigned to a year beginning in either March, June, September or December. Eligibility for National Insurance benefit was determined by the number of Class 1 contributions in the previous contribution year, and the year appropriate for benefit eligibility began five months after the end of the relevant contribution year. To qualify for the full flat-rate benefit an individual must have paid at least 26 contributions as an employed person (Class 1) since becoming 'insured', and must have paid or been credited with at least 50 Class 1 contributions in the contribution year to which the test applies. Reduced benefit, on a sliding scale, was payable to those with at least 26, but less than 50, contributions (paid or credited). Individuals were credited with a flat rate Class 1 contribution for each week which counted as a week of unemployment for benefit purposes, even if benefit had been exhausted.[5]

As a result of the 1975 Social Security Act, the contribution requirements have been altered in two respects. In the first place, the need for a minimum *number* of contributions has been replaced by a minimum *value* of contributions. Unlike the flat-rate principle established in the 1946 Act, contributions are proportional to earnings,[6] and the new requirement for full benefit

---

[4] The graduated pension scheme was introduced in 1961, and earnings related unemployment benefits in 1966. National Insurance benefit is actually administered by the Department of Employment for the Department of Health and Social Security, partly because of the close association between the Employment Service and unemployment registration.

[5] In certain circumstances, benefits could be raised for additional Class 2 contributions but Class 2 contributions alone were not sufficient to claim National Insurance benefit.

[6] The proportions are 5.5% for the employee and 8.5% for the employer, of all earnings up to the upper limit (but liability arises only after the basic minimum is achieved). The upper and lower limits in 1975 were £69 and £11 respectively, and the limits are raised regularly such that they are approximately $1\frac{1}{2}$ and $\frac{1}{4}$ of average male earnings.

is that in any contribution year a value of contributions equal to 50 times the value of contributions paid on earnings at the lower limit must be paid or credited. Thus, if the lower earnings limit is £10 a week, a person earning £50 weekly will have a sufficient value of contributions after only 10 weeks of any contribution year. For a reduced benefit of 50% of the full flat-rate benefit the requirement is 25 times the lower limit (and for 75% of the flat-rate, $37\frac{1}{2}$ times the lower limit). Eligibility for benefit is increased by this alteration so long as the lower limit is not set so high as to exclude a substantial proportion of wage earners. A further important condition is that credited contributions are only relevant to entitlement to the basic flat-rate benefit, not to Earnings Related Supplement. An additional amendment to the regime classifies the contribution year simply as the tax year, and the benefit year as the following calendar year.

There are other provisions common to both the old and revised schemes. Individuals who are eligible but on strike, left their job voluntarily or were dismissed for misconduct, cannot receive benefit for up to six weeks. Unemployment Benefit is not paid if the individual restricts 'unreasonably' the location or type of job he or she is willing to accept, or refuses 'without good cause' to take a job offered. These individuals, along with those with insufficient contributions, must apply to the means-tested Supplementary Benefit sector.[7] There are additional provisions covering new entrants to the labour force and working wives.

Another important regulation concerns what is known as the 'linked-spells' rule. Under this rule a person registering as unemployed must have worked for at least 13 weeks immediately preceding the unemployment spell, otherwise he or she will be treated as if the previous and current spells of unemployment were one spell of unemployment. In this case the claim for Unemployment Benefit will be exhausted before 52 weeks have elapsed in the current spell.

Earnings Related Supplement may be paid, in addition to flat-rate benefit, after two weeks and for a period of six months. The level of Supplement is based on income in the preceding tax year, with no adjustment for inflation.

It is immediately clear that this system bears very little resemblance to an 'insurance scheme', and it is not immediately clear how benefits and contributions are related to individual risks.[8] In examining how such a system may affect eligibility it is therefore important to use a model which explicitly

---

[7] However, persons not eligible for National Insurance benefit because of 'industrial misconduct' or 'voluntary unemployment' may have their Supplementary Benefit reduced for up to six weeks by 40% of the scale rate for single persons.

[8] Early schemes of unemployment benefit run, for example, by Trade Unions were operated on a risk pooling basis. Presumably these individuals faced similar types of risk, although Beveridge noted as early as 1909 that a relatively small proportion of individuals accounted for most of the insurance claims to these funds. See Garraty (1978, p. 138).

allows for differences between individuals. This is considered in the next section.

III. A model of unemployment flows

It is first important to stress that sufficient information about the benefit status of the unemployed cannot be obtained from the usual statistical sources which give details of the stock of registered unemployed at particular dates, and which may be compared with a 'snapshot' of a dynamic process. The characteristics of those individuals who are recorded by the snapshot will differ from those of the typical individual passing through the register. In particular, the distribution of complete spell lengths is positively skewed, so that the number of long duration unemployed on the register at any time is greater than in the total flow. The proportion of unemployed on the register who are receiving benefits will differ from the proportion of all unemployed passing through the register who receive benefits. For example, there may be a significant proportion of individuals who have short spells of unemployment but who are ineligible for benefits because of the 'linked-spells' rule. What is ideally required is a longitudinal study examining the employment of a cohort of individuals over a long period of time. Such a study is not at present available in Britain.[9]

(a) *The model*

The starting point of this section is a simple model in which each individual is assigned a constant probability of gaining employment if unemployed, say θ, and of becoming unemployed if employed, say λ. In particular, four groups of individuals stand out as posing distinct policy problems. Those with low values of both θ and λ suffer relatively few but on average long spells of unemployment. Few of the unemployed in this group will be ineligible for benefits at the beginning of the spell but a large proportion will suffer spells in excess of twelve months and thus exhaust their claim on unemployment benefit. This group probably contains a relatively large number of older workers. Another group, with low θ and high λ will, on average, suffer regular long spells of unemployment. They will suffer under the twelve months rule, the linked spells rule and the lack of paid contributions which will affect their eligibility for Earnings Related Supplement. A third group, with high θ and high λ suffer, on average, repeated short spells of unemployment and will be affected by the linked spells rule. This group will contain proportionately more young people. The final group, with low λ and high θ, obviously presents few problems because

---

[9] A study is, however, in preparation by the Department of Health and Social Security; although it is on a small scale and covers a rather short period.

TABLE 1
Joint distribution of λ and θ

| | | Probability of gaining employment | | |
		θ_1	θ_2	Total
Probability of becoming unemployed	λ_1	$P(\lambda_1, \theta_1)$	$P(\lambda_1, \theta_2)$	$P(\lambda_1)$
	λ_2	$P(\lambda_2, \theta_1)$	$P(\lambda_2, \theta_2)$	$P(\lambda_2)$
	Total	$P(\theta_1)$	$P(\theta_2)$	

individuals in this group are on average eligible for the full range of benefits in their short and infrequent spells of unemployment.[10]

The division of the population into these four groups is represented in Table 1, where

λ_i = probability of becoming unemployed for those in group i ($i = 1, 2$)

θ_j = probability of gaining employment for those in group j ($j = 1, 2$).

$P(\lambda_i)$ = proportion of population with $\lambda = \lambda_i$

$P(\theta_j)$ = proportion of population with $\theta = \theta_j$

$P(\lambda_i, \theta_j)$ = proportion with $\lambda = \lambda_i$ *and* $\theta = \theta_j$.

Thus, individuals characterised by low values of both λ and θ are placed in the group with $\lambda = \lambda_1$ and $\theta = \theta_1$. These people form a proportion $P(\lambda_1, \theta_1)$ of the population.

Two aspects of this framework require further discussion. First, it may be argued that the parameters of the model may be affected by the particular unemployment benefit regime in operation, but this can be examined by sensitivity analysis. The extent to which the benefit regime may affect search behaviour has been considered at length elsewhere.[11] Nevertheless the majority of studies of induced unemployment have assumed that all of the unemployed are always eligible for full benefits, making it difficult to integrate the behavioural models into the present framework, which is specifically designed to compare eligibility under alternative benefit regimes

---

[10] It may of course be argued that the model should allow for greater heterogeneity. However, realistic parameter values have been obtained for the four groups used here, and the results of the model can easily be interpreted. The choice of a functional form to represent a joint distribution of λ and θ would be rather arbitrary, and estimation would be impossible with available data for Great Britain. But for discussion of a possible functional form see Frank (1978).

[11] Empirical studies for Britain include Spindler and Maki (1975, 1979), Cubbin and Foley (1977) and Sawyer (1979). Some aspects of optimal unemployment insurance are considered in, for example, Bailey (1978) and Flemming (1978), who examine behavioural models with homogeneous individuals. As mentioned above, the effects of different behaviour (as a result of changes in the regime) in the present context can best be seen by examining results with different parameter values.

within a heterogeneous population. Secondly, the assumption that for any individual the probability of re-employment remains constant over the spell of unemployment is rather strong, although within a heterogeneous population this is consistent with the observed fall in the aggregate re-employment probability.[12] Changes in θ will of course also result from changes in the state of the economy, and again the present approach has the advantage of facilitating comparisons in the form of a sensitivity analysis of the effects of variations in the relevant parameters.

(b) *Parameter values*

The next step is to assign values to the four joint probabilities. Some information about the distribution of θ for males is given in Cripps and Tarling (1974, p. 304). It is, however, important to note that their estimates are based on samples of the unemployed, rather than of the total population, and therefore strictly relate to spells of unemployment, rather than to individuals. In the absence of suitable data which exactly correspond to the definitions given above, it is necessary to use the results of Cripps and Tarling while bearing in mind the possibility that they may be slightly biased. They show that in December 1955, a distinct group, accounting for approximately 10% of the flow, had a very low probability of leaving the unemployment register of 0.013 a week. In the following calculations, the low value θ_1 is therefore set at 0.013 a week, with $P(\theta_1) = 0.10$. The average duration of spells of unemployment among this group, given by $1/\theta_1$, is around nineteen months. The value of $P(\theta_2)$ is then 0.9 and the average value of θ for this group, again from Cripps and Tarling, may be calculated as approximately 0.4 a week. However, there was a particularly tight labour market in 1955, and it seems likely that the value of θ_2 has been very much lower in recent years. This is because variations in the level of unemployment are brought about largely by changes in the duration of unemployment; that is, changes in the probability of leaving, rather than that of entering, the register. In the spirit of the present model it is therefore suggested that changes in unemployment are brought about primarily through changes in the value of θ_2.[13]

Evidence for the distribution of λ is more tenuous, but an analysis of labour turnover using a two-probability model is given in Metcalf and

---

[12] See, for example, Cripps and Tarling (1974) and Salant (1977). The basic problem is that the available data cannot distinguish between the separate effects of composition and declining probabilities, as noted in the interesting discussion by Bartlett (1951, p. 27). More recent studies include Nickell (1979), Lancaster (1979) and McGregor (1978), although the latter wrongly interprets his regression results.

[13] Thus demand conditions are assumed to affect the probability of re-employment for the predominantly short-spell individuals. The lower value of θ is assumed to be relatively unaffected by demand changes, as this depends more on structural factors.

Tarling (1975, Appendix 1). For the group with low turnover, λ_1, they used a probability of 0.0006 a week. This implies an average time between spells of unemployment within this group of about 32 years. Having set this value, Metcalf and Tarling then proceeded to estimate values of λ_2 and $P(\lambda_2)$ using turnover data from the New Earnings Survey. Their estimates of $\lambda_2 = 0.036$ and $P(\lambda_2) = 0.15$ are used here. Thus for this group the average time between unemployment spells is about 27 weeks.

Unfortunately, even less is known about the joint probabilities $P(\lambda_i, \theta_j)$. With only four groups there is, however, only one degree of freedom available given the values of the marginal totals $P(\lambda_i)$ and $P(\theta_j)$. The implications of alternative assumptions can therefore easily be derived. Consider the conditional probability of a person having the low value of θ (that is, θ_1) given that he has the high value of λ (that is, λ_2). If those with a high probability of becoming unemployed also have a low probability of gaining employment, then the proportion with $\theta = \theta_1$, among those with $\lambda = \lambda_2$ would be higher than the proportion with $\theta = \theta_1$ in the general population.[14] If this conditional probability is denoted $P(\theta_1 \mid \lambda_2)$, then the joint probability may easily be obtained from $P(\theta_1, \lambda_2) = P(\theta_1 \mid \lambda_2)P(\lambda_2)$. If it is assumed, for example, that $P(\theta_1 \mid \lambda_2) = 0.2$ (rather than being equal to $P(\theta_1)$, which is 0.10) then the other joint probabilities may be obtained by appropriate subtraction from the marginal proportions, and the complete joint distribution is given in Table 2.

TABLE 2
Joint distribution $P(\lambda, \theta)$

	$\theta_1 = 0.013$	$\theta_2 = 0.30$	$P(\lambda)$
$\lambda_1 = 0.0006$	0.07	0.78	0.85
$\lambda_2 = 0.036$	0.03	0.12	0.15
$P(\theta)$	0.10	0.90	1.0

N.b. Obtained using $P(\theta_1 \mid \lambda_2) = 0.20$.

Now the equilibrium unemployment rate within each group is given by $\lambda_i/(\lambda_i + \theta_j)$ and the average number of spells of unemployment per period is given by $\lambda_i \theta_j/(\lambda_i + \theta_j)$.[15] Using the assumptions needed to calculate Table 2, the unemployment rate in the low risk group (low λ, high θ) is only 0.2% while for those with θ_1 and λ_2, the unemployment rate is 73%. This latter group, who in this case account for 3% of the population, experience on

---

[14] There is some evidence that this is the case. See Hill (1978, Table 4) who provides a joint distribution of unemployment length and unemployment frequencies. These results cannot be used directly here, however.

[15] In equilibrium the probability of being unemployed is constant.

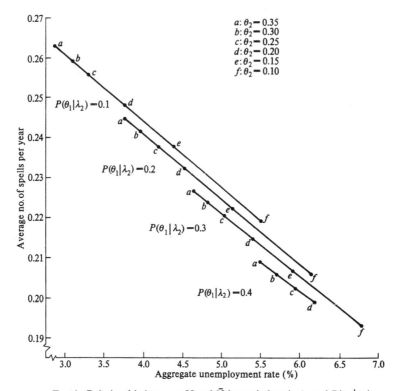

FIG. 1. Relationship between U and $\bar{N}$ for variations in θ_2 and $P(\theta_1 \mid \lambda_2)$.

average one spell of unemployment every 2 years. The group characterised by repeated spells (λ_2 and θ_2) experience, on average, 1.67 spells per year.[16]

Table 2 may be combined with the values of λ and θ in order to obtain the aggregate unemployment rate, U, and the average number of spells of unemployment per year, $\bar{N}$, over all groups. These are given by

$$U = \sum_i \sum_j \frac{\lambda_i}{\lambda_i + \theta_j} P(\lambda_i, \theta_j) \qquad (1)$$

and

$$\bar{N} = 52 \sum_i \sum_j \frac{\lambda_i \theta_j}{\lambda_i + \theta_j} P(\lambda_i, \theta_j) \qquad (2)$$

Under these particular assumptions it is found that $U = 3.9\%$ and $\bar{N} = 0.24$. Varying θ_2 and $P(\theta_1 \mid \lambda_2)$ gives different values of U and $\bar{N}$. This can be seen from Fig. 1 where, not unexpectedly, reducing θ_2 and raising $P(\theta_1 \mid \lambda_2)$ gives

---

[16] This may be compared with the values given in Disney (1979). It can also be noted that this group has an unemployment rate of 11%, because of the higher rate of flows through the register.

higher equilibrium rates of unemployment, and reduces the value of $\bar{N}$. This is because the longer average duration of spells of unemployment reduces the number of spells that can be undertaken in a given time period. Notice that the relationship between U and $\bar{N}$ is linear for variations in θ_2 for given $P(\theta_1 | \lambda_2)$ and that the slope is the same for each value of the latter conditional probability (and similarly for given θ_2 and variation in $P(\theta_1 | \lambda_2)$). The value of U may easily be contrasted with recent experience. Although estimates of $\bar{N}$ are more difficult to obtain, a value of approximately 0.24 seems to be appropriate for Great Britain.[17]

IV. Eligibility for benefits

Eligibility for National Insurance benefits largely depends on the value of contributions paid during the previous year, the length of the current spell of unemployment, and the time between spells of unemployment. A feature of the present model is that, within each of the four groups, the probability of a spell of unemployment or employment lasting a given number of weeks is independent of the time which has elapsed since the previous spell of unemployment. This property facilitates calculation of the equilibrium proportion of individuals within each group who are not eligible for benefits given the various regulations.

(a) *Benefit exhaustion*

One of the most important regulations is that concerned with the duration of the various unemployment benefits. If the individual has sufficient contributions, Earnings Related Supplement is payable for 26 weeks, and flat-rate unemployment benefit (leaving aside for the moment the linked-spells rule) for 52 weeks. Let

$P(U_j > t) = $ probability that a spell of unemployment exceeds t weeks for an individual in the group with $\theta = \theta_j$.

With constant probabilities this distribution is geometric, which is the discrete time analog of the exponential distribution. It is therefore convenient to use $P(U_j > t) = \exp(-\theta_j t)$. Then the proportion of the total unemployed who have been on the register for more than t weeks, $P(U > t)$ is given by

$$P(U > t) = \sum_{j=1}^{2} P(U_j > t) \left\{ \sum_{i=1}^{2} \frac{\lambda_i}{\lambda_i + \theta_j} P(\lambda_i, \theta_j) \right\} \Big/ U \qquad (3)$$

---

[17] By dividing the number of spells per year by the labour force a value of just under 0.2 is obtained. Further allowance for repeated spells (using estimates contained in Disney (1979)) gives a value of $\bar{N}$ of approximately 0.24.

J. CREEDY AND R. DISNEY   265

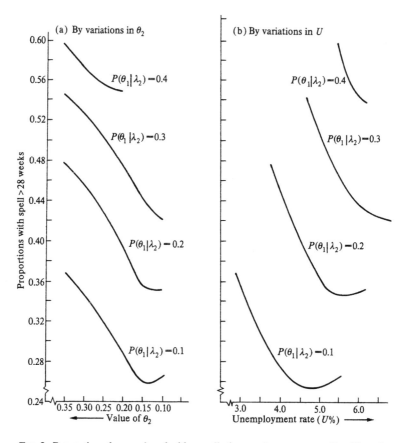

FIG. 2. Proportion of unemployed with a spell of unemployment exceeding 28 weeks.

Figure 2 depicts the results for $t > 28$ and Fig. 3 for $t > 52$ weeks under various assumptions about θ_2 and $P(\theta_1 \mid \lambda_2)$. In both cases it is noticeable that the proportions are rather sensitive to changes in the parameters and an increase in the unemployment rate, via a fall in θ_2, leads to a fall in the proportion of the unemployed with spells greater than 52 weeks, although of course the absolute number of individuals in this category shows a slight increase. The reason for this result is that the unemployment rate increases because the average duration of spells increases among those with relatively short duration unemployment; that is, with θ_2 rather than θ_1. Further falls in θ_2 would increase the proportion with $t > 52$. This can be seen by returning to Fig. 2 where the same pattern is shown for $t > 28$ until θ_2 falls below about 0.15. At this point the proportion nearing exhaustion of their entitlement to Earnings Related Supplement begins to rise as some of the θ_2 group begin to have spells exceeding 28 weeks.

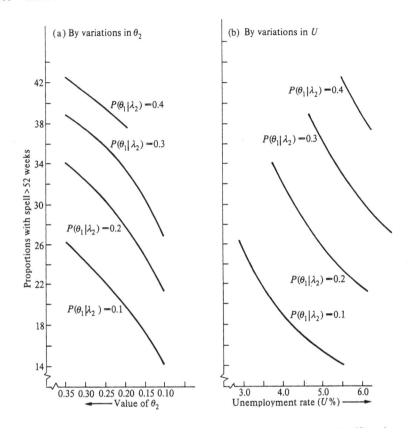

FIG. 3. Proportion of unemployed with a spell of unemployment exceeding 52 weeks.

The falling proportions in Figs. 2 and 3 for $\theta_2 > 0.15$ are partly a consequence of the assumption that re-employment probabilities are independent of duration. If the probability of leaving the register falls with duration, then the proportion with $t > 52$ will not fall so rapidly as the unemployment rate rises. However the probability would need to fall rapidly early in the spell of unemployment, and evidence suggests that this is not the case.[18]

Despite these qualifications, it is clear from these results that the rule concerning duration of benefit receipt cannot be the sole explanation of the low coverage of unemployment benefit. Unless unemployment is unrealistically low, the proportion of the unemployed who exhaust their entitlement to Unemployment Benefit because they are unemployed for longer than 52 weeks is much lower than observed proportions. This factor therefore only

[18] See, for example, Nickell (1979).

partly explains the large numbers among the stock of unemployed who are observed to be receiving Supplementary Benefit alone.

(b) *The linked-spells rule*

From the results of the previous section it seems that a significant proportion of the unemployed exhaust entitlement to benefits before 52 weeks have been completed in the current spell. As explained in Section II, the linked-spells rule means that spells of unemployment, which are not separated by at least 13 weeks, cannot be considered as separate spells for the purposes of qualifying for benefits. Now denote the probability that a spell of *employment* lasts less than t weeks, for individuals in the group with $\lambda = \lambda_i$, by $P(E_i < t)$. This is given by $1 - \exp(-\lambda_i t)$, and the probability of an unemployed individual having previously had a spell of employment of less than t weeks is given by

$$P(E < t) = \sum_{i-1}^{2} P(E_i < t)\left\{\sum_{j=1}^{2} \frac{\lambda_i}{\lambda_i + \theta_j} P(\lambda_i, \theta_j)\right\}\Big/U \qquad (4)$$

Equation (4) can then be used to examine the case where $t = 13$.

Figure 4 depicts the results for the present model. The proportion affected by this rule remains roughly constant at 30–35% of the unemployed. These individuals will exhaust their benefit before reaching 52 weeks in the current spell and it can be seen that they represent a substantial proportion of the unemployed. At certain rates of unemployment the linked spells rule can actually be a more important explanation of benefit exhaustion than the 52 week duration condition. Furthermore, the proportion of the unemployed with a previous spell of employment of less than 13 weeks is not sensitive to the aggregate unemployment rate. Exhaustion of benefits because of the linked-spells rule is therefore still important in periods of high demand.

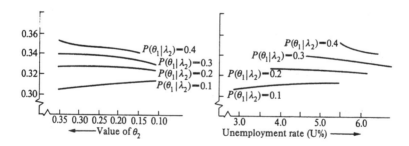

Fig. 4. Proportion of unemployed with a previous spell of employment of less than 13 weeks.

(c) *Contributions requirements*

The model has been used in Sections IV(a) and IV(b) to consider the reasons for benefit exhaustion. As noted in Section II, some of the unemployed do not receive National Insurance benefits for other reasons. Some will be excluded for a specified period of time for voluntary quitting and misconduct. Others do not have enough contributions and credits to qualify for flat-rate benefit, or enough contributions to qualify for Earnings Related Supplement. This section briefly considers these contributions requirements.

In its survey of recipients of Supplementary Benefit among the male unemployed in May 1977, the DHSS found that whereas 49% had exhausted their claims to Unemployment Benefit a further 38% had insufficient contributions to qualify.[19] This survey of course only shows a 'snapshot' of the stock of unemployed at that date but it is surprising that the latter proportion is so high, given that the regulations governing new entrants to the labour force have been liberalised recently and, following the 1975 Act, the eligibility requirements for National Insurance benefit are reduced for anyone receiving weekly earnings above the lower earnings limit. The main reason for insufficient contributions is that the individual has just entered or re-entered the labour market. The present model only contains two 'states', employment and unemployment, and cannot therefore be used to examine this aspect of eligibility.[20]

Eligibility for Earnings Related Supplement (ERS) depends on the value of contributions which have actually been paid, since credits only count towards flat-rate benefits. Having considered exhaustion of ERS in a previous section, it is of interest to examine separately the effect of the contributions requirement. The relevant legislation requires that the upper and lower earnings limits will be raised periodically so that they are approximately $1\frac{1}{2}$ and $\frac{1}{4}$ of average male earnings respectively. Let δ denote the contributions rate, $\bar{y}$ the average male weekly earnings and y an individual's weekly earnings while employed. The rules require that to qualify for ERS, the individual must have worked for at least t weeks in the relevant contributions year, where

$$t\delta y = 50\delta(\bar{y}/4) \quad \text{and} \quad t = 12.5(\bar{y}/y) \tag{5}$$

Thus it is necessary to earn at least $12\frac{1}{2}$ times the average weekly earnings, subject to a minimum of 9 weeks' contributions because of the upper earnings limit. Now the proportion of individuals working less than any given number of weeks can be calculated using the model of Section III. In equilibrium, the probability of being unemployed in any week, u, is equal to

[19] See Clark (1978, p. 338).
[20] Some information about other labour market flows is given in Creedy and Disney (1981).

$\lambda/(\lambda + \theta)$. The proportion of a group experiencing no unemployment over a period of T weeks (say one year) is therefore $(1-u)^T$, and in general it can be shown that the proportion experiencing no more that t weeks of unemployment, P_t is given by

$$P_t = \binom{T}{t} u^t (1-u)^{T-t} \tag{6}$$

and the distribution of total time in unemployment is binomial. Equation (6) refers to a specific group (characterised by λ and θ) and suitable earnings distributions for each group are not available. Thus the present model cannot be directly applied to this question.

However, there is a further interesting point in the present context which concerns the averaging procedure by which ERS is calculated. If an individual is eligible for ERS, the amount paid is calculated by dividing annual income by 50.[21] If ERS were instead assessed simply on the basis of 'normal' weekly income when in work, the amount paid would be much higher for those who suffer regular interruptions of employment. Using equation (6), and aggregating over the four groups, the equilibrium proportion of those becoming unemployed with no more than two weeks of unemployment in a year can be calculated.[22] The model suggests that only about one fifth of the unemployed satisfy this condition, even under the most favourable demand conditions (that is, when θ_2 is relatively high). Thus most of the unemployed probably have their ERS reduced, relative to the rate which would apply to their normal income in employment, by this procedure.

Finally, it should be noted that even for those who are eligible for the full rate of ERS, a further proportion of the unemployed have their claim disqualified as a result of the rule that the combined total of Unemployment Benefit and Earnings Related Supplement must not exceed 85% of previous earnings.[23]

V. Policy conclusions

One of the most important conclusions arising from Section IV concerns the question of benefit exhaustion. The results show that between one sixth

---

[21] See the annual HMSO publication *Social Security Statistics* for some details for the amount of ERS paid.

[22] Substitution for $t = 2$ in equation (6) gives

$$P_t = \left(\frac{\theta}{\lambda + \theta}\right)^T \left\{1 + T\frac{\lambda}{\theta} + \frac{T(T-1)}{2}\left(\frac{\lambda}{\theta}\right)^2\right\}.$$

This can then be aggregated over the four groups as before.

[23] See *Social Assistance: A Review of the Supplementary Benefits Scheme in Great Britain* (HMSO, 1978, p. 15).

and two fifths of the unemployed may have spells exceeding one year, and will exhaust their claim to National Insurance benefits. The model suggests, however, that the proportion of the unemployed exhausting their claim for this reason may fall as the unemployment rate rises because the lengthening of durations is concentrated initially among those who, on average, suffer shorter spells.

Previous studies have not introduced explicitly the probability of entering the register. Results from the present model suggest that when this is taken into account the linked-spells rule becomes a sizable reason for benefit exhaustion, with the proportion at risk of being affected by this rule accounting for up to one third of the unemployed. This proportion seems to be insensitive to changes in demand conditions and assumptions made about the joint distribution of λ and θ. Previous policy recommendations have therefore ignored the impact of this regulation. Neither the proportion of the unemployed affected by the linked-spells rule, nor by the rule limiting receipt of unemployment benefit to 52 weeks, are positively related to changes in the level of unemployment. Therefore, in answer to the question posed in Section I, this apparent failure of the National Insurance scheme must stem from a basic fault in the system, rather than being an unavoidable feature of high unemployment. The question then arises of how these regulations may be justified, if at all.

From the point of view of administrative efficiency, the actual operation of both rules requires information about previous and current spell durations. When National Insurance benefits are exhausted the savings obtained by excluding a minority from Supplementary Benefits by use of the means-test may well be offset by the extra administrative cost incurred. There are also small, and unnecessary, differences between the relevant basic rates for short-term National Insurance benefits and Supplementary Benefit, which increase administrative costs. The present rules are probably, therefore, more costly to administer than a regime without them.

The linked-spells rule is presumably intended to deter excessive job turnover on the grounds that it imposes costs on the economy. But insofar as turnover is voluntary, there are other regulations in the benefit regime which restrict the payment of benefit in such cases. On the other hand if short spells of employment are involuntary, it would appear to be inequitable to penalise individuals who already have little or no claim on other benefits such as Redundancy Payments.

A second aspect of the benefit regime examined here concerns the contribution requirements for Unemployment Benefit and Earnings Related Supplement. Now while National Insurance benefits are, generally, cheaper to administer than Supplementary Benefit, the need to establish the value of previous contributions plus, in the case of ERS, previous earnings, raises costs. The small value of ERS payments (just over £100 million) suggests that it has a rather high ratio of administrative costs to benefits paid.

A wider examination of these regulations would, of course, bring into question whether payments to the unemployed should be part of a system of 'National Insurance' at all, or, rather part of an 'unemployment compensation' scheme. Certainly the existing regulations and the exclusions resulting from them do not seem to be based on any clear economic rationale. The post-1975 rules have been described as

> a quagmire of contributions, credits and earnings factors . . . which . . . makes the continuance of the contributory principle harder to justify, when other methods exist for testing present attachment to the labour market. When there is a gap of nine months between contribution year and benefit year, the relevance of that past period to current entitlement is slim (Mesher (1976, p. 23)).

The contrast is therefore between the use of a pseudo-insurance system combined with a means-tested sector, and an unemployment compensation system which tests 'attachment' to the labour force and 'willingness to work'. Since, as shown in this paper, the means-tested sector is unlikely to have to deal with only 'residual categories', a thorough cost-benefit analysis of alternative methods would be extremely useful.

Finally, it is suggested that the approach taken here which explicitly considers population heterogeneity and flows in and out of unemployment, is potentially more useful than the analysis of single isolated spells in the context of a homogeneous population. Furthermore, those studies which attempt to examine the duration of spells of unemployment on the assumption that the unemployed are eligible for all forms of benefit at the beginning of the spell are likely to be highly misleading. The practical problems of designing an unemployment benefit regime which deals with the needs of particular groups remains the important and difficult task.

University of Durham and
University of Kent

REFERENCES

ATKINSON, A. B. and FLEMMING, J. S. (1978) Unemployment, social security and incentives, *Midland Bank Review*, Autumn.

BAILEY, M. N. (1978) Some aspects of optimal unemployment insurance, *Journal of Public Economics*, 10.

BARTLETT, M. S. (1951) Some remarks on the theory of statistics, *Manchester Statistical Society*, January.

CLARK, M. (1978) The unemployed on supplementary benefit: living standards and making ends meet on a low income, *Journal of Social Policy*, 7, no. 4.

CREEDY, J. and DISNEY, R. (1981) Labour market flows in Great Britain, *Scottish Journal of Political Economy*, 28, no. 1.

272   ELIGIBILITY FOR UNEMPLOYMENT BENEFITS IN GREAT BRITAIN

CRIPPS, T. F. and TARLING, R. J. (1974) An analysis of the duration of male unemployment in Great Britain, 1932–1973, *Economic Journal*, 84.

CUBBIN, J. S. and FOLEY, K. (1977) The extent of benefit-induced unemployment in Great Britain; Some new evidence, *Oxford Economic Papers*, 29.

DISNEY, R. (1979) Recurrent spells and the concentration of unemployment in Great Britain, *Economic Journal*, 89.

FLEMMING, J. S. (1978) Aspects of optimal unemployment Insurance, *Journal of Public Economics*, 10.

FRANK, R. H. (1978) How long is a spell of unemployment? *Econometrica*, 46, no. 2.

GARRATY, J. (1978) *Unemployment in History*, Harper and Row.

HILL, M. J. (1978) Evidence submitted to the *Royal Commission on the Distribution of Income and Wealth for Report No. 6: Lower Incomes*, HMSO.

MCGREGOR, A. (1978) Unemployment duration and re-employment probability, *Economic Journal*, 88.

MESHER, J. (1976) *Compensation for Unemployment*, Sweet and Maxwell.

METCALF, D. and TARLING, R. J. (1975) Labour Market Flows. *Department of Employment* (mimeo).

NICKELL, S. (1979) Estimating the probability of leaving unemployment, *Econometrica*, 47.

SALANT, W. (1977) Search theory and duration data: A theory of sorts, *Quarterly Journal of Economics*.

SAWYER, M. C. (1979) The effects of unemployment compensation on the rate of unemployment in Great Britain: A comment, *Oxford Economic Papers*, 31.

SPINDLER, Z. A. and MAKI, D. (1975) The effect of unemployment compensation on the rate of unemployment in Great Britain, *Oxford Economic Papers*, 27.

SPINDLER, Z. A. and MAKI, D. (1979) More on the effects of unemployment compensation on the rate of unemployment in Great Britain, *Oxford Economic Papers*, 31.

APPENDIX: THE MARCH 1980 BUDGET

The budget of March 1980 made some important amendments to the unemployment benefit regime in Great Britain. The first was to reduce the scale rate for payment of Earnings Related Supplement (ERS) from January 1981 and to phase-out ERS completely by January 1982. Unemployment Benefit was to be increased by 5 per cent less than long term benefits in the November 1980 uprating, and it was proposed to tax short term insurance benefits from April 1982 or as soon as possible thereafter. It was also planned to alter the linked spells rule, shortening the linking period from 13 to six weeks and instituting 'waiting days' for linked spells. However, these latter proposals were amended in committee by increasing the linking period to eight weeks and dropping the provision of 'waiting days' for linked spells. At the time of writing, the final form of this regulation is still unclear.

Section IV(c) above suggested that eligibility for full ERS has always been rather low, and implied that the grounds for maintaining ERS were rather slender. Nevertheless, the proposed changes in the regulations heighten the argument outlined in Section V, namely that the benefit regime is now excessively complex. Earnings-related contributions finance flat-rate benefits, which are supplemented by means-tested benefits financed from general taxation. An increasing proportion of the unemployed will require means-tested Supplementary Benefit which is more expensive to administer, as a result of the phasing-out of ERS and the increasing average duration of spells of unemployment as the current recession deepens. These amendments call into question the whole basis of the 'insurance' system for the unemployed.[1]

The possible effect of changes in the linked spells rule can be analysed by applying a sensitivity analysis to the calculations described in Section IV(b) and depicted in Fig. 4.

[1] For further discussion of the state of the 'insurance' system, see Metcalf (1980) and Disney (1981).

TABLE A1
The linked-spells rule

Weeks of employment, t	3	6	9	12	15	18
$P(E < t)$	0.09	0.17	0.24	0.31	0.37	0.42

Note: Value of $P(\theta_1 \mid \lambda_2) = 0.2$. See Section IV(b) for calculation of $P(E < t)$.

Again the results are not sensitive to the unemployment rate, and results are given in Table A1 for a single joint distribution of $P(\lambda, \theta)$. The results suggest that for the original proposal of six weeks, 17 per cent of the unemployed would be at risk of being affected by the linked-spells rule. The proportion rises to over 20 per cent for eight weeks. The impact of this amendment, subject to whether 'waiting days' are instituted for the linked spell, will therefore be to increase slightly eligibility for Unemployment Benefit.[2]

Furthermore, the higher unemployment rate of 1980, implying longer durations, suggests that an increased proportion of the unemployed will begin to experience spells exceeding 26 weeks and, possibly, 52 weeks. This will increase the numbers exhausting their claim on ERS prior to 1982 and may even raise the proportion as well as the absolute number of those eligible for only means-tested benefit because their spells exceed one year.

REFERENCES

METCALF, D. (1980) 'Goodbye to National Insurance' *New Society*, June 26th, 349–350.
DISNEY, R. (1981) 'Unemployment Insurance in Great Britain' in J. Creedy (ed.) *The Economics of Unemployment in Britain*, Butterworths.

[2] However, the new regulation will make it more difficult for the sick to become eligible for the long term rate of National Insurance benefit.

[6]

Applied Economics, 1983, **15**, 177–185

Firm formation in manufacturing industry

J. CREEDY and P. S. JOHNSON

Department of Economics, University of Durham, UK

I. INTRODUCTION

In 1971 the Bolton Committee of Inquiry on Small Firms attributed a vital economic function to new businesses. They stated that

> 'We believe that the health of the economy requires the birth of new enterprises in substantial number and the growth of some to a position from which they are able to challenge and supplant the existing leaders of industry.' (HMSO, 1971, p. 85)

This view, which does of course have strong overtones of Marshall's 'trees of the forest' analogy,[1] was backed by little supporting evidence.[2] Yet it served to increase both policy interest and research in the economic role of new firms. The present government now sees the encouragement of such enterprises as an important part of its industrial policy not least because they are regarded as a significant source of new jobs. On the research side, several studies have now been undertaken on new firms.[3] As a result of these studies the availability of data on the extent and nature of formation activity in particular regions and areas of the UK is now much improved. There has also been a very considerable increase in the management literature on new and small firms. However, relatively little attention has been given to the formal modelling of the formation decision (although there is no shortage of suggestions about why people form businesses). This paper represents an attempt to provide a step towards filling this gap. Section I outlines a very simple model of the for-

---

[1] It is interesting to note that in the sixth and following editions of his *Principles* Marshall admitted that the advent of the joint stock company might have modified the applicability of the analogy by increasing the adaptability of the established business which is challenged by younger rivals. Such a company 'often stagnate(s) but do(es) not readily die' (1920, p. 263). At the same time, it is still likely 'to have lost so much of its elasticity and progressive force, that the advantages are no longer exclusively on its side in its competition with younger and smaller rivals' (p. 264).

[2] It is perhaps surprising that although the committee stressed the lack of availability of satisfactory data on firm births (HMSO 1971, pp. 72–73) and attached considerable economic importance to births, none of its commissioned research reports was specifically concerned with the formation process.

[3] A number of studies of particular areas have been made, including Beesley (1955), Firn and Swales (1978), Gudgin (1978), Fothergill and Gudgin (1979), Johnson and Cathcart (1979a), Robinson and Storey (1981) and Cross (1981).

0003-6846/83 $03.00 + .12. © *1983 Chapman and Hall Ltd.* 177

mation decision which may be used in empirical work.[4] In Section II the model is applied to cross section data for manufacturing industry in the UK.

It is important to stress that the concern of this paper is with the formation of entirely new businesses and not with those formed as the result of diversification by existing businesses. Because of the paucity of data in this area, the approach must necessarily be rather basic, and the results regarded as suggestive rather than conclusive.

II. A FRAMEWORK OF ANALYSIS

The first basic element of the present approach is the argument that the formation of a new business involves the transfer, for the founder of the business, from the status of being an *employee* to being *self-employed*. The framework does not therefore apply to individuals who remain in employment while devoting their 'spare time' to a small business; such cases would be unlikely to employ other individuals (or be recorded in official data).

The potential founder may therefore be viewed as comparing his expected income from remaining an employee with his expected income which may result from setting up his own business.[5] While the comparison between employment and self-employment income is fundamental to the present analysis, and may indeed seem to be an obvious component of a model of firm formation, it is surprising that in the literature on both barriers to entry and the nature of the firm, areas in which new firm formation is central to the analysis, there is little explicit treatment of the earnings that the potential founder may obtain in paid employment.[6] For present purposes it is assumed that potential founders consider only prospective incomes within the industry in which they are currently employed. This assumption is not entirely unrealistic, since the majority of founders are likely to consider manufacturing possibilities only within the range of their own experience.

It is therefore suggested that the proportion of employees in an industry who successfully form a new business depends on the proportion for whom the expected income from self-employment exceeds the expected income from employment by a minimum amount. This minimum, or 'threshold', level depends on a number of factors, including barriers to entry within the industry. There are differences between individuals in their perceived prospects from employment and self-employment, and the distribution of the ratio of the latter to the former may be expected to follow a unimodal distribution which is positively skewed. It is clear that not all of those who would like to form a new business will succeed in doing so, or will manage to survive for a sufficient length of time, or grow to a sufficient size, to be included in official statistics. It is important to stress at this stage that the formation of new firms necessarily represents a *process* of adjustment, and the analysis is not concerned directly with the question of the *equilibrium* number of firms in an industry. Such an analysis would require a much more extensive model, and considerably more data.

[4]A general equilibrium analysis of firm formation is given by Kihlstrom and Laffont (1979).
[5]Knight (1921, p. 271) refers to the former as contractual income and the latter as residual income, but these terms are not used here.
[6]This is true of Bain (1952), Coase (1937), Alchian and Demsetz (1972) and Williamson (1975).

The above arguments suggest therefore that the 'formation rate' (the number of new firms recorded over a specified period as a ratio of the number of employees) in an industry is proportional to the percentage of individuals for whom expected self-employment income exceeds expected employment earnings by the minimum (threshold) amount. Further empirical content must of course be added to this simple statement, and it is first useful to examine the ways in which the framework may deal with a number of elements which are commonly associated with firm formation.

Comparison of prospects in self employment with those of employment in an industry may well be influenced by a number of non-monetary considerations. Such factors have long been acknowledged, and several authors have stressed considerations such as independence, prestige and power in self-employment.[7] These factors are of course notoriously difficult to measure quantitatively, though their importance is shown by questionnaire results. However, in the context of a cross-section analysis it may reasonably be supposed that non-pecuniary factors are associated with the status of self-employment itself, and are not industry specific. They may therefore be excluded from the statistical analysis.

It is often suggested that unemployment in an industry may stimulate firm formation, and there is some evidence from questionnaires that the threat of unemployment may sometimes affect the formation decision.[8] In the present framework the extent of unemployment in an industry may therefore be used in the construction of measures of expected earnings. There is the further point that the chances of survival in an industry (for sufficiently long to be recorded in official data) may also be related to unemployment. The present framework also allows for this kind of effect to be included in the specification.

It may also be thought that the structure of the industry in which an individual is employed has some effect on the formation decision. For example, there is some evidence which suggests that proportionately more founders come from smaller plants.[9] To the extent that earnings from employment and profits are affected by the size of firm, the structure of the industry will be reflected in the form of the distribution of the ratio of expected self-employment income to employment income. In this case the structure of the industry does not need to be introduced explicitly into the model. However, it may be argued that barriers to entry vary across industries. The approach taken here is to use a direct measure of the difficulty of forming an entirely new firm in an industry; namely the capital expenditure required.

III. EMPIRICAL RESULTS

The data

The very basic approach outlined in the previous section may in principle, after the addition of sufficient empirical content, be applied to single industries over a period of time,

[7]See the survey by Parnes (1970), McClelland (1961, p. 52), Boswell (1971, p. 55), Golby and Johns (1971, p. 59), Roberts and Wainer (1971) and Scott (1978).
[8]See Schumpeter (1939, p. 94, fn.), Oxenfeldt (1943, pp. 120–3) and Steindl (1945, p. 61).
[9]See Johnson and Cathcart (1979b) and Cross (1981, p. 220–2).

or to a cross-section of industries. However, time series data are not available, so that the results presented here apply to a cross-section. As with all cross-section analyses it is necessary to assume that the basic parameters of the model are the same in each industry.

The detailed specification of the model for empirical purposes is necessarily severely restricted by the available data. Indeed, very few data on formations by industry are available for the UK; for example, company and business name registrations are not broken down by industry. The formation data used in this paper are derived from the Department of Industry's monitoring of openings and closures in the U.K. regions. One of the categories used by the Department is that of 'Enterprise New to Manufacturing' (ENMs).[10] This category covers openings of establishments which do not have a manufacturing parent. Here attention is restricted further to ENMs without origin (ENMWOs), by excluding the opening of an establishment with any parent. Such ENMWOs come fairly close to the definition of the new firm used in this paper. The ENMWOs are allocated to orders under the 1968 Standard Industrial Classification. Unfortunately, the monitoring of ENMWOs is not entirely consistent in its coverage; while in most of the U.K., ENMWOs which reach 11 employees are included, the minima in the Greater London Council and the West Midlands Metropolitan County are 20 and 50 respectively. These two areas have, therefore, been excluded from consideration in this paper.

It is important to stress that only firms which reach 11 employees and which were in existence in 1977 are included in the analysis, so that the expression 'survival' (used in Section II) should be interpreted to mean 'grow to at least 11 employees and survive to 1977'. These formation data are available for the twelve-year period 1966 to 1977; the annual average value in each industry has been used here.[11] In calculating the formation rate the denominator is measured by the average number of full-time male employees in each industry over the period 1966–77.[12] These data are published in the Department of Employment *Gazette*. The formation rate is measured as an annual average rate of formation per 1000 male employees.

It is shown in the Appendix that the framework outlined in Section II, combined with a number of convenient simplifications, suggests that the formation rate is given as follows:

$$R = \beta_0 + \beta_1 \log \Pi - \beta_2 \log Y - \beta_3 \log C + u \qquad (1)$$

In Equation 1 R is the formation rate, Π is the geometric mean of expected income from self-employment, Y is the geometric mean of expected earnings from employment, and C is

---

[10]The Department's monitoring system does not, however, define a change of ownership *alone* as the formation of an ENM. A change in both ownership and activity is required. Thus, a new business that takes over existing premises and makes no change in that premises' activities is not classified as an ENM, although it comes within the definition given at the beginning of the paper. However, the number of cases involving such take-overs is likely to be small.

[11]The age distribution of firms which do *not* survive to 1977 is not, unfortunately, known. The firms included in R obviously vary in their ages. Also order IV (coal and petroleum products) was excluded from the analysis as no formations occurred over the period.

[12]Females account for a very small minority of founders in manufacturing. For example, there was only one female founder from 74 new businesses formed in the Northern Region; see Johnson and Cathcart (1979a).

the capital expenditure required to start a new firm in the industry. The term u is a stochastic term which is assumed to satisfy the usual conditions required for Ordinary Least Squares.

The measurement of the independent variables does of course present serious difficulties. For example, an ideal measure of Π would be the geometric mean of the distribution of discounted expected self-employment income resulting from founding a firm; where the distribution included *all* employees, not just those who became founders. The model of course explicitly allows for the fact that some individuals who expect less than average profits will become founders, depending on their expected employment income. Such an ideal measure cannot possibly be obtained, and this paper measures Π using data on the actual annual profits of firms in the smallest size category (1–99 employees), from the Census of Production. In fact only arithmetic means are available and suitable data are only provided for the years 1970–73 and 1975. Gross profits per enterprise (before depreciation and interest) were obtained as the difference between total Gross Value Added and Wages and Salaries in the smallest size group, divided by the number of enterprises in that group.[13] All values were converted to 1975 prices, and the average was calculated over the five years for which comparable data were available. All the usual problems associated with the use of *ex post* data will obviously apply, and the skewness of the distributions also means that arithmetic and geometric means are unequal.

Similarly the geometric mean of expected employment income in each industry was measured by the annual average value of the median earnings of full-time males (unaffected by absence), expressed in 1975 prices. Data were taken from the *New Earnings Survey* for years comparable with the profits data; that is, 1970–75 inclusive.

Finally, Census of Production data provide information about the total net capital expenditure in firms of 1–99 employees. The annual average, in 1975 prices, of the net capital expenditure per enterprise in this smallest group was therefore used as the measure of C for each industry.

Cross-section results

The data described above for 16 industries were then used to carry out an ordinary least squares regression based in Equation 1. The results are shown below, where t-values are given in parentheses immediately underneath parameter estimates.

$$R = 5.235 + 0.079 \log \Pi - 0.647 \log Y - 0.092 \log C + u \qquad (2)$$
$$ (4.202) \ (2.135) \quad\ (-4.973) \quad\ (-3.917)$$
$$R^2 = 0.791$$

All of the coefficients are highly significantly different from zero, and the goodness of fit is very good. The regression 'explains' almost 80% of the variation in formation rates across

---

[13]Gross Value Added (GVA) is derived by subtracting from the traditional Net Output measure (NO) the cost of certain services. Unfortunately the GVA measure is not available for all five years. The GVA/NO ratio for 1971 was therefore applied to NO figures in each year to provide an estimate of GVA.

industries. The coefficients have the appropriate signs, but the significant difference between the coefficients on log Π and log Y requires further comment. The framework developed earlier suggests that the formation of entirely new firms is related to expected profits and expected earnings from employment in a symmetric manner, but this is not supported by the results shown in Equation 2. Thus the elasticities of R with respect to Π and Y are 1.13 and -9.25 respectively where these are calculated at the average value of R of 0.0699 (thus on average over the period there were approximately 7 new firms formed each year, per 100,000 employees, of which each grew to employ at least 11 individuals and survived to 1977).

The use of a measure of realised profits of existing firms does not, as already noted, allow in any way for the expectations of those who do not form firms, and furthermore does not allow for optimism or pessimism. The 'error' in the measurement of Π is expected to be much greater than in the measurement of anticipated earnings, Y, and individuals generally have relatively much more information about earnings from employment and their distribution.[14] Also, the measure of profits does not allow for depreciation and interest, and these may be systematically related to gross profits (but if the relationship were proportional, and the same in each firm and industry, the effect would be to alter the constant term rather than the coefficient on log Π).

A further possibility is that there may be other significant barriers to entry which face the new firm and whose omission affects the regression results. It is also worth repeating that the cross-section application of the specification in Equation 1 assumes that the parameters of the model are the same for each industry. Bearing all these points in mind, the performance of the model as reflected in Equation 2 may perhaps be regarded as encouraging. The results suggest that the application of the general framework to improved data would be a useful exercise.

IV. CONCLUSIONS

The purpose of this paper has been to suggest a framework for the empirical analysis of the formation of entirely new firms in manufacturing industry. The formation decision was assumed to depend on a comparison of prospects in employment and in self-employment, and the capital expenditure required to form a new business was regarded as a major barrier to entry. The functional relationship (a semi-logarithmic form) between the relevant variables was derived explicitly from the model, and applied to cross-section data relating to U.K. manufacturing industry. Although the data have many acknowledged shortcomings, the empirical results are sufficiently encouraging to suggest that the model provides a useful basis for further analysis. Further refinements, such as more detailed specification of the chances of survival in an industry, and the inclusion of further barriers to entry, could be made once additional data become available.

---

[14]The measure of earnings for each industry was adjusted for the unemployment rate in the industry, but this did not improve the results.

ACKNOWLEDGEMENTS

We are grateful to S. Nunn for kindly providing the data on firm formations which are used in this paper and for helpful discussions. We have also benefitted from discussions with our colleagues in Durham.

APPENDIX

Further simplifications

In Section II it was suggested that the formation rate, R, is proportional to the proportion of employees for whom the expected self-employment income, π, exceeds expected employment income, y, by a sufficient amount, called the threshold, t. Thus

$$R = \theta[1 - F(t)] \qquad (A1)$$

where θ is a parameter and F is the distribution function of the ratio of π to y. The first stage in the simplification of Equation A1 is the specification of the form of F. It is assumed that a suitable functional form to describe both the distribution of π and of y is the lognormal distribution, which has been widely used in analyses of earnings and profits. The distributions may therefore be written as

$$\pi \text{ is } \Lambda(\pi \,|\, \mu_\pi, \sigma_\pi^2) \quad \text{and} \quad y \text{ is } \Lambda(y \,|\, \mu_y, \sigma_y^2) \qquad (A2)$$

where Λ denotes the lognormal distribution function, and μ_π and σ_π^2 are the mean and the variance respectively of the logarithms of anticipated profits. Similar definitions apply to μ_y and σ_y^2.

The lognormal distribution has the convenient property that the ratio of lognormal variables is also lognormally distributed (see Aitchison and Brown, 1957, p. 11), so that

$$F(\pi/y) \text{ is } \Lambda(\pi/y \,|\, \mu_\pi - \mu_y, \sigma_\pi^2 + \sigma_y^2). \qquad (A3)$$

From the definition of the lognormal, it can be seen that

$$F(t) = N([\log t - \mu_\pi + \mu_y]/v \,|\, 0, 1) \qquad (A4)$$

where N denotes the Normal distribution function and $v = (\sigma_\pi^2 + \sigma_y^2)^{1/2}$.

As this integral cannot be evaluated explicitly it is convenient for present purposes to use a linear approximation over the relevant range; that is, to write the function $N(x\,|\,0, 1)$ simply as $N(x\,|\,0, 1) = a + bx$. This approximation is perhaps reasonable, given the quality of the available data and the range of magnitudes involved. Thus

$$1 - F(t) = 1 - a + (b/v)(\mu_\pi - \mu_y - \log t). \qquad (A5)$$

It is also suggested that the threshold t is proportional to the amount of capital expenditure required to form a new firm, C. Thus

$$t = kC. \qquad (A6)$$

Now define Π and Y as the geometric means of anticipated self-employment and employment income respectively. Then by definition $\mu_\pi = \log \Pi$ and $\mu_y = \log Y$. Substitution of Equations A5 and A6 into the basic Equation A1 gives

$$R = \beta_0 + \beta_1 \log \Pi - \beta_2 \log Y - \beta_3 \log C \tag{A7}$$

where $\beta_0 = \theta[1 - a - (b/v) \log k]$, etc. It can also be seen that $\beta_1 = \beta_2 = \beta_3$.

REFERENCES

Aitchison, J. and Brown, J. A. C. (1957) *The Lognormal Distribution*, Cambridge University Press, Cambridge.

Alchian, A. and Demsetz, H. (1972) Production Information Costs and Economic Organisation. *American Economic Review*, **62**, 777–95.

Bain, J. S. (1952) *Barriers to New Competition*, Harvard University Press, Cambridge, Massachusetts.

Beesley, M. (1955) The Birth and Death of Industrial Establishments Experience in the West Midlands Conurbation, *Journal of Industrial Economics*, **4**, 45–61.

Boswell, J. L. (1973) *The Rise and Decline of the Small Firm*, Allen and Unwin, London.

Coase, R. H. (1937) The Nature of the Firm, *Economica*, **4**, 386–405.

Cross, M. (1981) *New Firm Formation and Regional Development*, Gower, Farnborough.

Firn, J. and Swales, K. (1978) The Formation of New Manufacturing Establishments in the Central Clydeside and West Midlands Conurbations, *Regional Studies*, **12**, 199–213.

Fothergill, S. and Gudgin, G. (1979) *The Job Generation Process in Britain*, Centre for Environmental Studies, Research Series No. 32, CES, London.

Golby, C. W. and Johns, G. (1971) *Attitude and Motivation*, Committee of Inquiry on Small Firms, Research Report No. 7, HMSO, London.

Gudgin, G. (1978) *Industrial Location Processes and Regional Employment*, Saxon House, Farnborough.

Firn, J. and Swales, K. (1978) The Formation of New Manufacturing Establishments in the Central Clydeside and West Midlands Conurbations, *Regional Studies*, **12**, 199–213.

HMSO (1971) *Report of the Committee on Inquiry on Small Firms* (The Bolton Report), Cmnd. 4811, HMSO, London.

Johnson, P. S. and Cathcart, D. G. (1979a) New Manufacturing Firms and Regional Development, *Regional Studies*, **13**, 269–80.

Johnson, P. S. and Cathcart, D. G. (1979b) The Founders of New Manufacturing Firms: A Note on the Size of their Incubator Plants, *Journal of Industrial Economics*, **28**, 219–24.

Kihlstrom, R. E. and Laffont, J. J. (1979) A General Equilibrium Entrepreneurial Theory of Firm Formation, *Journal of Political Economy*, **87**, 719–48.

Knight, F. H. (1921) *Risk Uncertainty and Profit*, Houghton Mifflin, Boston.

Marshall, A. (1920) *Principles of Economics*, 8th edn, Macmillan, London.

McClelland, D. C. (1961) *The Achieving Society*, Van Nostrand, Princeton.

Nunn, S. (1980) *The Opening and Closure of Manufacturing Industry 1966–75*, Department of Industry, London, mimeo.

Oxenfeldt, A. R. (1943) *New Firms and Free Enterprise*, American Council on Public Affairs, Washington.

Parnes, H. S. (1970) Labour Force Participation and Labour Mobility, *Review of Industrial Relations Research*, **1**, 1–78.

Roberts, E. B. and Wainer, H. A. (1971) Some Characteristics of Technical Entrepreneurs, *IEEE Transactions on Engineering Management* EM-18 3, 100–109.

Robinson, J. F. F. and Storey, D. J. (1981) Employment Change in Manufacturing Industry in Cleveland, 1965–76, *Regional Studies*, **15**, 161–72.

Schumpeter, J. (1939) *Business Cycles*, Vol. 1, McGraw-Hill, New York.

Scott, M. (1978) Independence and the Flight from Large Scale: Sociological Factors in the Founding Process. Paper given to the Smaller Business Research Conference, Durham University Business School (November).

Steindl, J. (1945) *Small and Big Business*, Oxford Institute of Statistics Monograph No. 1, Blackwell, Oxford.

Storey, D. (1980) *Job Generation and Small Firm Policy*, Centre for Environmental Studies Policy Series 11, CES London.

Williamson, O. E. (1975) *Markets and Hierarchies*, Free Press, New York.

Migration and Population Ageing in Australia

Jose Alvarado and John Creedy*
University of Melbourne

Much concern has been expressed in recent years regarding population ageing in industrialised countries, although it is often suggested that Australia's population will not age as much as that of others because of its high level of migration. In studying the ageing of the Australian population, the Office of EPAC (1994) offers the most recent analysis of the impact of immigration. It includes population projections for the next 60 years under six alternative migration scenarios, two of which set migration levels at a fixed proportion of the population. However, that study focuses only on migration *levels*. No analysis has been made regarding the impact of changing the *composition* of the net intake; that is, differentiating between the country of birth of migrants and the demographic and social characteristics associated with it. The same is true of other projections, including those of the ABS (1989a), the BIPR (1992), the National Population Council (1991, 1992) and the Office of EPAC (1988). The present paper extends the analysis of the impact of migration by considering the differences associated with birthplace, particularly differences in mortality and fertility rates.

To achieve that aim, a framework is needed for projecting population that allows for migration. The following section describes this framework and presents the benchmark projections. The main demographic differences among the Australian resident population according to country of birth are then presented. This is followed by a study of the impact of these differences on population growth and age structure. Finally, the main conclusions are presented.

Benchmark Projections

The number of people in a country at the beginning of a year is made up of people who lived in the country at the start of the previous year and neither died nor migrated to other countries during that year, plus the number of surviving people who migrated from other countries during that year, plus the births during the previous year. The flows can be represented in a social accounting framework which enables year-to-year projections to be made. Such population projections therefore require a large number of assumptions regarding birth, death, and migration rates, for males and females in each age group, along with the way in

*   We would like to thank a referee for detailed and constructive comments on earlier drafts.

which these rates are assumed to change over time. A simplifying assumption commonly made is that all migrants, once they arrive in the country, immediately acquire a common set of fertility and mortality characteristics so that the composition of the population can be ignored. The major contribution of the present paper is to modify this type of assumption, but for comparison purposes a 'benchmark' set of projections is presented which follows the standard approach. The social accounting framework used to produce the projections is described in detail in Alvarado and Creedy (1994), and the data sources are given in the appendix.

Assuming annual net migration of 125,000 persons, fertility rates constant at the 1990 level, and mortality falling as described by the long-term rates of annual change estimated by the ABS (1989a, Table 4.10, p. 27), the benchmark population projections are shown in Table 1. The results are grouped into nine age groups, corresponding to those used by the ABS. These projections show that although Australia has one of the youngest and fastest growing populations of the Western countries, it will grow older rapidly during the next few decades. The proportion of people younger than 40 years of age falls from 62 per cent in 1990 to 49 per cent in 2031, while those aged 65 years and over increases from 11 per cent to 20 per cent during the same period. Population ageing accelerates particularly after 2011. Thus, the proportion of people aged 65 years and over increases 27 per cent between 1990 and 2011, and 43 per cent during the following 20 years. The ageing increases to the point that the proportion of middle-aged people also starts to fall. Although the number of people between 40 and 64 years of age increases from 27 to 34 per cent of the total population between 1990 and 2011, it falls to 31 per cent by 2031. Similarly, whereas the number of people younger than 40 years rises 17 per cent between 1990 and 2031, people aged 75 years and over increases by more than 200 per cent during the same period. These trends can be explained by the combined effect of the assumed decline in mortality rates and the 'baby boom' generation entering retirement after 2011.

Population Decomposition

The majority of migrants come to Australia as adults, so their social and demographic characteristics differ from those of people born in Australia. However, the above projections assume that immigrants and Australian-born persons do not differ significantly in terms of fertility and mortality. The appropriateness of this assumption is discussed in this section.

It is reasonable to expect that people from different countries will display different characteristics. These differences range from demographic factors such as fertility and mortality rates, to economic variables such as unemployment and participation rates, although this article focuses on the most relevant demographic characteristics. If the fertility of immigrants is substantially higher than that of Australian-born females, population ageing could be offset by immigration.

Table 1

Projections of the Population of Australia by Sex and Age ('000s)

Age group	1990 Males	1990 Females	2001 Males	2001 Females	2011 Males	2011 Females	2021 Males	2021 Females	2031 Males	2031 Females
1-14	1917.8	1823.8	1975.4	1896.1	2022.2	1944.0	2100.9	2018.7	2222.5	2135.0
15-24	1413.8	1353.6	1370.1	1314.4	1503.1	1452.0	1546.6	1496.7	1586.3	1533.8
25-39	2080.0	2052.6	2248.9	2191.0	2231.2	2173.4	2385.0	2335.5	2492.2	2447.5
40-49	1154.0	1102.1	1458.4	1447.2	1590.0	1557.8	1554.5	1517.2	1646.7	1612.9
50-59	788.3	758.5	1206.9	1185.2	1435.5	1441.6	1569.2	1552.1	1539.9	1514.2
60-64	366.5	369.0	416.5	414.2	608.4	627.6	714.6	735.2	775.4	784.9
65-69	314.9	351.1	332.0	348.7	488.4	509.3	597.4	646.7	668.4	705.4
70-74	216.4	270.0	289.0	322.3	335.6	370.3	497.4	562.3	593.8	661.7
75-99	279.9	473.0	453.9	711.8	534.2	812.4	716.4	1032.1	996.7	1443.5
All ages	8531.7	8553.7	9751.1	9830.9	10748.6	10888.4	11682.0	11896.5	12521.9	12838.9

Note: Comparisons of the projections in Table 1 with those of the ABS (1989a) show that the differences are very small.

For many years the source of migrants was mainly Europe, particularly the United Kingdom and Ireland. Since the 1970s, ethnic diversity, and therefore a wider variety of social and cultural backgrounds, has been one of the main characteristics of migration. Similarly, these changes have been accompanied by a greater variety in entry categories as well as changes in the relative importance of each of these categories over time. In general, over the last two to three decades there has been a decline in the relative importance of skilled and unsponsored migrants in favour of family migration, and to a lesser extent, refugees. This has exerted an important effect on the age structure and status of migrants.

Age Structure

Wooden (1990) shows that the proportion of migrants sponsored by families increased from an average of about 30 per cent of adult migrants during the 1960s and 1970s to almost 45 per cent by 1986–87. Of those, 30 per cent were older than 54 years of age. These trends, together with the fact that the large intakes of migrants in the immediate post-war years have already reached retirement age, have resulted in a rapid ageing of the migrant population. Thus, in 1986 the median age of overseas-born persons was 40.7 years compared with 27.5 years for Australian-born persons. There are even larger differences between migrant groups by region and country of origin; for instance, the median age of people born in Europe was 45.2 years and those born in the USSR was 62.6 years (ABS 1989b). In 1989, 40 per cent of Australian-born were older than 34 years of age, while 64 per cent of the overseas-born were in that age group (see ABS 1990).

Fertility

There are significant demographic differences between the Australian-born and the overseas-born in terms of fertility rates. Table 2 shows that overseas-born women, particularly those from non-English speaking backgrounds (NESB), experience higher fertility rates in each age group than Australian-born females. According to the 1986 census, women from NESB had a total fertility rate almost 11 per cent higher than Australian-born females, and 10.3 per cent above that experienced by women migrating from English speaking backgrounds (ESB). Among the more fertile ethnic groups were those coming from the Middle East and Asian countries. Thus, for instance, 45 per cent of Lebanese, 40 per cent of Arab, 31 per cent of Khmer, and 27 per cent of Laos women had four or more children (see Kee 1992, p. 6).

Mortality

Overseas-born people have mortality rates lower than those of Australian-born persons. Table 3 shows that NESB migrants have the lowest rates. These mortality rates are much higher than those given in the Australian life tables that were used to obtain the benchmark population projections discussed in the previous section.

Table 2

Live Births per 1000 Females by
Age and Birthplace of Mother, 1986

Birthplace of mother	15-19 years	20-24 years	25-29 years	30-34 years	35-39 years	40-44 years	45-49 years	TFR
Australia	22.1	93.0	149.0	90.9	25.8	3.9	0.2	1,925
Overseas	24.6	101.9	144.8	96.5	33.7	5.9	0.3	2,039
Total	22.2	93.3	145.8	90.9	27.8	4.4	0.2	1,923
ESB	25.2	93.7	138.2	95.2	29.5	5.0	0.2	1,935
NESB	24.1	110.6	151.1	97.5	36.5	6.5	0.4	2,134

Source: ABS 1989, *Overseas Born Australians 1988, A Statistical Profile*, ABS Cat. No. 4112.0, Table 1.15, p. 63.

Table 3

Age-Specific Death Rates by Birthplace, 1986
(deaths per 1,000 population)

Birthplace	0-14 years	15-24 years	25-34 years	35-44 years	45-54 years	55-64 years	65-74 years	75+ years	Total Deaths
				Males					
Australia	1.0	1.4	1.4	2.0	5.5	15.4	38.0	106.2	45195
Overseas	0.4	1.1	1.3	1.6	4.1	13.1	35.2	100.8	16404
ESB	0.3	1.4	1.4	1.7	4.3	14.5	36.3	106.1	8745
NESB	0.4	0.9	1.2	1.5	3.9	12.2	34.2	92.9	7657
Total	1.0	1.3	1.4	1.9	4.9	14.6	36.7	101.9	62195
				Females					
Australia	0.8	0.5	0.6	1.1	3.1	7.8	20.6	80.2	40459
Overseas	0.3	0.4	0.5	0.9	2.5	6.8	19.0	74.5	11905
ESB	0.2	0.4	0.5	0.9	2.8	7.6	19.6	81.1	7252
NESB	0.3	0.4	0.5	0.9	2.2	6.2	18.2	63.1	4650
Total	0.7	0.5	0.5	1.0	2.9	7.5	20.0	76.6	52769

Source: ABS 1989, *Overseas Born Australians 1988, A Statistical Profile*, ABS Cat. No. 4112.0, Table 2.1, pp. 70-71.

It is clear from Tables 2 and 3 that overseas-born and Australian-born persons are heterogeneous groups, and Kee (1992) has shown that these characteristics persist for several generations. Therefore, it seems desirable to incorporate some allowance for these differences in projections. Although the heterogeneity between the Australian-born and the overseas-born is quite clear, the characteristics of ESB migrants are much closer to the Australian-born group than to those of NESB migrants. This is even more evident when social and economic aspects are taken into account. Hence, it seems appropriate to redefine the Australian resident population as made up of just two groups: those born in Australia and in other English-speaking countries and their descendants on the one hand, referred to as AESB, and NESB migrants and their descendants on the other hand. This population decomposition will be used in the next section.

Alternative Projections

The population projections mentioned earlier in this article were made under the assumption that, although overseas migration played a role in determining the size and growth of the Australian population, the only difference added by migrants was in terms of age and sex distribution. However, the above discussion showed that the Australian-born and the overseas-born, and particularly the NESB migrants, are quite heterogeneous. Hence, this section examines the effect on the population structure of changing the benchmark assumptions. Thus, while the benchmark framework assumed the extreme case of homogeneity, the other extreme, whereby the NESB migrants are treated as being a separate group from that of AESB people, is now assumed. The Australian resident population is thus made up of two main groups: Australian combined with ESB migrants and their descendants, giving AESB, and migrants from non-English speaking backgrounds (NESB) and their descendants. The Australian-born fertility and mortality rates are assigned to both Australian and ESB migrants.

Data availability becomes a severe constraint, given the high level of disaggregation required. Most of the data derive from the 1986 Census, while other data required the processing of unpublished data kindly made available by the BIPR.

Settler Arrivals

During the last five years, settler arrivals from both English and non-English speaking countries have reduced steadily, but while the former have shrunk to almost one-third of the 1988 level, the latter have only fallen by 36 per cent. It is estimated that in 1959 the proportion of NESB migrants first exceeded that of ESB migrants (BIPR 1991) and the gap has increased since then.

Table 4 shows the annual average of settler arrivals between 1988/89–1992/93 by country of birth and age groups. NESB arrivals have more than doubled those from English-speaking countries. Both groups have a similar age structure, but again NESB migrants are slightly more concentrated in the middle-aged group while ESB persons are a bit older.

Permanent Departures

While settler arrivals have been decreasing, out migration has increased, though not steadily, during the last five years. Out migration of AESB people reached its peak in 1990/91. The annual average of permanent departures during the last five years are presented in Table 5. Almost four times more AESB people left the country compared to NESB people. But 40 per cent of AESB persons leaving the country were born in Australia. There are also significant differences in age structure between emigrants born in English-speaking countries and NESB countries. The proportion of AESB persons younger than 20 years emigrating from Australia was twice that of NESB persons. On the other hand, while 22 per cent of emigrants born in English-speaking countries were older than 39, 40 per cent of NESB leaving Australia fell into that age group.

Table 4

Settler Arrivals by Sex, Age, and Country of Birth
(Average   1988/89–1992/93)

Age groups	English-speaking background		Non-English-speaking background	
	Males	Females	Males	Females
0-4	2298	2148	3886	3722
5-9	1731	1632	3663	3460
10-14	1283	1211	3086	2849
15-19	1154	1130	2594	3083
20-24	1735	1819	2987	4298
25-29	2969	2965	5243	6272
30-34	2423	2172	5529	5654
35-39	1710	1437	3939	3749
40-44	1184	904	2466	2224
45-49	570	475	1242	1159
50-54	366	334	833	970
55-59	290	323	726	932
60-64	286	387	680	815
65+	664	811	879	1018
Total	18663	17749	37753	40205

Source: Authors' calculations using BIPR unpublished data.

The differences in number and age structure between arrivals and departures, and between ESB and NESB persons, define the net migration gain. Thus, excluding Australian-born emigrants, there was an annual average migration gain of 95,593 people during the last five years. Of those, almost 25 per cent were born in English-speaking countries (other than Australia). That is, net migration gain is almost three times higher for NESB than for ESB people. Comparison of Tables 4 and 5 shows that the age distribution of ESB arrivals is very similar to that of departures. However, the average age of NESB departures is substantially higher than that of NESB arrrivals, so that the absolute levels of the flows have an effect on population ageing.

Table 5

Permanent Departures by Sex, Age, and Country of Birth
(Average 1988/89–1992/93)

Age groups	English-speaking background		Non-English-speaking background	
	Males	Females	Males	Females
0-4	1446	1372	94	97
5-9	879	831	114	119
10-14	667	665	127	134
15-19	527	594	111	131
20-24	849	1223	168	235
25-29	1426	1772	312	345
30-34	1385	1426	374	361
35-39	1022	946	345	317
40-44	787	679	307	241
45-49	502	446	228	173
50-54	336	281	181	127
55-59	235	191	133	115
60-64	177	194	124	132
65+	418	507	271	268
Total	10655	11126	2889	2794

Source: Department of Immigration and Ethnic Affairs, unpublished data.

The rest of the assumptions required, including the annual decline in mortality rates and the proportion of births that are male, are the same as used to make the benchmark projections. These assumptions are applied to both population groups, AESB and NESB persons.

Population Projections

The method used to project population under the new assumptions is to take each population group, AESB and NESB persons, with its corresponding set of data. Then, applying the population model, projections are made for each group as if they were two separate populations. Finally, the two groups are added together for each year of the projection period to obtain projections for the total Australian population.

This method assumes that each population group keeps its demographic characteristics constant during the projection period, and that they develop independently of each other so that later generations absorb the characteristics of the group in which they are born. In the case of NESB, second and later generations throughout the projection period are, obviously, Australian-born, but for present purposes they are referred to as NESB persons.

Table 6 presents the new set of projections, using the same assumptions employed to make the benchmark projections, that is, an annual net migration of

125,000 persons, fertility rates constant, and mortality falling as described by the long-term rates of annual change estimated by the ABS. Given that during the last five years 75 per cent of the migration gain corresponded to NESB persons and 25 per cent to ESB persons, the net intake of 125,000 is divided into those proportions, and each population group projected under this assumption.

Comparing the results in Table 6 with the benchmark projections of Table 1, it is found that the figures under the new scenario are lower than the benchmark. The most significant differences appear in the older age groups, though the gap becomes smaller as the projection period is extended. The total population is four per cent lower than the benchmark in 2031. One of the reasons for the lower population figures is that mortality rates used in the new scenario are higher than in the benchmark case. Also, the initial population of 1986 does not include almost a quarter of a million people born at sea and whose country of birth could not be determined. That fact together with the high levels of immigration, particularly during the second half of the 1980s, result in a base population for 1990 of 11.3 per cent lower than the one used to make the benchmark projections.

Table 6

Projections of the Australian Population by Sex and Age Groups

Age group	2001 Males	2001 Females	2011 Males	2011 Females	2021 Males	2021 Females	2031 Males	2031 Females
1-14	1918.96	1843.45	1997.09	1918.07	2101.58	2018.13	2240.02	2150.88
15-24	1325.77	1274.23	1440.26	1393.66	1503.71	1453.99	1566.96	1514.07
25-39	2121.77	2103.18	2149.40	2116.58	2285.54	2258.36	2420.92	2391.83
40-49	1279.24	1271.58	1508.00	1505.42	1517.51	1498.10	1584.05	1567.72
50-59	992.25	991.17	1257.62	1267.61	1483.48	1497.48	1498.96	1492.80
60-64	449.12	468.16	473.29	490.62	655.52	687.36	715.30	737.61
65-69	414.63	448.41	420.42	455.35	488.15	523.77	639.12	691.51
70-74	278.00	325.67	355.07	410.43	381.73	432.78	537.11	608.37
75-99	344.10	511.00	552.21	789.57	710.18	1039.80	850.74	1233.29
All ages	9123.84	9236.85	10153.36	10347.31	11127.40	11409.77	12053.18	1238.08

Alternative projections were based on the benchmark mortality by applying those rates to the AESB group. From the mortality rates shown in Table 3 the ratio of NESB persons to total mortality was taken to estimate corresponding rates for the NESB people. Since these mortality rates were lower, the population estimates obtained were on average one per cent higher than those shown in Table 6.

Changing the Level and Composition of Overseas Migration

Changing the level of overseas migration exerts a significant impact on the size and age structure of the population, but the effect is insignificant when only the composition of the intake is modified. Table 7 shows the age structure and size of the Australian population assuming a net migration of 125,000 but under two alternative scenarios. Case A has an intake of 125,000 ESB people and no NESB persons, and Case B has 125,000 NESB migrants and no ESB migrants.

Table 7

Projections of the Population Age Structure Under Two Scenarios
(Proportion of people in each age group)

Age group	2001 A	2001 B	2011 A	2011 B	2021 A	2021 B	2031 A	2031 B
1-39	0.5771	0.5765	0.5370	0.5374	0.5146	0.5160	0.4995	0.5036
40-64	0.2957	0.2973	0.3166	0.3174	0.3261	0.3255	0.3129	0.3101
65-99	0.1272	0.1262	0.1464	0.1452	0.1593	0.1585	0.1876	0.1862
75-99	0.0472	0.0464	0.0662	0.0652	0.0785	0.0774	0.0859	0.0851
Total ('000s)	18308.4	18379.3	20365.0	20547.1	22292.9	22619.4	24046.4	24574.8

Case B produces a slightly younger and bigger population. The widest gap between the two scenarios occurs in 2031 and for the youngest age group, but even then the difference is insignificant, reaching less than one per cent. Similarly, total population under Case B in 2031 is only two per cent higher than under Case A.

However, the composition of the net intake of overseas migration does play a role in the ethnic structure of the population. Under scenario A, NESB persons would shrink to just 5.2 per cent of the Australian population in 2031, from a base year level of 11.3 per cent, whereas under scenario B, NESB persons would jump to 36.5 per cent of the total population by the last year of the projection period. Similarly, the age structure of the NESB population is significantly altered in correspondence to the scenario adopted, as Table 8 shows.

Increasing the net intake of migrants reduces significantly the proportion of elderly people throughout the projection period. Table 9 shows the impact of changing the level of net migration on the proportion of people aged 65 and over. The net intake is raised assuming 25 per cent of migrants are ESB migrants, and the rest are NESB migrants. The impact increases with time. Thus, by 2031 a net intake of 80,000 migrants reduces the proportion of elderly people by 11 per cent compared with the case were no migration is allowed; it falls by 15 per cent with a net intake of 125,000; and with 170,000 migrants the proportion of people aged 65 and over decreases by 19 per cent in 2031, compared with a zero migration scenario. Similarly, compared with a zero migration scenario, total population increases substantially: in 2031 Australian population might be 29 per cent higher with a net migration of 80,000; 45 per cent higher with 125,000 migrants; and 61 per cent higher if net migration reaches 170,000 annually.

Table 8

Projections of NESB Population
(proportion of people in each age group)

Age group	2001 A	B	2011 A	B	2021 A	B	2031 A	B
1-39	0.34	0.54	0.31	0.54	0.38	0.56	0.41	0.55
40-64	0.44	0.35	0.37	0.33	0.23	0.31	0.19	0.29
65-74	0.22	0.12	0.32	0.13	0.40	0.14	0.40	0.15
75-99	0.08	0.04	0.15	0.05	0.21	0.06	0.26	0.07

Table 9

Impact of Changing Net Migration Intake on People Aged 65 and Over
(proportion of people)

Net migration	2001	2011	2021	2031
0	0.1382	0.1678	0.1868	0.2199
80,000	0.1303	0.1525	0.1670	0.1959
125,000	0.1265	0.1455	0.1587	0.1866
170,000	0.1229	0.1394	0.1517	0.1792

Immigration Versus Fertility

Immigration may be regarded as a substitute for fertility; the ageing and size of the population resulting from low fertility rates can be compensated to a certain extent by higher levels of immigration. The question arises whether fertility is in any sense more 'efficient' in retarding the population ageing process than migration. This question is examined here by considering alternative scenarios and comparing results with those of Young (1990).

Using the population model employed to produce the benchmark estimates and assuming mortality decline up to the year 2020, as described by the long-term rates of annual change estimated by the ABS (1989a), and a continuation of the 1985-86 age structure of migrants, projections of the population size and age structure since 1986 are made under three alternative scenarios. Scenario A assumes a total fertility rate (TFR) of 1.44 and a zero migration intake; scenario B keeps the level of migration at zero but increases TFR up to 1.85; and scenario C increases the net intake of migrants to 150,000 per year while keeping the TFR to the original level of 1.44. The results are presented in Table 10.

Table 10

Projections of the Population Size and Age Structure Under Different Migration and Fertility Assumptions (percentage of people in each age group)

Year and scenario	Aged 1–14	Aged 15–64	Aged 65+	Total ('000s)
2001				
Scenario A	15.2	70.5	14.3	16,617.4
Scenario B	18.7	67.6	13.7	17,340.3
Scenario C	16.2	70.8	13.0	19,045.3
2011				
Scenario A	14.0	68.7	17.3	16,581.1
Scenario B	17.0	66.9	16.1	17,808.8
Scenario C	15.3	69.8	14.9	20,818.2
2021				
Scenario A	12.2	64.9	22.9	16,085.9
Scenario B	15.9	63.6	20.5	17,989.1
Scenario C	14.0	67.3	18.7	22,237.9
2031				
Scenario A	11.0	60.8	28.2	15,112.0
Scenario B	15.4	60.6	24.0	17,791.0
Scenario C	13.1	64.5	22.4	23,198.4
2046				
Scenario A	10.4	56.1	33.5	12,833.6
Scenario B	15.0	59.3	25.7	16,711.4
Scenario C	12.7	61.7	25.6	23,651.1

Increasing either the fertility rates or the migrant intake produce the same effect on the proportion of people aged 65 years and over by the end of the projection period. However, higher fertility rates produce a smaller population size and an age pyramid broader at the base than with high levels of immigration. These results are similar to those obtained by Young (1990) who concludes that:

> ... increasing the level of fertility is a more efficient way of retarding the ageing of the population than increasing the level of immigration, because the same effect on the proportion aged 65 years or more would be achieved through a smaller increase in population.
>
> *Young 1990, p. 20*

However, it is important to note that immigration appears to slow down the process of ageing faster than higher fertility rates. While higher fertility reduces the proportion of elderly people by 1.2 percentage points in 2011, high migration levels decrease that proportion by 2.4 percentage points. Similarly, in 2021 and 2031 high migration levels reduce the proportion of elderly people by almost two percentage points more than high fertility rates (Table 10).

Additional gains in retarding the ageing of the population are achieved when account is taken of the demographic differences between AESB and NESB persons. On the other hand, although immigration produces a lower percentage of people in the youngest age group, it also generates a higher proportion of working-age persons, which could potentially lead to lower dependency ratios.

To illustrate the role of migration further, using assumptions similar to those employed by Young (1990), Table 11 presents additional estimates of the proportion aged 65 and over, using the benchmark model. Whereas with a 50,000 intake of migrants the proportion of elderly reaches 23.6 per cent by 2040, with 100,000 migrants or more that proportion can only be reached after several centuries have elapsed. Similarly, with a net intake of 150,000 migrants the proportion of elderly would reach 22.1 per cent by the year 2160, whereas that proportion is reached at the earlier year of 2031 when the intake is reduced to 50,000 net migrants per year.

Table 11

Impact of Changing Net Migration Intake on Total Population and Persons Aged 65 Years and Over

Year	Net intake 50,000			Net intake 100,000			Net intake 150,000		
	Aged 65+ ('000s)	Total pop. ('000s)	Aged 65+ %	Aged 65+ ('000s)	Total pop. ('000s)	Aged 65+ %	Aged 65+ ('000s)	Total pop. ('000s)	Aged 65+ %
2001	2411.4	18172.3	13.3	2448.0	19004.4	12.9	2484.3	19836.4	12.5
2011	2950.3	19285.3	15.3	3028.2	20761.8	14.6	3106.1	22238.2	14.0
2021	3840.5	20169.6	19.0	4001.7	22350.1	17.9	4162.9	24530.7	17.0
2031	4577.4	20713.9	22.1	4890.7	23636.7	20.7	5204.2	26559.6	19.6
2046	4880.1	20753.1	23.5	5465.2	24794.7	22.0	6050.0	28836.4	21.0
2081	4698.7	20069.0	23.4	5884.1	26504.3	22.2	7069.6	32939.6	21.5
2160	4395.0	18823.2	23.3	6678.2	29641.0	22.5	8961.6	40458.8	22.1

Conclusions

This paper has contributed to the study of migration and population in two ways. It has used a population projection model that allows for changes in specified demographic variables and assumptions, and produces results that are consistent with official estimates. Also the paper has studied in more detail the impact of net migration on population projections. On the basis of census data that show that the fertility and mortality characteristics of overseas migrants do not adjust immediately but take several generations, the paper has extended traditional analyses of migration by proposing a decomposition of the Australian population. This decomposition made it possible to study the impact on population structure of changing not only the level but also the composition of the migration intake.

The analysis showed that although the composition of the net intake does play a role in determining the ethnic structure of the population, it is the level of overseas migration that exerts the most significant impact on the size and age structure of the population. Increasing the intake of migrants reduces significantly the proportion of elderly people throughout the projection period. For instance, with an annual intake of 170,000 migrants the proportion of people aged 65 and over decreases by 19 per cent and the size of the population rises by 60 per cent by 2031, compared with a zero migration scenario. The role of migration in relation to fertility was also contrasted.

Appendix: Data Sources

The population projection model requires the age distributions to be given by single years of age. Whenever the data were not available in this form, the total number included in each age group was divided by the number of years in the age group and the same value was assigned to each age within the group. The base year is 1990, but in some cases the average of the years 1988–90 appeared to be more appropriate.

The estimated resident population of Australia by sex and single year of age at 30 June 1990 is given in *Estimated Resident Population by Sex and Age, States and Territories of Australia, 1991*, ABS Catalogue No. 3201.0, Table 1, p. 3-6.

Emigration data are given by the average 1988–90 age and sex distribution of permanent departures, in *Overseas Arrivals and Departures, Australia*, 1991, ABS Catalogue No. 3404.0, Table 10, p.14.

Mortality data are taken from the *Australian Life Tables 1985-87* estimated by the Office of the Australian Government Actuary (1991). Multiplying the probability of a person of a given age dying within a year by the resident population gives the number of deaths for the initial year by sex and single year of age.

Subtracting from the resident population the number of deaths and emigrants, and dividing by resident population gives the survival rates. These survival rates change over time with decreasing mortality rates. The long-term rates of annual change in age-specific death rates estimated by the ABS (*Projections of the Population of Australia, States and Territories 1989 to 2031*, ABS Cat. No. 3222.0, Table 4.10, p. 27) were used.

The average 1988–1990 permanent overseas arrivals (immigrants) by sex and age were taken from *Overseas Arrivals and Departures, Australia, 1991*, ABS Catalogue No. 3404.0, Table 9, p. 13. New settlers are younger than people emigrating from Australia. Similarly, while 38 per cent of the total population in 1990 were younger than 25 years of age, 45 per cent of new arrivals were in this age group.

Age specific birth rates are taken from *Births Australia, 1991*, ABS Catalogue No. 3301.0, Table 4, p. 5. Fertility rates in Australia are still higher than in most developed countries, and in recent years the total fertility rate experienced a slight increase from 1.84 in 1989 to 1.90 in 1990. The highest number of births is concentrated in the 25–29 age range, followed by the 30–34 age group. Hence, most of the 'baby boom' generation has not yet passed the peak childbearing ages which guarantees high levels of natural increase of the population during the early and mid 1990s (see NPC 1991 and 1992 and BIPR 1992). For women younger than 15 and older than 49 years, a zero fertility rate was assumed.

The average 1988–90 proportion of total births that are male was 0.51, given in *Births Australia, 1991*, ABS Catalogue No. 3301.0, Table 2 , p. 4.

References

Alvarado, J. and Creedy, J. (1994), 'Migration and Australian Population Projections', Research Paper No. 421, Department of Economics, University of Melbourne.

Australian Bureau of Statistics (1989a), *Projections of the Population of Australia States and Territories 1989 to 2031*, ABS Cat. No. 3222.0, Canberra.

Australian Bureau of Statistics (1989b), *Overseas Born Australians 1988, A Statistical Profile*, ABS Cat. No. 4112.0, Canberra.

Australian Bureau of Statistics (1990), *Estimated Resident Population by Country of Birth, Age and Sex, Australia*, ABS Cat. No. 3221.0, Canberra.

Australian Bureau of Statistics (1991), *Births Australia*, ABS Cat. No. 3301.0, Canberra.

Bureau of Immigration and Population Research (BIPR) (1991), *Community Profiles* (various issues), AGPS, Canberra.

Bureau of Immigration and Population Research (BIPR) (1992), *Australia's Population Trends and Prospects*, AGPS, Canberra.

Economic Planning Advisory Council (EPAC) (1988), 'Economic Effects of an Ageing Population', Council Paper No. 29, AGPS, Canberra.

Economic Planning Advisory Council (EPAC) (1994), 'Australia's Ageing Society', Background Paper No. 37, AGPS, Canberra.

Kee, P. (1992), *Social and Economic Attainment of Immigrants and Later Generation Australians*, AGPS, Canberra.

National Population Council (NPC) (1991), *Population Issues and Australia's Future*, AGPS, Canberra.

National Population Council (NPC) (1992), *Population Issues and Australia's Future, Environment, Economy and Society*, (Consultant's Reports), AGPS, Canberra.

Office of the Australian Government Actuary (1991), *Australian Life Tables 1985–1987*, AGPS, Canberra.

Wooden, M. (1990), *Migrant Labour Market Status*, AGPS, Canberra.

Young, C. (1990), *Australia's Ageing Population – Policy Options*, AGPS, Canberra.

[8]

The Choice of Early Retirement Age and the Australian Superannuation System

M.E. Atkinson and John Creedy
The University of Melbourne

Abstract

This paper uses a lifetime simulation model to examine the optimal (utility maximising) choice of both the retirement age and the allocation of assets at retirement, for a cohort of males in Australia. Given the complexity of the income tax, superannuation and age pension system, the incentives facing individuals are far from clear. The results suggest that there is a substantial incentive for individuals to retire early and that this, along with the allocation of assets, is strongly influenced by the means-testing of the age pension. Experiments suggest that a universal age pension would encourage later retirement. Furthermore, lower mandatory contribution rates provide an incentive for later retirement ages. Reforms to the superannuation system are required if it is desired to encourage later retirement.

Acknowledgements

The support of an ASFA grant is gratefully acknowledged by Creedy. We have benefited from the comments of two referees on an earlier version.

Introduction

This paper uses a lifetime simulation model to examine the choices made by individuals concerning both the age at retirement and the allocation of accumulated savings and superannuation assets[1]. Individuals approaching retirement are faced with a dual decision problem concerning both the age at which to retire and the manner in which to allocate accumulated assets. The complexity of the tax and superannuation system in Australia makes it difficult to disentangle the incentive structure influencing this decision. For this reason, analytical results cannot be established and lifetime simulations are required.

The Australian system has been described in terms of a 'retirement maze'; see Atkinson, Creedy and Knox (1995). By considering the implications of a large number of routes through this maze, using alternative evaluation criteria, Atkinson and Creedy (1996) examined optimal choices for a simulated population on the assumption that each individual retires at age 65. The assets modelled consisted of accumulated superannuation contributions (from employers and employees) made over the working life as part of the Superannuation Guarantee Charge (SGC) along with any additional private savings. The population group consisted of a large number of males in a single cohort, assuming that the SGC scheme is fully mature. It was found, for example, that there is very little incentive inherent in the tax and age pension system for individuals to use their assets to purchase annuities. The government's stated objective in introducing the SGC was, however, to encourage the private provision of retirement incomes in order to reduce reliance on the means-tested age pension.

The purpose of the present paper is to extend the previous analysis to allow for the retirement age to vary between the ages of 55 and 65 years. The analysis does not allow for the transition to part time work, and retirement is treated as being irreversible and total. Although voluntary early retirement may affect longevity, this type of interdependence is also ignored. The standard form of labour supply model in a multi-period context is of little value in this context given the complexity of the tax and transfer systems.

The analysis focuses on two main questions. First, to what extent does the system in Australia, in its mature form, offer an incentive for individuals to retire early? Second, to what extent is optimal behaviour at retirement regarding the use of assets affected by the retirement age?

The retirement options, or routes through the maze, are described in section 2. Simulation results are presented in section 3, with brief conclusions in section 4. First, however, some features of the tax and superannuation system in Australia, as modelled here, are described; this inevitably involves a simplication of the actual system.

The Tax and Superannuation System

Each individual is modelled as having accumulated assets at the time of retirement which may be classified in three ways. First, there is the sum of superannuation contributions arising from employee contributions, assumed to be 3 per cent of gross earnings throughout the working life. Secondly, there are accumulated employer contributions, known as deducted contributions, assumed to be 9 per cent of gross earnings in each year, plus all other investment income earned by the fund. These contribution rates correspond to those recommended for a mature version of current policy and have bipartisan political support. These two components are treated in different ways for tax purposes and are known as the *undeducted benefit* and the *taxable benefit* respectively. Thirdly, each individual has other accumulated savings; these are assumed to be made at the rate of 5 per cent of disposable income in each year. These assets are disposed of at retirement, and the initial disposal identifies amounts put to various uses thereafter. Further details are given in Table 1. The various thresholds reflect conditions in force in 1994, with indexation of thresholds and pension levels at the rates indicated in the appendix.

Table 1 The Tax Structure in Australia

Contribution rates	Employer 9%, Employee 3%
Contribution tax	15% on tax deductible Employer contributions
Employee contribution rebate	10% of employee contributions, subject to tests on income (maximum rebate $100, maximum salary $31,000) and age related maxima on total contributions. Rebate may not exceed tax liability.
Superannuation Fund Earnings	Nominal rate of tax of 15% (assumed to be an effective rate of 7.5%, after allowance for credits).
Lump Sum Tax	Undeducted contributions are not subject to lump sum tax. The taxable benefit included in the lump sum is subject to 16.4% tax on amounts in excess of a threshold ($77,796 in 1993-94). Excessive amounts taxed at 48.4%. Rates include the Medicare levy.
Age Pension	Taxable age pension payable subject to income and asset means-tests. Income tax rebate depending on income. Single pension: $8,115
Annuities in payment	Superannuation annuity taxed as income, except UPP exempt. Other annuities taxed as income, except the purchase price allowance which is exempt.
Superannuation pension rebate	15% rebate associated with contribution tax.

Retirement Decisions

The simulation model enables, for each of 11 retirement ages, 46 different routes through the 'retirement maze' to be evaluated in terms of lifetime utility; the best combination for each individual of the 506 alternatives of age and routes is selected. This section describes the 46 'routes' through the maze and the method used to model the choice of the age of retirement.

Working an extra year involves giving up leisure in favour of work in return for extra consumption, during that year and following years, as a result of the further accumulation of assets. This may perhaps suggest a simple marginal condition in terms of the equality of marginal utility from an extra year of work and that from an extra year of leisure. However, such a simple 'flow' condition is not operational in this context. Kingston (1995) argued that this flow condition is a necessary but not a sufficient condition for retirement. He examined a 'stock' condition in a model of labour supply and portfolio choice. The approach followed below also amounts to a stock condition.

The Range of Routes Available

The superannuation assets may initially be used in a combination of two ways. They may be used to purchase a lifetime annuity, or may be taken as a lump sum which is subject to lump sum tax. The other savings, and any superannuation lump sum taken, may be used in one of three ways. The simulation model allows for the after-tax cash amounts to be used to purchase an annuity, to be deposited in an interest-bearing bank account, or to be put to immediate consumption. These three destinations are available in any combination and to various degrees. Any annuities purchased are identified throughout retirement according to the source of the money which is used to purchase them. This distinction governs the income tax rules which apply to them, and also the treatment under the operation of the age pension means tests. Annuities purchased by lump sum proceeds from the superannuation benefit are treated in the same way as annuities purchased from other savings; both are considered to be purchased by after-tax money.

The simulation model allows for two basic methods of retirement income provision, the money purchase method, and the defined benefit method. In the former method, a proportion of the available amount used to purchase an annuity is specified, and in the latter method a level of required income is specified. Defined benefit levels are described as a proportion of the average of the final three years' earnings before retirement.

After the purchase of annuities from pre- or post-tax money, an amount may be placed in an interest bearing bank account; the amount is specified as a proportion of the money available. The account attracts taxable interest payments at a constant rate, and is subject to annual drawings. The amount withdrawn at the end of each year is calculated as the balance of the account divided by the number of years remaining to age 80; thus the account is assumed to be extinguished at age 80. This is an arbitrary assumption, but it is made in the absence of an explicit model of bequest behaviour and the formation of expectations of length of life. This assumption approximates to the conditions governing the draw-down of allocated pensions and provides an appropriate alternative to the other choices available here. Hence, bequests exist in some cases, but their provision is modelled as a residual rather than as deliberate decision of individuals. Under the assumption of common mortality, when all individuals are assumed to die aged 79, this approach implies that there are no bequests. The final allocation of resources at the time of retirement is to consumption. All money remaining after the above provisions for income and investment is spent immediately.

Given the complexity of the system, there is in principle an infinitely large number of routes which may be taken at retirement. A catalogue of 46 routes through the maze has been constructed. The range of routes from which each individual makes the optimal choice are described in Tables 2 and 3 for defined benefit and money purchase cases respectively. The defined benefit is specified in relation to average earnings in the three years immediately before retirement; this average is referred to as the 'final salary'. In Table 2, column 2 indicates the first call on the use of pre-tax superannuation assets. The initials 'LS' signify that the superannuation assets are taken as a lump sum. The initial 'A' signifies that the superannuation assets are used to provide an annuity to the defined level of income described in column 4. If the superannuation assets are insufficient to purchase an annuity to the required level, then savings are drawn upon until the level is reached. Any balance of pre-tax money is then taken as a lump sum, and added to other post-tax money. If there is insufficient money to purchase the defined level of income, the individual buys as much as possible, so that all assets are devoted to annuity purchase.

Table 2 Routes 1-24: Defined Benefit Cases

Route	Super pre-tax destination	Savings and post-tax destination	Defined benefit: % of final salary	% of balance to bank	% of balance to consumption
1	A	A	85	-	100
2	A	A	75	-	100
3	A	A	65	100	0
4	A	A	65	50	50
5	A	A	65	-	100
6	LS	A	65	100	-
7	LS	A	65	50	50
8	LS	A	65	-	100
9	LS	A	60	-	100
10	A	A	50	100	-
11	A	A	50	50	50
12	A	A	50	-	100
13	LS	A	50	100	-
14	LS	A	50	50	50
15	LS	A	50	-	100
16	LS	A	45	-	100
17	A	A	35	100	-
18	A	A	35	50	50
19	A	A	35	-	100
20	LS	A	35	100	-
21	LS	A	35	50	50
22	LS	A	35	-	100
23	A	A	25	-	100
24	A	A	10	-	100

Table 3 Routes 25-47: Money Purchase Cases

Route	% of Super to annuity	% of Savings and post-tax to annuity	% of balance to Bank	% of balance to consumption
25	100	100	0	0
26	100	0	100	0
27	100	0	50	50
28	100	0	0	100
29	50	50	100	0
30	50	50	50	50
31	50	50	0	100
32	50	0	100	0
33	50	0	50	50
34	50	0	0	100
35	LS	100	0	0
36	LS	85	100	0
37	LS	70	100	0
38	LS	70	50	50
39	LS	50	100	0
40	LS	50	50	50
41	LS	50	0	100
42	LS	0	100	0
43	LS	0	75	25
44	LS	0	50	50
45	LS	0	25	75
46	LS	0	10	90

It is assumed that the age pension becomes payable only at age 65, and no provision is made for other social transfer payments. Thus, those retiring earlier than the age pension eligibility age must rely entirely on their own resources to provide income. They may be eligible to receive the low income earners rebate, in addition to a rebate linked to the age pension. The age pension is paid subject to means-tests on both income and assets.

Fringe benefits associated with the age pension or low income levels are not modelled. It would be difficult to make such allowance in a reasonable way, since such benefits reflect to a large extent the consumption pattern, as well as the income level of an individual. However, the inclusion of such an allowance would exaggerate rather than moderate the incentives revealed below, since it would be inclined to increase the relative value of the low annuity income and high consumption options; options which are already preferred by the low income and high mortality groups.

In Table 3, column 2 indicates the percentage of pre-tax superannuation assets used to purchase an annuity. The balance of superannuation assets is taken as a lump sum and later pooled with any balance of the savings accumulation. If the superannuation assets are converted entirely to a lump sum, as in routes 35-46 inclusive, then the post-tax money is added to the savings accumulation and the stated percentage applied to the purchase of an annuity. Thus, for example, route 35 specifies that all superannuation is taken as a lump sum and all the money then available is used to buy an annuity. Route 25 specifies that all benefits are used to purchase annuities, but one annuity arises from pre-tax superannuation assets while the other arises from post-tax savings and therefore involves a different tax and age pension treatment.

The route which has the highest value of lifetime utility, as defined below, is the one chosen by an individual. If there is more than one route with the same value, the highest route number is preferred.

Evaluation of Retirement Choice

The criterion for evaluating the retirement choice is specified in terms of a utility function based on net consumption and leisure in each year. Total leisure available in each year is normalised to unity, so that leisure is specified as a proportion of the available time. During retirement years this proportion is set equal to one in each year, and for working years it is set equal to a fixed value less than one (the sensitivity to this assumed value is examined below). If c_t and h_t respectively denote the amount of consumption and the proportion of time in leisure in year t, utility in that year is defined as the following Cobb-Douglas form:

$$U_t = c_t^\alpha \, h_t^{1-\alpha} \tag{1}$$

where $\alpha < 1$. If there is a bequest, its value is added to consumption in the final year of life. Lifetime utility is then defined as the present value, at entry to the workforce, of the stream U_t.

Individuals are assumed not to save from any disposable income during retirement. The amount of net consumption in any year in retirement is the sum of income from any purchased annuities, plus the age pension received where relevant, plus the amount taken from the bank account, less the amount of income tax paid, allowing for the appropriate income tax rebates due. This amount is not the same, in general, as the net income in the year. Net income includes the interest earned on the bank account, but does not include the capital amount withdrawn from it. The amount of the bequest, if any, is the balance of the bank account at the time of death. Since the bank account is reduced to zero by age 80, any individual who survives this age provides no bequest.

The evaluation of each route for each individual is made *ex post*. That is, the criterion refers to the consumption stream and bequest actually received by the individual over the whole of the retirement period. Hence the optimal route is the one that 'turned out' to be the best in the end.

These results do not therefore directly indicate which routes are optimal *ex ante*, since it would be necessary to model explicitly the formation of expectations by individuals about the length of life. The two concepts coincide only if individuals know at retirement how long they will live[2].

Annuity Rates

Individuals who retire early and purchase an annuity receive benefits over a longer period than if they retire later. The purchase rate of annuities depends on the age from which they become payable. The rate in Australia for a whole-life annuity escalating at 5 per cent per year for a male aged 65 is 12.5 (from the Rice-Kachor Rollover/Annuity League Table consistent with the values used). That is, the cost of an annuity which pays $1 in the first year on retirement at age 65 is $12.50. Annuity purchase rates have been constructed for other ages consistent with this base value. This was done using the software package ADVANCE (Actuarial and Demographic, Visual And Numerical Curricula Enhancement) developed at the University of Melbourne.

The market for whole-life annuities in Australia is currently quite small, but as the Superannuation Guarantee Charge matures it is expected, if the government intention is realised, that this market will increase to include individuals previously absent from the annuity market. Hence the mortality characteristics of those purchasing retirement annuities are expected to change. The following simulations therefore use purchase rates based on differing mortality assumptions. Two sets of rates are used in this study, as follows.

The first set of annuity rates for early retirement, A1, assumes that the underlying mortality experience is that of typical annuitants, and is based on the mortality table a(90) males. Current rates would be expected to reflect the effects of self-selection exercised by purchasers of annuities. On this mortality assumption, a purchase price of 12.5 at age 65 implies an underlying real rate of interest of 1.90 per cent allowing for escalation at 5 per cent. Assuming that all expense allowances and other costs are implicitly allowed for in this real rate of interest, ADVANCE was used to calculate the corresponding rates for ages 55 to 64, on the basis of the a(90) males mortality table.

The second set of annuity rates, A2, is based on the same real rate of interest implied by current market rates, that is 1.90 per cent, but uses a different assumption of mortality experience, the Australian Life Table 1985-87, males. This mortality table is representative of a wider population than the annuitants mortality table used for the first set of rates, and the mortality rates are in general higher.

Annuitants' mortality is lower than the general population since it represents a group self-selecting on the basis of expectation of longer than average survival. If the purchase of retirement annuities becomes much more common than it is at present, then purchase rates would be expected to reflect the higher mortality experience of a wider group of purchasers of annuities. Thus, the second set of purchase rates is intended to be representative of market rates which might apply when the Superannuation Guarantee Charge scheme is mature and the purchase of retirement annuities is much more widespread than it is at present. The two set of rates are shown in Table 4.

Table 4 Annuity Purchase Rates

Age	A1	A2
55	17.57	16.92
56	17.04	16.40
57	16.52	15.87
58	16.00	15.35
59	15.48	14.83
60	14.97	14.32
61	14.47	13.80
62	13.97	13.30
63	13.48	12.80
64	12.99	12.30
65	12.50	11.81

Simulation Results

Some further comments on the population group are warranted at this stage. In view of the complexities involved in modelling households and female income dynamics, a model of age-earnings profiles was estimated for Australian males, using data for all occupations and household types; see Creedy (1992). When calculating the tax paid and the age pension, the simulated individuals were, however, treated as if they were single and home owners in order to classify them for purposes of the assets and income means tests. It would be desirable to model household formation and joint decision-making, where appropriate. It is argued that the present approach is sufficient to demonstrate the complexity of the system in Australia and the nature of the incentive structure created. All individuals are assumed to enter the workforce at age 20 and no deaths are assumed to occur before age 65.

The model is used to simulate the lifetime experience of each of 3000 individuals. In each case the value of discounted lifetime utility, based on the Cobb-Douglas form, is evaluated for each of the 46 routes through the maze and each retirement age from 55 to 65, and the combination of age and route giving the maximum value of utility is recorded. The simulation is carried out both for the assumption of common mortality, such that all individuals live to age 79, and for differential mortality whereby the relatively richer live, on average, relatively longer (and the expectation of life for the median individual is 79 years), following the specification described in the appendix. Any effect which early retirement may have on life expectancy is not modelled.

The choice of values of h_t (the proportion of time spent in leisure during each year) and α must be somewhat arbitrary. All that can be done is to choose sensible values as a base case and then to consider the sensitivity of results to variations. The coefficient α is the exponent on consumption. The form of U_t implies that, within each year, utility is constant if a 1 per cent increase in leisure is matched by a reduction in consumption of $\{(1 - \alpha)/\alpha\}$ per cent. Hence if α is set at 0.5, a 1 per cent increase in h_t accompanied by a 1 per cent reduction in c_t results in no change in utility. If α is increased to 0.6, for example, an increase in h_t of 1 per cent must be matched by a reduction in c_t of 0.667 per cent to maintain the same utility, reflecting a higher weight attached to consumption. If α is instead 0.4, a similar change in h_t implies a fall in consumption of 1.5 per cent if utility is to be constant. The central value of $\alpha = 0.5$ is taken as the base case, along with the assumption that $h_t = 0.25$ during each of the working years. After retirement a value of $h_t = 1$ is used.

Common Mortality

Tables 5 and 6 respectively show the optimal route choices for the A1 and A2 annuity rates, and the base values of $h_t = 0.25$ and $\alpha = 0.5$, on an assumption of common mortality (CM). Each table shows the number of members of the cohort selecting each age and route combination. Only routes which are chosen are included.

Table 5 Retirement Age and Choice of Route
(h = 0.25; α = 0.25; α = 0.5; A1; CM)

No.	55	56	57	58	59	60	61	62	63	64	65
1	11	-	-	-	-	-	-	-	-	-	-
2	25	-	-	-	-	-	-	-	-	-	-
5	69	51	10	2	-	3	1	-	-	-	-
8	24	6	1	1	-	-	-	-	-	-	-
9	17	28	28	33	40	23	17	-	-	-	-
12	166	207	197	105	19	20	20	22	23	8	4
15	26	32	57	79	143	225	207	113	27	2	-
16	2	3	6	13	44	106	129	135	85	25	1
19	10	10	6	1	-	-	-	-	-	-	-
22	-	-	-	-	1	3	21	38	24	15	2
25	63	35	17	14	14	15	12	10	4	3	4
28	15	13	3	-	-	-	-	-	-	-	-
35	13	-	-	-	-	-	-	-	-	-	-
Total	441	385	325	240	261	395	407	318	163	53	12

Column header above: "Age of retirement"

Table 6 Retirement Age and Choice of Route
(h = 0.25; α = 0.25; α = 0.5; A2; CM)

No.	Age of retirement 55	56	57	58	59	60	61	62	63	64	65
1	12	-	-	-	-	-	-	-	-	-	-
2	35	-	-	-	-	-	-	-	-	-	-
5	90	55	39	7	7	11	3	3	-	1	1
8	24	10	5	6	-	-	-	-	-	-	-
9	19	25	35	34	56	43	27	13	1	-	-
12	171	210	214	119	38	11	15	17	14	3	3
15	19	15	45	60	116	199	224	105	35	6	-
16	5	4	2	5	25	49	79	93	72	15	-
19	5	6	8	-	-	-	-	-	-	-	-
22	-	-	-	-	-	-	4	12	12	7	2
25	107	52	33	23	25	22	36	22	12	14	6
28	11	9	5	-	-	-	-	-	-	-	-
35	17	-	-	-	-	-	-	-	-	-	-
Total	515	386	386	254	267	335	388	265	146	46	12

The essential features of the two tables are the same. The most preferred retirement age is 55, with a second mode at age 61. The preferred routes all involve using a proportion of the available funds to purchase an annuity and allow for the immediate consumption of any cash balance. Of the routes chosen, all (apart from 25, 28 and 35) are defined benefit routes and all involve the consumption of the balance of funds after the defined level of income has been met. These results, because based on common mortality experience, do not favour any use of the bank account, since the persisting capital value of this as an estate is only relevant when individuals die before age 80. The lower annuity purchase rates A2 involve more individuals taking routes 5, 9 and 25, and fewer taking routes 16 and 22, compared with the rates A1. Due to space constraints, later comparisons are shown only for the set A1.

The results shown in Tables 5 and 6 reflect the combined action of different effects and there is no single reason which explains the pattern of choices. A more detailed study was made of individuals and their optimal choice and, from the detail, it was found that patterns emerge. Looking at the defined benefit choices, it appears that the major part of the cohort are opting to buy a level of income which maximises their receipt of the income and asset means-tested age pension. Thus, in general, those choosing to retire with 50 per cent of final (average three years) salary rather than 35 per cent, for example, are retiring with similar levels of annuity income, but have a lower average salary over the final three years of work. Some routes purchase an annuity of the same proportion of final average salary, (for example, the pairs of routes 5 and 8, 12 and 15, 19 and 22) but from different sources (using pre- or post-tax money). These pairs of routes differ only in the tax treatment of the annuity income purchased and the way in which the annuity is treated for the purposes of the age pension means-test. Routes 12 and 19 are preferred by those retiring earlier, whereas routes 15 and 22 are preferred by those who retire relatively later. Hence those retiring later find it advantageous to take their superannuation assets as a lump sum (and pay any tax if appropriate) before purchasing an annuity.

Consider the money purchase routes chosen. Route 28 allows for all superannuation benefits to be put to annuity purchase and the balance of assets to be spent immediately. This route is, effectively, preferred by individuals whose optimal percentage salary replacement is not represented in the defined benefit options. Similarly route 35 and route 25, which provide for all assets to be used to purchase annuity income, are distinguished by the fact that route 25 involves all superannuation assets being used to purchase an annuity, and route 35 specifies taking a lump sum and using after-tax money to purchase an annuity. Thus, the optimal routes chosen fall into associated pairs, and each member of the pair is distinguished by the associated tax and means-test operation.

The general trend is that those whose income level is such that the operation of the age pension means-test may have an effect, purchase a level of income which will maximise their benefit. This constitutes the majority of the cohort: this majority arrange affairs such that they just get under the means-test thresholds.

There is a small group whose level of earnings are so low that the workings of the means tests are irrelevant, in that they are never able to purchase an income in excess of the thresholds. For this group, the optimal behaviour is to retire as early as possible, since there is no relative advantage in remaining in low paid employment.

There is another small class of individuals who are always able to purchase income well in excess of the means-test thresholds. These individuals arrange their net income according to the relationship between the annuity purchase rates and their level of income.

The effects on the optimal retirement age of changing the values of α and h_t from the base case, are quite straightforward. The effect of increasing α alone, that is, attaching more weight to consumption compared with leisure, is to reduce the extent of early retirement. However, a less obvious result is that the importance of different routes through the maze changes substantially. With $\alpha = 0.6$, very few select routes 12, 5, and 27. Those retiring in their early 60s select mainly routes 8 and 9, along with 35. Later retirees prefer 25 and 44. The higher value of α also eliminates the bimodality in the distribution of optimal age at retirement. Increasing h_t to 0.3 does not eliminate the bimodality. The effect of a higher value of h_t during the working life is to produce a movement towards later retirement ages, resulting from the smaller increase in leisure on retirement, but there is little effect on the optimal choice of route.

A Universal Pension

The above results suggest that a substantial proportion of individuals in the cohort are affected by the age pension means-test, particularly the income test, which influences not only the allocation of assets but also the optimal age of retirement. It is therefore useful to examine the effects of abolishing the means-test. Table 7 shows that the optimal choice of the same cohort under conditions which are the same as those for Table 5, except that the age pension is universal and subject to no means-testing. The differences in choice are thus entirely due to the removal of the means-test. Obviously, those few individuals beneath the effects of the means-test do not change their behaviour. The distribution of retirement ages becomes unimodal with the universal age pension. This eliminates the mode at the lowest age, but the single mode is slightly lower than the highest mode when there is means-testing. The arithmetic mean optimal retirement age is the same in each case, at 59 years.

Table 7 Universal Pension (h = 0.25; α = 0.5; A1; CM)

					Age of retirement						
No.	55	56	57	58	59	60	61	62	63	64	65
1	13	1	-	-	-	-	-	-	-	-	-
2	36	6	3	-	-	-	-	-	-	-	-
5	83	99	120	117	79	35	7	-	-	-	-
9	-	1	-	5	3	1	1	-	-	-	-
12	94	159	266	324	364	294	170	121	64	13	2
15	-	-	-	-	-	-	-	1	1	2	1
16	-	-	-	1	-	-	1	-	-	15	3
19	1	-	1	3	2	8	3	1	1	-	1
22	-	-	-	-	-	-	-	-	-	1	2
25	36	26	47	46	64	41	27	29	4	4	3
28	1	-	4	13	24	38	34	12	10	4	-
35	-	-	-	-	-	-	-	-	-	-	2
Total	265	292	441	509	536	417	243	164	80	39	14

The result is that the removal of means-testing leads more individuals to replace a higher proportion of income and/or to retire later. The majority of the cohort is within the reach of the existing age-pension means-test and, when this is removed, these people are encouraged to purchase higher levels of income and to work longer in order to do so.

Comparison of Tables 5 and 7 also shows that almost all of those choosing to buy annuities with after-tax money rather than directly from superannuation, in Table 5, were doing so because the means-test distinguishes between them rather than because the income tax rules make a distinction. With a universal pension, very few continue to choose routes 8, 15, 19 and 22, which all involves commutation of superannuation funds to a lump sum and a level of annuity purchase. Similarly, more choose routes 25 and 28 which both use all superannuation funds to purchase an annuity.

One argument made against the introduction of a universal pension is that it involves higher expenditure. However the results presented here show that, in the context of early retirement choices, the universal pension produces an incentive for higher levels of income provision and an associated delay in retirement age. This incentive may give rise to additional taxation to offset the costs of a universal pension[3].

Differential Mortality
Tables 8 and 9 show the optimal choices of the members of the cohort when subject to differential rather than common mortality, for annuity routes A1. Thus differences between the pair of Tables 5 and 8, and the pair 6 and 9 arise entirely from the change in mortality assumption. As might be expected, routes involving the bank account are chosen under the assumption of differential mortality. Those who die before the age of 80 retain a capital asset by using the bank account and would otherwise, if purchasing an annuity, experience a loss due to mortality.

With differential mortality there is also a drift towards retirement at the later ages (particularly 64 and 65) though the broad bimodal pattern is still observed, with modes again at age 55 and 61. The general pattern is unchanged, but those with mortality much higher than the average choose the bank options, and those whose longevity significantly exceeds the norm choose higher levels of annuity purchase. The number of individuals choosing Route 25 (all assets used to purchase an annuity) doubles.

Another major difference when there is differential mortality is that some of the money purchase routes, notably 27, 35, 43 and 44, become optimal for a significant minority of the cohort. Further analysis of individuals and their characteristics suggest the following patterns. First, the money purchase routes involving bank accounts are only used by those of below average life expectancy, who leave an estate. Second, route 25, the 100 per cent annuity route, is strongly favoured by high income, high longevity individuals. Third, earlier retirement ages are typically associated with those on low earnings, and with low ages of survival.

Table 8 Differential Mortality (h = 0.25; α = 0.5; A1; DM)

					Age at retirement						
No.	55	56	57	58	59	60	61	62	63	64	65
1	7	-	-	-	-	-	-	-	-	-	-
2	19	1	-	-	-	-	-	-	1	-	-
3	-	-	-	-	-	-	-	-	-	-	-
4	4	-	-	-	-	-	-	-	-	-	-
5	49	34	13	10	1	4	2	1	2	-	1
7	4	-	-	-	-	-	-	-	-	-	-
8	13	1	1	1	3	7	22	28	10	1	1
9	15	13	8	4	13	27	53	56	19	3	2
11	34	-	-	-	-	-	-	-	-	-	-
12	124	144	128	45	6	3	3	2	1	-	2
14	4	1	-	-	-	-	-	-	-	-	-
15	17	29	32	26	44	75	85	72	37	13	4
16	6	8	13	21	41	55	70	61	36	19	5
18	47	52	56	49	10	-	2	3	-	-	-
19	7	10	4	3	-	-	-	-	-	-	-
21	-	-	1	-	3	4	6	1	-	3	-
22	-	-	-	2	2	7	12	22	5	5	-
25	35	31	29	5	5	14	21	33	44	30	110
27	22	14	3	3	-	-	-	-	-	-	-
28	7	7	2	-	-	-	-	1	-	-	-
30	8	3	19	39	36	25	1	1	-	-	-
33	-	-	2	2	1	-	-	-	-	-	-
35	1	-	-	-	-	-	3	8	1	-	3
38	101	1	2	-	2	5	5	5	1	-	1
40	-	-	-	-	-	-	1	8	15	4	-
43	-	-	6	17	39	63	68	32	8	5	-
44	-	-	-	-	-	-	-	-	-	31	66
Total	433	349	319	227	206	289	354	334	214	146	129

Table 9 Choice with Differential Mortality (h = 0.25; α = 0.5; A2; DM)

No.	55	56	57	58	59	60	61	62	63	64	65
					Age at retirement						
1	7	-	-	-	-	-	-	-	-	-	-
2	30	-	3	-	1	-	1	1	1	1	-
5	68	37	35	12	3	2	4	4	3	-	1
7	3	-	-	-	-	-	-	-	-	-	-
8	21	2	3	1	4	9	31	35	6	2	-
9	15	11	8	8	12	17	41	57	33	9	3
11	41	1	-	-	-	-	-	-	-	-	-
12	149	145	140	74	15	2	3	2	2	-	2
14		5	-	-	1	-	-	-	-	-	-
15	27	14	25	26	45	54	87	46	29	8	4
16	6	10	11	13	29	41	53	40	31	7	2
18	57	35	49	43	17	2	2	2	-	-	-
19	7	6	9	1	-	-	-	-	-	-	-
21	-	2	-	-	1	1	1	3	-	-	-
22	-	-	-	2	2	1	6	12	6	1	1
25	62	34	47	23	11	17	32	35	53	41	131
27	32	12	11	5	-	-	-	-	-	-	-
28	8	5	5	3	-	-	1	1	-	-	-
30	-	7	12	21	27	22	3	-	-	-	-
33	-	-	2	1	1				-	-	-
35	2	-	-	-	-	1	1	7	5	1	1
38	16	-	1	2	-	3	4	4	-	-	-
40	-	-	-	-	-	-	-	9	8	2	-
43	-	-	1	4	28	54	54	20	1	3	-
44	-	-	-	-	-	-	-	-	31	64	-
Total	560	321	362	240	196	226	324	278	209	139	145

A general result with differential mortality is that the lower the earnings, the earlier the preferred age at retirement and vice versa. Thus the introduction of differential mortality has the following general effects by comparison with common mortality. First individuals with high incomes and low mortality are inclined to buy more annuity income and retire later. Second, individuals with low incomes and high mortality are inclined to buy less annuity income and retire earlier. The net effect is a flattening of the distribution of the age of retirement. This is a complimentary net effect to that of introducing a universal pension.

The two fringe classes who lie outside the means-test influence are simply able to buy a higher level of income than before. The lower purchase rates, associated with Table 9, result in a slight shift in that some will be brought up into the range of income influenced by the means-test and some will rise beyond it.

**Table 10 Differential Mortality and Universal Pension
(h = 0.25; α = 0.5; A1; DM)**

No.	Age at retirement										
	55	56	57	58	59	60	61	62	63	64	65
1	6	-	-	-	-	-	-	-	-	-	-
2	23	2	9	9	6	4	3	2	1	-	-
4	4	-	-	-	-	-	-	-	-	-	-
5	64	46	47	58	39	32	16	21	7	5	-
9	2	2	-	1	1	-	-	-	-	-	-
11	28	2	-	1	-	-	-	-	-	-	-
12	101	123	183	151	143	119	70	39	17	6	2
14	1	-	-	-	-	-	-	-	-	-	-
16	-	-	1	1	-	-	-	-	-	1	-
18	39	33	46	46	34	30	15	5	2	2	1
19	2	2	3	7	5	10	4	2	-	-	-
25	16	21	31	56	73	102	86	84	61	47	98
27	41	25	18	12	7	4	-	-	-	-	-
28	9	5	23	23	34	32	21	11	1	1	-
30	3	2	2	1	3	12	9	14	6	4	-
33	-	-	-	3	8	6	8	1	1	1	-
38	6	-	-	-	-	-	-	-	-	-	-
43	-	-	6	14	39	57	55	24	3	8	-
44	-	-	-	-	-	-	-	1	25	49	-
Total	345	263	369	383	392	408	287	204	124	124	101

Table 10 shows results of combining a universal pension with differential mortality. A combination of the features of differential mortality and abolition of the means-testing of the age pension result in a combination of various effects. There is a more even distribution of optimal retirement ages, though modes at age 55 and 60 are still obtained.

Earnings Profiles
It was suggested above that a factor in the determination of the optimum retirement age, in addition to the tax and transfer structure, is the shape of the individual's earnings profile. The benefits of an extra year's earnings must be balanced against those of an extra year of leisure in retirement and the impact of the means-tested pension. Each individual in the simulations experiences a unique earnings profile, based on the use of a stochastic model of earnings estimated using Australian data; see the appendix. The model implies that, on average, those with relatively higher earnings experience their peak earnings relatively later than those with relatively lower earnings; for further discussion of this phenomenon, see Creedy (1985, p.68). The parameters used in the above simulations imply, however, that an individual who experiences the median income of the cohort in each year of working life receives peak real earnings at about

age 50 years, although nominal median earnings never fall over the relevant period. Arithmetic mean real earnings reach a peak about 3.5 years later.

Table 11 Steeper Earnings Profiles (h = 0.25; α = 0.5; A1; CM)

No.	55	56	57	58	59	60	61	62	63	64	65
					Age at retirement						
2	2	-	-	-	-	-	-	-	-	-	-
5	9	12	3	-	1	1	2	-	-	-	-
8	1	2	1	-	1	-	-	-	-	-	-
9	3	7	6	10	9	17	7	2	-	-	-
12	45	53	69	68	10	17	29	46	51	52	57
15	-	6	15	30	68	149	211	143	55	20	-
16	-	2	3	6	17	58	165	269	203	115	14
19	-	4	1	-	-	-	-	-	-	-	10
22	-	-	-	-	-	5	44	116	163	193	75
25	13	5	8	2	9	15	21	18	18	11	95
28	2	5	5	-	-	-	-	-	-	-	-
35	2	-	-	-	-	-	-	-	-	-	8
38	-	-	-	-	-	-	-	-	-	1	9
Total	77	96	111	116	115	262	479	594	490	392	268

It is therefore worth considering the effects of somewhat steeper age-earnings profiles. Simulations were accordingly carried out for alternative parameters; the values of θ and δ were changed to 0.04 and 0.0006. These imply that the median value of real earnings reaches a peak at about 62 years. The upper deciles reach a maximum substantially later, of course. Results are given in Table 11 for common mortality and annuity purchase rates A1. As expected the modal age of retirement increases and the lower mode disappears, although there remains a substantial amount of early retirement.

The effect of making the age pension universal is that the distribution of age at retirement becomes more widely dispersed. The mode falls by one year although the lower tail contains fewer people. The average optimal retirement age is 61 for both means-tested and universal systems, however. Routes 25 and 28 become substantially more popular, especially among late retirees, as does route 12. The number for whom routes 15 and 16 are optimal falls dramatically; these involve the taking of lump sums (before purchasing an annuity) and consuming all that remains after purchasing a specified proportion (50 and 45 per cent respectively) of final salary, and are driven by the existence of the means-tests.

Contribution Rates

An important issue, not mentioned so far, concerns the desirable level of the contribution rates in a mandated superannuation scheme such as the Superannuation Guarantee Charge. The scheme is introduced on the (paternalistic) argument that individuals are generally myopic and will not otherwise save enough for retirement. However, there is a possibility that some people are thereby forced to 'oversave'. Decreasing marginal utility implies a preference for a smooth consumption stream, and contribution rates that are 'too high' tend to encourage early retirement rather than higher consumption during retirement. Any attempt to increase aggregate savings with such a mandatory scheme would thus be frustrated. It is therefore of interest to examine the implications of a mature scheme in which individuals are faced with lower contribution rates and save less out of disposable income in each year of the working life.

Suppose that the employee and employer contribution rates are reduced to 2 and 6 per cent respectively (from the 3 and 9 per cent used above), and that individuals reduce their additional saving rate to 2.5 per cent (from 5 per cent assumed above). With the base values of $h_t = 0.25$ and $\alpha = 0.5$, and using the annuity rates A1, the average optimal age at retirement, with common mortality, is increased to 62, with the (single) mode increasing to age 64 (when almost a third of the cohort retire). The choice of routes through the maze is dominated by routes 15, 16 and 22 (the most popular among the late retirers). Each of these defined benefit routes involves the superannuation assets being taken as a lump sum before an annuity is purchased (to achieve 50, 45 and 35 per cent respectively of the average earnings over the final three working years), with the remaining assets (if any) being consumed at retirement.

The fact that the bank account is not used is driven by the assumptions of common mortality and the draw-down of the account, but the use of the lump sums is driven by the tax treatment of annuities and the means test for the age pension. Where the age pension is universal, the average optimal retirement age is reduced by one year to 61, which in this case is also the mode. With a universal pension the optimal routes are dominated instead by 12, 19 and 28 since individuals are not penalised for replacing a higher level of income. The two defined benefit routes 12 and 19 use pre-tax money to purchase an annuity, while route 28 involves all superannuation funds being used to purchase an annuity and all additional savings being consumed at retirement.

The alternative assumption of differential mortality introduces, as before, a richer range of optimal routes through the maze as more of the money purchase alternatives become optimal and the use of a bank account in retirement is more common. With differential mortality the average age at retirement continues to be 62 (with the mode at 64). Routes 15, 16 and 22 continue to be popular (as with common mortality), though the money purchase routes 40, 43 and 44, which involve the use of a bank account and possible bequests, are frequently used (the modal combination of age and route is in fact age 64 and route 44). The latter two routes do not involve the purchase of an annuity. The choice of routes 15 and 16 is clearly driven by the means test relating to the age pension; with a universal pension these routes virtually disappear and routes 25 and 28 (giving a high proportion of income replacement) become very popular, with 30 and 33 also being used more frequently. In this case the universal pension has the same mean and modal optimal retirement age, but the distribution is, as before, more widely dispersed. The question of the appropriate contribution rate (along with the profile of the rate over the life cycle) warrants further investigation.

Conclusions

This paper has used a lifetime simulation model in order to examine the optimal choice both of the retirement age (between the ages of 55 and 65) and the allocation of assets at retirement, involving the route through what has been referred to as the retirement maze. Each simulated member of the cohort was assumed to maximise a lifetime utility function defined in terms of the present value of utility, with each years' utility independently defined as a Cobb-Douglas function of consumption and leisure in the year.

In view of the fact that individuals' preferences are not known and the simulation model requires a number of strong simplifications and assumptions, the results must be treated with caution. However, they suggest the existence of a significant incentive towards early retirement and a substantial impact of the age pension means-tests on the allocation of resources and optimal retirement age of individuals. The extent and nature of incentives were found to vary with the mortality assumption used, and depend on the means tests associated with the age pension. The assumption of a universal pension encourages later retirement in a substantial proportion of the cohort. The simulations apply to a fully mature Superannuation Guarantee Charge scheme, such that the contribution rates apply for each year of the working life. This will not apply until individuals are retiring after approximately the year 2040.

The analysis raises the important question of the appropriate level of contribution rates in a mandated scheme. Results suggest that lower contribution rates encourage a later preferred retirement age.

In the policy debate relating to the provision of retirement incomes in Australia, it has often been argued that there is a need to encourage later retirement rather than early retirement (in view of expected population ageing) along with the use of annuities rather than reliance on the age pension. The simulations reported in this paper suggest that reforms to the superannuation system will be required in order to achieve these objectives.

Appendix

The Simulation Model

Earnings Profiles

Gross earnings in each year of working life are generated using a model of age-earnings profiles in which earnings in age group t are lognormally distributed as $\Lambda(\mu_t, \sigma_\tau^2)$, where μ_t and σ_τ^2 are respectively the mean and variance of the logarithms of earnings. These two parameters are assumed to be quadratic and linear functions of t respectively, so that:

$$\mu_t = \mu_1 + (\theta + g) t - \delta t^2 \qquad (2)$$

$$\sigma_t^2 = \sigma_1^2 + \sigma_u^2 t \qquad (3)$$

where g is the nominal growth rate of earnings which affects all age groups equally. The five parameters μ_1, σ_1^2, θ, δ and σ_u^2 were estimated using data for Australian males and are $\mu_1 = 9.98064$, $\theta = 0.0385$, $\delta = 0.00086$, $\sigma = 0.1817$, $\sigma_u^2 = 0.00575$; $g = 0.06$; see Creedy (1992).

Age at Death

The number of years the ith individual survives after retirement, d_i, is obtained, following Creedy (1982), using the following formula:

$$d_i = \bar{d} + \beta \log \frac{\bar{X}_i}{M} + u_i \qquad (4)$$

where $\bar{X}_i$ is the individual's annual average real earnings, M is the geometric mean value of the $\bar{X}_i$s, $\bar{d}$ is the average number of years individuals in the general population survive after retirement and u_i is a random normal variable $N(0, \sigma_u^2)$. The values used are: $\bar{d} = 14.6$, $\beta = 8$ and $\sigma_u^2 = 50$.

Other Assumptions

The major assumptions used in the simulation are as shown in Table 12.

Table 12 Economic Assumptions

Tax on super fund investment income	7.5%
Tax on savings fund investment income	25%
Annual increase in Average Earnings	6%
Annual increase in income tax thresholds	5.5%
Annual inflation rate	5%
Gross annual rate of return on Super fund	9%
Gross annual return on Bank account	5%
Annuities escalate in payment at	5%

Notes

1 The model is a modified version of LITES (Lifetime Income, Taxation, Expenditure and Superannuation), described in Atkinson *et al.* (1994).

2 Hammermesh (1985) examined the differences between expectations and actual longevity for a sample of individuals in the U.S.

3 The additional revenue cannot be estimated with the current model, which examines just a single cohort.

References

Atkinson, M. E., Creedy, J., Knox, D. M., (1994) Lifetime income, taxation, expenditure and superannuation (LITES) : a life-cycle simulation model. *Centre for Actuarial Studies Research Paper No. 9.*

Atkinson, M.E., Creedy, J., Knox, D.M. (1995) Planning retirement income in Australia: routes through the maze. *Australian Economic Review*, 4'95, pp. 15-28.

Atkinson, M.E. and Creedy, J. (1996) Modelling optimal retirement decisions in Australia. *Australian Economic Papers*, 35, pp. 39-59.

Creedy, J. (1982) *State Pensions in Britain*. Cambridge: Cambridge University Press.

Creedy, J. (1985) *Dynamics of Income Distribution*. Oxford: Basil Blackwell.

Creedy, J. (1992) Income, Inequality and the Life Cycle. Aldershot: Edward Elgar.

Hammermesh, D. S. (1985) Expectations, life expectancy and economic behaviour. *Quarterly Journal of Economics*, 100, pp. 398-408.

Kingston, G. (1995) Retirement flexibility and portfolio choice. *University of New South Wales, Department of Economics.*

PART II

SKILLED LABOUR MARKETS

Earnings and Job Mobility:
Professional Chemists in Britain

by J. Creedy
and K. Whitfield*
*University of Durham
and University of Sydney*

Examining the process of job mobility and its effect on earnings, the authors find that this particular labour market is characterised by a high incidence of specific training, that upward mobility is largely experienced within the same organisation and is mainly of the osmotic type. It is felt that a technique must be devised to measure osmotic mobility accurately.

Introduction

The main purpose of this article is to examine the process of job mobility and its effects on the earnings of a group of professional employees; that is, members of the Royal Society of Chemistry. A special feature of the analysis is that it uses specially conducted sample surveys, carried out in the mid-1970s, which provide detailed information about the career histories of the respondents. Surveys of this type are still rare, especially in Britain, and the empirical analysis of such data raises a number of problems.

The first section of this article examines the analysis of mobility and earnings which has been conducted within the human capital framework and, following a summary of the main criticisms of this approach, explores the possibility that it may be more fruitful to base analysis on the observed mobility process, as suggested by internal labour market theory. The second section then describes the surveys of professional chemists and discusses the special problems raised by the empirical analysis of career mobility. The third section contains the substantive results of the article, relating earnings to previous job mobility; this deals with both the relation between various types of job change and short-term changes in earnings, and the longer-term relation between mobility patterns and relative earnings at the time of the survey. A fourth section concludes the article.

Mobility and Earnings

The relationship between job mobility and earnings has been the subject of much analysis by economists. Contemporary work on this relationship has been undertaken

* We are very grateful to Barry Henman, Registrar of the Royal Society of Chemistry, for his considerable help and co-operation with the surveys used here. We should also like to thank the trustees of the Bank of England's Houblon/Norman Fund, for providing financial assistance towards the second mobility survey, and a referee of this journal for constructive comments on an earlier draft of the article.

24   Journal of Economic Studies 13,2

largely within the human capital framework and concerns not only the benefits of changing organisations but also of organisational stability. This work has yielded satisfactory statistical results and certainly improves the explanatory power of the human capital earnings equation. However, this approach to the analysis of earnings has been subject to severe criticism and, moreover, its main adherents have been unsure about some of its interpretations. Hence it seems useful to stand back from the equations and examine the processes being conceptualised in order to ascertain whether the current approach requires only minor changes or whether it would be useful to develop an alternative framework which by-passes the major problems of human capital theory.

Current research on mobility and earnings within the human capital framework is a simple extension of the analysis of on-the-job training which was developed by Becker in the early 1960s. The essence of this analysis is that post-school investments in human capital can be divided into the following three categories. First, there is investment in general training, the returns to which can be obtained in organisations other than that of acquisition. Consequently the bulk of payment for this training will be made by the worker concerned, usually by a wage which is equal to the level of marginal product during training. Secondly, there is investment in specific training, the returns to which can be obtained only in the organisation in which it is acquired. The bulk of the costs of this training will be incurred by the organisation although it may share some of the costs with the employee in return for an increased post-training wage. The objective of this sharing principle is to reduce turnover and increase the probability that the organisation will recoup its investment. Thirdly, there is investment in job search, the returns to which are realised on changing the job.

Borjas (1981) has drawn out the implications of this trichotomy for the relationship between job mobility and earnings. First, turnover will cause a shift in the level of the worker's experience-earnings profile. Secondly, there is less investment in specific on-the-job training and hence less earnings growth, when a job is not expected to be permanent. Borjas, however, then makes a large conceptual leap when he concludes that, "job mobility will tend to flatten the slope of the experience-earnings profile within the job" (1981, p. 366). The problem here is that *ex ante* has become *ex post*.

Borjas's empirical analysis is based on the US National Longitudinal Survey for Mature Men. He found a negative relationship between workers' level of job mobility and the growth of earnings within each job; labour turnover usually leads to a higher wage rate in the new job but the short-run advantages of turnover were more than offset for most workers by lower rates of wage increase within each job, thus the least mobile middle-aged men were the highest earners.

Borjas concludes that, "the explanatory power of the human capital approach was significantly increased by accounting for the effects of job mobility" (1981, p. 376). However, this conclusion is tempered with the cautionary statement that, "it is very likely that the empirical findings are consistent with many alternative explanations" (1981, p. 376). Other economists, even while generally supporting the human capital approach to earnings analysis, have been much less willing to accept the human capital interpretation. For example, Blaug (1976) has argued that an explanation couched in terms of the assignment of *all* intra-firm pay changes to a process of rational self-investment is implausible. Thurow (1983) has been even more sceptical of the whole on-the-job training extension of human capital theory. Not only does this extension

Professional Chemists in Britain   **25**

convert the approach into a tautology but postulates a process for the allocation of on-the-job training which differs substantially from that observed. Thurow states that "employers usually allocate such opportunities not based on a willingness to work for less than one's free market wage but on seniority or merit for having performed well in a job previously held" (1983, p. 175).

The implausibility of the current human capital interpretation of earnings change and mobility suggests that some analysis needs to be made of the actual *processes* which the theory seeks to model. Human capital theory itself gives little insight as to the exact form which such an investigation should take. However, internal labour market (ILM) theory, which was developed contemporaneously with human capital theory and has much in common with Borjas's development of it, is more fruitful in this respect. Thus the next sub-section isolates key insights of ILM theory which relate to the mobility process.

Internal Labour Markets
While the internal labour market has a long intellectual history, its most explicit introduction into the labour economics literature was by Doeringer and Piore (1971). In this study the authors defined an ILM as "an administrative unit, such as a manufacturing plant, within which the pricing and allocation of labour is governed by a set of administrative rules and procedures" (1971, pp. 1-2). The utility of the concept is seen to depend upon "the *rigidity* of the rules which define the boundaries of internal markets and which govern pricing and allocation within them" (1971, p. 5).

In their study, Doeringer and Piore offered an explanation for the development of the ILM which integrated ideas from the theory of specific human capital and from research on occupational mobility. The low turnover and internal mobility characteristics of such institutions were seen as reflective of the acquisition of specific skills. However, they departed from the strict human capital explanation by dropping the assumption that the costs of such skills are shared on the basis of some optimisation principle. Instead, firms are seen to possess a fairly rigid internal pricing and allocation structure which is dictated by the nature of the technology used and the need to integrate promotion and training ladders. A similar model has been presented by Thurow who has argued that firms deliberately suppress wage flexibility so as not to disrupt on-the-job training. In short, the internal requirements of the firm are seen to prevent the wage flexibility which is central to the human capital explanation.

Rather than develop a tautological framework which is seemingly at variance with the operation of the labour market, ILM theory suggests that analysis should be concentrated on the actual mobility processes which take place within organisations. That is, it recommends the opening of the "black box" which labour economists have been wary of examining. However, in contrast to the human capital analysis, no established methodology has emerged from ILM theory to form the basis of such an investigation. Therefore, the present study must be extremely tentative and at this stage can only be regarded as exploratory.

The most important reason for the neglect of the ILM in applied economic research is the lack of suitable data. ILM analysis is concerned with particular occupations and organisations and with processes which occur over long time-periods. Most available data, however, relate either to wider aggregates (such as the general move-

26   Journal of Economic Studies 13,2

ment of workers between organisations and into and out of the labour force) or to cross-sections. Both are inappropriate for the task at hand. There is a consequent need to collect work histories, which give detailed information about the career patterns of individuals in selected cohorts.

ILM theory offers a number of implications for the analysis of the relationship between labour mobility and earnings. First, it suggests that there will be a high level of organisational stability and that the more stable workers will generally be the most highly paid. A similar conclusion can be derived from human capital theory. Secondly, inter-firm mobility will be concentrated among workers in the early stages of their working lives who will be searching for the most advantageous job ladder as part of a process of "job shopping". Hence external mobility will decline with age. Again this prediction is shared with human capital theory. Thirdly, the bulk of upward mobility in a labour market with well-developed ILMs will be of the internal variety and, moreover, it will be characterised by its gradual or "osmotic" nature, reflecting the gradual accumulation of skills during on-the-job training and the consequential movement up the internal job hierarchy[1]. Some researchers have suggested that osmotic mobility processes may constitute the bulk of its mobility process (Hunter and Reid, 1968; White, 1970). This aspect of the mobility process is ignored by human capital theory which relates changes in earnings between the beginning and end of each job to self-investment in specific and general training. Finally, involuntary mobility will be very costly to the workers concerned. This is because their skills are likely to be so specific that they will be less productive in other firms or because of the existence of institutional rules which restrict recruitment to the lower rungs of the job ladder.

The Analysis of Job Mobility

Jobs and Firms

The foregoing discussion has suggested that any examination of the generation of earnings requires an understanding of mobility processes within firms. The empirical analysis of such processes is complicated by the fact that terms used in the theoretical analyses, even apparently simple terms like "job", are often very difficult to specify in a particular context. Within-organisation mobility is an extremely difficult concept to measure for two main reasons. First, there is no generally accepted methodology for deciding which changes in job duties should be regarded as job changes. Secondly, following the earlier discussion of osmotic mobility, a great deal of internal mobility results not from discrete job changes but from the gradual accumulation of a number of small changes in job duties. None of these changes may be sufficiently wide-ranging in itself to constitute a job change but, when viewed over a long time horizon, a series of changes may result in a substantial change in the nature of the tasks being undertaken.

The problem of distinguishing between changes in job duties which are job changes from those which are not has been addressed in two main ways. The first and most common method is to define within-organisation mobility as a change in occupational status, according to a well specified occupational classification, which nevertheless does not involve a change of firm. However, this technique tends to underestimate the incidence of internal mobility relative to external mobility. First, it involves an asymmetry in that internal mobility can only occur when there is a change of occupational status (according to the classification used), whereas external mobility is counted as a job change whether or not there is such a change in status (see also Cole, 1979). Secondly, the incidence of reported internal mobility depends crucially on the occupational classification adopted. These tend to be extremely narrow and not always closely related to the occupation under study. Thirdly, even with a good classification, this technique may fail to detect those small-scale changes in job duties mentioned above.

An alternative technique for measuring the incidence of internal mobility is the self-reporting technique. The decision as to whether or not a change in job duties constitutes a job change is left to the respondent. While this technique overcomes many of the problems inherent in the use of occupational classifications, it encounters the difficulty that workers' perceptions of what constitutes a job can vary among workers. Moreover, there are reasons to believe that such perceptions are inherent within the mobility pattern itself. For example, in a study of American and Japanese workers, Cole (1979) found, contrary to his expectation, that the incidence of intra-firm mobility reported by workers in the two countries differed only minimally. Given the lifetime employment system in Japan and the very different ideology of the USA, Cole expected workers in the former country to report more internal mobility. This paradox can perhaps be explained in terms of a broader conception of what constituted a job within the Japanese context. An interpretation is that occupational differentiation was less important to a Japanese worker than an American. In general, it can be expected that this will be a smaller problem in a national, as opposed to a cross-national, investigation and in a study based on a homogeneous as against a heterogeneous group. It is not, therefore, thought to create problems in the present context.

A further, less difficult, issue to be resolved is how to define the term "firm", and hence where to place the dividing line between inter- and intra-firm mobility. The word "firm" has been defined in the literature in three main ways; an establishment, enterprise or organisation. The broader the definition chosen, the greater the incidence of intra-firm mobility reported. Which definition is chosen depends partly on the object of the analysis and partly on the nature of the labour market under study. Thus a study of, say, the effects on executive productivity of movement between locations would more likely take the narrow definition. However, the present study, concentrating on movement within an internal labour market, is more appropriately based on the wider definition. Thus in the following analysis the term "firm" should be regarded as synonymous with organisation.

Surveys of Professional Chemists
The present article is based on two surveys undertaken under the aegis of the Royal Institute of Chemistry, RIC (now the Royal Society of Chemistry, RSC) in the mid-1970s. The first survey was conducted in late 1973 and early 1974 among 435 members of the Institute who were aged 47 years on 1 January 1973. The second was undertaken in late 1975 and was based upon 2,000 members who were aged between 25 and 44 years at the time of the survey[2].

Both surveys asked respondents to give details of each job held in their working lives. Information included, for example, income, type of work undertaken, level of responsibility held, year of commencement and completion of job. The data were, therefore, collected by the retrospective technique, whereby respondents provide a summary of their work history. This technique has often been criticised for yielding inaccurate information due to faulty recall and *ex post* rationalisation of job changes. While it is not possible to check the accuracy of the replies, there is every reason to believe that they are reasonably correct. The respondents exibited background characteristics, such as having high education levels, being male and middle-aged, which place them among the more accurate of survey respondents. Further, the RSC is one of the most active and experienced sample surveyors in Britain; and the mobility surveys used a classification and a format which resembled the Society's triennial remuneration surveys of its total membership. An extremely useful characteristic of the members is that those who move into management retain their membership. This has arisen largely from the great foresight shown by the Professional Affairs section of the Royal Society at an early stage in its growth.

There are two features of the RIC mobility surveys which make them appropriate for the study of mobility in the internal labour market. First, both obtained information on within-organisation job mobility using the self-reporting technique. Secondly, it is possible to obtain from the work histories returned an estimate of the incidence of the "osmotic" form of labour mobility which some researchers have suggested to be important.

Both surveys made an explicit request for information on within-organisation mobility. The first survey offered a category in its section on "reason for change of location" entitled "transfer within organisation". The second survey was even more explicit and not only offered two categories for internal mobility (transfer within and promotion within organisation), but also headed the coding schedule with the request that, "if you have held two or more separate posts with different job titles within the same establishment, please treat each one as a separate job".

Both surveys also requested information on the type of work undertaken and the level of responsibility held at the beginning and the end of each job in the work history. From this information it is possible to obtain an estimate of the more gradual form of labour mobility which occurs without a discrete job change being perceived. To distinguish it from within-organisation job changing, this phenomenon may be called "within-job" mobility. It can be regarded as a measure of the osmotic mobility which was examined earlier.

Types of Mobility
This section provides a brief description of the main characteristics of the mobility patterns of professional chemists, as a preliminary to the main analysis of the following section. It provides a highly aggregative and condensed summary of survey results, but gives initial support for the relevance of the internal labour market framework for this profession. As explained above, this article distinguishes three main types of job mobility: between-organisation (or inter-firm) mobility; within-organisation (or intra-firm) mobility; within-job mobility. The first two types of mobility were

Professional Chemists in Britain **29**

distinguished using the section of the questionnaires giving the reasons for each change. Each questionnaire contained a section on transfer or promotion within the same organisation, and these were considered to be synonymous with internal mobility. The replies could also be used to subdivide between-organisation moves into the two categories "voluntary" and "involuntary" mobility, thereby distinguishing between two aspects of the phenomenon which have differing motivations and consequences.

The responses to both surveys showed that the respondents exhibited a high level of organisational stability. It was possible to calculate the number of changes of organisation reported per man year which the respondents have spent in the labour force. The "turnover rate" so obtained was 0.075 changes per year for the respondents to the first survey and 0.102 for second survey respondents. Given that the average age of first survey respondents was 47 years and of second survey respondents was 35 years and that inter-organisation mobility declines with age, these figures suggest that the labour market for chemists would be classified as "manorial" on the Kerr/Alexander classification; that is, a market which contains well-developed, enterprise-specific internal labour markets (Kerr, 1954; Alexander, 1974)[3]. Low turnover is also compatible with the human capital interpretation of a high incidence of specific training.

Between-organisation mobility and within-organisation mobility show differing lifetime patterns; the former shows a tendency to decline with age, whereas the latter does not. As a result, the relative magnitudes of the two types of mobility for the older age groups is much closer than for the younger. For example, disaggregation of the second survey responses, by age at time of job change, reveals that inter-firm mobility outnumbers intra-firm by three to one for respondents under 25. However, figures for the age group 40 and over show an almost equal magnitude for the two mobility types. These differing lifetime patterns of inter- and intra-firm mobility suggest that a large proportion of the movement between organisations represents a process of "job shopping"; that is, the movement of labour market entrants between jobs during a period of experimentation and search.

Changes in Earnings over the Career
This section summarises the main empirical results relating earnings to the nature of job mobility over the career. Both of the mobility surveys obtained the annual earnings of each respondent at the time of the survey, and a regression analysis of earnings against suitable measures of the mobility characteristics for which data are available is presented below. The first survey also obtained information about the annual rate of earnings at the beginning and end of each job, and these data are also examined. It is clear that the movement into management and into higher levels of responsibility over the career are important factors in the receipt of relatively high earnings. The basic features of such moves are, therefore, described first. It has to be emphasised that the analysis does not purport to provide rigorous hypothesis tests comparing alternative and well formulated theories of age-earnings profiles and internal labour markets. Rather, it provides a description of several neglected features of a professional labour market, motivated to some extent by insights contained within the basic framework of the theory of internal labour markets. It is argued that the results are sufficiently encouraging to warrant further investigations along similar lines.

Movement into and out of Management

The regular cross-sectional remuneration surveys carried out by the Royal Society of Chemistry show that chemists in managerial or administrative work-roles earn more, on average, than those in non-management and non-administrative work-roles. Thus it can be assumed that the *movement* into management is financially important; but before examining such gains it is useful to consider briefly the way in which the moves can be made.

Movement into management or administration can take two main forms; namely, movement into "general management" and movement into a managerial or administrative role more closely connected with a chemistry-related type of work. An example of the latter is the movement into an administrative role within "research and/or development" activity[4].

All movements into managerial or administrative work-roles were recorded, using the information provided about the type of work performed at the beginning and end of each job. Following the line of argument presented in earlier sections of this article, the moves were then divided into the four categories mentioned earlier: within-job; between-jobs (but within the same organisation); voluntary between organisations; involuntary between organisations.

The results are summarised in the upper half of Table I, and show the number of recorded moves of each type, for each survey[5]. It is clear that the majority of moves into managerial or administrative work-roles took place within the same organisation, rather than as a result of moving between organisations. Moves within the same organisation include both those resulting from an explicit job change within the organisation *and* a movement made within the confines of the same job. The ratio of within-organisation to between-organisation moves into management was 2.1 for the first survey and 4.8 for the second, larger, survey. Furthermore, the large majority of the within-organisation moves were actually reported as taking place within the same job (111 and 255 moves respectively in the first and second survey). Thus for many professional chemists the movement into management or administration was not actually perceived as involving a change of job, when it occurred within the same organisation. This finding is, of course, highly relevant to the discussion of "osmotic" mobility processes, the importance of which was emphasised earlier. It is also worth adding that such changes in work-role, related to the growth of earnings over the career, would not have been observed by the more usual surveys which concentrate on between-organisation job changes.

The responses also revealed a number of moves *out* of managerial or administrative work-roles, as shown in the lower half of Table I. It can be seen that very few of the moves out of management were made within the same organisation. The majority were made voluntarily on a change of organisation. It is interesting to note that for the second survey, the number of between-organisation moves *out* of management is greater than that *into* management. This may perhaps be interpreted as supporting the hypothesis that much voluntary mobility between organisations is a form of "job shopping"; those chemists involved may be trading short-term positional advantages for longer-term gains. This point is examined further in a later sub-section[6].

Professional Chemists in Britain **31**

Table I. Moves into and out of Management/Administration

Type of move	Survey	Within job	Job change within organisation	Job change between organisations Voluntary	Involuntary
Into management	First survey	111	21	59	2
	Second survey	255	73	59	9
Out of management	First survey	6	4	20	9
	Second survey	10	27	80	9

Changes in Responsibility

Although it is uncontroversial to state that there is a positive relationship between income and level of responsibility, it is by no means a straightforward matter to investigate the precise nature of the association. The measurement of an individual's level of responsibility within any professional group presents awkward problems, but the present results are obtained from classifications based on the job title of the person to whom the respondent is directly responsible. The coding schedule for the second survey used a total of 32 job titles, and these were grouped into six categories[7]. Information about responsibility levels was unfortunately not obtained from the first, smaller, mobility survey. Each "level of responsibility" is therefore quite broad, and it is possible that there is some unrecorded mobility among positions of slightly differing responsibility within each of the categories. The present sub-section describes briefly the ways in which changes in responsibility levels are made, while their effect on earnings is examined later.

All recorded changes in responsibility levels were decomposed in the same way as movements into or out of management. The results are shown in Table II. The first row of the table shows that of the 1,516 upward changes in responsibility, 35 per cent took place within what was perceived by respondents to be the same job, and 24 per cent resulted from a change of job within the same organisation. The remaining 41 per cent occurred as a result of a movement between organisations, the majority of which were voluntary moves. Downward changes in responsibility are shown along the second row of Table II, where it can be seen that downward movement is much more likely to be associated with a between-organisation job change, than with the other categories. Only 65 downward changes were made within the same organisation, while 296 such changes resulted from mobility between organisations.

Table II. Upward and Downward Changes in Levels of Responsibility: Second Survey

Type of move	Within job	Job change within organisation	Job change between organisations Voluntary	Involuntary
Upward	537	362	561	56
Downward	23	42	247	49

The analysis of change in responsibility level, therefore, provides a similar picture of mobility to the analysis of movement into and out of management. First, within-organisation mobility processes are predominant in the upward mobility of chemists, and rarely involve a fall in responsibility level. Secondly, voluntary mobility between organisations is more heterogeneous in its effects but is, on average, upward. Thirdly, involuntary mobility is also heterogeneous but is neither upward nor downward in net terms. Again it is worth stressing that many features would have been ignored in a mobility survey which concentrated on movement between organisations, to the neglect of within-organisation, and, particularly, within-job changes.

Changes in Earnings on Job Change
The first mobility survey requested information about the annual rate of earnings received at the beginning and end of each job. The results of this sub-section, therefore, refer only to the first survey. In the present context it is of interest to compare the types of income change made by those changing jobs within and between organisations. A basic comparison is made in Table III, which shows simply the proportions of jobs giving each direction of income change for each type of move. It is clear that voluntary job changes between organisations are much more likely to yield an increase in income than any other change in job; 78 per cent of such moves involved an increase. Furthermore, it was found that, on average, voluntary job changes between firms yielded an income increase of 22 per cent. This, as expected, contrasts with involuntary moves between organisations, where less than half of such moves resulted in an increase, over one quarter resulted in a decrease, and the overall average percentage income change was −1 per cent.

Table III. Direction of Change in Earnings on Job Change (percentages)

	Within-organisation	Between-organisation	
		Voluntary	Involuntary
Increase	42	78	43
No change	52	9	30
Decrease	6	13	27

Column totals add to 100.

Table III also shows that about half of the job changes made within organisations do not result in any change in income, although the average change in income resulting from such changes was found to be 8 per cent[8]. These fairly broad descriptive statistics do show clearly that the largest short-term pecuniary gains are generally made from voluntary moves between organisations[9]. However, the "quality" of a given type of move depends not only on the immediate income change, but also on the pattern of income over the succeeding career. The importance of taking a longer-term view is examined further in the next sub-section, and it is worth adding here that it is not sufficient merely to consider experience only in the immediately succeeding job. For example, it was found that of all the within-organisation job

Professional Chemists in Britain   **33**

changes, 77 per cent experienced an increase in earnings in the following job, and the subsequent annual average increase in that job was 3.4 per cent. For all voluntary between-organisation moves, the same proportion experienced a further increase, but the annual average increase during the tenure of the following job was slightly higher, at 4.3 per cent[10]. This partial view might suggest that between-organisation moves are advantageous from both a short-term and a longer-term perspective but, as shown below, such an inference would not be correct.

Mobility and Earnings at Time of Survey
In examining the effects of various types of mobility process on earnings in a particular profession it may perhaps be suggested that attention should be paid to some measure of lifetime or career earnings, or at least a fairly long-term measure of earnings. However, appropriate data do not exist and the present sub-section attempts to relate earnings at the time of the survey to the pattern of mobility over previous years. The method used is ordinary least squares regression analysis, and it must immediately be accepted that, given the current state of theory, the specification inevitably contains *ad hoc* elements. Data limitations are inevitably important, and for this reason the two surveys must be considered separately.

For the first survey all respondents were the same age so that attention can be focused largely on previous mobility. However, a dummy variable, set equal to unity if the respondent had a higher degree (zero otherwise), was included. The need to allow for movement into management or administration has been discussed earlier, and an additional dummy variable was, therefore, included. In view of the relative importance of within-job moves into management (shown in the first sub-section above), the dummy variable was set equal to unity if the respondent experienced such a move at any stage in his career. The other variables used are fairly straightforward and simply reflect the number of within-organisation, and between-organisation, moves made over the career (with the latter divided into voluntary and involuntary).

The results are shown in Table IV. The value of R^2 is quite respectable for this type of cross-sectional regression using individual data, but most importantly the coefficients on all the independent variables are significantly different from zero, with the interesting exception of that relating to voluntary moves between organisations. The latter coefficient is both relatively low and insignificant, showing that between-organisation moves, even when voluntary, do not provide a significant positive contribution to earnings at the time of the survey (in this case in the respondent's late 40s). Involuntary moves are clearly harmful, and the results show the advantages of within-organisation mobility: each reported internal job change resulted, on average, in an extra £179.3 at the time of the survey.

This finding should be compared with those reported earlier concerning the immediate earnings change on job change, and the annual average rate of earnings change in the subsequent job. The earlier results seemed to indicate that between-organisation (voluntary) job changes were most advantageous, but this is now seen to be merely a short-term gain. More substantial and significant gains result from internal job changes. The other variable designed to reflect internal mobility, the dummy variable relating to within-job moves into management or administration, has a large and highly

**Table IV. Regression Analysis of Earnings at Time of Survey:
First Mobility Survey**

Variable	Coefficient (Standard error)
Constant	3999.3 (238.54)
Education level	1254.6 (222.94)
Number of transfers within organisation	179.3 (83.45)
Number of voluntary job changes	60.3 (66.46)
Number of involuntary job changes	− 834.4 (219.81)
Within-job move to management	1033.8 (223.02)
R^2	0.251

Number of observations = 246.

significant coefficient. The level of education is, of course, also important; a higher degree contributing on average an extra £1,254.6 to annual earnings at the time of the survey.

More information was obtained from the larger second survey, which also included all ages between 25 and 45. Because of the variation in ages, two additional and familiar variables, age and age squared, were used. Information about the education level was not, however, available in this case. The variables which are common to both surveys include the dummy variable for within-job movement into management, the number of job changes made within organisations, and the number of voluntary and involuntary job changes made between organisations.

As discussed above, the second survey also provided information about responsibility levels. The second regression therefore included a variable for the initial level of responsibility in the first job and a further reflection of internal mobility was provided by a variable measuring the number of promotions made on job changes within the same organisation. In view of the problems of measuring responsibility levels in absolute terms, the initial level was measured using a dummy variable. This was set equal to unity if the person to whom the respondent was directly responsible was either a Principal Scientific Officer, Senior Research Scientist, Technical Service Manager, Group Leader, Chief Chemist, or above[11].

Professional Chemists in Britain **35**

In addition, a dummy variable was added to reflect the size of establishment at the beginning of the first job; this was set equal to unity if the establishment employed 1,000 or more people (and was zero otherwise).

The results for the second survey are given in Table V. The coefficients on the age variables are significantly different from zero and of the expected sign, while the coefficient on the dummy variable for size of establishment is not significant. As with the first survey, all the variables relating to internal mobility (including the additional variable for number of promotions) are highly significant, and voluntary job changes between organisations have a much smaller impact on earnings at the time of survey than do internal moves. The results also show that the negative effect of involuntary job changes is greater for respondents to the first survey. It is possible that this reflects the high average age of respondents to that survey, and an increase in the negative effects of involuntary mobility with age. There can be little doubt, from Tables IV and V, that internal mobility processes play a very important role in the determination of earnings, and that the information provided by detailed career histories is vital to an understanding of those processes.

Table V. Regression Analysis of Earnings at Time of Survey: Second Mobility Survey

Variable	Coefficient (Standard error)
Constant	-3074.3 (1003.30)
Age at time of survey	277.1 (56.95)
Age (squared)	-2.2 (0.79)
Size group of establishment at start of first job	88.7 (80.56)
Level of responsibility in first job	332.8 (80.30)
Number of transfers within organisation	138.5 (54.75)
Number of promotions within organisation	176.8 (37.51)
Number of voluntary job changes between organisations	55.8 (27.75)
Number of involuntary job changes	-303.9 (85.56)
Within-job move to management	316.7 (87.86)
R^2	0.344

Number of observations = 987.

Conclusions

Four main conclusions arise from this article. The first is that the labour market for professional chemists has the characteristics of what human capital theorists call a market with a high incidence of specific training and ILM theorists a manorial market. Secondly, it was shown that the bulk of upward mobility experienced by the respondents occurs within the same organisation and the majority of upward moves are of the osmotic type. Moves between organisations were generally of the type which is associated with "job shopping". Thirdly, the analysis has indicated that cross-sectional analyses can often give a misleading picture of the main processes generating earnings growth. Future work in this area must be based on work histories and longitudinal data. Finally, concentration on the mobility process rather than the human capital approach gives greater realism to the analysis but poses many problems for the investigator. In particular, a technique must be devised to measure osmotic mobility accurately. Nevertheless, the results of this tentative investigation are sufficiently encouraging to indicate that further work along these lines should attempted.

Notes

1. Doeringer and Piore (1971, p. 18) suggest that osmosis is most important in blue-collar manufacturing. "For blue-collar manufacturing jobs, the hallmark of on-the-job training is its informality." The process is variously described as 'osmosis', 'exposure', 'experience' or 'working one's way up through promotion'.

2. More comprehensive details of these surveys can be found in Creedy (1975), Creedy and Whitfield (1980, 1982) and Whitfield (1982).

3. Kerr divided labour markets into three main types — manorial, guild and unstructured. Alexander suggested that manorial markets would show firm mobility of less than 10 per cent *per annum,* that guild markets would show a figure for firm mobility minus industry mobility of more than 10 per cent and unstructured markets would show a figure for firm mobility of more than 20 per cent (and a mobility pattern which was not that of a guild market).

4. In each survey the coding schedule for the type of work performed included, in addition to a classification for general management, a code for primarily managerial or administrative activities within the following work-types: research and/or development; production; other scientific or technical work; and educational work.

5. This, and the following tables, necessarily provide a highly condensed summary of results. They mainly demonstrate the usefulness of the distinctions among types of mobility, mentioned earlier in this article. The most important differences between proportions, mentioned in the text, are so clearly highly significantly different that it would be otiose to present details of hypothesis tests. For further details, see Creedy and Whitfield (1980, 1982).

6. For evidence that such changes, or job shopping, occur largely in the early years of the career, see Creedy and Whitfield (1980).

7. Titles included, for example, (in decreasing order of seniority) chief scientific officer, research manager, technical service manager, section leader, research chemists, and so on. The titles and grouping used result from the long experience of the Royal Society of Chemistry; it would not be possible to carry out such a survey without this detailed knowledge of the nature of the profession. The coding schedule is given in Creedy and Whitfield (1980).

8. The finding that many intra-organisation job changes result in no change in earnings may be compared with the contention of Williamson (1975) that one of the distinctive characteristics of internal labour markets is that wages are attached to jobs rather than persons. More research is clearly required into the details of wage determination.

Professional Chemists in Britain   **37**

9. Further decomposition in order to distinguish moves made when respondents were 35 years old or less, compared with those made when they were over 35 years, also gave interesting results. Age at time of move had a negligible effect on the average income change resulting from within-organisation job changes, but voluntary between-organisation moves were less beneficial when made at a later age. The average change was 25 per cent for the youngest age group, but 14 per cent for the older group. For involuntary moves the average income changes were 4 per cent and −4 per cent respectively.

10. Only 52 per cent of involuntary between-organisation job changes resulted in an increase during the following job, and the annual average change in that job was also much lower than for the other categories, at 1.7 per cent.

11. The Royal Society of Chemistry has recently devised a 20-point classification of responsibility levels, and it is hoped to use this in future analyses.

References

Alexander, A.J., "Income, Experience and Internal Labour Markets", *Quarterly Journal of Economics,* Vol. 56, 1974, pp. 63-86.

Blaug, M., "The Empirical Status of Human Capital Theory: A Slightly Jaundiced View", *Journal of Economic Literature,* Vol. 4, 1976, pp. 287-855.

Borjas, G.J., "Job Mobility and Earnings over the Life-Cycle", *Industrial and Labor Relations Review,* Vol. 34, 1981, pp. 365-376.

Cole, R.E., *Work, Mobility and Participation,* University of California Press, Berkeley, 1979.

Creedy, J., *Careers in Chemistry: Report of a New Survey,* London, Royal Institute of Chemistry, 1975.

Creedy, J. and Whitfield, K., "An Analysis of the Job Mobility of Professional Chemists in Britain", *Monash University Department of Economics, Seminar Paper,* 17/80, 1980.

Creedy, J. and Whitfield, K., "Professional Chemists: The First Three Jobs", *Chemistry in Britain,* Vol. 18, 1982, pp. 352-358.

Doeringer, P.B. and Piore, M.J., *Internal Labor Markets and Manpower Analysis,* Lexington, Heath, 1971.

Hunter, L.C. and Reid, G.L., *Urban Worker Mobility,* Paris, Organisation for Economic Cooperation and Development, 1968.

Kerr, C., "The Balkanization of Labor Markets", in E.W. Bakke *et al.* (Eds.), *Labor Mobility and Opportunity,* Cambridge, Massachusetts, MIT Press, 1954.

Thurow, L.C., *Dangerous Currents: The State of Economics,* Oxford, Oxford University Press, 1983.

White, H. *Chains of Opportunity: Systems Models of Mobility in Organisation,* Cambridge, Massachusetts, Harvard University Press, 1970.

Whitfield, K., *The Study of Occupational Labour Market Structures in Selected British Scientific Professions, 1945-75; with special reference to the Socio-Economic Characteristics of Supply Determinants,* D.Phil. thesis, Oxford University, 1982.

Williamson, O.E., *Markets and Hierarchies,* New York, Free Press, 1975.

[10]

J. R. Statist. Soc. A (1987)
150, *Part 1, pp. 57–68*

Variations in Earnings and Responsibility

By JOHN CREEDY†

Department of Economics, The Pennsylvania State University, USA

SUMMARY

The paper investigates, using data collected by the Royal Society of Chemistry, the relationship between earnings and a cardinal measure of responsibility designed to reflect an individual's level of autonomy in four different areas of work. A close relationship between the logarithm of earnings and responsibility is found. It is shown that this result, along with the characteristics of the growth of responsibility with age, can be integrated into a model of age-earnings profiles. The complete model generates the well-established results that mean log-earnings increase quadratically, while the variance of log-earnings increases linearly, with age. The approach would appear to be widely applicable since the responsibility measure can easily be applied to a wide variety of occupations, unlike measures based on job titles.

Keywords: HIERARCHY; CARDINAL MEASURE OF RESPONSIBILITY; ROYAL SOCIETY OF CHEMISTRY; AGE-EARNINGS PROFILE; AGE-RESPONSIBILITY PROFILE

1. INTRODUCTION

It is widely accepted that high earnings are generally associated with high levels of responsibility, and that a component of the systematic variation in earnings with age is the tendency for responsibility to increase with age. However, there is very little detailed information available about these relationships. Several 'hierarchical' models of the distribution of earnings have been produced, in which earnings are related to the number of individuals in each hierarchical position, but they have not been tested directly. Hierarchical models in which earnings are related to the number of subordinates (a rather poor cardinal measure of responsibility) include those by Simon (1957) and Lydall (1968). These may seem to offer a method of relating the personal distribution of earnings to the size and growth of firms, and thereby perhaps to the 'functional' distribution of income, but developments along these lines have not been made. An alternative, less well known, hierarchical model is by Tuck (1954), which generates a log-normal distribution of earnings in contrast with the Pareto upper tail of Lydall's model. Studies have also been made of the probability of promotion, and its relationship with various individual characteristics, but again these have not been directly concerned with the variation in earnings with responsibility. There have been many studies of promotion, such as Wise (1975) and Marshall (1975). Using a social accounting model based on Stone (1973), Creedy (1977) examined earnings in a model where promotion depends on past success and an incremental payment system operates at each hierarchical level.

A basic difficulty arises because of the problem of defining responsibility in a practically useful manner. In addition to the number of individuals over which a person has 'authority', it may also seem natural to think of responsibility in terms of job titles, and indeed many job titles are explicitly designed to reflect levels of status or seniority within an occupation or organisation. It is therefore not surprising that official statistics provide little help in this context, since they would have to deal with thousands of job titles; the classification problems are enormous. However, the use of titles is not unambiguous, and makes comparisons very difficult.

---

† *Address for correspondence*: Dept of Economics, The Pensylvania State University, 613 Kern Graduate Bldg, University Park, PA 16802, USA.

0035-9238/87/150057 $2.00

Even among the professional bodies, covering for example scientists and engineers, very little information is gathered about remuneration in relation to responsibility. This is perhaps surprising in view of the fact that one of their important roles is to provide detailed and up-to-date information about the conditions of employment of their members, not only for individual use but to monitor the 'status' of the profession in society, and to help discussions with employing organisations. The Royal Society of Chemistry (RSC) is by far the most advanced in this respect, and since 1971 their regular surveys have requested information about each individual's level of responsibility. Between 1971 and 1978 the responsibility level was defined according to a six-fold classification depending on the job title of the individual's immediate superior, using titles such as, 'works chemist', 'senior chemist', 'chief chemist', and 'works manager'†.

The use of job titles produces a set of *levels* which is unambiguously *ordinal* in nature. A chief chemist is recognised as having more responsibility than a works chemist, and having less responsibility than a member of the Board, or managing director. But no attempt is made to measure differences between levels on a *cardinal* scale; for example, it is not claimed that one person has two, or three, times the amount of responsibility of another person. Any attempt statistically to relate earnings to a number of explanatory variables must necessarily specify responsibility using one or more dummy variables.‡ Similarly, any attempt to examine variations in responsibility over individuals' careers must use statistical techniques which have been specifically developed for such 'dichotomous' variables.

In 1978 the RSC's survey contained a major innovation, in the form of a question designed to produce a 'responsibility score' for each individual. Henman (1978, 1979) describes the use of the responsibility assessment schedule. Instead of relying on the use of job titles the question examined the extent of an individual's *autonomy* within his employing organisation, and produced 'scores' ranging from four to twenty. This question is described in more detail in the following subsection, but the essential feature of the approach is that it produces a cardinal measure of responsibility. The purpose of this paper is, then, to examine the characteristics of the RSC's responsibility scale, and to consider its possible use in further analyses of earnings. Because the scale does not rely on specific job titles, it may easily be used for other professional groups of employees. Serious consideration of its properties therefore seems warranted. Section II considers the relationship between earnings and the responsibility score, and then Section III goes on to examine the use of such scores in a model of age-earnings profiles. First, however, the nature of the scale is described.

1.1 *The RSC responsibility score*

The basic principle of the RSC's cardinal measure of responsibility is the assessment of an individual's *level of autonomy* exercised in four areas of work. These four areas are 'job duties', 'technical decisions and recommendations', 'supervision exercised', and 'supervision received'. Within each of these headings are five separate statements describing the extent of autonomy, and these are given scores from one to five. The full assessment schedule is shown in Table 1. Each individual has to work out his or her appropriate score for each aspect of work, and then *add* the four separate scores together. Thus the full range of possible scores runs from four to twenty. If 'scores' for each aspect of work were recorded separately on the questionnaire, then of course these could, if desired, be regarded as four separate sets of ordinal rankings. But the addition of the separate scores to produce a total responsibility score immediately introduces an element of cardinality into the assessment, irrespective of how these total scores may ultimately be used.

---

† The surveys used 32 job titles, grouped into 6 categories. Examples include (in decreasing order of seniority) chief scientific officer, research manager, technical services manager, section leader, and research chemist.
‡ Analyses of earnings using dummy variables based on the RSC's earlier ranking method, and individual observations, are reported in Creedy (1977a) and Creedy and Whitfield (1986).

TABLE 1
Responsibility assessment schedule

DUTIES

I receive on the job training working on simple projects or assisting more senior staff.	1
I perform responsible and varied assignments within projects.	2
I plan, conduct and co-ordinate projects of some complexity.	3
I undertake long term and short term planning and supervision of projects plus decisions on work programmes, together with budgetary control of projects.	4
I have full managerial responsibility for a function with full responsibility for the operation of a budget and long term planning.	5

SUPERVISION RECEIVED

My work is assigned with detailed instructions, guidance being always available. My results are subject to close scrutiny	1
My work is assigned in terms of detailed objectives and priorities, guidance being available on problems and unusual features. My work is subject to scrutiny.	2
My work is assigned in terms of general objectives and priorities, guidance being available on policy or unusually complex problems. My work is reviewed for effectiveness only.	4
My work is such that I receive executive instruction on broad overall objectives and it is reviewed only for its general effectiveness and adherence to policy.	4
My work is unsupervised, other than that I comply with thepolicy decided with the governing body.	5

TECHNICAL DECISIONS AND RECOMMENDATIONS

I am responsible for minor technical details only, all other matters being checked.	1
I am responsible for technical detail which is reviewed overall.	2
I am responsible for technical matters but am subject to occasional review.	3
I have full technical responsibility for projects.	4
I am responsible for all technical matters, including the delegation of responsibility.	

SUPERVISION EXERCISED

I have no authority but may give technical guidance to juniors working on the same project.	1
I have no managerial responsibilities for qualified staff but may be assigned graduates, technicians or other juniors as assistants from time to time.	2
I supervise a group of qualified staff, technicians and other employees; I assign and review their work; I can recommend on the selection, discipline, rating, training and perhaps rates of pay.	3
I am responsible for leaders of groups containing qualified staff, technicians and other employees, I give guidance on policy and complex technical matters delegating responsibility for discipline, rating training and rates of pay.	4
I have full control over senior staff who are in turn responsible for groups of qualified staff and other employees.	5

Source: Royal Society of Chemistry

The assumptions used to obtain the responsibility score are therefore very strong. For example, a reducation in the score for 'supervision received' of unity (irrespective of whether the change is from 5 to 4 or, say, 2 to 1) is regarded as being exactly balanced by an increase of unity in the score for 'technical decisions and recommendations' (or any of the other three areas of responsibility), irrespective of the initial position. Not only are the four areas regarded as directly comparable according to the numbers given, but the use of simple addition (that is, a linear scale) is also thought to be appropriate. It is worth noting some features of the scale based on multiplication, rather than addition. If the responsibility score were obtained by multiplying together the four numbers obtained, then the scores would run from 1 to 625. The scale is therefore very much longer, but of course not all the integers would be relevant. For example 625 is the score of someone with 5 points for each of the four areas, but an individual with three values of 5 and one value of 4 would achieve a score of 500; the next value in the series would be 400, and soon. Furthermore, a reduction of one point in any area of responsibility has different implications according to the values in the three other areas. For example, 4 points in each of the four areas gives a 'total' score of 256, and a fall from 4 to 3 in one area would reduce the score by 64 to 192. But from above a drop from 5 to 4 points in one area, when all the other areas have 5 points, would cause a drop of 125. While the linear scale involves strong assumptions, and despite the fact that the early training of economists inculcates a scepticism towards any type of cardinal scale, the approach taken in the present paper is partially to suspend disbelief and to investigate as far as possible the properties of the scale used by the RSC. From the point of view of the applied economist it would be extremely useful to have a cardinal scale which would allow individual measurement in a wide variety of occupations and organisations.

The precise meaning of 'responsibility' has received surprisingly little attention by economists; those using the number of subordinates as a cardinal measure have not seriously examined the nature of the concept. However, reference may usefully be made to the work by Jaques (1956), based on an extensive study of the Glacier Metal Company. Jaques found that the simple 'measures' of responsibility were inadequate and developed a measure based on the 'time-span' of work. This was defined as the maximum length of time during which an individual was allowed to exercise discretion before being subject to direct supervision. He then discovered that pay scales were systematically related to the time-span of jobs, and that dissatisfaction with pay could generally be resolved into anomalies between individuals with similar time-spans. Jaques (1956, p. 48) argued that the firm

"had been applying, without knowing it, a systematic pattern of salaries and of ranks—a pattern that could be observed once level of work was measured by time-span. But because this pattern was unrecognised, it could not be used as a conscious aid to planning; and divergencies from the pattern, although intuitively felt as such, could not be readily pinpointed".

Jaques (1956, p. 50) suggested that changes in responsibility can take place gradually over time although an individual retains the same job title, and (1956, p. 74) that where a person's skill or experience was greater than the level of work performed, he or she was paid according to the work. Both these points are of course part of the more modern 'alternative' theories of pay ('osmotic' labour mobility, and the 'job competition' models)

The measurement of the time-span of each individual's job required extensive investigations and lengthy discussions; individuals had some difficulty assessing their own time-span. This experience contrasts with the use of the self-assessment score used by the RSC, the introduction of which has generally been welcomed by members. The point of similarity is of course that Jaques's cardinal measure was based fundamentally on discretion or autonomy allowed to each individual in performing his or her duties. Although it is argued here that the extent of autonomy is basic to the concept of responsibility, the purpose of the following discussion is entirely objective. Thus although the paper concentrates on the observed relationship between measured responsibility and earnings, and their variation over age, no normative judgement is attempted.

Jaques's early discussion of responsibility was highly tentative, but his finding that people thought it 'fair' that those with the same time-span are paid the same, soon developed into the argument that a complete pay structure if based on an observed relationship between pay and time-spans, was itself 'fair'. He also speculated that pay was based on a percentage (based on the rate of interest) of the possible loss from exercising discreton during the time span (or the value of resources entrusted to the discretionary control of each person). Jaques later expanded his views, along with arguments about peoples' ability to exercise discretion over their expenditure, into a grand normative view of pay; see Jaques (1961).

2. EARNINGS AND RESPONSIBILITY

2.1. *The RSC Regressions*

Following the first survey (1978) in which the responsibility scores were used, the general results were described further by Henman (1978), who stated that, 'high responsibility showed a marked degree of linearity with high earnings' (Henman, 1978, p. 157). The sample responses were in fact divided into age groups, and linear regressions of annual earnings against responsibility score were run, showing high correlation coefficients.† However, it was reported that a relatively small number of individuals with very high earnings had responsibility scores as low as 4 and 5. It is believed that these observations may result from certain senior employees working alone on one-person projects, or from some self-employed members in one-person businesses. Thus it was recognised at an early stage that the assessment schedule does not work very well for the very low scores, and those with scores of 4 or 5 were omitted from later regressions. (In 1983 this involved dropping only 155 observations from a total sample of 12,386).

The most recent set of results is for the 1983 Remuneration Survey (1983, p. 16, Table 21). Information is given, for eight separate age groups, about the median and lower and upper quartile earnings within each responsibility score. The RSC then present results for what are described as the 'coefficient of correlation' and the 'equation of line' (no standard errors are reported). Two points can be made about these results: the first concerns the method of estimation, and the second concerns the form of the fitted equation. These points are examined below.

Although the RSC Survey report is not explicit about the statistical approach used, it can be found (using the published data) that the 'equation of line' was obtained by carrying out an ordinary least squares regression analysis for each age group using median earnings as the dependent variable, and responsibility score as the independent variable (omitting information about scores 4 and 5). For example in the lowest age group (25–29) median earnings are given for responsibility scores 6–17 inclusive (that is, 12 classes or 'observations'). The method used was 'unweighted' least squares, since no allowance was made for the fact that there is a considerable variation in the number of observations within each responsibility score. Furthermore, the 'coefficient of correlation' is not, as may be thought, the linear correlation coefficient between earnings and responsibility score, but is simply the conventional R^2 for the regression based on medians. The former correlation coefficient based on individual observations would of course be much lower. After re-running the regressions, the full results are given for comparison purposes on the left hand part of Table 2 below.‡

It is however more appropriate in this context to use the method of weighted least squares in order to allow for the fact that the various medians are based on very different numbers of observations. Although the frequencies are not published in the report, they were kindly provided by the RSC for the present analysis (and are given in Section III). The weighted regressions are reported on the right hand side of Table 2, where it can be seen that the results are very different, especially the values of the constant terms for the higher age groups. It should be noted that the standard errors in the weighted regressions are much lower than in the unweighted regressions, mainly because of the much larger number of 'observations' used in the former.

Having estimated linear relationships between median earnings and responsibility, using a more satisfactory procedure, it is then necessary to consider the appropriateness of the specification. From Table 2 it can be seen that both the constant term and slope coefficient vary systematically with age; the constant decreases steadily while the slope increases with age, but at a decreasing rate. These results may simply be interpreted as showing that although median earnings are linearly related to the responsibility score, higher levels of the latter make a larger contribution to earnings in the older age groups. But this is not a very satisfactory statement, as the responsibility score does not seem to be measuring the same type of phenomenon for the different age groups. However, it is important to recognise that the problem is not necessarily the responsibility of the assessment method used to measure

---

† Henman (1978) argued, on the basis of comparisons of regressions, that the assessment schedule was equally appropriate for those whose class of employment is education. A brief comparison was made of classifications using job titles and responsibility scores (Henman, 1978, p. 158); it seems that job titles exaggerate 'autonomy' in many cases.
‡ There are slight differences between these results and those on page 16 of the RSC *Remuneration Survey* (1983), arising from the rounding used by the RSC; the larger differences for age group 35–39 may be noted, however.

TABLE 2

Linear regressions of annual earnings on responsibility score: 1983

Age Group	Unweighted regressions			Weighted regressions		
	Constant	Slope	R^2	Constant	Slope	R^2
25–29	5691.57 (238.77)	238.78 (11.65)	0.977	5703.59 (13.18)	237.10 (1.22)	0.963
30–34	4123.58 (862.35)	520.75 (62.95)	0.840	4989.23 (49.83)	428.48 (4.00)	0.861
35–39	3773.43 (677.07)	638.00 (48.06)	0.936	3758.08 (51.57)	622.80 (3.76)	0.920
40–44	3282.57 (635–95)	752.57 (46.42)	0.953	2428.55 (62.26)	794.07 (4.36)	0.946
45–49	2506.15 (606.25)	857.31 (41.84)	0.975	2336.03 (57.64)	860.18 (3.91)	0.970
50–54	1071.54 (867.08)	1019.84 (59.83)	0.964	−112.97 (79.85)	1086.65 (5.24)	0.966
55–59	512.31 (874.74)	1087.69 (60.36)	0.967	−370.16 (127.20)	1144.27 (8.27)	0.949
60–64	307.27 (1489.79)	1046.73 (97.183)	0.928	−1157.88 (247.56)	1144.80 (15.19)	0.943
All ages Combined	369.10 (819.51)	948.43 (59.82)	0.951	−661.94 (27.49)	998.83 (1.99)	0.953

Standard errors are given in parentheses immediately below the parameter estimates. Those in responsibility groups 4 and 5 (130 individuals over all age groups) were omitted.

responsibility; rather, the results suggest that further investigation into the nature of the relationship is required.

2.2. *An Alternative Specification*

The use of a linear relationship between earnings, y, and responsibility, x, immediately raises two points. First, the method of assessing the responsibility score imposes a maximum value of x beyond which no individual can move, yet there is no such constraint on the level of earnings. This suggests that the relationship between y and x may become relatively steeper as x approaches its maximum possible value (with x on the horizontal axis). The second, related, point is that the observations for younger age groups will be concentrated nearer the lower responsibility scores, while those for the older age groups will be spread about higher levels. Thus if the 'true' relationship between y and x is curvilinear, the linear regressions will simply provide approximations over different ranges of the observations.

Alternative specifications cannot be examined using individual data, since the RSC Remuneration Survey provides only summary measures of the earnings distribution for the each age group and responsibility score. However, a good idea of the relationship can be seen from Fig. 1, which shows the median annual earnings plotted against responsibility score, for all age groups combined. Similar plots for other age groups show very similar results, except for the youngest age groups where the rate of change of earnings with responsibility is not as systematic.

The form of the relationship displayed in Fig. 1 suggests that it may be more appropriate to regress the logarithm of median earnings against the responsibility score (as easily seen by plotting median earnings on a logarithmic scale rather than the linear scale of Fig. 1). Thus if y_m denotes median earnings and x denotes responsibility score, a weighted regression of

$$\log (y_m) = \alpha + \beta x \tag{1}$$

may be carried out for each age group. Results are presented in Table 3. Comparison with the right hand side of Table 2 shows that the coefficients in the non-linear form are estimated with much greater precision (the 't' values are considerably higher), and the values of R^2 are

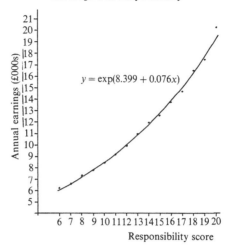

Fig. 1.   Median earnings and responsibility score (All age groups: 1983)

higher†. A very important further result is that there is a much greater similarity between age-groups than indicated from the estimates of the linear specification (although the youngest age groups have significantly lower values of β). This result is encouraging from the point of view of the method used to measure responsibility since, as observed earlier, large differences between age groups would otherwise seem to indicate that the responsibility score is not consistently measuring the same phenomenon (even if a close relationship between y and x can be found *within* each age group).

Thus, although the earlier part of this Section was critical of the statistical methods used in the RSC report, the further analysis actually offers greater support for the use of the assessment schedule devised by the RSC. In view of these encouraging results the following section considers the integration of the relationship into the further analysis of the variation in earnings over the working life.

It may perhaps be thought that the above results suggest the use of a multiplicative scale, as discussed earlier. It would be interesting to compare results, if the scores for the four different areas of responsibility were recorded separately. A multiplicative system at least has the 'advantage' (as shown in Section 1) of reflecting a greater value attached to obtaining high scores in *all* areas of responsibility. It may be that some younger individuals can rapidly attain autonomy in just a few areas of responsibility, and that the difficulty of achieving a wider spread of autonomy should be reflected in the measuring scale.

3. AGE AND EARNINGS

3.1. *The Age-earnings Profile*

Since 1919 the Royal Society of Chemistry has published detailed information about the distribution of its members' earnings, decomposed into a number of age groups, and its reports

---

† Other functional forms were tried, such as the double-log form, but the specification used in the text out-performed all others. There may, in addition, be some reluctance to work in terms of log x, when x is an arithmetic measure. If x were obtained by multiplying together the four separate scores, then the use of logarithms may well be appropriate.

TABLE 3
Weighted regressions of log $(y_m) = \alpha + \beta x$

Age Group	α	β	R^2
25–29	8.709 (0.0016)	0.029 (0.0002)	0.961
30–34	8.734 (0.0036)	0.040 (0.0003)	0.913
35–39	8.724 (0.0030)	0.050 (0.0002)	0.957
40–44	8.689 (0.0029)	0.058 (0.0002)	0.977
45–49	8.746 (0.0029)	0.058 (0.0002)	0.984
50–54	8.645 (0.0034)	0.068 (0.0002)	0.984
55–59	8.676 (0.0053)	0.069 (0.0003)	0.975
60–64	8.636 (0.0120)	0.068 (0.0007)	0.962
All ages Combined	8.399 (0.0008)	0.076 (0.0001)	0.993

have presented diagrams showing the age profiles of various summary measures (in particular the octiles and the highest and lowest deciles)†. The main characteristics of these age-earnings profiles can be easily summarised: the distribution of earnings in each group is approximately lognormal (that is, the logarithms of earnings follow the Normal distribution); the arithmetic mean of the logarithms of earnings in each age group is a quadratic function of age; and the variance of the logarithms is a linear function of age. The 1983 RSC Remuneration Survey provides information about the earnings of approximately $8\frac{1}{2}$ thousand Fellows and members, grouped into eight age groups (ignoring those less than 25 and those over 64), and 27 income groups (1983, Table 8, p. 5). Unfortunately it is not possible to obtain age and earnings distributions for precisely the same group of individuals included in the tables for responsibility and earnings. The age-earnings profiles are estimated for a sub-sample of the group used earlier. These data can be used to obtain the following results:

$$\hat{\mu}_t = 7.642 + 0.0705t - 0.00058t^2 \qquad (2)$$
$$\phantom{\hat{\mu}_t = } (0.0648) \quad (0.000041) \quad (0.00317)$$

$$\hat{\sigma}_t^2 = -0.0687 + 0.0040t \qquad (3)$$
$$\phantom{\hat{\sigma}_t^2 = } (0.00410) \quad (0.00011)$$

where μ_t and σ_t^2 are respectively the arithmetic mean and the variance of the logarithms of earnings at age t, and the 'hat' denotes estimated values along the fitted line. The parameters in (2) and (3) were estimated simultaneously using an iterative technique based on the method of Maximum Likelihood. This is more efficient that the separate estimation of profiles for the mean and variance of log-earnings using Ordinary Least Squares.‡

3.2. *Basic Relationships*

The main objective of the present Section is to try to combine the information about the relationship between earnings and measured responsibility, discussed in Section 2, with the above well-established results concerning the growth of earnings with age. An important factor

---

† The Remuneration surveys for 1956 to 1971 inclusive have been examined in detail in Creedy (1974).
‡ For further discussion of the estimation procedure see Creedy (1985). It should also be mentioned that the usual problems of interpretation apply, when using cross-sectional data.

influencing the pattern of earnings change is the variation in responsibility with age, and of course any analysis must ensure that the three aspects are treated consistently. A valuable feature of the responsibility scale produced by the RSC, which is not possessed by the more usual ranking procedures, is that responsibility can be treated as a quasi-continuous variable. Thus there is a much greater potential for the integration of responsibility into formal analyses of earnings distributions.

The basic inter-relationships may easily be seen as follows. From Section 2, the logarithm of median earnings was found to be linearly related to responsibility, as in equation (1). The form of the relationship was very similar for all age groups (except for the youngest). From above, the mean of the logarithms of earnings is a quadratic function of age.

There has been no difficulty about estimating the mean of the logarithms of earnings directly for each group, as full frequency distributions are published by the RSC, but the fact that the logarithm of median earnings has been regressed against responsibility may initially appear to create a problem of inconsistency. However, there is one situation in which such a problem does not exist. The lognormal distribution has the convenient property that the mean of the logarithms of earnings and the logarithm of median earnings are equivalent; this is because log-earnings are Normally distributed and hence have equal mean, mode and median. If the distribution of earnings within each responsibility level may be regarded as following the form of the lognormal distribution, then the estimates in Section 2 may be regarded as equivalent to regressions of mean log-earnings on responsibility. (It would obviously be desirable to test this assumpt directly, but the required data are not available).

For presentaton purposes it is most convenient to consider explicit functional forms relating y to x, and x to t, and then to examine their implications for the relationship between y and t. It is also useful to begin by considering *individual* earnings, although separate subscripts need not be used. Using the results obtained earlier, each individual's earnings are assumed to be related to that individual's responsibility score according to:

$$\log y_t = \alpha + \beta x_t + u_t \tag{4}$$

where the coefficients α and β are the same for all individuals and age groups, and u_t is a stochastic term that governs individual variations, with $E(u_t) = 0$. Now suppose further that changing responsibility with age can be described by the following:

$$x_t = a + bt - ct^2 + \varepsilon_t \tag{5}$$

where a, b, and c are parameters and ε_t is stochastic with $E(\varepsilon_t) = 0$. Thus the average responsibility score is a quadratic function of age. The empirical appropriateness of these assumptions about x_t will be examined in the following subsection, since the purpose of the present analysis is to concentrate on the possible inter-relations in the generation of earnings distributions. Substitution of (5) into (4) gives:

$$\log y_t = (\alpha + a\beta) + (\beta b)t - (\beta c)t^2 + (\beta \varepsilon_t + u_t) \tag{6}$$

Taking expectations then produces, with $\mu_t = E(\log y_t)$,

$$\mu_t = (\alpha + a\beta) + (\beta b)t - (\beta c)t^2 \tag{7}$$

This is precisely the quadratic equation which has been estimated above, in (2). The result in (7) shows clearly how the coefficients in (2) depend on combinations of the coefficients in (4) and (5). Taking variances of (6), with $\sigma_t^2 = V(\log y_t)$, gives:

$$\sigma_t^2 = E(\beta \varepsilon_t + u_t)^2 \tag{8}$$
$$= \beta^2 E(\varepsilon_t^2) + E(u_t^2) + 2\beta E(\varepsilon_t u_t)$$

Since individuals are concentrated in the lower responsibility scores at younger ages, the process of increasing responsibility with age is likely to increase the dispersion of x_t as t

increases. Hence it may be assumed that:

$$E(\varepsilon_t^2) = \sigma_0^2 + \sigma_\varepsilon^2 t \qquad (9)$$

(Again, this will be examined further below). Suppose, furthermore, that $E(u_t^2) = \sigma_u^2$, for all t, and that $E(\varepsilon_t u_t) = 0$. Thus (8) reduces to

$$\sigma_t^2 = (\beta^2 \sigma_0^2 + \sigma_u^2) + (\beta^2 \sigma_\varepsilon^2)t \qquad (10)$$

which is of course precisely the equation that has been estimated in (3) above. The result in (10) shows how the extent to which the dispersion of earnings increases with age is affected by $\beta^2 \sigma_\varepsilon^2$; that is, it depends on the increasing spread of the distribution of responsibility scores with age, and on the coefficient relating responsibility to log-earnings. The above model therefore generates the well established pattern of age-earnings profiles (the variation in both μ_t and σ_t^2 with t), and allows a much richer interpretation of the coefficients in terms of responsibility changes†. The empirical relevance of (4), (7) and (10) has already been established, so it remains to consider the important assumptions reflected in (5) and (9).

3.3. *Age and Responsibility*

As mentioned earlier, the RSC provided details of the unpublished frequency distributions of responsibility scores for each age group, from the 1983 survey. These are shown in Table 4. The last two rows give the arithmetic mean and variance of the responsibility score in each age group. These distributions of the cardinal measure of responsibility can then be used to test the assumptions made earlier, but instead of carrying out separate least squares regressions using only the means and variances, an iterative procedure based on maximum likelihood,

TABLE 4
Distribution of responsibility scores by age

Responsibility score	< 25	25–29	30–34	35–39	Age groups 40–44	45–49	50–54	55–59	60–64
6.00	20	22	18	5	11	6	3	2	1
7.00	35	79	40	22	17	7	7	4	3
8.00	43	164	97	62	35	25	23	16	1
9.00	43	226	136	98	56	34	37	18	6
10.00	25	249	220	192	125	81	76	54	15
11.00	18	242	261	247	189	135	94	84	19
12.00	14	218	319	347	273	170	165	95	24
13.00	3	96	245	323	204	150	133	87	32
14.00	2	61	184	299	215	186	164	117	26
15.00	0	41	118	236	161	159	160	77	38
16.00	0	27	86	209	176	169	139	112	26
17.00	0	16	62	138	157	114	157	94	23
18.00	0	4	40	95	129	113	135	91	41
19.00	0	0	15	51	64	70	95	58	37
20.00	0	2	17	68	92	88	136	128	62
Arithmetic mean	8.76	10.60	12.16	13.39	13.93	14.35	14.85	14.99	15.75
Variance	3.31	5.27	7.40	8.25	9.68	9.43	10.24	10.90	11.35

† With three inter-related functions, only two can be set independently. For example if it were found that the best relationship between y and x is the double-log form, then the mean of log-responsibility score would need to be a quadratic function of age in order to produce an age-earnings profile with mean log-earnings a quadratic function of age.

involving all the information available in the table, was used.† The results are as follows:

$$\hat{\bar{x}}_t = -1.138 + 0.5767t - 0.0051t^2 \tag{11}$$
$$(0.4135)\ \ (0.00025)\ \ (0.0209)$$

$$\hat{\sigma}^2_{xt} = 0.256 + 0.2052t \tag{12}$$
$$(0.2935)\ \ (0.00780)$$

where $\hat{\bar{x}}$ and $\hat{\sigma}^2_{xt}$ denote respectively the estimated mean and variance of responsibility at age t (σ^2_{xt} is of course equivalent to $E(\varepsilon^2_t)$ in equation 9).

These results show that the assumption that responsibility score is a quadratic function of age is well supported, along with the linear increase in the variance of responsibility score with age. Although further analysis of the present data does not seem warranted, it can be argued that these results indicate a strong potential for the inclusion of the RSC's measure of responsibility into the analysis of earnings (of other groups of employees). It offers the prospect of a richer interpretation of the characteristics of age earnings profiles than formerly.

4. CONCLUSIONS

The main purpose of this paper has been to investigate, using special data collected by the Royal Society of Chemistry, the relationship between earnings and a cardinal measure of responsibility (designed to reflect an individual's level of autonomy within an organisation). The relationship has been shown to be much closer than initially envisaged by the Royal Society. The paper has also shown how 'responsibility' can be integrated into a model of age-earnings profiles, something which presents considerable problems when using an ordinal ranking.

Although an approach based on the use of a cardinal scale may perhaps meet with some scepticism among economists, it can claim a number of advantages. For example it emphasises autonomy, which seems to be closer to what most people understand by responsibility, rather than using titles that may vary between organisations. It can be used for a wide variety of occupations; indeed chemists themselves are to be found in many classes of employment, types of work, and kinds of employing organisations. It produces a quasi-continuous variable that is easier to deal with than discrete variables giving only rankings. Furthermore, as shown above, in analysing the generation of the earnings distribution it allows concentration on a fundamental determinant that can be conveniently integrated into existing models. It would thus be useful to examine the characteristics and determinants of changes in responsibility over the working life in more detail, hopefully using data on career histories rather than cross sections.

ACKNOWLEDGEMENTS

I should like to thank Diana Bartlett of the Royal Society of Chemistry for kindly providing the data used in this paper, and Jill Peters for computing assistance. In preparing the paper I benefitted from discussions with Keith Whitfield.

REFERENCES

Creedy, J. (1974) Earnings in Chemistry: past and present. *Chemistry in Britain*.
Creedy, J. (1977) Earnings in an hierarchical structure. *University of Reading Discussion Paper in Economics*, Series A, No. 92.
Creedy, J. (1977a) A multivariate analysis of earnings in chemistry. *Chemistry in Britain*, 13, No. 4, pp. 146–148.
Creedy, J. (1985) *Dynamics of Income Distribution*. Oxford: Basil Blackwell.
Creedy, J. and Whitfield, K. (1986) Earnings and job mobility: Professional Chemists in Britain. *J. Economic Studies*, 13, No. 2, pp. 23–37.

†The procedure used is in fact a varient of that used earlier to estimate the parameters of the age-earnings profile.

Henman, B. (1978) Remuneration for responsibility. *Chemistry in Britain*, **14**, No. 4, 157–159.

Henman, B. (1979) Close comparisons for commensurate compensation. *Chemistry in Britain*, **15**, No. 4, pp. 165–167.

Jaques, E. (1956) *Measurement of Responsibility*. London: Tavistock.

Jaques, E. (1961) *Equitable Payment*. London: Heinemann.

Lydall, H. (1968) *The Structure of Earnings*. Oxford: Oxford University Press.

Marshall, M. L. (1975) Equilibrium age distributions for graded systems. *J. R. Statist. Soc.* A, **138**, 000–000.

Royal Society of Chemistry (1983) *Remuneration Survey 1983*. London: RSC.

Simon, H. (1957) The compensation of executives. *Sociometry*, **20**, No. 1, 32–45.

Stone, J. R. N. (1973) Transition and admission models in social demography. *Social Science Research*, **2**.

Tuck, R. H. (1954) *An Essay on the Economic Theory of Rank*. Oxford: Basil Blackwell.

Wise, D. A. (1975) Personal attributes, job performance and probability of promotion. *Econometrica*, **56**, 913–932.

[11]

Bulletin of Economic Research 40:4, 1988, 0307-3378 $2.00

THE ECONOMIC ANALYSIS OF INTERNAL LABOUR MARKETS*

John Creedy and Keith Whitfield

I. INTRODUCTION

The internal labour market (ILM) has attained an established position within the economics literature since its initial development over 30 years ago. This paper reviews the analyses of the ILM which have been undertaken by economists and evaluates the progress made in this area. Limitations of space preclude the examination of non-economic research although some references will be made to work by sociologists and industrial relationists which is relevant to the main themes.

The most frequently cited definition of the ILM was made by Doeringer and Piore, who stated that it is:

> an administrative unit, such as a manufacturing plant, within which the pricing and allocation of labour is governed by a set of administrative rules and procedures. The internal labour market, governed by administrative rules, is to be distinguished from the external labour market of conventional economic theory where pricing, allocating, and training decisions are controlled directly by economic variables (1971, pp. 1–2).

The economic literature on the ILM has concentrated on a number of characteristics which make it distinctive. These are, *inter alia*, high employment stability, the restriction of entry to lower level positions, the filling of higher level positions by internal promotion, a heavy emphasis on seniority in promotion, the according of major importance to internal factors in wage determination and the attachment of wages to jobs rather than workers. Theoretical analysis has concentrated on the forces generating these characteristics and empirical analysis on measuring them.

The ILM raises a number of issues for economic analysis. First, to what extent is the pricing and allocation of labour within firms controlled by non-economic variables? Secondly, to the extent that non-economic vari-

*We would like to thank a referee of this journal for extremely constructive comments on an earlier version of this paper. Helpful suggestions were also made by Mark Casson, Keith Crocker, Richard Disney, Peter Elias, David Shapiro, George Strauss and participants at a seminar at the University of Sydney.

ables are important, what are the implications for economic theory? Thirdly, are the conventional methods of economics appropriate for empirical research on the ILM or is it necessary to develop alternative approaches? The objective of this paper is to outline how economists have responded to such questions.

Major Themes

The importance of the ILM concept is that it suggests that there are significant areas of the labour market where the processes emphasized in the model of wage competition do not operate or operate only to a very limited extent. Economists have responded to this observation in two distinct ways. One group has searched for rationales for the existence of ILMs which utilize concepts from the neoclassical paradigm on which wage competition is based. The result is the development of a model which emphasizes the departure of real world markets from wage competition while indicating that the principles underlying wage competition are sound. A second group is more critical of wage competition and suggests that the real world is so different that a new model is needed for labour market analysis. Central to the debate on whether the ILM is compatible with basic neoclassical principles is the issue of whether it can be explained by economic factors alone or whether it can only be understood by an analysis combining economic, sociological, political and psychological factors. This is a recurring theme in debates between authors from different schools within economics.

Some writers have questioned whether ILMs can be considered as markets at all. For instance, Marsden (1986) argues that ILMs have quite different transaction arrangements to the external labour market and that the use of the market analogy is misleading. An alternative position is held, however, by Blandy and Richardson (1982) who argue that a market exists where willing sellers trade with willing buyers and where there is a mechanism for allocating tasks to persons. On such a definition the ILM is a market although, '. . . labour markets are not like transposed vegetable markets' (1982, p. 1).

The early ILM literature suggested that the formation and character of ILMs reflected the influence of unions. There has, however, been increasing emphasis on the role of management in promoting ILMs as part of a policy to enhance labour productivity. This partly reflects the recognition that ILMs exist in sectors that are not unionized. Contemporaneously it has been argued that unions themselves have contributed to productivity gains at the workplace (Freeman and Medoff, 1979). This further complicates the problem of isolating factors promoting the growth of the ILM.

A major theme concerns the efficiency aspects of the ILM. Much of the early work suggested that ILMs, by introducing rigidities which constrain labour market adjustments, prevent allocative efficiency being achieved and deliberately trade efficiency for equity. However, later work has viewed the ILM as an efficient response to uncertainty in a market containing an idiosyncratic factor of production; the firm's internal market is seen to operate more efficiently than the external market. Other models introduce competitive elements and examine the implications of alternative labour contracts for Pareto efficiency. Nevertheless, some inefficiency is found to exist due, for example, to over-investment by individuals in 'signals' to employers concerning their quality.

A closely related aspect concerns the motivation of workers, although different authors use their own special vocabulary, making precise comparisons difficult. Some stress the 'negative' aspects of moral hazard and the enforcement of compliance with the firm's rules, while others stress more 'positive' aspects whereby individuals identify their own interests in terms of the performance of the enterprise. Despite these differences of emphasis, most authors agree that questions of work effort and motivation are central to the analysis of the ILM and its rationale.

The ILM approach has changed the focus of much labour market analysis. In particular, it has opened the 'black box' of the employing organization which was formerly regarded as the province of industrial sociologists, industrial relationists and organization theorists. It is no longer appropriate for the labour economist to deal with market operations while ignoring the internal workings of employing organizations.

Empirical work on the ILM by economists has been limited and is much less than that undertaken by other social scientists. A major reason for this seems to be the difficulty of applying standard econometric techniques to such a complex institution as the ILM. A related issue concerns the inappropriateness of aggregate data for ILM analysis; this imposes the need for researchers on the ILM to collect their own data. Economists have been more reluctant to undertake data collection than other social scientists and physical scientists. Empirical work has only occasionally been guided by an explicit model and has rarely moved beyond the classification stage towards the testing of the ILM approach against alternative theories.

II.   THE ORIGIN AND NATURE OF THE ILM

The ILM concept was developed by economists in the institutionalist tradition. It represents the integration of a wide range of ideas on labour market structure, labour mobility, wage determination and adjustment mechanisms. A common element was a belief that the labour market is so distinctive that the use of the simple price-auction model for theory formulation and policy advice was inappropriate. Consequently institutionalists attempted to develop a more realistic model of the labour market and thought that research should study the distinctive institutions of the labour market so that its idiosyncrasies could be more fully understood. However, much of the early work was descriptive and showed little concern for theoretical issues. The development of the ILM concept was therefore seen as a major step from pure empiricism towards the formulation of a model richer in institutional detail than the wage competition model.

Labour Market Structure

The most important early work was that of Kerr (1951, 1954) who distinguished between two types of labour market — structured and structureless. Structureless markets were defined as those in which there is no attachment between the worker and the employer except the wage; such markets resemble the wage competition model. Structure was seen to occur when rules governing the pricing and allocation of labour are introduced and different treatment is accorded to the 'ins' and 'outs'. Hence a distinction is made between the internal and the external market. Kerr further distinguished between internal markets based on crafts ('guild' markets) and those based on manufacturing plants ('manorial' markets).

Kerr postulated that the admission policies of employers and unions were of key importance in introducing structure into labour markets. Such policies were seen to be more important with regard to the distribution of jobs than in wage setting. This emphasis was later to be fundamental to the theories of job competition. It marks a shift from the emphasis on supply side factors (such as the possession of various attributes by individuals) to the demand side of the market; that is, attention shifts from the market for persons to the market for jobs. It also recognizes that the investment by individuals in the acquisition of desirable characteristics, emphasized by human capital theory, will only be worthwhile to the extent that suitable jobs are available and attainable.

The direction of attention towards rigidity in the distribution of jobs promoted considerable research on the question of how labour markets adjust to changing economic conditions. This has emphasized that labour economists should no longer think in terms of a market in which the characteristics of jobs are simply the outcome of the preferences of their occupants.

Labour Mobility

A building-block of ILM research was the work on labour mobility that raised the question of whether mobility between firms was as prevalent as might be predicted from the wage competition model. Workers were found to exhibit low rates of mobility even when opportunities for advancement existed. The level of inter-firm mobility was deemed insufficient to promote the equalization of net advantages that is central to wage competition. Studies of local labour markets, such as Hunter and Reid (1968), also found workers undertaking similar jobs in different firms, but with very different earnings. Moreover, there seemed to be few processes promoting the elimination of these differences.

Such observations could be explained in a number of different ways, including measurement inaccuracies, imperfect information or worker inertia. However, those who believed that the explanation was more deep-seated directed their attention towards the nature of the employing organization. The major work was by Doeringer and Piore (1971), who explained low mobility by the efforts of employers to reduce turnover because of the presence of skill-specificity; that is, the existence of skills which are only useful in a small range of jobs. The consequence of such skills is that firms draw a distinction between incumbents and otherwise similar workers outside the firm. Rules develop to distinguish between 'ins' and 'outs' and prevent the firm from responding to economic events in the manner predicted by the basic wage competition model. The pricing and allocation of labour is determined by these rules rather than by the external market.

The most important rules are those governing entry and promotion. Skill-specificity is seen to promote the restriction of entry into ILMs to the lower job classifications. The criteria for entry to the lower jobs are controlled by management and are free to vary with conditions in the external market. Internal mobility is seen to represent a compromise between promotion by seniority and by ability; it is suggested that the former is more acceptable to the worker and the latter to the employer.

A major insight of Doeringer and Piore's analysis is the notion that the bulk of labour mobility (defined as changes in the nature of jobs undertaken by workers) occurs within the firm rather than as a result of changing firms. In particular, they stress the process of 'osmotic mobility' in which the nature of the tasks undertaken changes gradually. However, when viewed over a long time-span, the accumulation of such changes results in a major change in the type of work undertaken. This type of mobility has major implications for manpower planning and for policies designed to improve the level of skill formation in the labour market.

Wage Determination

The institutional work on wage determination was also important for ILM research. Dunlop (1957) concentrated on the concepts of the job cluster and the wage contour. The former was defined as a stable group of job classifications or work assignments within a firm that have common wage-making characteristics. The latter was defined as a stable group of wage-determining units that have common wage-making characteristics.

Dunlop argued that wages are not determined by suppply and demand in the external market but by processes involving comparisons, both within and between firms, among particular types of job. He suggested that rigidity was introduced into wage determination by formal rules or customs that kept wage relativities within a given job cluster (in a firm) in close alignment. Similarly, the existence of wage contours kept wage relativities between firms in close alignment. In these processes attention focused on key rates within the job clusters; these could be the highest rate in a cluster, the rate paid at the top step in a promotion ladder or the rate paid for a job at which a large number of workers are employed. Wage determination concentrated on fixing key rates and then passing on equivalent wage increases to other rates in the cluster.

Dunlop's work was developed by Doeringer and Piore (1971) who suggested that there are three principal elements of the ILM wage structure: (i) the plant wage level; (ii) the vertical differentiation and (iii) the horizontal differentiation of the wage structure. These are determined by job evaluation techniques, community wage surveys and engineering production standards. Much more emphasis is placed on getting internal relativities correct than ensuring that the plant is in line with others in the local labour market; that is, firms take job evaluation surveys much more seriously than community wage surveys.

Doeringer and Piore postulated that there are three main influences on wage determination. The first is the external labour market, but this simply sets a wide range within which wages must be set. The second influence results from the firm's need to allocate labour. Wage structures must be related to internal promotion lines, acting as a constraint to prevent wages from responding to changes in the external labour market. The third relates to the development of customary relationships within ILMs and the role of wages as an indicator of social status.

Labour Market Adjustment

A persistent theme in the institutional literature has been that the labour market does not adjust according to the wage competition model and, in particular, that the wage is not the principal adjustment mechanism. Emphasis is instead placed on the constraints which prevent the wage from responding to changing conditions and on the alternative adjustment mechanisms used.

A distinction was made by Doeringer and Piore (1971) between 'the more constrained' and 'the less highly constrained' adjustment mechanisms. The 'more constrained instruments' include wages, the job structure and the internal allocative structure — the conventional methods that are the focus of wage competition. Wages are said to be constrained by 'the exigencies of internal allocation and customary law' which cause adjustments in the entry wage to exert a leverage upon all wages in the enterprise and thereby make wage adjustment costly. Changes in the job structure are seen to be dominated by engineers, 'who seldom have direct contact with external market conditions and are only rarely attracted by the problems which such conditions cause' (1971, p. 98). Finally, the degree to which the internal allocative structure is flexible is reduced by the value which the existing structure has to the labour force and the effect of customary law.

The 'less highly constrained instruments' are job vacancies, subcontracting, overtime, recruitment procedures, hiring standards, screening procedures and training. These are regarded as the principal adjustment mechanisms used by firms to obtain a balance between the internal and external labour markets. The major factor determining the adjustment method selected is the relative cost and effectiveness of each.

Efficiency

The institutional literature tended to stress that many labour market structures prevent the attainment of allocative efficiency. To some extent, this reflected a reaction to those orthodox economists who emphasized the efficiency aspects of market processes. It also reflected a view that static Pareto efficiency is rather narrow and that other features of organizations are more important for the development of a high productivity labour market.

Kerr argued that institutional markets 'operate so imprecisely in allocating resources to their most efficient uses and in setting wages' (1951, p. 285). Doeringer and Piore (1971) were, however, less concerned than Kerr to stress the inefficiency aspects of ILMs. They stated that the ILM reflects the employer's interests in allocative efficiency, employee interest in job security and advancement and custom. The first of these is said to relate primarily to the need of employers to reduce training and turnover costs in the presence of skill-specificity. The second and third are seen to reduce the employer's ability to respond to these dictates.[1] The early literature did not examine efficiency in depth, so that direct comparisons with later views are difficult to make.

The Challenge of the ILM

The preliminary work on ILMs was solidly based on empirical research and the experience of policy formulation. However, while presenting a strong challenge to conventional modes of analysis, it failed to produce an alternative theoretical framework that could stand on its own. Doeringer and Piore's contribution brought a disparate literature together and thereby focused attention on the distinctive nature of the employing

[1] Doeringer and Piore were ambivalent about efficiency aspects; though stressing the *rigidity* of administrative rules used in the ILM (1971, p. 5), they suggested that rules are capable of 'gradual erosion' despite employees' resistance to change (1971, p. 32; see also 1971, p. 7). They also stated that pay and productivity 'need not be equated in any pay period or on any particular job classification' (1971, p. 89).

organization. Responses to this challenge can be divided into two main types. Neoclassical work has largely concentrated on integrating the ILM into orthodox theory and explaining its existence in terms which are compatible with the key principles of the neoclassical paradigm. This is examined in Section III. An alternative response has been to search for theories which are more broadly based and to develop a model which eschews wage competition. Analyses of this type are considered in Section IV.

III. NEOCLASSICAL ANALYSES

A theme which clearly emerges from the neoclassical literature is an unwillingness to give up some form of the marginal productivity theory, combined with a strong desire to work in terms of models which imply efficient organizational structures, rather than using frameworks in which efficiency is traded for other characteristics. There seems to be a predominant tendency to see the search for efficient institutions as a driving force in industrial development. Furthermore, there has been an unwillingness to take seriously the concepts of 'power' and 'atmosphere' which have been of concern to sociologists.

In dealing with the ILM, neoclassical economists have concentrated on only a small number of the characteristics which distinguish it from wage competition, such as low turnover, internal promotion and seniority. There is a propensity for analyses to reduce the ILM to a number of constituent parts which are analysed in isolation. This form of reductionism contrasts with the more holistic approaches adopted by institutionalists and radicals.

In recent years the microeconomic analysis of the labour market has witnessed many changes which have involved modification of the wage competition model in an attempt to introduce greater reality. Many of these analyses have not examined internal labour markets directly but have concentrated on phenomena which have been associated with them. Prime examples are the analyses of specific human capital and implicit contract theory. The former suggests that both employers and employees favour long term employment relationships. Employers benefit because of their investment in specific training (in skills which are only useful in that firm) and employees favour it because of the premium they receive over their alternative wage. Implicit contract theory developed to explain the high level of wage rigidity in labour markets. Such rigidity was explained as a result of an understanding between employers and employees that wages would not be reduced in response to falls in the demand for labour. This reduces the riskiness of investment in human capital for employees and is said either to reduce the wage bill of employers or increase the work effort of employees (Okun, 1981).

While the bulk of the neo-classical literature has only indirectly examined the ILM, two related strands have examined it more directly. The most direct analysis is the work of Williamson (1975). This research has variously been called the transaction cost approach or the theory of idiosyncratic exchange. The second type of direct analysis is the more disparate literature on market signalling, selection models and principal/agent analyses.

Transaction Costs

The starting point of the transaction cost approach, originating from Coase (1938), is the question of when it is more efficient to replace market transacting with internal organization. Unlike the institutional approaches Williamson emphasizes the development of procedures to handle trans-action costs (Williamson, 1975; Williamson, Wachter and Harris, 1975). He argues that the fundamental feature of labour markets is uncertainty, without which adaptive decision making problems would not be posed (Williamson, 1975, p. 80).

Two basic behavioural assumptions are made. First, individuals are assumed to have 'bounded rationality' (although intendedly rational, they have limited information processing capabilities), making it impossible to construct the complex contracts that would be required to cover all con-tingencies in the absence of some form of organizational structure. Secondly, workers are assumed to be 'opportunistic'; they would not hon-estly disclose all the information they have. Williamson suggests that indi-viduals will acquire a monopoly of knowledge regarding their jobs, resulting from 'task idiosyncrasy'. Thus bargaining problems of bilateral monopoly arise. Some alternative to spot market contracting is therefore required, and the ILM is seen as the structure that simultaneously econo-mizes on bounded rationality and weakens opportunism. Williamson (1975, p. 73) views the ILM in terms of a cooperative solution (arising from some sort of social contract) in order to avoid the problems of the individual pursuit of self interest in organizations. Hence restrictions on opportunistic bargaining are recognized to be in the interest of the system as a whole, in which all have a common interest.

One method of reducing such bargaining is to attach wages to jobs rather than individuals, so that small adaptations that are good for the system can be introduced without a great deal of haggling. There are also group pressures on individuals to accept small changes in their job duties when other members are indifferent. The use of low ports of entry into the organization provides an efficient screening device. Internal promotion to senior positions is seen to encourage 'consummate' rather than just 'per-functory' cooperation from workers, as the interests of workers are tied to those of the system in a continuing way. Their use also means that indi-viduals cannot mislead a number of organizations by moving among firms, and the use of internal promotion has 'experience rating' implications (similar to insurance).

These three characteristics emphasized by the transaction cost minimizing approach are therefore similar to those described in the earlier institutionalist literature. However, Williamson's approach gives the appearance of being based on a more formal economic model; he rejects the suggestion that any elements of ILMs are introduced for reasons of justice rather than efficiency. Furthermore, concepts such as 'power' and 'atmosphere' are not allowed to play any role on the grounds that, unlike transactions, they cannot be 'dimensionalized'. The possible inefficiency aspects of ILMs, mentioned by some of the earlier writers, are denied. Williamson argues that this brings the analysis of the ILM more into the mainstream of economic literature.[2]

In terms of marginal productivity, Williamson (1975, p. 78) suggests that the attachment of wages to jobs means that there is not necessarily a close relation between productivity and pay. The use of internal promotion based on seniority, and the payment of earnings above marginal productivity at higher ages in order to encourage attachment to the organization, introduces a need for compulsory retirement. This type of argument was later formalized by Lazear (1979). He argues that a rising earnings profile, with mandatory retirement, in which earnings exceed the value of the marginal product in later years is desired *ex ante* by workers. This is because the present value of the marginal product and hence pay is higher than otherwise, because of incentives that prevent dismissal and the loss of deferred pay. But workers *ex post* will not actually wish to retire; hence the need for a contract in which retirement is mandatory. Lazear argues that firms will not cheat because of the loss of reputation.

The transaction cost approach to the ILM can be criticized on several grounds. Despite appearances to the contrary, it has not rigorously demonstrated that the three ILM features necessarily result from the basic premises. It has also not clarified precisely the concept of efficiency used; indeed, this is complicated by the recognition of dynamic aspects and the potential importance of conflicts of interests between workers and managers. A further important criticism is that it neglects the problem of moral hazard on the side of employers.

Signalling and Incentives

It has been seen that Williamson placed great stress on uncertainty and the special access to information about their jobs that workers have. However,

---

[2] Williamson and his co-authors Wachter and Harris did, however, overstress the degree to which early writers mentioned inefficiency in explaining ILMs. This is indicated in Piore's response to a paper by Wachter. Piore (1974, p. 684) states, 'I am not arguing that the firm operates inefficiently and certainly not that management fails to minimize cost. However, when tastes and technology are made endogenous to the economy, the term "efficiency", as it is understood in neoclassical theory, loses its meaning'.

there is yet another branch of the literature that takes as its starting point imperfect, and especially asymmetric, information. The fact that the seller of a good has more information about its quality than potential buyers involves the use of various signals. Such signalling involves self-selection processes — whereby the course of action taken by the seller differs according to the quality of the good being sold. It must be unprofitable for low quality sellers to imitate the signals of the higher quality sellers. Despite the somewhat different focus of this literature (for example, no role is allowed for bounded rationality, opportunism and imperfect competition) many contributions have been explicitly concerned with labour markets and have described their results as producing features of ILMs.

An early analysis of signalling in the labour market, by Salop and Salop (1976), involves the self-selection of workers to firms according to their propensity to quit. If firms have a rising earnings profile then only those with low propensities to quit would wish to join, so that where firms have differential turnover costs this type of self-selection provides a better matching of workers to firms. An early example of over-investment in signals was provided by Akerlof's (1976) analysis of a 'rat race' in which workers signal their higher ability by their willingness to work at higher speeds (and ability is judged only by speed). At slower speeds a worker must share the output with workers of lower ability, whereas at higher speeds output is shared with workers of higher ability (but judged to be the same). The result is that lower ability workers select a higher than optimal speed.

One of the most comprehensive models in this tradition is that of Malcomson (1984), who examines a two period contracting system. In this model firms offer contracts in which a specified proportion of workers will be paid a higher wage in the second period. Such 'promotion' is based on a ranking of individuals according to the firm's assessment of performance in the first period. The firm has an incentive to promote those who perform relatively better than others because this provides the greatest incentive for employees to work hard in the first period. This type of contract works where asymmetric information about performance would prevent performance based contracts from being enforceable and, drawing on the literature of repeated games, Malcomson argues that firms cannot afford to lose reputations for keeping to their side of the contract.[3] It is shown that wages rise with seniority by more than productivity.

The approach is of course highly stylized and its links with ILMs are somewhat artificial. For example, the internal promotion gives rise to a horizontal hierarchy rather than one based on authority or autonomy.

---

[3] On reputations, see Carmichael (1984). On competitive ranking procedures, see Nalebuff and Stiglitz (1983) and Rosen (1986). Contractual models are also examined in Holmstrom (1981).

Furthermore, an important feature that distinguishes the model from ILM frameworks is the explicit introduction of competition among workers for a limited number of promotions based on a ranking of performance. This kind of competition was deliberately ruled out by early proponents of ILM theory on grounds that it would hinder the informal process of on-the-job training, involving the sharing of knowledge among workers and internal promotion by seniority. It does seem that neoclassical economists are generally unhappy with incentive devices which do not rely on competition.

The disparate contributions to the signalling/incentive literature have been synthesized and termed efficiency wage models (Akerlof and Yellen, 1986). Efficiency wage models explain why firms find it unprofitable to reduce wages when there is high unemployment. In brief, wage cuts are said to harm productivity and therefore, while they would reduce total labour costs, they may increase labour costs per efficiency unit. This simple hypothesis has been used to explain the rigidity of real wages, the existence of dual labour markets, the payment of differing wages to similar workers and discrimination between distinct groups. While not explicitly mentioned by Akerlof and Yellen, ILMs can be interpreted as institutions which reflect the interdependence of wages and productivity. This inter-dependence is seen to reflect either the incentive, signalling or turnover problems which are stressed by neoclassical theorists or sociological factors such as group norms based on social conventions and principles of appropriate behaviour (1986, p. 8). The latter have been more fully articulated by economists adhering to the institutional and radical schools of thought.

IV.   ALTERNATIVE APPROACHES

A number of differences emerge between the neoclassical models and those of the alternative schools. The rationales offered for the existence of ILMs are much broader, involving concepts drawn from a range of social sciences. Analyses are much less formal than their neo-classical counter-parts, placing more importance on descriptive reality than analytical rigour. The methodology adopted is much more inductive than the deduc-tive, neoclassical approach. Theories are more likely to be developed from observations and inferences made about the general case from specific studies than is the case in neoclassicism. Furthermore, there is an explicit attempt to develop an alternative model of the labour market to wage competition; the main examples are the job competition model and the dual labour market hypothesis. Finally, much emphasis is placed on the motivation of workers, although writers have not compared their argu-ments with, for example, Williamson's concern with attenuating opportunism or the need expressed by others to design contracts that minimize moral hazard problems. Each strand of the literature has tended to develop its own argot.

A basic divide can be observed between institutionalists and radicals. This mainly relates to the degree to which ILMs are explained as reflections of the dictates of technology on work organization or attempts by employers to gain greater control over the production process. The institutional explanations are firmly grounded in the pluralist tradition of social thought which conceives the employing organization as a coalition of competing interest groups which are kept in equilibrium by management. The radical explanations are linked to Marxian theory and view the structure of the labour market as reflecting the conflict between the owners of capital and the suppliers of labour power; management is seen as representing the interests of capital owners rather than simply as organizers.

Institutional Analyses of the ILM

The institutional analysis of the ILM has been most fully developed by Doeringer and Piore (1971). The main elements of their early work were summarized in Section II. They discussed several rationales for the existence and character of ILMs including employer attempts to reduce turnover in the presence of specific training, worker pressure to enhance job stability and the development of custom and practice in the workplace. In contrast with the neoclassical theorists, Doeringer and Piore accorded a role to unions in the establishment of labour market structure. However, it can be argued that they failed to establish the relative importance of the various factors.

While Doeringer and Piore's analysis has much in common with that of neoclassical theorists, a crucial difference is the rejection of the notion that the labour market works even remotely like a wage competition model. A consequence of this difference is the rejection of that model for manpower analysis and support for the dual labour market hypothesis. This hypothesis argues that the labour market can be divided into two sectors — a primary sector composed of 'good' jobs and a secondary sector composed of 'bad' jobs. Some formulations make a distinction between an upper and lower tier in the primary sector. The primary sector is seen to consist of a series of well-developed ILMs (Doeringer and Piore, 1971, p. 167). Secondary jobs are those outside ILMs, those in poorly developed ILMs (that is, possessing formal internal structures but many entry ports, short mobility clusters and unpleasant/low-paying work) and those in well-developed ILMs but not attached to formal promotion lines. It is suggested that secondary jobs occur because employers have little incentive to reduce turnover, because of the technical aspects of the job or because the labour force places little value on job security. This model is based on a great deal of rigidity in the job structure and suggests that there are few competitive processes to eradicate qualitative differences between jobs. Indeed, it has been argued that these differences are intensified; those in 'bad' jobs acquire behavioural traits such as lateness and absenteeism which make it increasingly difficult for them to move into 'good' jobs. In more recent work Piore (1979) has offered a more general explanation for the emergence of dualism which suggests that the differing characteristics of jobs primarily reflect the cognitive processes inherent in them. Jobs where a clear understanding must be made between ends and means are seen to generate employment characteristics similar to those in the upper tier of the primary sector. Those involving more routine thought processes are linked to the lower primary sector. All other jobs are located in the secondary sector.

Thurow (1975) also locates the development of the ILM in on-the-job training but, in contrast to Doeringer and Piore, the key link is the willingness of workers to transmit their knowledge to newcomers. The essence of Thurow's hypothesis is that the bulk of training occurs on the job and that it is crucial for employing organizations to maximize the acquisition of skills. It is argued that unless employers suppress wage and employment competition, workers will fear that the transmission of their knowledge will generate an increase in competition for their jobs. This will result in decreased job security and the undermining of their bargaining positions. Wage and employment competition which is postulated to promote labour market efficiency in the neoclassical model, is therefore seen by Thurow to give workers an incentive to hoard knowledge. He concludes that:

> the types of wage and employment competition that are the essence of efficiency in simple, static neoclassical models may not be the essence of efficiency in a dynamic economy where the primary function of the labour market is to allocate individuals to on-the-job training ladders and where most learning occurs in work-related contexts (1975, p. 84).

The job competition model therefore emphasizes quantity adjustment rather than wage adjustment. It not only draws on the ILM literature but also on the screening hypothesis which developed as a critique of human capital theory. Thurow contends that there are sectors of the labour market in which workers compete for jobs on the basis of background characteristics rather than relative wages. Within these sectors workers are ranked for available jobs according to their expected training costs; this ranking forms a 'labour queue'. The characteristics of applicants for entry level jobs (such as age, sex, IQ, education) are used as proxies for trainability; work experience is used to rank applicants for higher level jobs. Those at the top of the labour queue obtain the best jobs and those at the bottom obtain either the worst jobs or none at all. It should be stressed that Thurow is less dismissive of the principles of wage competition than Doeringer and Piore. First, he accepts the notion of competition in the process of labour allocation, although for jobs rather than for wages. Secondly, he suggests that those sectors not subject to job competition operate in a manner similar to wage competition.

Radical Analyses

A more far-reaching approach has been developed by radical economists. Edwards (1975), for example, has contended that firms established ILMs to prevent the development of class consciousness among workers and to allow employers to maintain control over the production process. The ILM is therefore said to maximize the amount of labour (effort expended in production) obtained from a given amount of labour power (the capacity to perform useful work). This requires bureaucratic control, involving the development of formal definitions for the direction of work tasks and the use of institutionalized power to enforce compliance. Thus work habits become consistent with the form of bureaucratic control rather than with the actual work tasks.

Edwards distinguishes three principal modes of compliance. The first is 'rules orientation' in which workers are made aware of the rules and are expected to follow them in an unambiguous manner. A more sophisticated form of control is based on the encouragement of habits of predictability and dependability; workers are expected to perform their tasks according to the spirit rather than the letter of work criteria. The most sophisticated form of control involves the internalization of the enterprise's goals and values; the worker is encouarged to be loyal, committed and thus self-directed.

The generation of these behavioural characteristics is said to involve both the firm's hiring and firing policy and the use of differential internal promotion. Potential rules orientation is an important determinant of whether or not a person is hired and career ladders are designed to foster and reward dependability and/or the internalization of the firm's goals.

This bureaucratic control hypothesis has been subject to considerable criticism by other writers in the radical tradition, who view employers as acting not as a class but as individuals in a competitive environment. Furthermore, Edwards sees labour force homogenization as a problem for employers, whereas others argue that it is most threatening to the bargaining position of workers. Some radical theorists suggest that the ILM results from the defensive reaction of organized workers to employer efforts to de-skill the workforce. Such action could take the form of union-organized apprenticeship schemes or promotion based on seniority. The theory suggests that the most effective tactic for workers is to differentiate themselves from potential competitors. This could involve the maintenance of skill status long after the original skill divisions become irrelevant. Hence Rubery (1980, p. 260) has argued that 'the existence of a structured labour force, where jobs are strictly defined, and workers are not interchangeable, provides a bargaining base for labour against management's attempts to increase productivity and introduce new technology'.

Most radical analyses have used the concept of labour market segmentation, which is a development of the dual labour market hypothesis. The distinction between the primary and secondary sectors and the upper and lower tiers of the primary sector are common to both. Major differences involve the explanation offered for the development of ILMs (as noted above) and in the precise nature of labour market segmentation. In particular, segmentation theorists emphasize that racial minorities and women are confined to the poorer jobs within any sector of the market.

V. EMPIRICAL STUDIES

The ILM has not given rise to a large amount of empirical work by economists, particularly those working in the neoclassical tradition. A major problem is that the literature has not provided a framework for the empirical analysis of ILMs and the testing of its features against particular alternative models. In comparing models, Doeringer and Piore argued that:

> The requisite measures of neoclassical economic variables are unavailable at the microeconomic level, and the administrative rules which control internal labour markets in practice cannot be defined with sufficient precision to permit quantitative testing of their compatibility. As a result, the case for the internal labour market must rest on less satisfactory heuristic evidence (1971, p. 5).

Although Doeringer and Piore made some suggestions for a more heuristic procedure, requiring information from individual firms, research generally has not moved beyond taxonomy and general description and only on limited occasions can it be said to have gone beyond the classification stage.

It would be unfair, however, to criticize only ILM theorists for a failure to carry out appropriate data collection and empirical work. The same is true of a great deal of economic research and is particularly true of research in the same general area as ILM research. A prime example is work on the question of why the earnings profile rises with experience. Most analyses of this phenomenon have postulated a close relation between productivity and earnings, particularly the human capital approach. However, there are few direct attempts to test the theory.[4]

The ILM poses special problems for empirical analysis. First, it is a complex phenomenon which cannot be reduced to a small number of measures. Secondly, its characteristics have been shown to vary considerably across space and time in a manner that is not readily understandable. Thirdly, many of its principal dimensions are longitudinal in nature and cannot be analysed using cross-sectional data. The major consequence of these problems is that the types of data normally used by economists are

---

[4] The extent to which the firm specific human capital approach implies a wage profile that rises faster than productivity is examined by Carmichael who states that the derived wage profile 'corresponds closely to those we observe' (1983, p. 251); yet no empirical work is reported.

not useful for ILM research. In particular, ILM research requires that researchers collect their own data. However, this is not common among economists, although it is more common in sociology and industrial relations, where the bulk of the empirical work on the ILM has been undertaken.[5] Leontief (1983, p. viii) pointed out that only 0.8 and 1.4 per cent of articles published in the *American Economic Review* from 1972 to 1976 and from 1977 to 1981 respectively contained analyses based on data generated by the author's initiative.

Types of Approach

Empirical research on the ILM has generally adopted three main types of approach. The first involves the analysis of highly aggregative data; the second is based on case studies of particular firms and industries, using data collected specially by researchers; the third type concentrates on the analysis of career histories, usually of particular occupational groups.

Studies which use highly aggregative data can at most offer a broad description of the distribution of ILMs across industries, occupations or regions. They usually concentrate on one element of the ILM, typically the low turnover rate, and use it as a classification device. The prime example of this approach is by Alexander (1974), who divides industries into Kerr's trichotomy of unstructured, manorial and guild on the basis of their inter-firm mobility rates. A manorial industry is arbitrarily defined as having less than 10 per cent per year; a guild industry has a value of inter-firm minus inter-industry mobility of more than 10 per cent per year; an unstructured industry is a non-guild industry in which inter-firm mobility is more than 20 per cent per year.[6]

The major problem with such highly aggregative work is that it is so arbitrary. It largely concentrates on the turnover rate, to the exclusion of other aspects such as internal promotion, the use of non-wage adjustment mechanisms and the emphasis on internal considerations in wage-fixing. This is mainly due to the failure of aggregate data to relate to these factors. The case study approach is more appropriate and can provide detailed pictures where large-scale simplification can be misleading, suggest hypotheses which may not emerge from deductive reasoning and provide orders of magnitude for details which cannot be isolated in aggregative analysis (Blandy and Richardson, 1982). The major problem with case-studies is that their results do not necessarily have general applicability.

Case-studies have generally concentrated on examining whether employing organizations exhibit the characteristics ascribed to ILMs.

[5] Medoff and Abraham (1981, p. 215) note that, 'Unlike physical scientists, economists typically are not involved in the collection of the data they use, and, unlike other social scientists, economists usually avoid having contact with their unit of observation'.

[6] Osterman (1984) also stresses the ILM's low turnover rate. A recent such study is Collier and Knight (1985).

Mace (1979), for example, surveyed engineers in 12 firms and attempted to establish whether the firms had low turnover-rates, entry ports at the lower level jobs, a preference for current employees in filling vacancies, well-developed mobility clusters, and a willingness of firms to provide general training. He also examined whether salary differentials existed between firms employing similar types of labour over long periods and the relative importance of Doeringer and Piore's 'less constrained' adjustment mechanisms. Nowak and Crockett (1983) studied three large organizations in Western Australia in order to 'gain detailed information on the structure and dynamic responses in the labour market of particular firms and to investigate the interaction of this and employee career patterns' (1983, p. 448). The standard technique for undertaking such a case study has been to conduct a series of interviews of personnel managers and to supplement this with information obtained from company records and/or employee questionnaires. The information obtained provides a detailed picture of how firms organize their workforces and how they adjust to changing economic conditions.

A more direct attempt to address economic issues can be found in ILM orientated research using the career history method. It usually involves the replacement of the assumptions of human capital theory by an empirical analysis of the *process* of mobility within organizations. Nowak and Crockett (1983) sent questionnaires to staff in the three large organizations mentioned earlier. Creedy and Whitfield (1986, 1988) used retrospective surveys of professional scientists who are members of national scientific institutes. The questionnaires elicited information which could be used to measure both internal job mobility and the phenomenon which Doeringer and Piore termed osmotic mobility. The latter is essentially the result of gradual changes in the nature of the work performed and can be measured by the extent of changes in job duties taking place within the same job.

A problem with the career history approach is the difficulty involved in obtaining accurate information. First, accurate yet widely applicable classifications need to be developed for comparing jobs. Secondly, information must be collected relating to a long period of time, so that retrospective work histories are usually involved. Thirdly, some of the key concepts of ILM theory are extremely difficult to measure; for example, the measurement of osmotic mobility depends crucially on worker perceptions.

The Main Empirical Results

While the empirical research on ILMs is limited, it has produced a number of important results. Indeed, many of the features stressed in the ILM literature have been shown to exist across a wide range of occupations, industries and regions; the evidence suggests that many workers are

employed under ILM conditions. It has also been shown that ILM structures are considerably more complex and wide-ranging than earlier writers
suggested.

Low turnover rates have been found in many sectors and occupations.[7]
Steinberg (1974) found that approximately half of US workers were with
the same firm in 1970 as in 1965 and that lengthy attachment was greatest
for higher income earners and older workers. The restriction of entry to
lower levels of job classifications has been shown to be very common.
Mace (1979) found that the average age of entry into nine of the firms surveyed was 25 or below and for the other three it was below 30. Nowak and
Crockett (1983) found that the lowest job classification was the entry point
for the majority of employees of the firms studied. Osterman (1984) found
that the restriction of entry to the lower job classifications varied considerably between occupations. Managerial jobs were unlikely to be entered
above the lower classifications but computer programming and clerical
jobs were most likely to be entered at higher levels. Sales positions were
situated between the two types.

The filling of upper level positions by internal promotion has been
shown to be a very common practice. Mace (1979) found that every firm in
his survey preferred internal to external appointments and that in 11 firms
90 per cent of promotions went to internal candidates. This pattern was
explained as resulting from the need to maintain morale, provide a career
pattern for new recruits and to appoint engineers with known and relevant
experience. Nowak and Crockett (1983) also found a strong preference for
internal promotion, although the emphasis placed on it varied considerably between firms. Internal mobility has also been shown to be important
for the upward mobility and earnings of professional chemists. Almost
60 per cent of the upward changes of responsibility level reported in
Creedy and Whitfield (1986) were made within the same organization and
the majority were made within the same job, confirming the importance of
osmotic mobility. Furthermore, it was shown that the experience of internal mobility is a key determinant of earnings.

A number of researchers have identified the existence of job clusters
along the lines suggested by Doeringer and Piore. Mace (1979) found that
10 of the 12 firms surveyed had elaborate job description schemes and
that all 12 had some job description scheme. Osterman (1984) found that
movement between job ladders was relatively easy at the entry position but
less so at higher levels, although the degree of upper level openness seems
to vary between occupations, largely depending on the technical nature of
the skills used.

The empirical research has also shown that wages are tied to jobs within
ILMs and that they are not very responsive to changing labour market con-

[7] On low turnover in the US see Hall (1982); for Australia see Foster and Gregory (1983,
p. 130) and Nowak and Crockett (1983); for UK engineers see Mace (1979, p. 55); for UK
and Australian chemists see Whitfield (1982, p. 163) and Whitfield (1981).

ditions. Mace (1979, p. 57) found that, 'in setting salaries within firms, attention was primarily directed to fitting the hierarchy of salaries to the hierarchy of jobs. This was usually legitimized through job evaluation, and once the hierarchy was set it was not possible for firms to move outside the relevant salary band for a job'. Furthermore, Osterman (1984) and Nowak and Crockett (1983) found that firms operating ILMs exhibited rigid salary structures but showed a great deal of flexibility in moving workers between jobs at differing points on the classification: that is, the wages for workers were more flexible than the wages for jobs.

The ILM research has also complemented research on labour market adjustment and, in particular, has indicated that the wage competition model is at variance with reality. The key finding is that wages represent a highly constrained adjustment mechanism. Such a conclusion was reached by Mace (1979), Nowak and Crockett (1983) and by more general labour market analyses by Thomas and Deaton (1977) and Blandy and Richardson (1982). Moreover, a number of firms in Mace's study said that they would curtail production rather than use one of the adjustment mechanisms emphasized in competitive theory.

VI. CONCLUSIONS

As suggested in the introduction to this paper, the ILM has raised three principal questions for economic analysis. These concern the relevance of non-economic factors, their implications for economic theory and the possible need to develop alternative empirical approaches.

Economists are divided on the first question; some stress economic determinants and others a mixture of economic and non-economic determinants. However, even those stressing economic factors have utilized ideas and concepts which were formerly the province of non-economic disciplines such as sociology, organizational behaviour and industrial relations. In particular, the ILM has prompted economists to examine more closely questions of work effort and motivation and to recognize that labour is a qualitatively different factor of production from capital.

The main differences between economists in their rationales for the ILM relate to their analysis of efficiency. Neoclassical theorists tend to see the ILM as an efficiency-orientated response to the idiosyncrasies of labour as a factor of production. The ILM is the institution which equates wages and marginal productivity in a situation where market pressures would be insufficient to do so. Institutionalists question whether the neoclassical concept of efficiency is appropriate in a setting in which wages and productivity are interdependent and where social factors influence both. They emphasize a broader notion of efficiency which incorporates social, political and psychological factors as well as economic. Radicals question whether the concept of efficiency is as value-free as the other schools suggest. They suggest that efficiency is defined so as to be identical to the interests of capital and therefore it is an instrument which is used in the capital/labour conflict.

The recognition of non-economic determinants of the ILM (or, at least, a wider range of economic determinants) has evoked a mixed response from economists in terms of theory construction. Neoclassicists have suggested the ILMs slow down the basic processes which are outlined in the wage competition model but that the model when modified is still applicable. Institutionalists have searched for alternative models, such as job competition and dual labour markets, but have not been able to convince the bulk of economists of the utility of these constructs. Radicals view the ILM as confirming the superiority of an economic model grounded in Marxian rather than neoclassical concepts. The ILM has thus simply re-oriented the debate between the schools of thought.

Developing out of the institutionalist tradition, the ILM might have been expected to have had its major impact on the methods used in empirical analysis. Paradoxically, this is the area in which the least development has taken place. The ILM poses serious questions for the appropriateness of conventional economic methods based on highly aggregated data sets. These questions have, however, been ignored by most economists, who have either failed to undertake empirical work on the ILM or have adopted conventional and inappropriate methods. There is a need for economists to undertake detailed and disaggregated research on the relationship between the ILM and the traditional concerns of economics, such as wage determination, the distribution of earnings and employment change. To date, the ILM has been more thoroughly researched at the empirical level by non-economists.

University of Melbourne   *Invited paper, received January 1988*
and
Institute for Employment Research,
University of Warwick/University of Sydney

REFERENCES

Akerlof, G. (1976). 'The Economics of Caste and of the Rat-race and other Woeful Tales', *Quarterly Journal of Economics*, Vol. XC, pp. 599, 617.
Akerlof, G. and Yellen, J. (1986). *Efficiency Wage Models of the Labor Market.* Cambridge; C.U.P.
Alexander, A. J. (1974). 'Income, Experience and the Structure of Internal Labor Markets', *Quarterly Journal of Economics*, Vol. 88, pp. 63–86.

Blandy, R. J. and Richardson, S. (eds.) (1982). *How Labour Markets Work.* Melbourne; Longman Cheshire.

Carmichael, H. L. (1983). 'Firm Specific Human Capital and Promotion Ladders', *Bell Journal of Economics*, Vol. 14, pp. 251–8.

Carmichael, H. L. (1984). 'Reputations in the Labor Market', *American Economic Review*, Vol. 74, pp. 713–25.

Coase, R. H. (1937). 'The Nature of the Firm', *Economica*, Vol. 4, pp. 386–405.

Collier, P. and Knight, J. B. (1985). 'Seniority Payments, Quit Rates and Internal Labour Markets in Britain and Japan', *Oxford Bulletin of Economics and Statistics*, Vol. 47, pp. 19–32.

Creedy, J. and Whitfield, K. (1986). 'Earnings and Job Mobility: Professional Chemists in Britain', *Journal of Economic Studies*, Vol. 13, pp. 23–37.

Creedy, J. and Whitfield, K. (1988). 'Job Mobility and Earnings: An Empirical Analysis Using the Internal Labour Market Approach', *The Journal of Industrial Relations*, Vol. 30, pp. 100–17.

Doeringer, P. B. and Piore, M. (1971). *Internal Labor Markets and Manpower Analysis.* Lexington; D. C. Heath.

Dunlop, J. T. (1957). 'The Task of Contemporary Wage Theory'. in Taylor, G. W. and Pierson, G. W. (eds.), *New Concepts in Wage Determination*, New York; McGraw-Hill, pp. 117–39.

Edwards, R. C. (1975). 'Industrial Traits and Organizational Incentives: What Makes a Good Worker?' *Journal of Human Resources*, Vol. 11, pp. 51–68.

Foster, W. F. and Gregory, R. G. (1983). 'A Flow Analysis of the Labour Market in Australia', in Blandy, R. J. and Covick, O. (eds.), *Understanding Labour Markets*, Sydney; George Allen and Unwin, pp. 111–36.

Freeman, R. and Medoff, J. (1979). 'The Two Faces of Unionism', *Public Interest*, Vol. 57, pp. 69–93.

Hall, R. E. (1982). 'The Importance of Lifetime Jobs in the U.S. Economy', *American Economic Review*, Vol. 72, pp. 716–24.

Holmstrom, B. (1981). 'Contractual Models of the Labor Market', *American Economic Review*, Vol. 71, pp. 308–13.

Hunter, L. C. and Reid, G. L. (1968). *Urban Worker Mobility.* Paris; Organisation for Economic Cooperation and Development.

Kerr, C. (1951). 'Labor Markets; Their Character and Consequences', *American Economic Association. Papers and Proceedings*, Vol. 40, pp. 278–91.

Kerr, C. (1954). 'The Balkanization of Labor Markets', in Bakke, E. W. (ed.), *Labour Mobility and Economic Opportunity*, Cambridge; The MIT Press, pp. 92–110.

Lazear, E. P. (1979). 'Why is There Mandatory Retirement?' *Journal of Political Economy*, Vol. 87, pp. 1261–84.

Lazear, E. P. (1981). 'Agency, Earnings Profiles, and Productivity and Hours Restrictions', *American Economic Review*, Vol. 71, pp. 601–20.

Leontief, W. (1983). 'Foreword', in Eichner, A. S. (ed.), *Why Economics is Not Yet A Science*, London; Macmillan, pp. vii–xi.

Mace, J. (1979). 'Internal Labour Markets for Engineers in British Industry', *British Journal of Industrial Relations*, Vol. 17, pp. 50–63.

Malcomson, J. M. (1984). 'Work Incentives, Hierarchy, and Internal Labour Markets', *Journal of Political Economy*, Vol. 92, pp. 486–507.

Medoff, J. L. and Abraham, K. G. (1981) 'Are Those Paid More Really More Productive/ The Case of Experience', *Journal of Human Resources*, Vol. 16, pp. 186–216.

Nalebuff, B. J. and Stiglitz, J. E. (1983). 'Prizes and Incentives: Towards a General Theory of Compensation and Competition', *Bell Journal of Economics*, Vol. 14, pp. 21–43.

Nowak, M. J. and Crockett, G. V. (1983). 'The Operation of Internal Labour Markets: Three Case Studies', *Journal of Industrial Relations*, Vol. 25, pp. 445–64.

Okun, A. M. (1981). *Prices and Quantities: A Macroeconomic Analysis*. Oxford; Basil Blackwell.

Osterman, P. (ed.) (1984). *Internal Labour Markets*. London; The MIT Press.

Piore, M. J. (1979). *Unemployment and Inflation: Institutionalist and Structural Views*. White Plains, NY; Sharpe.

Piore, M. J. (1974). 'Comments and Discussion', *Brookings Papers in Economic Activity*, Vol. 3, pp. 684–8.

Rosen, S. (1986). 'Prizes and Incentives in Elimination Contracts', *American Economic Review*, Vol. 76, pp. 701–15.

Rubery, J. (1980). 'Structural Labour Markets, Worker Organization and Low Pay', in Amsden, A. H. (ed.), *The Economics of Women and Work*, Harmondsworth; Penguin, pp. 242–70.

Salop, J. and Salop, S. (1976). 'Self-selection and Turnover in the Labor Market', *Quarterly Journal of Economics*, Vol. XC, pp. 619–27.

Steinberg, E. (1974). 'Upward Mobility in the Internal Labour Market', *Industrial Relations*, Vol. 15, pp. 259–65.

Thomas, B. and Deaton, D. (1977). *Labour Shortage and Economic Analysis*. Oxford; Basil Blackwell.

Thurow, L. C. (1974). *Generating Inequality*. London; Macmillan.

Whitfield, K. (1981). 'The Job Mobility of Professional Chemists in Australia and Britain', *Chemistry in Australia*, Vol. 48, pp. 277–82.

Whitfield, K. (1982). *Occupational Labour Market Structures*. D. Phil. thesis (Oxford).

Williamson, O. E. (1975). *Markets and Hierarchies*. New York; Free Press.

Williamson, O. E., Wachter, M. L. and Harris, J. E. (1975). 'Understanding the Employment Relation: The Analysis of Idiosyncratic Exchange', *The Bell Journal of Economics*, Vol. 61, pp. 250–80.

Job Mobility and Earnings: An Internal Labour Market Analysis

JOHN CREEDY* AND KEITH WHITFIELD**

The analysis of job mobility and earnings has been dominated by human capital theory. This approach has been subject to considerable criticism in recent years, particularly about the manner in which it conceptualizes the processes that take place between the start and end of a job. An alternative is the internal labour market approach, which focuses on the very processes which are so problematic for human capital theory. Information from three specially designed surveys of professional scientists in Australia and Britain suggests that the processes that are central to internal labour market theory are crucial to generating the distribution of earnings. While the evidence presented is not necessarily incompatible with human capital theory, it does suggest that future research on the earnings distribution could usefully involve the development of the internal labour market approach.

It has long been recognized that the generation of observed differences in earnings is closely related to the pattern of job mobility. The economic analysis of this relationship is dominated by human capital theory, which views the bulk of earnings differences as reflective of differential investment in productivity-augmenting skills. This approach is solidly grounded in the neoclassical theory of labour supply, which conceives the activities of workers in terms of individual utility maximization over the life cycle.

An alternative to human capital theory is internal labour market theory, which was developed at a similar time to human capital theory and has some features in common. However, it exhibits many features in contrast to those of human capital theory. These differences are principally methodological and are outlined below.

While a standard regression approach has been adopted by human capital theory analysts, internal labour market theorists cannot so far be said to have developed a complete set of formal empirical methods. Hence the principal objective of this paper is to develop an empirical analysis of mobility and

* Department of Economics, University of Melbourne, Parkville, Vic. 3052.
** Institute for Employment Research, University of Warwick and Department of Industrial Relations, University of Sydney, NSW 2006.
The Australian surveys were financed by a grant from the Bureau of Labour Market Research and the postal and printing costs of the British survey were financed by grant No. F00232206 from the Economic and Social Research Council, for which we are grateful. We are very grateful to the Royal Australian Chemical Institute, the Australian Institute of Physics and the Royal Society of Chemistry for their considerable help and co-operation. We should also like to thank Mark Dziegielewski and Jill Peters for computing assistance, Kylie Nomchong for research assistance with the Australian surveys and Braham Dabscheck, Flora Gill, Rob Wilson and two anonymous referees of the *JIR* for helpful comments on an earlier version.

earnings using the internal labour market approach rather than the human capital theory approach as its focus. This implicitly involves an assessment of the key relationships of the internal labour market theory. The paper also provides information about the actual processes which human capital theory ignores. It must be acknowledged, however, that rigorous tests of the competing elements of internal labour market and human capital theory cannot be carried out at this stage.

The data on which this paper is based result from three surveys of male scientists in Australia and Britain, carried out by the authors in 1985. These surveys, of members of three professional institutes, concentrated on the collection of information about individual work histories. A special effort was made to obtain data on mobility within firms as well as mobility between firms. This reflected the emphasis of internal labour market theory on the role of internal mobility in generating earnings differentials and, in particular, on a type of mobility that involves small-scale and gradual change to the job duties undertaken, or osmotic mobility.

The type of statistical information used in this study is extremely rare, particularly outside the United States. First, data pertaining to a long period and which allow job changes at differing points in the life cycle to be related have not been common. The United States National Longitudinal Study is the most notable survey to have collected this type of information and it has consequently been the focus of much empirical research on mobility and earnings (e.g., see Borjas 1981). Second, few data are available on the processes operating within the confines of the employing organization. Most information has related to movement between organizations, and researchers have made ad hoc inferences about what happens between such changes.[1]

Job mobility and earnings in theory

Internal labour market theory and human capital theory are very different in their approaches to job mobility and earnings. These differences principally relate to methodology and focus.

Human capital theory is based on a deductive methodology that involves the development of broad theories from a particular set of axioms and the fitting of data to resulting models. The internal labour market approach is more inductive in its stance: theories are often developed from observations generated from detailed empirical investigations. Thus the emphasis on theory and evidence is different in the two approaches. A related difference concerns the focus of the analysis. Whereas human capital theorists see the labour market as operating in a similar manner to that postulated by the wage competition model, internal labour market theorists believe that the labour market contains major institutions which prevent wage competition from operating. Consequently, distinctive institutions such as the internal labour market develop and persist in labour markets and are able to influence the manner of adjustment to changing conditions. The greater the influence of

---

1. The prime example is human capital theory which conceives all changes in income and job status between intra-firm job-changes as reflecting investment in on-the-job training.

such institutions, the more important it is that they are included in theory construction, empirical analysis and policy advice.

Human capital theory

The basic postulates of human capital theory are extremely simple and are based on the concept of the utility maximizing supplier of labour investing in education, training, or job search in order to maximize his or her lifetime utility. Individuals are assumed to compare the expected returns from such investment to its costs. In essence, persons with a preference for high current earnings rather than high future earnings will undertake little investment and vice versa.

Most formulations of the theory divide investment in human capital into three main types: investment in formal education, investment in on-the-job training and investment in job search. Investment in on-the-job training is divided into general training (resembling formal education) and investment in specific training. Investment in formal education and general training are financed by workers who forego earnings during training in return for higher earnings after training. The costs of specific training are divided between workers and employers in a manner not fully specified by the theory. Investment in job search yields a return through a discrete jump in the level of earnings at the time of job change.

In the human capital theory analysis of job mobility, internal mobility is not analysed directly but is assumed to reflect investment in human capital. Those investing heavily in on-the-job training will achieve considerable upward mobility and will receive higher earnings growth to accompany their promotion.

The human capital theory approach to mobility and earnings is founded on the assumption that the labour market works such that workers are able to choose from among alternative amounts of general and specific training. Furthermore, the wage rate is seen to adjust so as to yield the optimal cost-sharing arrangement between employers and employees—that is, there is no free learning. Thus Mincer (1976, 140) has stated that:

> Given differential learning options among jobs and no insuperable barriers to labour-mobility, present values of earnings among the various learning options will tend towards equalisation among workers with similar capacities. Thus labour mobility will impose opportunity costs of learning, by reducing the initial earnings of the steeper profiles below the initial earnings of the flatter profiles.

Some economists have, however, questioned whether the labour market works in this manner and, in particular, whether workers freely choose between learning options that are rationed by price. For example, Thurow (1983, 175) has argued that:

> Human-capital theory . . . cannot account for the fact that many of the on-the-job training markets where one is supposed to bid for opportunities to acquire informal training don't seem to exist. Employers usually allocate such opportunities not based on a willingness to work for less than one's free-market wage, but on seniority or merit for having performed well in a job previously held.

The human capital approach to mobility and earnings has, therefore, been seen by some economists to be at variance with the processes actually operating within employing organizations. This has led some researchers to attempt to develop an alternative approach based on a more realistic model of such internal processes.

Internal labour market theory

Internal labour market theory represents a substantial change of focus from human capital theory. Attention is centred on the mobility process. It is suggested that the bulk of job mobility results from the gradual accumulation of small changes in the job duties undertaken. None of these changes in themselves are sufficiently large to constitute a job change but, when viewed over a long time, they represent a major change in the nature of the work undertaken. This gradual form of mobility was termed 'osmosis', 'exposure', 'experience', and 'working one's way up through promotion' by Doeringer and Piore (1971, 18), but the first term has been most commonly applied to denote this form of mobility. It is suggested by internal labour market theorists that the discrete job changes emphasized by the human capital theorists are just a minor part of the mobility process and that any empirical analysis of mobility and earnings should include some measurement of both internal and osmotic mobility.

Despite its importance in the theoretical literature, the theory of internal labour markets has prompted very little empirical work. Most research has examined particular organizations using a case study approach and has made little attempt to link internal and osmotic mobility to earnings. This seems to reflect the lack of suitable data for such an analysis. For instance, very few attempts have been made to obtain information on internal mobility, and the studies that have made such an effort have tended to define it very narrowly (e.g. Cole 1979, ch. 2). There are also major problems encountered in measuring on a consistent basis differing aspects of the internal mobility process, and consequently research in the area has often bypassed such questions. Nonetheless, there is growing evidence that internal labour markets are prevalent in labour markets and that they are likely to have a major impact on the outcomes of labour market processes (see, for example, Osterman 1984). Hence, there is a need to assess how the key concepts of internal labour market theory can be measured and integrated into empirical analysis.

The measurement of job mobility

Types of mobility

The theoretical literature on internal labour markets has indicated that it is useful to distinguish three main types of mobility: inter-firm mobility, intra-firm mobility and within-job mobility. The divide between inter-firm and intra-firm mobility depends crucially on the definition of 'firm' that is adopted. The broader the definition, the greater is the incidence of internal relative to external mobility recorded. Within-job mobility differs from the other two types of mobility mainly because it is continuous rather than discrete.[2]

---

2. The importance of this form of mobility has been stressed by, for example, White (1970) and Hunter and Reid (1968).

Mobility between firms has been the subject of most analysis, reflecting the relative availability of data on labour turnover (usually defined in terms of inter-firm mobility). It is conventional to divide inter-firm mobility into 'voluntary' and 'involuntary' mobility. The distinction between voluntary and involuntary mobility is not always definite, however, since some 'voluntary' job changes may be prompted by pressure from employers or because of the poor quality of the job. For present purposes, a movement between firms was described as voluntary if it was made for 'immediate salary improvement', 'long-term prospects in fresh employment' or 'frustration'. It was classified as involuntary if it was made because of redundancy, dismissal or closure. Other reasons for changing jobs used in the surveys include 'transfer within organization' and 'promotion within organization'.

Mobility within firms has been much less comprehensively studied and is extremely difficult to measure. This is because there is no generally accepted method for deciding which changes in job duties are job changes and which are not. This problem has been addressed in two main ways. The first and most common method is to define intra-firm mobility as a change in occupational 'status', according to some occupational classification, which does not involve a change of firm. However, this technique under-estimates the incidence of internal mobility for the following reasons. First, it involves an asymmetry in that internal mobility can only occur when there is a change of occupational category, whereas external mobility is counted as a job change whether or not there is a change in status. [3] Second, the incidence of reported internal mobility depends crucially on the occupational classification adopted. These are often broad and not always relevant to the occupation under study. Third, this technique is unlikely to detect the frequent but small-scale changes in job duties that may not constitute job changes in themselves but, when viewed over a long period, may result in a substantial change in the nature of the tasks being undertaken.

An alternative method of measuring the nature and incidence of internal mobility is the 'self-reporting' technique. The decision as to whether a change in job duties constitutes a job change is left to the respondent. While this technique overcomes many of the problems inherent in the use of occupational classifications, it encounters the difficulty that worker's perceptions of what constitutes a job may vary. Furthermore, such variations may be related to the nature of the mobility process itself, that is, workers in situations of large-scale mobility are likely to have a broader conception of what constitutes a job than those in situations of limited mobility. This problem is, however, more severe for international comparisons involving very different cultures and types of work, but in the present context is unlikely to create serious problems. [4]

By recording various characteristics of work at the beginning and end of

3. In a study of intra-firm job changing in Detroit and Yokohama, Cole (1979, 36) found that over one-quarter of the changes reported by respondents were within conventional census occupation categories.
4. This type of problem is discussed by Cole (1979), who considered the different perceptions of United States and Japanese workers.

each job, a measure of 'within-job' mobility can be obtained. This may be regarded as reflecting the extent of the gradual or osmotic mobility mentioned earlier. Within-job mobility has been the subject of very little analysis, mainly because it only becomes evident after some time, unlike the discrete inter-firm and intra-firm changes, and is, therefore, difficult to measure without the kind of survey used here.

The surveys of professional scientists

The design of the questionnaires for the surveys of professional scientists was explicitly based on the need to measure the types of job mobility outlined above. Particular attention was paid to the measurement of intra-firm and within-job mobility. In consequence, the results can be used to assess the applicability of the internal labour market approach to the analysis of the generation of earnings differences.

The first Australian survey was sent to 1957 members of the Royal Australian Chemical Institute (RACI) in June 1985. There were 1284 replies, of which 1195 were usable, yielding an effective response rate of 61 per cent. The second Australian survey was sent to 1000 members of the Australian Institute of Physics (AIP) in July 1985. There were 621 usable replies, giving an effective response rate of 62 per cent. The British survey was sent to 6000 members of the Royal Society of Chemistry (RSC) in September 1985 and yielded an effective response rate of 50 per cent. These response rates can be considered high in view of the length and complexity of the questionnaires, particularly the British questionnaire, which contained a complex scale for measuring responsibility. The slightly higher response rate for the Australian surveys mainly reflects the use of a follow-up letter which was sent to all members of the survey populations one month after the questionnaire was distributed. Complete anonymity was maintained at all time.[5] It is important to stress that the present paper uses only the data for males.

The purpose of the surveys was to obtain information about the job mobility of individuals from the beginning of the first job to the time of the survey. This required respondents to list a wide variety of details about conditions at the beginning and end of each job held during their working lives, including income, type of work undertaken, level of responsibility held and the relevant dates. Respondents were also asked to give a reason for each job change and to think of the term 'job' broadly, defining posts with different titles within the same organization as separate jobs. This can be regarded as a variant of the self-reporting technique. Intra-firm and inter-firm mobility could be distinguished by reference to the reason given for each change, which could also be used to differentiate between voluntary and involuntary changes and transfers and promotions within the same firm. Within-job mobility could

---

5. Some replies were rejected for present purposes because the respondents were students, retired, not in the labour market or unemployed at the time of the survey, or had submitted incomplete forms. Not all questionnaires were complete, and consequently the numbers used in some of the analyses are less than the basic response rates suggest. In many analyses the unit of analysis is the job or job change, rather than the individual. The appropriate numbers are reported in each case.

be measured by comparing the level of responsibility held and the type of work undertaken at the beginning and end of each job.

Analysis of the relationship between mobility and earnings using the internal labour market approach requires the collection of information over a long time span. This could be based on an analysis that surveyed the same individuals at different times in their working lives. However, this poses so many problems that it is rarely used and most studies, including the three surveys analysed here, use the retrospective technique in which respondents are asked to recall details about their working lives. Other examples of retrospective surveys include Nowak and Crockett (1983) and Osterman (1984). The use of the retrospective technique may have imparted some inaccuracy into the analysis because of faulty recall and *ex post* rationalizations. However, the characteristics of the respondents and their familiarity with the format used suggest that the responses are quite accurate. [6]

Mobility and earnings in the short term

The bulk of the literature on mobility and earnings has concentrated on the immediate impact of inter-firm job changing on earnings. This research has generally found that most inter-firm job changes yield significant increases in earnings: voluntary moves are more likely to yield earnings increases than involuntary inter-firm moves, and voluntary mobility is most likely to be associated with an earnings increase if the new job is obtained before quitting the old job (see, for example, Borjas 1981). Very little work has been undertaken on either intra-firm job mobility or on the effects of mobility on job status and the duties undertaken. Such information is, however, essential if a comprehensive picture of the mobility process is to be obtained, particularly if an assessment is to be made of the utility of the internal labour market approach to mobility and earnings.

The aim of this section is to examine the relationship between mobility and earnings in the short term. The section begins with an examination of the effects of each type of job change on earnings. The relationships between the main types of mobility (voluntary and involuntary inter-firm changes, internal and within job), change in responsibility level and earnings change are then examined. This is followed by an analysis of the link between mobility, managerial/administrative work and earnings change.

Earnings and type of mobility

The relationship between the type of job change and the median percentage change in earnings is shown in table 1. It indicates that a substantial proportion of the job changes reported were of the internal variety. Both the Australian and British chemists reported that approximately 40 per cent of all job changes were internal and the Australian physicists reported a figure of approximately 30 per cent. These figures offer strong support for the internal labour market

---

6. In addition, comparisons made with cross-sectional data collected by the relevant professional institutes showed (where appropriate) that the mix of respondents was quite representative of the population.

approach and indicate that analyses of job turnover neglect a great deal of the mobility process. The slightly lower figure for the physicists possibly reflects the higher proportion of academics among the Australian Institute of Physicists' membership. Previous research has shown that the market for academics exhibits less internal mobility than those for other workers.

Table 1 Percentage earnings change by type of job change

Type of change	British chemists		Australian chemists		Australian physicists	
	No.	Median increase	No.	Median increase	No.	Median increase
Voluntary						
(a) Immediate salary improvement	454	25.0	144	24.7	37	26.3
(b) Long-term prospects in fresh employment	911	14.3	757	10.0	381	16.3
(c) Frustration in present employment	470	10.0	318	7.3	93	10.0
Involuntary Redundancy, dismissal or closure	328	4.0	208	6.3	82	4.4
Within-organization Transfer within organization	514	0	358	0	103	0
Promotion within organization	1065	11.1	674	5.8	190	9.0
Other	335	n.a.	117	n.a.	64	n.a.

Table 1 also reveals that voluntary job changes yield, on average, the largest increases in earnings. Not surprisingly, this is particularly strong when a voluntary job change is primarily motivated by the desire to obtain an immediate improvement in salary. Both internal promotions and involuntary moves yield positive average earnings increases but the magnitude of the median increase is less than for voluntary changes. For each sample, internal transfers result in a zero median income change.

Changes associated with promotion and demotion

The questionnaires requested information on the level of responsibility at the beginning and the end of each job. Combining this with information about the reason for the job change, it was possible to examine the degree to which each of the types of job mobility outlined above was associated with changes in levels of responsibility. Changes in responsibility within jobs could also be observed, although the precise path taken to a new level of responsibility within a job is not known.

The British and Australian surveys used different classifications for responsibility level, mainly reflecting the differing classifications used by the respective professional institutes in their remuneration surveys. Since 1978 the British Royal Society of Chemistry has used a detailed assessment schedule to obtain a responsibility 'score' for each of its members. It attempts to assess the level of autonomy in four areas of work. The four areas are 'job duties', 'technical decisions and recommendations', 'supervision exercised' and 'supervision received'. Within each of these headings are five separate statements describing the extent of autonomy; these are given a score from one to five. Each individual has to work out his or her appropriate score for each aspect of work and then add the four separate scores. The full range of possible scores thus runs from four to twenty; the lower the score, the lower the level of responsibility.[7]

The Australian surveys used a responsibility classification based on that used by the Royal Australian Chemical Institute. It involves a five-part classification based on the tasks undertaken by the individual, with emphasis on the extent of supervision given and received. The survey of physicists added an extra sentence to the statement of job duties which linked the responsibility scales to the usual academic scales. For present purposes it was only necessary to distinguish job changes that involved no change, or an upward or downward movement in responsibility change. The Australian surveys, using just five groups, are likely to record relatively fewer changes of responsibility than the British survey.

The principal objective of the analysis was to determine whether the internal mobility processes emphasized by the internal labour market theorists were predominant in producing changes in responsibility level. A decomposition based on the direction of change in responsibility, summarized in table 2, revealed that the most frequent improvements in responsibility were made within jobs. It can be seen that 48 per cent of the increases in responsibility level reported by British and Australian chemists and 50 per cent of those reported by Australian physicists occurred within the confines of the same job. Furthermore, very few of the reported downward changes in responsibility occurred within the same job. The figures were 3 per cent for both British and Australian chemists and 2 per cent for Australian physicists. Thus within-job mobility can be characterized as predominantly positive and rarely negative.

Table 2 Direction of change in responsibility

Type of movement	British chemists			Australian chemists			Australian physicists		
	Down	No change	Up	Down	No change	Up	Down	No change	Up
Within-job	24	4645	3010	11	3118	966	2	1385	382
Intra-firm	175	878	1467	56	687	553	21	229	164
Inter-firm (voluntary)	364	736	1257	216	888	429	73	472	198
Inter-firm (involuntary)	209	242	394	69	221	57	16	129	23

7. For further discussion of the properties of the Royal Society of Chemistry's responsibility scale see Creedy (1987).

Intra-firm job changing was also a major contributor to upward change in responsibility level. In the British survey and the Australian chemists' survey, it was the second most important form of upward change. Intra-firm mobility was also predominantly positive, and the ratio of upward changes in level to downward changes was 8.4 for the British chemists, 9.9 for the Australian chemists and 7.8 for the Australian physicists.

Voluntary inter-firm mobility was also a major contributor to upward change in responsibility level and a predominantly positive force in this respect. However, such changes were less likely to be positive than either of the two forms of internal mobility. The ratio of upward to downward changes were 3.5 for British chemists, 2.0 for Australian chemists and 2.7 for Australian physicists. Furthermore, in all surveys but that for Australian physicists, voluntary inter-firm mobility was less important for upward mobility than either of the two internal forms.

Involuntary inter-firm mobility was the least likely form of mobility to yield an increase in responsibility. Only 6 per cent of the improvements reported by British chemists, 3 per cent of those reported by Australian chemists and 3 per cent of those reported by Australian physicists came from involuntary inter-firm mobility. Furthermore, a large proportion of such moves resulted in a fall in responsibility. The ratio of upward to downward changes was 1.9 for British chemists, 0.6 for Australian chemists and 1.4 for Australian physicists.

It is instructive to compare the income changes associated with an increase in responsibility for the different types of job mobility. Internal labour market theory predicts that a change in responsibility level from a change of firm would probably yield a higher increase in earnings than an internal job change and that a within-job change would yield only a small change, if any, in earnings. These outcomes result from the process of wage fixing within internal labour markets. First, the process concentrates on internal, as opposed to external, wage relativities and thereby permits the growth of wage differentials between similar jobs in differing organizations. Second, it relates wages to the particular job undertaken rather than the person.

The relationships among the type of mobility, change in responsibility and change in earnings are shown in table 3. Since the changes made within jobs can occur over quite different time periods, the percentages in that category refer to annual average changes in earnings adjusted for price changes over the period during which the job was held. This table reveals that voluntary inter-firm moves that involved an increase in responsibility were likely to be approximately twice as remunerative in terms of the associated income change as intra-firm job changes and four to five times as remunerative as within-job changes. In the British survey, involuntary inter-firm job changes involving an increase in responsibility were, on average, as remunerative as voluntary job changes, but were less remunerative in the Australian cases. The downward changes in responsibility level were in general less likely to be remunerative in the short term and only voluntary job-changes involving a fall in responsibility showed a median increase in earnings in all three surveys. Involuntary job changes involved a zero median change in earnings in the chemists' surveys and a fall in the physicists' survey.

Table 3 Distribution of percentage earnings changes on responsibility change

Type of move	British chemists				Australian chemists				Australian physicists			
	No.	Q_L	*M*	Q_u	*No.*	Q_L	*M*	Q_u	*No.*	Q_L	*M*	Q_u
					Upward responsibility changes							
Within-job	1713	1.4	5.1	11.2	761	0.7	4.1	9.1	284	1.1	3.8	7.0
Intra-firm	920	1.7	10.7	20.0	441	0	7.1	16.7	121	3.6	8.7	20.0
Inter-firm (voluntary)	958	8.3	20.0	34.5	338	4.7	18.5	40.0	143	2.0	19.1	57.9
Inter-firm (involuntary)	293	2.6	20.0	59.1	46	-2.0	11.1	33.3	17	0	16.1	50.0
					Downward responsibility changes							
Within-job	9	-2.2	0.6	1.7	9	0	2.6	28.1	—	—	—	—
Intra-firm	114	0	0	11.1	43	0	0	5.0	14	-6.3	0	0
Inter-firm (voluntary)	295	0	10.0	25.5	172	-10.0	2.9	17.0	51	-29.8	11.1	40.9
Inter-firm (involuntary)	170	-13.0	0	12.5	57	-17.4	0	11.6	12	-21.1	-11.3	10.3

Notes: The figures for within-job changes give the annual average percentage increase in earnings, adjusted for price increases, between the beginning and end of the job. Other values give the percentage change from the end of a job to the beginning of the next job.
Q_L = lower quartile; M = median; Q_u = upper quartile percentage change.

Managerial and administrative work

An alternative perspective on the process of upward mobility is to examine the movement of the workers into managerial and administrative work. The regular remuneration surveys of the Royal Society of Chemistry, Royal Australian Chemical Institute and Australian Institute of Physics have continually shown that one of the key elements in obtaining a high income in a scientific career is the move into managerial/administrative work.[8] An important feature of these professional institutes is that people who move into management or administration during their career retain their membership. Without this feature the present surveys would have much less value.

The results of the analysis of moves into and out of management are shown in table 4. They are broadly similar to those for change of responsibility level, to which they are closely related. Moves into managerial/administration positions predominantly occurred within the same organization, and in the Australian surveys these moves were more likely to have occurred within the same job than as a result of change of job within the same organization. Movement out of management largely occurred from inter-firm job changes and it is notable that involuntary changes were more likely to involve such moves than moves into management.

The income changes associated with moves into and out of management, also shown in table 4, were on average higher for external as opposed to internal moves. The median increase in earnings resulting from a voluntary inter-firm move into management/administration was approximately twice that of a similar intra-firm move. Movements out of management/administration were not usually accompanied by earnings increases although those changing organizations voluntarily and moving out of management/administration did, on average, experience an earnings increase.

Assessment

The results of this section have indicated that from a short-term viewpoint it seems more rewarding to achieve promotion by moving between organizations than by obtaining promotions or transfers within an organization. It was also shown that the bulk of the mobility process takes place within the organization and that the osmotic or within-job type of mobility is predominant in this respect. However, internal mobility and, in particular, within-job mobility are associated with relatively low rates of increase in real earnings.

The work of Borjas (1981) on the United States National Longitudinal Study has shown that workers who exhibit low levels of inter-firm mobility earn more, on average, than workers undertaking a great deal of such mobility, despite the fact that these inter-firm changes usually result in significant improvements in earnings. Borjas explains this paradox as a reflection of differential investment in specific training by those anticipating a lengthy

---

8. Managerial and administrative work includes general management, general administration (for example as a buyer or personnel officer) and primarily managerial and administrative work in other areas such as research or development, analytical work, quality control and so on.

Table 4 Managerial and administrative work and earnings changes

Type of move	British chemists				Australian chemists				Australian physicists			
	No.	*Q_L*	*M*	*Q_u*	*No.*	*Q_L*	*M*	*Q_u*	*No.*	*Q_L*	*M*	*Q_u*
	Movement *into* management or administration											
Within-job	247	2.1	5.7	10.5	256	0.8	4.3	9.8	66	0.5	2.8	6.1
Intra-firm	288	2.7	11.6	23.1	172	0	7.1	14.3	46	3.7	7.9	17.1
Inter-firm (voluntary)	233	9.1	19.2	35.1	145	1.4	13.3	27.8	27	8.1	18.8	42.9
Inter-firm (involuntary)	59	0	11.1	33.3	14	0.7	8.6	40.0	8	0	2.8	33.9
	Movement *out* of management or administration											
Within-job	28	−1.1	2.0	7.2	12	2.3	3.6	9.8	3	—	—	—
Intra-firm	120	0	0	10.5	42	0	0	4.4	14	−6.3	0	3.3
Inter-firm (voluntary)	143	0	9.2	21.4	98	−9.1	1.9	18.2	21	7.1	33.5	78.3
Inter-firm (involuntary)	76	−10.0	0	10.0	38	−25.9	−4.0	12.5	5	−33.3	−12.5	5.6

Notes: The figures for within-job changes give the annual average percentage increase in earnings, adjusted for price increases, between the beginning and end of the job. Other values give the percentage change from the end of a job to the beginning of the next job.
Q_L = lower quartile; M = median; Q_u = upper quartile percentage change.

period in the same job. It should be noted, however, that Borjas does not attempt to substantiate his hypothesis by the measurement of investment in specific training and is consequently forced to accept that his findings are compatible with other explanations.

One of the major alternative explanations to that advanced by human capital theorists is that of internal labour markets theory. This would view the earnings advantage of the less mobile workers as reflective of greater internal mobility. It can, therefore, be expected that the most highly paid persons in a given sample will exhibit both high levels of within-job and within-organization mobility. This hypothesis can be examined by comparing the earnings reported by each respondent at the time of the survey to the mobility pattern they reported. This is the subject of the next section.

Mobility and earnings in the long term
A basic approach

The examination of the long-term effects of mobility on earnings reported here involves the use of linear regression analysis in which the dependent variable is the logarithm of annual earnings at the time of the survey. The use of earnings at the time of the survey is of course less desirable than using a longer term definition. The implication is therefore that the value of annual earnings at the time of the survey is a reasonable indicator of earnings in the long term. [9] Respondents obviously have differing degrees of experience at the time of the survey and this could be expected to influence the level of their earnings. This factor can be partly allowed for by adding experience and experience squared as independent variables, as in conventional earnings equations.

The independent variables can be divided into those concerned with processes unrelated to mobility and those relating to the mobility process itself. The former are a dummy variable taking the value of 1 if the respondents held a PhD and 0 if not; experience and experience squared (as suggested above); responsibility at the start of working life (for the British survey this variable was the responsibility score at the beginning of the first job and for the Australian surveys it was based on two dummy variables indicating whether or not respondents were in either responsibility levels 2 and 3 or 4 and 5); and a dummy variable taking the value of 1 if the respondent was in managerial/administrative work in his first job and 0 if not.

The mobility variables were based on the four types of mobility outlined earlier and whether or not the respondent had spent a period out of the labour market. The number of within-organization promotions, the number of within-organization transfers, the number of voluntary, between-organization job-changes and the number of involuntary, between-organization job-changes were included as separate independent variables. A dummy variable was also included which took the value of 1 if a move into management/administration occurred within any job. All of the surveys included a dummy variable taking

---

9. It is not really possible to use the data on annual earnings at various earlier points in the career to build up a longer term measure, as there are too many missing years.

the value of 1 if the respondent had spent a period of unemployment and 0 if he had not. The British survey had an additional dummy variable based on whether or not the respondent had spent a period out of the labour market.

The regression results

The regression results for the three surveys are given in table 5. All of the R^2s are above 0.4 and are relatively high for this type of cross-sectional analysis. Many of the coefficients are significantly different from zero, except for the mobility variables of Australian physicists. It seems, therefore, that the market for physicists differs from that for chemists. For physicists the mobility pattern seems less important for obtaining a high income than other variables such as experience and whether a respondent holds a doctorate. As suggested earlier, it is likely that this reflects the large number of academics in the physics sample relative to the predominance of persons in industry and commerce among the chemists.

Among the non-mobility variables both the possession of a doctorate and the level of responsibility held at the beginning of the first job (in the British survey) are positively related to earnings at the time of the survey. The equivalent variables for the Australian surveys are more ambiguous and less strong in their relationships.

The mobility variables all take their expected signs, with the exception of the variable for voluntary inter-firm changes in the Australian physicists' survey, although this is not significantly different from zero. Interpretation of the coefficients is made easier if it is noted that, if b is the estimated coefficient on a variable, then $100[\exp(b)-1]$ estimates the percentage increase in current earnings resulting from a unit increase in the variable. [10]

These regression results on earnings and mobility pattern offer very strong support for the internal labour market explanation. Individuals who move into management/administration within any job during their working lives are likely to earn considerably more than their counterparts who did not. For example, respondents to the British chemist survey making such a move earned 11.1 per cent more than those who did not; the equivalent figures for Australian chemists and physicists were 6.6 per cent and 8.7 per cent respectively. [11] Similarly, moves within the same organization were positively linked to earnings at the time of survey. Each promotion within the same firm yielded a 7 per cent increase in earnings for British chemists and each internal transfer yielded 4.2 per cent. The benefits from such internal mobility were less for Australian physicists and chemists but were still substantial.

In all of the surveys, each voluntary inter-firm job-change was less remunerative than either of the intra-firm types of job change. Thus the higher

10. It should be noted that in small samples the expression given for the percentage effect is a biased estimator, but the small sample adjustment has no noticeable effect in the present context. For further discussion and references see Derrick (1984).

11. Each regression coefficient shows, of course, the partial effect of a change in the relevant variable, with other variables held constant. The results cannot therefore be directly compared with the earlier results. As usual in this type of regression, interaction terms give rise to multicollinearity problems.

Table 5 Regression analysis of current earnings on job mobility (dependent variable: logarithm of earnings in 1985)

Variable	British chemists	Australian chemists	Australian physicists
Constant	8.787	9.845	9.481
	(296.33)	(322.04)	(189.01)
Doctorate (=1 if PhD; otherwise)	0.170	0.200	0.214
	(10.76)	(7.20)	(5.13)
Experience	0.030	0.030	0.069
	(17.02)	(12.56)	(13.07)
Experience squared	− 0.00032	− 0.00031	− 0.0012
	(− 10.08)	(− 7.60)	(− 11.35)
Responsibility at start	0.024	—	—
	(8.60)		
Responsibility 2 and 3 at start	—	0.048	0.109
		(1.66)	(2.35)
Responsibility 4 and 5 at start	—	0.138	− 0.109
		(0.80)	(− 0.26)
No. of promotions within organization	0.068	0.046	0.034
	(12.84)	(5.30)	(1.81)
No. of transfers within organization	0.041	0.021	0.023
	(5.57)	(1.80)	(0.99)
No. of voluntary between-organization changes	0.034	0.009	− 0.012
	(5.83)	(1.01)	(− 0.81)
No. of involuntary between-organization changes	− 0.038	− 0.029	− 0.010
	(− 4.31)	(− 2.49)	(− 0.49)
Management in first job (=1 if man./admin.)	—	0.106	0.121
		(1.78)	(1.20)
Move to man./admin. within any job	0.105	0.064	0.083
	(6.31)	(2.61)	(1.64)
Period of unemployment	− 0.018	− 0.054	− 0.145
	(4.88)	(− 1.93)	(0.262)
Period out of labour market	− 0.058	—	—
	(− 2.85)		
R^2	0.414	0.416	0.426
N	1895	794	520

Note: 't' values are given in parentheses, immediately underneath parameter estimates.

immediate increase in earnings associated with such voluntary mobility, reported above, is offset in the long run by other factors associated with inter-firm mobility. These include, for example, a lower rate of increase of earnings in the new job, a lower possibility of future promotion or a greater possibility of involuntary mobility.

Each involuntary inter-firm job change was negatively related to earnings at the time of the survey. In the British survey each job change of this type resulted in earnings which were 3.7 per cent lower on average than would otherwise have been the case. The equivalent figures for the Australian chemists and physicists were 2.9 per cent and 1.0 per cent. It was also found that a period of unemployment at any stage in the career had a major negative impact on earnings at the time of the survey. For British chemists, earnings were 10.2 per cent lower for those indicating a period of unemployment, 5.3 per cent lower for Australian chemists and 13.5 per cent lower for Australian physicists.

These results show that movement between organizations has short-term benefits but long-term costs. They also offer strong support for the internal labour market hypothesis that the key to understanding the processes generating earnings inequality lies in the internal mobility process. While it is difficult to measure internal mobility, the effort has been shown to be worthwhile, in that it reveals important characteristics of the process of earnings generation. Rather than viewing differential earnings growth within organizations as reflecting the effects of an unobserved and unmeasured (and, for some, implausible) process of investment in specific training, the internal labour market approach concentrates on the actual mobility processes and thereby is able to show how such differences are generated. Moreover, internal labour market theory concentrates on those processes that have been seen to be of most importance in the relationship between mobility and earnings.

Conclusions

The objective of this paper has been to undertake an empirical analysis of the relationship between job mobility and earnings, using the insights of the internal labour market approach. The analysis in turn allows a partial assessment of the approach itself. This assessment was based on the analysis of three specially designed surveys which were undertaken in Australia and Britain in 1985. These surveys contained questions which allowed the measurement of both inter-firm and intra-firm mobility, including the gradual or osmotic mobility that internal labour market theorists have emphasized.

The results offer support for the internal labour market framework applied to professional scientists although certain problems encountered suggest the need for caution. It was discovered that the bulk of the mobility process (defined in terms of change of job duties) occurred within the same organization and that the gradual or osmotic mobility process taking place within jobs was predominant in this respect. Furthermore, examinations of differing types of job mobility on earnings revealed that internal job changes were the key to high earnings in chemistry. These results suggest that internal labour market theory does indeed concentrate on processes which are central to the generation of observed differences in earnings.

The need for caution, however, results from the fact that the processes emphasized by internal labour market theory are extremely difficult to measure. This is particularly true of the gradual or osmotic form of mobility which proved so important in the current analysis. Furthermore, with the available information it has not been possible to devise conclusive tests that compare the human capital and internal labour market models in detail. The rigorous testing of these theories raises fundamental issues that must form the subject of future research.

Nonetheless, the empirical assessment of the internal labour market approach that forms the basis of this paper suggests that further work should be undertaken within this framework. Research adopting the internal labour market perspective requires detailed information about jobs, firms and occupations and this poses numerous definitional and measurement questions for the researchers. This will require not only a different approach to existing data but also the collection of information more suited to examine the processes emphasized by internal labour market theory.

References

Borjas, G. J. (1981), 'Job mobility and earnings over the life-cycle', *Industrial and Labor Relations Review* **34**, 365–76.
Cole, R. E. (1979), *Work, Mobility and Participation*, Berkeley, University of California Press.
Creedy, J. (1987), 'Variations in earnings and responsibility', *The Journal of the Royal Statistical Society* A **150**, 57–68.
Derrick, F. W. (1984), 'Interpretation of dummy variables in semilogarithmic equations: small sample properties', *Southern Economic Journal* **50**, 1185–8.
Doeringer, P. B. & Piore, M. J. (1971), *Internal Labor Markets and Manpower Analysis*, Lexington, Heath.
Hunter, L. C. & Reid, G. L. (1968), *Urban Worker Mobility*, Paris, Organisation for Economic Co-operation and Development.
Mincer, J. (1976), 'Progress in Human Capital Analyses of the Distribution of Earnings' in A. B. Atkinson (ed.), *The Personal Distribution of Income*, London, George Allen & Unwin.
Nowak, M. L. & Crockett, G. V. (1981), 'The operation of internal labour markets: three case studies', *Journal of Industrial Relations* **25**, 445–64.
Osterman, P. (ed.) (1984), *Internal Labor Markets*, London, MIT Press.
Thurow, L. C. (1983), *Dangerous Currents: The State of Economics*, Oxford, Oxford University Press.
White, H. (1970), *Chains of Opportunity: Systems Models of Mobility in Organisations*, Cambridge, Mass, Harvard University Press.

[13]

Opening the Black Box: Economic Analyses of Internal Labour Markets

JOHN CREEDY AND KEITH WHITFIELD*

Recent years have seen the increasing interest of economists in the behaviour of firms in relation to their employees. The result is a reduction in the dichotomy of subject matter between industrial relations and labour economics. Despite this, substantial differences still exist, particularly between the approach of neoclassical economists and those (both economists and others) working outside this tradition. These differences are both theoretical and methodological and suggest a need for researchers examining the internal labour market to build bridges in their efforts to understand how firms price and allocate their labour. It is also suggested that a greater emphasis on the testing of competing hypotheses would be useful in this respect.

1. Introduction

The economic analysis of labour has undergone a significant transition in recent years. Of particular note has been the work concerning the most appropriate way to examine the behaviour of firms in relation to their employees. A major consequence of this transition is that the strong dichotomy between industrial relations and labour economics, where the latter merely regarded the employing organization as a 'black box' and concentrated on larger aggregates, has been eradicated. The breakdown of this dichotomy has been largely associated with work under the general title of the analysis of 'internal labour markets'.[1] A central tenet of this work is that the pricing and allocation of labour are determined by forces in addition to those associated with supply and demand in external labour markets. These pressures are seen to arise from a variety of sources, some of which are specific to the employing organization, while others are specific to the occupation of the workers concerned. Firms and other labour market organizations are seen not as passive transmitters of supply and demand conditions but also as active strategists in labour markets. This suggests that much labour market behaviour

---

* Department of Economics, University of Melbourne, Parkville, Vic. 3052, and Economics Section, Cardiff Business School, Aberconway Building, Colum Drive, Cardiff, CF1 3EU, United Kingdom. The authors would like to thank the anonymous referees of the *JIR* for comments on an earlier draft of this paper.
1. The formal introduction of the concept into the literature can be traced to Doeringer and Piore (1971). However, this work draws on a large literature on the pricing and allocation of labour within employing organizations. Some researchers (for example, Marsden, 1986, p. 143) have criticized the use of the term on the grounds that the activities analyzed are not market relations, whereas others use a much broader notion of what constitutes a market as any setting in which exchange takes place.

455

occurs independently of the external labour market and also that the latter is heavily influenced by internal markets.

Despite the reduction in the dichotomy between industrial relations and labour economics, substantial differences still exist. Moreover, within the labour economics domain there are substantial differences of opinion as to the most appropriate way to analyze the internal labour market. Such differences broadly correspond to those between researchers adopting a neoclassical approach to theory and methodology and those employing approaches within the institutional and radical traditions. Whereas neo-classicism has been predominant in the recent economic analysis of internal labour markets, the alternative approaches have been more important in industrial relations.

This paper has four main objectives. First, section 2 briefly surveys economic analyses of the internal labour market. Secondly, section 3 evaluates efforts by economists to develop theoretical structures incorporating the internal labour market. Section 4 examines the problems encountered in undertaking empirical analyses of the internal labour market. Finally, section 5 discusses implications for future research on the internal workings of the employing organization.

Major themes in internal labour market research

The internal labour market concept developed from empirical analyses of labour markets undertaken predominantly by American institutional labour economists soon after the Second World War. [2] This research paid little heed to theoretical development and, at most, efforts were made to construct middle-level theories involving the reduction of phenomena to broad analytical constructs but not to the behaviour of individuals. A major theme was the large distance between orthodox economic theory and reality.

During the late 1970s and the 1980s the focus of economic research on internal labour markets changed and theoretical issues were brought to the fore. A major contribution was the attempt to explain some of the features outlined by the institutionalists in terms that were compatible with orthodox economic principles. These analyses nevertheless acknowledged the functional role of a wide range of labour market institutions; that is, if an institution has lasted a long time, it is seen to have a role in the functioning of the labour market, otherwise competitive processes would have eliminated it. This approach has been variously termed the 'new institutional labour economics' and the 'new efficiency-oriented institutional labour economics'. Major contributions are the theory of idiosyncratic exchange, efficiency wage models, specific human capital theories, job market signalling theories and implicit contract theories. A key theme in the internal labour market literature concerns the degree to which the existence of and variations in internal labour markets can be explained by such theories.

Attempts have also been made to develop theories of the internal labour market using principles drawn from institutional and radical economics, using

2. For overview of this literature see McNulty (1980), Strauss and Feuille (1981), Kerr (1954).

a different set of behavioural assumptions from those of neoclassical theory. This has increasingly become identified with the labour market segmentation literature. Of particular note has been research concerned with building bridges between economic and sociological research on the internal labour market (see, for example, Farkas & England, 1988).

Empirical research within the internal labour market tradition has offered evidence that the majority of labour markets differ substantially from the wage competition model and are more complex than even the early institutionalists suggested. It has been suggested that theories have been developed on the basis of, at best, crude stylized facts and, at worst, misconceptions of the real world. [3] Empirical work has not, however, been much directed towards testing between the various theories.

2. The nature of internal labour markets

There has been considerable research on the forms which internal labour markets take. This has generally involved an attempt to make operational Doeringer and Piore's definition of an internal labour market as 'an administrative unit, such as manufacturing plant, within which the pricing and allocation of labour is governed by a set of administrative rules' (1971, pp. 1–2).

Early internal labour market research distinguished between two types of internal market. The first was based on organizations and the second on occupations. However, the predominant approach in more recent research is to focus on internal labour markets within employing organizations and to view occupational characteristics as constraints within which the firm shapes its internal labour market. Such occupational forces rank alongside those resulting from government legislation, trade union and product market pressures.

Research has also tended to focus on three main quantitative dimensions of internal markets. These are: (i) the level of labour turnover; (ii) the degree to which entry into organizations is restricted to lower level positions and the extent to which and the reasons why higher level positions are filled by internal promotion; and (iii) the factors that determine changes in wages within internal labour markets. On the basis of these dimensions, a series of internal labour market typologies has been constructed, becoming more complicated as information, particularly pertaining to differing countries, has accumulated.

There is considerable evidence that *employment stability* characterizes the majority of labour markets. [4] Case study analyses of firms, surveys of workers and aggregate data all suggest that low turnover rates are the norm rather than the exception not only in countries such as Japan, in which long-term employment guarantees are formally recognized, but also in countries such

---

3. Thus Jacoby (1990, p. 338) has stated that, 'Too often New-Institutional Labour Economics (and other) economists rush into print theories based on partial or incorrect factual knowledge; only later do the empiricists come to clean up the mess.'
4. Researchers have typically used a turnover rate of 10 per cent per annum or less as indicative of the presence of internal labour markets, although little justification has been offered for such a figure (Alexander, 1974).

as Australia and the United States, where such guarantees have been less prevalent. [5]

Case studies of individual organizations have indicated that the *restriction of entry to lower-level job classifications* is a common, though by no means universal, practice and that most upper level positions are filled by internal promotion rather than external recruitment. [6] This is commonly justified by personnel managers as an essential element in the development and maintenance of morale and because of its positive screening characteristics (Mace, 1979). There is also evidence of job clusters (jobs that are defined as part of common job ladders), which structure the internal mobility pattern within firms. Movement between clusters is generally relatively easy at the entry position but less so at higher levels, although the degree of upper-level openness seems to vary among occupations (Osterman, 1984); this depends largely on the technical nature of the skills used.

A key finding is that *wages are a highly constrained adjustment mechanism* and that some firms curtail production rather than adjust wages in response to a labour shortage (Mace, 1979). One of the main reasons given by employers for such behaviour is the cost of using wage adjustment, given that wages need to be increased for workers other than those in short supply (Thomas & Deaton, 1977). The principal adjustment mechanisms used are changes in recruitment and promotion rates, and variations in hours worked. In extreme cases firms may respond to labour market shortages by reorganizing their internal training and promotion arrangements (Blandy & Richardson, 1982). Moreover, it has been found that firms are capable of continuing for substantial periods with internal and external labour market conditions out of line and, in particular, wages that are higher than are needed to recruit a given workforce (Osterman, 1987; Brown, 1989).

The attachment of wages to jobs has been shown to be a common practice and there is substantial evidence that many internal wage structures are rigid. [7] Firms obtain flexibility of wages between workers not so much by varying the wage structure as by moving workers between jobs within a rigid wage structure (Osterman, 1984; Nowak & Crockett, 1983). Even in the presence of substantial shortages, firms seem to be unwilling to widen skill differentials (George & Shorey, 1985).

Types of labour market

Four different *types of labour market* have been identified (Kerr, 1954; Osterman, 1987). The first, the unstructured or secondary market, exhibits

5. See, for example, for the United States, Hall (1980, 1982); for Australia, Foster and Gregory (1983) and Nowak and Crockett (1983); for the United Kingdom, Main (1982), Mace (1979), Whitfield (1981).
6. Mace (1979) found that the average age of entry into nine of the United Kingdom engineering firms he surveyed was twenty-five or below and for the other three it was below thirty. Furthermore, in eleven firms 90 per cent of higher-level positions were filled by internal candidates. Similar findings were made by Nowak and Crockett (1983) in Australia and Osterman (1984) in the United States.
7. Mace (1979, p. 57) found that, 'in setting salaries within firms, attention was primarily directed to fitting the hierarchy of salaries to the hierarchy of jobs'.

high turnover and minimal employment structure. The second, the industrial or manorial market, exhibits low movement between firms, the restriction of recruitment to lower-level positions, promotion by seniority, and the attachment of wages to jobs. The third is the salaried market, which has low turnover but more flexibility in internal deployment than the industrial market and more emphasis on individual characteristics in wage determination. The fourth type, the craft or guild market, exhibits considerable turnover between firms, a high level of promotion by movement between firms and occupation-specific pay structures. Such markets are typically associated with the existence of professional or trade qualifications.

The nature of the labour market is seen to depend predominantly on decisions made by employing organizations, within the constraints set by technology, the available workforce and the role played by unions, professional associations and governments in regulating the labour market. Of particular importance is the interplay between employers, who generally favour 'vertical' structures within employing organizations, and professional associations and craft unions who generally favour 'horizontal' structures between employing organizations. Where associations or unions are able to impose entry qualifications for the undertaking of specific jobs, the development of vertical structures is frequently attenuated and replaced by more horizontal structures (Marsden, 1990; George & Shorey, 1985).

A major element in the recent literature is the recognition that internal labour markets are not synonymous with firms. There is evidence that a number of different internal labour markets can operate within the same firm. Such differences are closely related to occupational factors and seem to reflect the breadth of skills inherent in specific jobs (rather than the nature of the skill) and the nature of the work undertaken. Thus Osterman (1984) found that among white-collar occupations a key variable in promoting internal recruitment within an internal labour market was the degree of initiative shown by individuals, and the use of merit considerations in promotion and wage determination was associated with the importance of the occupation concerned for the firm's success.

Much of the early literature suggested that internal labour markets were only to be found in large firms, but recent research has indicated that many small firms exhibit the key characteristics of the internal labour market. For example, Siebert and Addison (1991) show that many small plants exhibit long tenure, wide coverage by a pension scheme and low numbers of part-timers: they suggest that this indicates the existence of an internal labour market.

It has also been suggested that there are substantial *international variations* in internal labour markets and that such differences reflect the history and culture of the country concerned. In particular, countries vary in the degree to which labour markets are organized along vertical and horizontal lines,[8] depending on the systems of vocational education and training that are

---

8. For example, Osterman (1987) found that United States and United Kingdom labour markets exhibited a much greater tendency to be organized along horizontal lines than Japanese and German markets. Marsden (1990) found that British and German markets have more horizontal internal labour markets than French and Italian markets.

prevalent in each country. The horizontal form is most important where there are well-developed apprenticeship systems and where occupational organizations have been able to impose and enforce job demarcation systems. In such countries there is a tension between employer efforts to develop vertical systems of training based on a narrow range of skills and union or profession pressure to develop horizontal systems based on broad skills, the qualifications for which are used to define the entry requirements for particular jobs.

3. The internal labour market and theory

Early institutional analysis of the internal labour market favoured the development of middle-level theory using methods and concepts from a wide range of disciplines and an approach that emphasized the search for empirical regularities or patterns, based on extensive observation. Such an approach is still followed by many internal labour market researchers but is by no means the dominant approach. The more prevalent approach has been generally termed the 'new institutional labour economics' and essentially involves the application of neoclassical methods and principles to explain key features of the internal labour market. It is more deductive than the institutional approach and much less prone to using multidisciplinary concepts. Such an approach contrasts not only with that of the institutional labour economists but also with that of the more orthodox neoclassical approach, which views the internal labour market as a market imperfection resulting from influences such as unions or wage-fixing bodies.

New institutional hypotheses

The 'new institutional' literature displays an unwillingness to give up some form of the marginal productivity theory, combined with the use of models that imply efficient organizational structures. Its focus is mainly on labour allocation rather than utilization. There is also an unwillingness to take seriously concepts such as power and atmosphere, which have been of concern to sociologists; indeed, at times there is a strong hostility to the use of these concepts.

   New institutional economists have typically concentrated on a small number of the characteristics, such as wage rigidity, low turnover, internal promotion and the use of seniority in promotion, which distinguish the internal labour market from the wage competition model. In that model, wages adjust freely to reflect supply and demand pressures in the external labour market and employers strive to employ the least costly combination of factors of production. Moreover, within the new institutional literature, the internal labour market has been reduced to a number of parts, which are analyzed in isolation. This contrasts with the more holistic approaches adopted by those outside the neoclassical tradition.

   The most comprehensive attempt to explain the internal labour market in neoclassical terms is Williamson's (1975) theory of idiosyncratic exchange, which builds on transaction cost theory. More partial approaches are those concerned with market signalling, self-selection, principal/agent analyses, skill specificity, efficiency wages and implicit contracts. These theories, despite many differences, exhibit some common themes, particularly attempts by employers to handle uncertainty.

The theory of idiosyncratic exchange conceives of the internal labour market as an institution that arises, where there is incomplete information, because of the need to respond to two main factors. Individuals have limited information processing capabilities, making it impossible to construct complex contracts required to cover an uncertain future. Workers acquire a monopoly of knowledge about their jobs, so they have an incentive to conceal information and use it strategically to bargain over adaptations to their work. The internal labour market limits the ability to exploit this type of knowledge.

The attachment of wages to jobs rather than individuals is said to allow adaptations to job duties without a great deal of haggling. The use of low ports of entry and internal promotion is seen to provide an efficient screening, as well as an incentive device, as workers have a long-term interest in the success of the organization. Williamson (1975, p. 78) suggests that the result of such arrangements is a closer correspondence between wages and marginal productivity for higher-level jobs.

A major criticism of this analysis has been that it involves a bias against workers by implying that opportunism emanates solely from them and not from employers (Willman, 1983). It has also been criticized for failing to embed the internal labour market within the social system in which it operates (Granovetter, 1988). Furthermore, the existence of internal labour markets seems not to be closely related to task idiosyncrasy, as jobs with similar levels of idiosyncrasy have different employment structures (Jacoby, 1988). Finally, it is questionable whether marginal productivity has much meaning in a setting in which team accommodations are important and productivity is endogenous to the form of the employment relation.

The *market signalling approach* to the internal labour market also takes as its starting point imperfect and asymmetric information. Where a seller has more information about quality than potential buyers there is a need for signals. For such signals to be useful it must be unprofitable for low-quality sellers to imitate the signals of higher quality sellers. Signalling in the labour market often involves the self-selection of workers to firms according to their propensity to quit (Salop & Salop, 1976). If firms have a rising earnings profile, only those with low propensities to quit would wish to join, so that where firms have differential turnover costs this type of self-selection provides a better matching of workers to firms.

A related theme emerges in the *principal/agent* literature, which has been concerned with the nature of the employment contract where the principal (employer) has difficulty in monitoring the performance of the agent (employee). Payment on the basis of performance is not possible, and alternative incentive schemes must be devised. Lazear and Moore (1984) suggested that a rising age–earnings profile achieves this objective, and Malcolmson (1984) has developed a two-period contracting system in which principals offer contracts whereby a specified proportion of agents will be paid a higher wage in the second period. Such 'promotion' is based on a ranking of individuals according to the principal's assessment of performance in the first period, thereby providing an incentive for agents to work hard in the first period. However, the explicit introduction of competition into the analysis seems at odds with evidence that internal labour markets often develop because of attempts to attenuate the negative effects of competition.

A more radical departure can be found in the *efficiency wage* literature, which suggests that firms use high wages to economize on supervision costs; see Akerlof and Yellen (1986). The effectiveness of supervision is seen to depend on the cost of dismissal to the worker. Hence, the higher the wage is, the more costly is dismissal and the lower is the level of shirking. Thus profit-maximizing firms will set wages above market clearing levels if they believe that the productivity gains from increased work effort are greater than the additional wage cost incurred. In many respects efficiency wage models depart more substantially from orthodox analysis than other models in the new institutional labour economics tradition, especially in the area of preference-endogeneity, and many models in this area have a sociological flavour; see, for example, Akerlof (1982) and Solow (1980).

Implicit contract theory is often used to explain wage rigidity in the face of changing labour market conditions, and assumes that workers and employers negotiate an implicit long-term contract involving a commitment by employers not to lower average wages if there is a fall in demand for labour. The most popular explanation of such contracts is the preference of workers to accept lower average wages in return for rigid wages over the period of the contract. Firms are constrained to keep their side of the bargain by their need to protect their reputations so that they can negotiate further implicit contracts; see Azariadis (1975), Baily (1974), Gordon (1974). An alternative explanation sees rigid wages as a reflection of employer efforts to appear fair, as part of their motivation strategies (Okun, 1981). However, implicit contract theory is unable to explain why firms generally prefer internal promotion to external recruitment. Further, it is not clear that wage rigidity is in practice traded for lower wages; wage rigidity is often greatest, all other things being equal, in high-paying jobs. It is also not clear why workers respond to risk aversion by negotiating rigid wages rather than job security arrangements.

The theory of *specific human capital* is based on a distinction between general skills, which are widely useful, and specific skills, which are only useful in the firm of acquisition; see Becker (1964). Firms are willing to bear the costs of specific training but not general training and, having provided specific training, they have an incentive to reduce turnover. It is suggested that this explains features of internal labour markets such as low turnover and promotion by seniority. However, Thurow (1983, p. 175) has argued that 'Human capital theory . . . cannot account for the fact that many of the on-the-job training markets where one is supposed to bid for opportunities to acquire informal training don't seem to exist. Employers usually allocate such opportunities not on a willingness to work for less than one's free market wage, but on seniority or merit for having performed well in a job previously held.' Furthermore, empirical measures of specific human capital have not been developed and this has prevented discrimination between human capital and other hypotheses about low turnover and internal promotion.

Criticisms of the new institutionalism

Some of the new institutional labour economics rationales for the internal labour market are complementary, while other are competitive. In consequence, considerable research is needed to discriminate between competing hypotheses. This has been minimal and seems to reflect both a difficulty in developing empirical counterparts for many of the key new institutional labour economics concepts and the reticence of researchers in the area to engage in empirical research.

Criticisms of the approach centre on four main issues. First, the theories are said to be based on too narrow a set of behavioural assumptions, particularly concerning the motives of employers and employees (see Jacoby, 1990). Secondly, labour market interactions are not located in a particular historical or geographical context, despite evidence that internal labour market variations reflect historical and cultural specificity.[9] Thirdly, the approach has been criticized for a failure to incorporate important details of labour market institutions into models, despite evidence that such details are crucial for explaining labour market performance. Fourthly, new institutional labour economics has been criticized, especially by radical economists, for a failure to deal with the concept of power.

Alternative internal labour market models

Features that distinguish alternative analyses from new institutional are: an explicit attempt to model preferences as endogenous rather than exogenous; the use of assumptions that contain a high degree of descriptive realism; and the use of a wide range of concepts such as power and fairness. The result is the development of models that are more fully grounded in institutional detail at the cost of theoretical rigour.

Alternative explanations of internal labour markets have generally been associated with labour market segmentation theory. The essence of this theory is that qualitative differences can be observed between jobs, resulting from the failure of competitive processes in the labour market to equalize the net advantages of differing employments. Consequently, it is suggested that the market consists of different segments and the internal labour market is a major cause of the process that produces this segmentation. The internal labour market is therefore seen to operate according to principles that obstruct the competitive processes. Those adopting a segmentation approach can be divided into those who seek to extend neoclassical theory to include a variety of institutional factors and those who have attempted to develop a new paradigm (McNabb & Ryan, 1990). The former group has much in common with the new institutionalists and the latter have generally adopted concepts from Marxian economics.

The focus of early segmentation research was upon the dual hypothesis that divided the market into a primary segment, composed of 'good' jobs,

---

9. Thus Granovetter (1988) has complained of the failure to consider the 'embeddedness' of human behaviour by orthodox labour economists and Jacoby has criticized the 'synchronicity' of much new institutional labour economics theorizing.

which have high wages, secure employment and career potential, and a secondary segment, composed of 'bad' jobs. By contrast, more recent research has concentrated on the processes causing distinct segments to develop in labour markets and has tended to downplay the strict dualist approach.

The major difference between neoclassical and segmentation theorists lies in the emphasis of the former on the supply side of the labour market and that of the latter on the demand side. Attention is paid to the characteristics of jobs rather than individuals and, moreover, the process of job-creation is seen as analytically prior to job filling (Peck, 1989). The failure of the competitive pressures to eradicate qualitative differences between jobs results in the rationing of 'good' jobs according to rules laid down by employers. Consequently, these rules are the focus of segmentation analysis.

Thurow's *job competition model* departs from the wage competitive model in its postulate that employers constrain wage and employment competition in order to facilitate on-the-job training. It is suggested that employees would otherwise have a disincentive to transmit their knowledge to trainees for fear that it would increase competition for their jobs. Thurow also suggests that wage determination is heavily influenced by sociological factors, but is less dismissive than other non-neoclassical economists of the principles of wage competition. First, he accepts the notion of competition in the process of labour allocation, although for entry jobs rather than for wages. Secondly, he suggests that sectors with low levels of on-the-job training operate in a manner similar to wage competition.

Thurow's model has been used extensively in empirical work (see, for example, Raffe (1988), Shelly (1988), Whitfield & Bourlakis (1991), and Hoskyns, Sang & Ashton (1989)), but has not had much impact on the theoretical debate on internal labour markets. The new institutional research has suggested that the apparent contradictions Thurow outlines can be explained within neoclassical theory, and it has been questioned whether the transmission of on-the-job training is the sole or even principal cause of the suppression of wage competition. Thurow's model therefore sits uneasily between neoclassical and non-neoclassical analyses of the labour market.

Doeringer and Piore (1971) were among the earliest writers to develop a dualist approach. Their work made an explicit link between the primary segment and the internal labour market. They suggested that internal labour markets develop where workers acquire firm-specific skills, thereby encouraging employers to seek to retain their services. Where these employers operate in stable product markets, they are able to offer employment stability and develop internal labour markets. The secondary sector is composed of firms that are unwilling or unable to develop internal labour markets.

Doeringer and Piore argued that workers are recruited to internal labour markets on the basis of their potential stability. Members of demographic groups with high turnover records are less likely to be employed than those with lower turnover. Furthermore, they suggested that a feedback mechanism operates in which those initially excluded from the primary jobs acquire the traits of high-turnover individuals, thereby further reducing their chances of primary sector employment. Such a process intensifies the primary/secondary division. Doeringer and Piore suggested that, in the short run, the labour market would operate very differently from the neoclassical competitive model, but in the long run the forces of competition would reassert themselves. They stated that 'many of the rigidities which impede market forces in the short run are eventually overcome, and there is probably a tendency to adjust, in time, in a direction consistent with the predictions of competitive theory' (Doeringer & Piore, 1971, p. 7).

Radical segmentationists have been highly critical of such an attempt to forge a bridge between neoclassical theory and dualism, and are sceptical of Doeringer and Piore's focus on the technological factors for the development of the internal labour market. Reich, Gordon and Edwards (1973) regarded the internal labour market as resulting from a strategy by employers to divide and rule their workforces. They attempt to forestall the development of class consciousness resulting from the homogenization of labour. This segmentation process focuses on existing differences between workers, especially gender and race.

Much recent work on segmentation has developed within the radical approach, and has often been allied to work based on the labour process paradigm (see, for example, Bray & Littler, 1988). A number of themes have emerged from this literature. First, there has been a tendency to move away from a dualist formulation towards those which suggest that dualism is simply a heuristic device (McNabb & Ryan, 1990). Second, the mono-causal approaches of early authors have been superseded by multi-causal theories (Peck, 1989). Third, much more emphasis has been placed on the supply side of the labour market. Fourth, the conditions that produce internalization of labour market activity are seen as permissive rather than deterministic (McNabb & Ryan, 1990).

Criticisms of alternative approaches

A major question remains as to whether the alternative models represent genuine alternatives to the new institutional labour economics. Those attempting to develop alternative models have not been able to develop a comprehensive theoretical framework. The result has been a growing tendency for labour economists to use the empirical work of the alternative theorists as a starting point for theoretical analyses aimed at making neoclassical theory more realistic. The role of those critical of neoclassical theory has thus become one of producing fresh 'stylized' facts for the new institutional theorists. Moreover, many researchers critical of neoclassical analyses have moved into other related disciplines such as industrial sociology and industrial relations, resulting in the dominance within economics of neoclassical theory (McNulty, 1980).

A major problem is that it has proved impossible to develop a decisive test between the neoclassical and alternative approaches. Those tests that have been conducted have generally questioned simplistic versions of both approaches, while suggesting that both are supported to some degree (McNabb & Ryan, 1990). This issue has been further complicated by the fact that neoclassical researchers have increasingly accepted dualism as a stylized fact and have explained it in terms compatible with neoclassical principles (see, for example, Dickens & Lang, 1988).

4. The internal labour market and empirical analysis

The large amount of empirical work on internal labour markets has focused on taxonomy and general description and has rarely gone beyond the classification stage. For example, there has been little work attempting either to discriminate between competing explanations of the internal labour market or to use the insights of internal labour market theory to develop new empirical approaches. Part of the problem lies in the nature of the underlying theoretical debate, which has developed concepts with few empirical counterparts and hypotheses, which are inherently difficult to test. The corollary of such a position is that empirical research guided by a given theoretical perspective is unable to show that the results develop unambiguously from that theoretical perspective rather than any one of a number of others.

A problem is that the data normally used by economists are not very useful for the analysis of as complex and micro-level a concept as the internal labour market. The internal labour market is a complex phenomenon that cannot be reduced readily to a small number of measures. Second, many of its principal dimensions are longitudinal in nature and cannot be analyzed using cross-sectional data. Third, many internal labour market insights relate to institutional details that are not readily identifiable. Data that can cater for these problems are extremely rare.

Empirical research on the internal labour market has used three main types of data. The first is highly *aggregative data*. This can, however, offer at most a broad description of the distribution of internal labour markets across industries, occupations or regions. Studies using such data have a tendency to focus on one element of the internal labour market, typically the low turnover rate, and use it as a classification device (see, for example, Alexander, 1974). By their nature, such classifications are arbitrary and concentrate on one or a small number of elements to the exclusion of others such as internal promotion, the use of non-wage adjustment mechanisms or the emphasis on internal considerations in wage determination.

Second, the *case study approach* has been sometimes employed in internal labour market research. It can provide detail and orders of magnitude for phenomena that cannot be isolated in aggregative data, although the results do not necessarily have general applicability. Case study research on internal labour markets has concentrated on examining whether employing organizations exhibit the characteristics ascribed to them in basic internal labour market theory. The standard technique used has been to conduct a series of interviews of personnel managers and supplement this with information obtained from company records and/or employee questionnaires; see Mace (1979) and Nowak and Crockett (1983).

Third, the *work history approach* has been used by internal labour market researchers. It examines the behaviour of workers and suggests whether it is consistent with the existence of internal labour markets. It is particularly useful if it obtains information about changes in phenomena such as job duties, remuneration and location during a continuous period with the same employing organization. However, such data are difficult to obtain. First, accurate, yet widely applicable, classifications need to be developed for comparing jobs in different employing organizations and occupations. Second, information must be collected relating to a long period, so that retrospective work history surveys are usually involved; these need to be carefully designed and conducted. Third, many of the key concepts of internal labour market theory on which work histories focus are extremely difficult to measure. A prime example is the concept of osmotic job changes. There is evidence that most changes of job function are not discrete job changes but result from gradual changes in duty; none of the changes is important in itself but they accumulate into fundamental change over a period. Cole (1979) and Creedy and Whitfield (1986, 1988) attempt to measure this phenomenon.

The main area in which empirical research has progressed beyond the classification stage towards the testing of conflicting theories and the development of a distinctive internal labour market approach is the analysis of *wage equations*. At the microeconomic level, much of this work has been motivated by a reaction against the human capital approach to life-cycle earnings. The human capital hypothesis is that a major cause of variations in wages is differential investment in on-the-job training. Internal labour market theorists have questioned whether the markets required for such investment exist and have suggested alternative hypotheses based on movement within an internal job structure. However, research has shown how difficult it is both to test competing hypotheses in this area and to develop alternative analyses based on internal labour market concepts. For example, Medoff and Abraham (1981) have questioned whether wages increase in line with productivity as human capital theory suggests, while Creedy and Whitfield (1986, 1988) have raised doubts about the hypothesized link between skill specificity and high earnings. However, both sets of authors find it difficult to propose tests that would unambiguously support or reject the human capital hypothesis. In short, they conclude that it is sufficiently malleable to be compatible with a wide range of supporting evidence.

The analysis of wage equations at the macroeconomic level has also paid attention to internal labour market research. Research in this area has been associated with the 'insider–outsider' literature, which suggests that those within internal labour markets (the 'insiders') are not highly influenced by conditions in the external labour market in the determination of their wage levels; see, for example, Solow (1980). This has been seen as a reason for the failure of wage equations that include unemployment as an explanatory variable to predict changes in aggregate wages (Gregory, 1986). Equations replacing unemployment rates by 'internal utilization rates', such as the level of overtime hours worked, have been shown to yield a better statistical fit and have promoted the incorporation of a wide range of proxies for labour market demand in the specification of empirical wage equations (see, for example, Mitchell, 1987).

5. Implications for future research

The broadening of the focus of labour economics to cover the internal labour market raises three main questions for labour market research. These concern the degree to which internal labour market research has improved understanding of economic paradoxes, the compatibility of orthodox theory and the internal labour market, and the contribution that economic research on the internal labour market could make to research in cognate disciplines, and vice versa.

A great deal of the research outlined above was motivated by a perception that the internal labour market is pivotal in explaining some phenomena that posed problems for economic analysis. The contribution of internal labour market research to resolving such problems, however, has been limited. A wide variety of theoretical models has been developed to explain phenomena such as wage rigidity in the presence of unemployment and low levels of turnover. These explain such phenomena as being integral to labour market operation rather than as aberrations, and are therefore more satisfactory than explanations alleging market imperfection. However, they have also promoted a situation where each theorist has his or her own specific resolution of the paradox in question. Moreover, the internal labour market research has not made a major contribution to improving the level of empirical analysis. In short, internal labour market research has promised more than it has delivered in this area.

The question of whether the internal labour market is compatible with orthodox economic principles has produced a mixed response. There is no consensus on how economists can best respond to the challenge set by the internal labour market. Thus the debate initiated by the institutional labour economists in the 1950s and 1960s is still alive, despite concerted attempts to develop an all-encompassing economic theory of the internal labour market. The major change has been in the nature of the debate. It has moved from being primarily concerned with subject matter to one in which methodology has come to the fore (see Jacoby, 1990).

Four main areas of disagreement among economists can be discerned. The first concerns the exogeneity or endogeneity of preferences. While certain innovations such as efficiency wage theory have introduced a limited form of preference endogeneity into neoclassical analysis, this is insufficient to counter the criticisms of many non-neoclassical theorists and considerably less than is inherent in sociological analyses of the internal labour market (Farkas & England, 1988). Second, there is a marked divergence in the degree to which the wage competition model of the labour market is viewed as a legitimate representation of the real world. Neoclassicists have tended to see market outcomes as strongly influenced by those factors outlined in wage competition, whereas others have emphasized the limited effect of the external market on labour pricing and allocation. Third, neoclassicists have adopted a narrow concept of power in their analyses, whereas others have suggested that power inequalities lie at the heart of understanding how the internal labour market operates. The latter view postulates that workers do not have free choices in their labour market activities but are heavily constrained by power structures. Fourth, non-neoclassicists have been concerned to develop partial theories of the labour market through the identification of empirical regularities in the data, while neoclassicists have been more deductive and primarily concerned with developing general laws.

The question of whether economic research has made or can make a contribution to research in cognate disciplines must also be answered in a largely negative manner. Certainly many non-economists working on issues relating to the internal labour market are sceptical about much economic research in the area, particularly that undertaken by neoclassicists. In this they share much in common with those economists proposing a broader theoretical stance than is currently dominant in economics. While there is evidence of some building of bridges between the different groups, this is strictly limited and generally takes the form of neoclassicists using selected 'stylized facts' uncovered by non-neoclassicists as the basis of new theories derived from neoclassical principles.

This review of the current state of internal labour market research therefore suggests three main implications for future research in this area. The first concerns the axioms about human behaviour. The narrow assumptions of neoclassical economics have been criticized for a long time. There is considerable survey evidence that some characteristics of the internal labour market result from factors such as notions of fairness. As Phelps Brown (1980, p. 12) has pointed out, 'Economic "aspects" may be detached analytically; "the economy" may be separated conceptually from society, but the behaviour of "economic agents" is affected by influences from which the theorist abstracts. Effective policy recommendations must take account of these influences.' A loss of analytical rigour in the use of broader axioms about human behaviour could be a small price to pay for greater relevance.

A second feature of internal labour market research is the paucity of testing between competing hypotheses. The consequence is the generation of a plethora of theories purporting to explain the same or similar phenomena. This is an unsatisfactory way for a research programme to develop. Part of the problem lies with those who develop models from a set of axioms with scant regard for empirical analysis. The concepts, such as specific human capital, are inherently difficult to operationalize. While this serves to protect the hypothesis from critical scrutiny, it does little to help its development as an operational theory. Thus the balance could usefully be shifted towards empirical operationalization and ultimately to the testing of the theories underlying internal labour market research.

Finally, there is an urgent need to improve the data underlying internal labour market research. The Australian Workplace Industrial Relations Survey will certainly help in this respect. It has extensive information on some of the key phenomena associated with internal labour markets and a wide coverage of organizations. This will help bridge the gap between aggregative and case study research in this area. However, due to its strict set of objectives, it was unable to collect information on many of the key dimensions of the employing organization, such as internal promotion patterns, that are at the centre of the internal labour market debate.

References

Akerlof, G. A. (1982), 'Labour Contracts as Partial Gift Exchange', *Quarterly Journal of Economics* 97, 543–69.

Akerlof, G. and Yellen, J. (1986), *Efficiency Wage Models of the Labor Market*, Cambridge, Cambridge University Press.

Alexander, A. J. (1974), 'Income, Experience and the Structures of Internal Labor Markets', *Quarterly Journal of Economics* 88, 63–86.

Azariadis, C. (1975), 'Implicit Contracts and Underemployment Equilibria', *Journal of Political Economy* **83**, 1183–1202.

Baily, M. (1974), 'Wages and Employment under Uncertain Demand', *Review of Economic Studies* **41**, 37–50.

Becker, G. S. (1964), *Human Capital*, New York, National Bureau of Economic Research.

Blandy, R. J. and Richardson, S. (eds) (1982), *How Labour Markets Work*, Melbourne, Longman Cheshire.

Borjas, G. J. (1981), 'Job Mobility and Earnings over the Life-Cycle', *Industrial and Labor Relations Review* **34**, 365–76.

Bray, M. and Littler, C. R. (1988), 'The Labour Process and Industrial Relations: Review of the Literature', *Labour and Industry* **1**, 551–87.

Brown, W. (1989), 'The Paradoxical Role of Pay in Eliciting Labour Productivity', *Labour Economics and Productivity* **1**, 1–7.

Craig, C., Rubery, J., Tarling, R. and Wilkinson, F. (1982), *Labour Market Structure, Industrial Organisation and Low Pay*, Cambridge, Cambridge University Press.

Cole, R. E. (1979), *Work, Mobility and Participation*, Berkeley, University of California Press.

Creedy, J. and Whitfield, K. (1986), 'Earnings and Job Mobility: Professional Chemists in Britain', *Journal of Economic Studies* **13**, 23–37.

Creedy, J. and Whitfield, K. (1988), 'Job Mobility and Earnings: An Internal Labour Market Analysis', *Journal of Industrial Relations* **30**, 110–17.

Dickens, W. and Lang, K. (1988), 'Neoclassical and Sociological Perspectives on Segmented Labor Markets', in G. Farkas and P. England (eds), op. cit., 65–88.

Doeringer, P. B. and Piore, M. J. (1971), *Internal Labor Markets and Manpower Analysis*, Lexington, D. C. Heath.

Edwards, R. C. (1975), 'Industrial Traits and Organizational Incentives: What Makes a Good Worker?', *Journal of Human Resources* **11**, 51–68.

Farkas, G. and England, P. (eds) (1988), *Industries, Firms and Jobs: Sociological and Economic Approaches*, New York, Plenum.

Foster, W. F. and Gregory, R. G. (1983), 'A Flow Analysis of the Labour Market in Australia', in R. J. Blandy and O. Covick (eds), *Understanding Labour Markets*, Sydney, George Allen & Unwin, 111–36.

George, K. and Shorey, J. (1985), 'Manual Workers, Good Jobs and Structured Internal Labour Markets', *British Journal of Industrial Relations* **23**, 425–47.

Gordon, D. F. (1974), 'A Neo-Classical Theory of Keynesian Unemployment', *Economic Inquiry* **12**, 431–59.

Granovetter, M. (1988), 'The Sociological and Economic Approaches to Labor Market Analysis', in G. Farkas and P. England (eds), op. cit., 187–216.

Gregory, R. G. (1986), 'Wages Policy and Unemployment in Australia', *Economica* **53**, 553–74.

Hall, R. E. (1980), 'Employment Fluctuations and Wage Rigidity', *Brookings Papers on Economic Activity* **1**, 91–123.

Hall, R. E. (1982), 'The Importance of Lifetime Jobs in the United States Economy', *American Economic Review* **71**, 308–13.

Hoskyns, M. D., Sang, J. and Ashton, D. (1989), 'Job Competition and the Entry to Work', University of Leicester, Department of Economics, Discussion Paper, 111.

Jacoby, S. (1990), 'The New Institutionalism: What Can It Learn from the Old?', *Industrial Relations* **29** (2), 316–59.

Kerr, C. (1954), 'The Balkanisation of Labor Markets', in E. W. Bakke (ed.), *Labor Mobility and Economic Opportunity*, Cambridge, MIT, 92–110.

Lazear, E. and Moore, R. L. (1986), 'Incentive, Productivity and Labor Contracts', in Akerlof and Yellen, op. cit., 135–56.

Leontief, W. (1983), 'Foreword', in A. S. Eichner (ed.), *Why Economics is Not Yet a Science*, London, Macmillan, vii–ix.

Mace, J. (1979), 'Internal Labour Markets for Engineers in British Industry', *British Journal of Industrial Relations* **17**, 50–63.

McNabb, R. and Ryan, P. (1990), 'Segmented Labour Markets', in D. Sapsford and Z. Tzannatos (eds), *Current Issues in Labour Economics*, Basingstoke, Macmillan, 126–51.

McNulty, P. (1980), *The Origins and Development of Labor Economics*, Cambridge, MIT.

Main, B. G. M. (1982), 'The Length of a Job in Great Britain', *Economica* **49**, 325–33.

Malcolmson, J. M. (1984), 'Work Incentives, Hierarchy and Internal Labor Markets', *Journal of Political Economy* 92, 486–507.

Marsden, D. (1982), 'Career Structures and Training in Internal Labour Markets in Britain— and Comparisons with West Germany', *Manpower Studies* 4, 10–17.

Marsden, D. (1986), *The End of Economic Man? Custom and Cooperation in Labour Markets*, Brighton, Wheatsheaf.

Marsden, D. (1990), 'Institutions and Labour Mobility: Occupational and Internal Labour Markets in Britain, France, Italy and West Germany', in R. Brunetta and C. Dell'Aringa (eds), *Labour Relations and Economic Performance*, Basingstoke, Macmillan.

Medoff, J. L. and Abraham, K. G. (1981), 'Are Those Paid More Really More Productive? The Case of Experience', *Journal of Human Resources* 16, 186–216.

Nowak, M. J. and Crockett, G. V. (1983), 'The Operation of Internal Labour Markets: Three Case Studies', *Journal of Industrial Relations* 25, 445–64.

Okun, A. M. (1981), *Prices and Quantities: A Macroeconomic Analysis*, Oxford, Basil Blackwell.

Osterman, P. (ed.) (1984), *Internal Labor Markets*, London, MIT.

Osterman, P. (1987), 'Choice of Employment Systems in Internal Labor Markets', *Industrial Relations* 26, 46–67.

Peck, J. A. (1989), 'Labour Market Segmentation Theory', *Labour and Industry* 2, 119–44.

Phelps Brown, H. (1980), 'The Radical Reflections of an Applied Economist', *Banca Nazionale del Lavoro Quarterly Review* 132.

Raffe, D. (1988), 'The Story So Far: Research on Education, Training and the Labour Market from the Scottish Surveys', in D. Raffe (ed.), *Education and the Youth Labour Market*, London, Falmer, 40–65.

Rees, A. (1973), *Economics of Work and Pay*, New York, Harper.

Reich, M., Gordon, D. and Edwards, R. (1973), 'A Theory of Labor Market Segmentation', *American Economic Review* 63, 359–65.

Rubery, J. (1980), 'Structured Labour Markets, Worker Organization and Low Pay', in A. H. Amsden (ed.), *The Economics of Women and Work*, Harmondsworth, Penguin, 242–70.

Thomas, B. and Deaton, D. (1977), *Labour Shortage and Economic Analysis*, Oxford, Basil Blackwell.

Thurow, L. C. (1975), *Generating Inequality*, London, Macmillan.

Salop, J. and Salop, S. (1976), 'Self-Selection and Turnover in the Labor Market', *Quarterly Journal of Economics* 90, 619–27.

Shelly, M. (1988), 'Has the Bottom Dropped Out of the Youth Labour Market?', in Raffe, op. cit., 100–16.

Siebert, W. S. and Addison, J. T. (1991), 'Internal Labour Markets: Causes and Consequences', *Oxford Review of Economic Policy* 7 (1), 76–92.

Solow, R. (1980), 'On Theories of Unemployment', *American Economic Review* 91, 848–66.

Stigler, G. J. and Becker, G. S. (1977), 'De Gustibus Non Est Disputandum', *American Economics Review* 67, 76–90.

Strauss, G. and Feuille, P. (1981), 'Industrial Relations Research in the United States', in Peter B. Doeringer (ed.), *Industrial Relations in International Perspective*, London, Macmillan, 76–144.

Whitfield, K. (1981), 'The Job Mobility of Professional Chemists in Australia and Britain', *Chemistry in Australia* 48, 277–82.

Whitfield, K. and Bourlakis, C. A. B. (1991), 'An Empirical Analysis of YTS: Employment and Earnings', *Journal of Economic Studies* 18, 14–56.

Williamson, O. E. (1975), *Markets and Hierarchies*, New York, Free Press.

Willman, P. (1983), 'The Organisational Failures Framework and Industrial Sociology', in A. Francis, J. Turk and P. Willman (eds), *Power, Efficiency and Institutions*, London, Heineman, 117–35.

[14]

114

Changes in the Responsibility and Earnings of Professional Scientists*

by JOHN CREEDY

1. Introduction

This paper describes the responsibility and earnings changes of a highly trained group of employees, professional scientists. The empirical analysis is based largely on the insights obtained from the literature on internal labour markets. However, it is not possible to produce conclusive tests of competing theories, which produce very similar qualitative results concerning earnings profiles, promotion and mobility. It is argued that such a description is nevertheless useful, since few detailed data are available about internal mobility processes.

The results are based on a special survey of members of the Royal Society of Chemistry (RSC) in the UK, carried out by the author. In concentrating on the pattern of changes in responsibility and the influence of those changes on earnings both in the short term and over a longer period, attention is given to the potential importance of gradual or 'osmotic' mobility processes. This contrasts with studies of mobility which only consider changes between organisations, and therefore ignore a great deal of information about career structures. The measure of responsibility used and the survey are described briefly in the following subsections. Section II examines the main patterns of responsibility change, and Section III presents the results relating to earnings changes.

The Measurement of Responsibility

A feature of the paper is the use of a detailed assessment schedule designed to obtain a 'responsibility score' for each individual. Responsibility is associated with an individual's level of autonomy exercised in four areas of work, described as 'job duties', 'technical decisions and recommendations', 'supervision exercised' and 'supervision received'. Within each of these headings are five separate statements describing the extent of the autonomy, and these are given scores from one to five; the detailed schedule is given in Creedy (1987). The four separate scores are added together; thus the full range of possible scores runs from four to twenty. The responsibility score is therefore a cardinal measure.

115

It seems that little work has been carried out by economists on the measurement of responsibility, despite the work on income distribution, such as that by Lydall (1968) and Simon (1957), which uses a simple cardinal measure of responsibility based on the number of subordinates. Hill (1980), following Wolf and Fligstein (1979) looked at authority (to hire and fire, to have a say in others' pay, to supervise others' work) rather than autonomy. The present approach may be compared with that of Jaques (1956), who found that measures such as the number of subordinates or job title were inadequate.   He developed a measure based on the 'time-span' of work, defined as the maximum amount of time during which an individual was allowed to exercise discretion before being subject to direct supervision. However, the measurement of time-spans was very complex, in contrast with the approach used here, which has the additional merit that it may be applied directly to a wide range of occupations.

The Mobility Survey

In September 1985 a questionnaire was set to 6000 members of the Royal Society of Chemistry (RSC), including all 1721 female members and a random selection of 4279 male members between the ages of 25 and 64. The response rates were 50.5% and 48.5% for men and women respectively, which is high in view of the length and complexity of the questionnaire and the fact that anonymity meant that no reminders were sent. Furthermore it is not known how many forms were sent to individuals who were students or retired, or otherwise not in the labour market. In view of the retrospective nature of the survey, the results have, where possible, been compared with regular cross-sectional surveys carried out by the RSC, which has extensive experience of remuneration surveys since 1919.   The members are completely familiar with the classifications used in the survey.

The survey obtained information about the mobility of individuals from the beginning of the first job to the time of the survey. A problem arises of how the term 'job' should be defined. In the present context it was important to obtain as much information as possible about the gradual movement of individuals within large organisations, so that defining a job change in terms of a change of employer would be much too narrow. Respondents were encouraged to regard a change of job as being associated with a change of 'job title', whether or not they changed firms. Hence much information about internal mobility was obtained. The extent of gradual, or 'osmotic' mobility was measured using information about those changes which took place within the same job. It must however be recognized that within-job changes represent only a partial measure of osmotic mobility, since

116

information is available only at the start and finish of each job.

In much of what follows the 'unit of analysis' is the job or job change rather than the individual. However, not all respondents gave full details about every job held; thus the total number of observations used in the calculations varies depending on the nature of the question. It is appropriate at this point to mention a well known difficulty in the interpretation of the data relating to women. The data necessarily refer to those who have remained continually in the profession, or who have left but re-entered. The female respondents may thus be dominated by 'stayers' who are relatively more successful, although some may plan to leave the labour market in the future for family or household reasons. Despite this problem the results are presented here, since so little is known about the careers of professional women, but they should not be interpreted as necessarily applying to all women who enter the profession. For further longitudinal studies of female earnings, see Corcoran et al (1983), Dex (1984), and Main (1985).

ii. Patterns of Responsibility Change

Promotion as a Reason for Job Changing

Individuals were asked to give the major reason for each job change over their career, and among the eight categories was 'promotion within organisation'. The nature of moves made for other reasons will be examined below, but promotion within the same organisation is the single most important reason given for all job changes. It was found that 29% of (almost 6000) job changes made by men, and 26% of (approximately 1200) changes made by women were for that reason alone.

Promotion within the organisation becomes more important as a factor in job changing as the job number, labour market experience, and the level of responsibility increase. For men, 18% of moves from the first, and 28% of moves from the fourth job were made for promotion within the same organisation: the comparable figures for women are 19% and 28%. For those moving with five or fewer, and more than twenty, years of experience the proportions moving primarily for internal promotion are respectively 19% and 37%: for women the comparable figures are 18% and 40%. This represents an increasing proportion of a decreasing number of moves.

Although fewer moves are made by those already in relatively high positions

117

of responsibility, within-organisation promotion is more important as a reason for change: the percentage changing jobs for that reason increases from 25% for those with responsibility score from 4 to 10 before the move, to 32% for those with responsibility score 16-20 (23% and 31% respectively for women). Fewer job changes are made by those in management or administrative work roles, but internal promotion is more important as a reason for change; the relevant figure is 36%, compared with 26% for those in non-administrative positions (34% and 24% respectively for women).

Types of Job Change Involving Responsibility Changes

Although internal promotion is the single most important reason for job changing, and increasingly so as the career progresses, many other job changes involve an increase in responsibility. Indeed, 54% of male, and 51% of female job changes involved an increase in the level of responsibility. Furthermore, many increases in responsibility are made within the same job. It must also be remembered that many individuals experience a decrease in their level of responsibility, often from a voluntary job change. This subsection examines more closely the pattern of changes in responsibility, distinguishing certain types of movement according to the information given about the reason for that move.

In addition to 'promotion within organisation', many job changes were attributed to 'transfer within organisation', some of which involved a change in level of responsibility. Job changes made for both of these reasons were simply grouped as 'within-organisation' changes. Three other reasons were 'immediate improvement of salary', 'long term prospects in fresh employment', and 'frustration in present employment': any job change attributed to these reasons were classified as a 'voluntary between-organisation' move. An 'involuntary between-organisation' move was made if either 'redundancy, dismissal or closure or department or organisation' of 'health considerations' were given as the reason.

The implications for promotion of each type of job mobility are shown in Table 1. Within-job promotion was the single most important method of increasing responsibility, despite the fact that within the majority of jobs there was no change in the level of responsibility. The within-job changes are taken from the difference between the level of responsibility at the end and at the beginning of the job; it is not known precisely when the change or changes took place. The level of responsibility within a job could change more than once, so that the figures in the first row of Table 1 perhaps understate the importance of within-job mobility. Even so, 49% of upward

118

changes in responsibility of men took place within the same job; the corresponding figure for women is even higher at 55%. When these are added to the within-organisation upward movements, 73% and 75% respectively of mens' and womens' upward mobility took place within the same organisation.

Downward changes in responsibility were made in quite different ways. For men and women respectively, 74% and 88% of downward changes in responsibility were made as a result of moving between organisations. The effect of involuntary between-organisation moves is quite severe; 25% of men and 24% of women who make such moves experienced an immediate fall in responsibility. Of those who move between organisations voluntarily, 15% of men and 17% of women had a reduction in their level of responsibility.

For each type of job change, the extent of the increase in responsibility is similar. This is measured by the difference between responsibility scores between the end and start of the same job, or between the start of a new job and the end of the previous job. In all categories the median number of increases in responsibility score was 2, both for men and women. For downward movements the median number of reductions was 2 for all types of move except within-job 'demotions', for which it was 1.

Table 1   Type of Job Change and Responsibility Change

Type of job change		Direction of change in responsibility					
		Male			Female		
	down	no change	up		down	no change	up
Within-job	24	4645	3010		1	1057	729
Within-organisation	175	878	1467		19	158	257
Voluntary Between organisation	364	736	1257		70	143	204
Involuntary Between organisation	209	242	394		72	100	130

Note: The entries indicate the number of job changes in each category.

The Importance of Internal Mobility

The results shown above illustrate the considerable importance of increases in responsibility within organisations, involving both job changes and within-job movements, relative to external mobility. In contrast, most reductions in responsibility occurred as a result of moving between organisations. However, the number of between organisation promotions is not negligible, representing a quarter of upward movements. Using different approaches, Kalleberg and Hudies (1979) and Sandefur (1981) have found strong support for the influence of internal mobility. The former was restricted to a five year sequence for middle-aged men, while the later used retrospective histories of males between 20 and 39 to examine 'prestige'.

The recruitment to higher levels of responsibility of individuals from other organisations can be seen from the distribution of responsibility levels on entry into a new organisation. For example, of the 784 between-organisation moves made by men in management or administration, the median responsibility level after the move was 13. For the 2464 moves by those not in management or administration, the corresponding median was 9. The median values were also found to increase for those moves made with more years of experience. For women, the median responsibility level on entry to a new organisation was 11 and 8 respectively for those in and those not in management or administration (of 95 and 634 moves respectively). The question arises of the extent to which mobility at the higher levels of responsibility has an effect in preventing the wage structures of large organisations from becoming insulated from the external market, as sometimes suggested by internal labour market theorists.

Responsibility and Managerial/Administrative Work

The implications for responsibility of movements into and out of management/administration are shown in Table 2 for men and women. Managerial and administrative work includes general management, general administration (for example as a buyer or personnel officer), and primarily managerial and administrative work in other areas such as Research and/or Development, analytical work, quality control and so on. The importance of moving into management/administration and the role of internal movements can be seen. For men, 83% of moves into management/administration involved an increase in responsibility, and of those, 73% were made within the same organisation (including within-job and within-organisation job changes). Only 3.5% of moves into management/administration involved a reduction in the responsibility score, but 69% of those reductions were made

120

as a result of moving between organisations. The moves out of management did not involve such a predominant movement in responsibility: 37% of outward moves involved a reduction, and of those 74% were made between organisations. However, 36% of outward moves involved an increase in responsibility, of which 66% were made by changing jobs within the same organisation. However, 66% of involuntary moves out of management involved a reduction in responsibility.

The results for women are broadly similar to those for men. Indeed, the similarity in the experience of males and females is perhaps more striking than the differences. These results also add support to those of Felmlee (1982) and Lewis (1986), who used United States data. Felmlee used the National Longitudinal Survey of Young Women (1968-73), and found (using a socioeconomic status score) that internal labour markets gave significant advantages. Lewis used Federal personnel records (1973-83), finding similar promotion probabilities for white men and women, although women made fewer upward steps and suffered slightly more demotions.

III.   Earnings Changes and Responsibility Changes

Short Term Earnings Changes

The earnings changes resulting from job changes are summarised in Table 3. This table shows, for each category, the distribution of the percentage difference between annual earnings at the end of the previous job and the beginning of the next job. The summary measures reported for the distributions are the lower and upper quartiles, QL and Qu respectively, and the median, M. The experience of women was again similar to that of men, except for changes made for 'other' reasons, 'health' reasons, and 'redundancy, dismissal or closure'. The main result is that earnings changes experienced as a result of 'promotion within the organisation' are not as large as for some of the other positive reasons for job changing. Voluntary movements between organisations result in larger average percentage earnings increases than within-organisation job changes. Whether or not they result in higher earnings in the long run will be examined later in this section.

121

TABLE 2

Movements Into and Out of Management/Administration and Responsibility Changes (all jobs).

	Type of responsibility change					
	MEN			WOMEN		
Type of movement	down	no change	up	down	no change	up
Movements into management/administration						
Within-job	1	47	405	0	11	39
Within-organisation	13	71	369	3	7	54
Voluntary Between-organisation	19	42	240	7	6	31
Involuntary Between-organisation	12	12	47	3	4	13
Movements out of management/administration						
Within-job	3	20	38	0	2	4
Within-organisation	43	56	77	2	5	4
Voluntary Between-organisation	78	42	48	12	10	10
Involuntary Between-organisation	55	17	11	7	4	3

122

The summary measures of the distribution of percentage earnings changes obtained as a result of both upward and downward changes in responsibility, according to the type of move, are shown in Table 4. The changes made within jobs can occur over quite different time periods, so the percentage in that category refer to average annual changes in earnings, adjusted for price changes over the period during which the job was held. The damaging effect on earnings growth of demotion, especially resulting from involuntary mobility, can be seen. However, when involuntary mobility is accompanied by promotion it produces (on average) relatively large increases. Furthermore the distribution of percentage changes is highly positively skewed.

From a short-term point of view it seems more rewarding to achieve promotion by moving between organisations. The promotion taking place within jobs is associated with a relatively low annual average rate of increase in real earnings. This result may perhaps be interpreted as supporting the argument of internal labour market theorists that wages are attached to jobs rather than individuals.

Longer-Term Effects on Earnings

The above results show that while the large majority of upward changes in responsibility are made within the same organisation, individuals who move between organisations obtain relatively large percentage increases in earnings on moving. This does not necessarily show that higher long-term gains are made by external mobility, only that large discrete gains are available. It is necessary to consider how the different types of mobility contribute to earnings when a longer time horizon is used. The approach used here is to carry out a regression analysis where earnings at the time of the survey are related to variables designed to capture different aspects of each individual's mobility pattern. This method has its obvious limitations, partly arising from the use of annual earnings which may not accurately reflect long run relative positions even after making an allowance for systematic life-cycle factors. It would be more desirable to use a longer accounting period, but this is not possible with the available data.

Table 3

Distribution of Percentage Earnings Changes by Reason for Job Change
(All job changes)

Reason for job change	Men				Women			
	QL	M	Qu	No.	QL	M	Qu	No.
Immediate salary improvement	14.3	15.0	40.0	454	15.2	25.0	36.8	73
Long term prospects in fresh employment	4.2	14.3	28.6	911	2.9	13.3	27.4	115
Frustration in present employment	0	10.0	22.2	470	0	11.1	20.0	109
Transfer within organisation	0	0	10.0	514	0	0	9.0	74
Promotion within organisation	3.5	11.1	20.0	1065	3.4	9.1	20.0	178
Redundancy, dismissal or closure of department	-4.0	4.0	16.7	328	0	8.9	22.2	51
Health considerations	-6.7	3.4	14.3	22	-10.7	0	9.7	8
Other	0	20.5	70.0	313	0	5.7	26.7	144

Notes: (i) QL, M and Qu denote the lower quartile, median and upper quartile respectively.

(ii) The total number of job changes recorded here is less than used in earlier calculations because information about earnings at the beginning and end of each job was less than other information.

124

Table 4

Distribution of Percentage Changes in Earnings by Type of Move and
Responsibility Change

Type of move	Upward responsibility changes				Downward responsibility change			
	QL	M	QM	No.	QL	M	Qu	No.
				Men				
Within-job	1.4	5.1	11.2	1713	-2.2	0.6	1.7	9
Within organisation	1.7	10.7	20.0	920	0	0	11.1	114
Voluntary between - organisation	8.3	20.0	34.5	958	0	10.0	25.0	295
Involuntary Between - organisation	2.6	20.0	59.1	293	-13.0	0	12.5	170
				Women				
Within-job	0	3.3	7.7	317	-	-	-	-
Within organisation	3.6	8.4	20.0	143	0	7.4	12.5	12
Voluntary Between - organisation	7.5	17.8	31.5	142	0	15.2	23.3	54
Involuntary Between - organisation	2.4	14.3	40.0	91	-20.0	1.1	20.0	46

Note: (i)   QL, M and Qu denote the lower quartile, median and upper quartile respectively.

(ii)   The percentages for within-job changes refer to average annual percentage changes in earnings adjusted for price changes over the period during which the job was held.   Other figures relate to percentage changes from the end of the job to the start of the next job.

Broad life-cycle variations were captured by including experience and the square of experience as independent variables.   The main variables

125

describing the mobility of each individual relate to the number of different types of move; that is, within-organisation promotions and transfers, voluntary and involuntary between-organisation job changes. The results, using the logarithm of earnings in 1985 as the dependent variable, are reported by Table 5. All the coefficients (except those on the female unemployment dummy variable and involuntary job changes between organisations) are significantly different from zero. Interpretation of the results requires the fact that if b is the coefficient on a variable, then $100\{\exp(b) - 1\}$ is the percentage increase in current earnings resulting from a unit increase in the variable.

Promotion within the same organisation has the largest effect on earnings at the time of the survey, although the immediate effect on earnings of a single such move was found to be generally lower than for other types of mobility. Each additional promotion within the organisation implies, on average, a 7% higher value of earnings in 1985 for men, and a 6% higher value for women. In each case this is double the effect of an additional voluntary job change between organisations. Transfers within the organisation also have a larger long run effect on earnings than between-organisation mobility, although their short run effect is much lower. While an isolated voluntary job change between organisations may have a larger immediate impact than a single within-organisation change, the latter is now seen to be generally part of a longer-term cumulative process of upward mobility.

The main differences between the results for men and women involve the effect of an involuntary move between organisations (which is less harmful for women than for men) and the effect of a period spent out of the labour market. The earnings of men who have experienced a spell out of the labour market are on average 5.6% lower than those who have been continuously in the labour market, whereas the corresponding figure for women is 14.7%. Numerous studies have been carried out on the 'depreciation of human capital', but the coefficient on the present dummy variable cannot be directly interpreted in those terms without further examination of the reasons for the spell out of the labour market, and appropriate treatment of the time spent in this state. For an analysis that concentrates on work interruptions, see Stewart and Greenhalgh (1984).

126

Table 5

Regression Analysis of Earnings and Career Mobility
(Dependent variable: logarithm of annual earnings 1985)

Independent Variables	Men(N=1895)	Women(N=603)
Constant	8.787 (296.33)	8.735 (240.00)
Ph.D. (=1 if PhD. 0 otherwise)	0.170 (17.02)	0.210 (12.37)
Experience	0.030 (17.02)	0.030 (12.37)
Experience squared	-0.00032 (-10.08)	-0.00033 (-9.31)
Responsibility at start	0.024 (8.60)	0.010 (2.19)
No. of within-organisation promotions	0.068 (12.84)	0.058 (4.67)
No. of within-organisation transfers	0.041 (5.75)	0.054 (30.5)
No. of voluntary job changes between organisations	0.034 (5.83)	0.030 (2.77)
No. of involuntary job changes between organisations	-0.038 (-4.31)	-0.004 (-0.262)
Move to management within any job (=1 if moved)	0.105 (6.31)	0.111 (2.75)
Period of unemployment (=1 if unemployed any time)	-0.108 (4.88)	-0.052 (-1.50)
Period out of labour market (=1 if out of market any time)	-0.058 (-2.85)	-0.159 (-4.84)
R2	0.414	0.414

't' values are given in parentheses underneath parameter estimates.

127

The earnings of men who have been unemployed at any time are on average 10% lower than those without any unemployment, but for women the reduction is 5%. Also notable in Table 5 is the importance of moving into management within any job (the dummy variable is set equal to unity if the individual experienced such a move at any time in his or her career), which increases current earnings by 11.1% and 11.7% for men and women respectively. It has been seen that the majority of such moves into management involved an increase in responsibility score. Higher earnings are thus achieved by those who are highly mobile within, rather than between, organisations.

IV. Conclusions

This paper has examined the pattern of changes in responsibility and earnings over the careers of male and female professional chemists in Britain. The results were based on a special survey of members of the Royal Society of Chemistry carried out by the author. The survey collected information from each respondent about several characteristics of his or her work at the beginning and end of each job held over the career, and captured details about the internal mobility both within jobs and organisations that is so often ignored by mobility surveys. A special feature of the paper is the use of a cardinal measure of responsibility based on the individual's level of autonomy in four aspects of work.

The results were found to be very similar for men and women. Over a quarter of job changes were made for 'promotion within the organisation'. However, many changes in responsibility took place within what respondents regarded as the same job. One half of recorded increases in responsibility were made within jobs, and three quarters of the increases were made within organisations. Moves between organisations were quite different, and of involuntary moves between organisations, one quarter involved a reduction in the level of responsibility. The survey also indicated the importance for scientists of movement into management, as has been recognised for many years by the Royal Society of Chemistry. Indeed, four fifths of moves into management involved an increase in the level of responsibility, and of those, three quarters were made within organisations.

When examining earnings changes associated with job changes, it was found that earnings increases were on average larger for those increases in responsibility arising from a movement between organisations, compared with those who increased their responsibility within the same job. However, the cumulative effect of internal promotion was found to be stronger than for

128

external movements: each additional increase in responsibility within an organisation had approximately double the effect on earnings, measured at the time of the survey. The results have generally confirmed the importance of internal mobility, although as stressed earlier it is not possible with these data to provide direct tests of competing theories of age-earnings profiles. The results apply to a particular group of highly trained employees, although the responsibility measures could be applied to a wide range of workers. It would be of much interest to compare these results with other groups.

Department of Economics,
The University of Melbourne.

References

Corcoran, M.E., Duncan, G.J. and Ponza, M. (1983) A longitudinal analysis of white women's wages. Journal of Human Resources, 18, pp. 499-520.

Creedy, J. (1987) Variations in earnings and responsibility. Journal of the Royal Statistical Society, A, 150, pp. 57-68.

Dex, S. (1984) Women's Work Histories: An Analysis of the Women and Employment Survey. London; Department of Employment Research Paper, 46.

Doeringer, P.B. and Piore, M. (1971) Internal Labour Markets and Manpower Analysis. Lexington; D.C. Heath.

Felmlee, D. (1982) Women's job mobility processes within and between employers. American Sociological Review, 47, pp. 142-151.

Hill, M.S. (1980) Authority at work: how men and women differ. In Five Thousand American Families, Vol. VII. (ed. by G.J. Duncan and J.N. Morgan), pp. 107-146. Ann Arbor; Institute for Poverty Research.

Jaques, E. (1956) Measurement of Responsibility. London; Trvistock.

Kalleberg, A.L. and Hudis, P.M. (1979) Wage changes in the late career: A model for the outcomes of job sequences. Social Science Research, 8, pp. 16-40.

Lewis, G.B. (1986) Gender and promotions: promotion chances of white men and women in Federal white collar employment. Journal of Human Resources, 21, pp. 406-419.

Lydall, H. (1968) The Structure of Earnings. Oxford; Oxford University Press.

Main, B.G.M. (1985) Women's hourly earnings: the influence of work histories on rates of pay. University of Edinburgh, Department

129

of Economics Working Paper, 1985; VIII.

Sandefur, G. (1981)   Organisational boundaries and upward job shifts. Social Science Research, 10, pp. 67-82.

Simon, H. (1957)   The compensation of executives.   Sociometry, 20, pp. 32-35.

Stewart, M.B. and Greenhalgh, C.A. (1984)   Work history patterns and the occupational attainment of women.   Economics Journal, 94, pp. 493-519.

Wolf, W.C. and Fligstein, N.D. (1979)   Sex and authority in the workplace: the causes of sexual inequality.   American Sociological Review, 44, pp. 235-252.

*I should like to thank Barry Henman and Diana Bartlett of the Royal Society of Chemistry for their cooperation, Jill Peters for computing assistance, and Keith Whitfield and a referee for helpful comments on an earlier draft.

PART III

TRADE UNIONS AND WAGES

[15]

A NOTE ON THE ANALYSIS OF
TRADE UNIONS AND RELATIVE WAGES

By John Creedy*

I. Introduction

The purpose of this note is to examine the method used by a number of recent studies which have attempted to estimate the effect of trade unions on relative wages within occupations in Great Britain.[1] These studies raise many difficult problems associated with data and the interpretation of results, but this note is confined to some statistical aspects of the work.[2] The estimation of the union/non-union differential is examined in section (II), while section (III) then considers some further difficulties where hours of work are variable.

II. Estimation of the Average Union/Non-Union Differential

The fundamental problem is, of course, raised by the fact that direct information about differentials is not available from published data.[3] The usual estimates are obtained from a single equation model which is based on a simple identity which decomposes the average wage within the jth occupation, $\bar{w}_j$, into a weighted average of the average union wage $\bar{w}_j^c$ and the average non-union wage $\bar{w}_j^{nc}$, where the weights depend on the proportion of workers who are 'covered' by the union negotiated wage, t_j. Thus

$$\bar{w}_j = t_j \bar{w}_j^c + (1 - t_j)\bar{w}_j^{nc} \tag{1}$$

A similar decomposition is obviously available for the logarithms of wages, where $\bar{w}$ etc. are re-defined in terms of the respective logarithms of the geometric means.[4] An immediate problem is raised if average hourly earnings are approximated by the ratio of average weekly earnings to average weekly hours, since the latter is not equal to the former and the discrepancy will be different in each occupation.

To simplify notation it is convenient to drop the subscripts and rewrite equation (1) as

$$z = tx + (1 - t)y \tag{2}$$

where the definitions of z, x and y are obvious by comparison with (1). The usual method then proceeds by rewriting (2) as

$$z = y + tD \tag{3}$$

---

* I should like to thank K. Mayhew for comments on an earlier version of this note.
[1] These include Pencavel (1974), Mulvey (1976, 1977, 1978), and Layard et. al. (1978), who describe their results as 'relatively reliable' and 'very approximate' in the same paragraph (*ibid*, p. 287).
[2] A survey of some of the difficulties is given in Metcalf (1977). Particularly important are problems of dealing with different levels of skill (especially where unions influence labour training), and the effect of size of establishment.
[3] Mulvey (1978, p. 106) actually makes the strange assertion that the non-union wage is 'obviously not directly observable', but this is only true if by 'non-union' is meant the wage in complete absence of any unions.
[4] In fact only arithmetic means are available, a problem which has been considered in a different context in Prais and Houthakker (1955, p. 14).

235

with $D=x-y$. Using information about z and t for each occupation it is argued that a cross-section regression of z against t and a number of measurable characteristics of each occupation which 'determine' y, would give the average value of D as the coefficient on t. However, y also appears as part of D, and it is not immediately clear that the procedure enables the coefficient on t to be interpreted in this way.

Define the proportional differential as $d=D/y$, and write

$$d=\bar{d}+\xi \quad \text{and} \quad y=f(c)+\varepsilon \tag{4}$$

so that

$$E(d)=\bar{d}=E\left(\frac{x}{y}\right)-1,\; E(\xi)=0,\text{ and } E(y)=f(c) \tag{5}$$

Here c is a vector of observable characteristics of each occupation. Substitution into (3) gives

$$z=y(1+td)$$

$$=f(c)+t\{\bar{d}f(c)\}+\eta \tag{6}$$

where $\eta=t\{\bar{d}\varepsilon+\xi f(c)+\xi c\}$ and clearly does not satisfy the conditions required for ordinary least squares estimation. More important, however, is the fact that $\bar{d}f(c)$ is not equal to $E(D)$, since from (5)

$$\bar{d}f(c)=E(y)\left\{E\left(\frac{x}{y}\right)-1\right\}$$

$$\neq E(x)-E(y) \tag{7}$$

The reason for the inequality in (7) is simply that the ratio of averages is again not equal to the average of ratios. The statement by Mulvey (1976, p. 425) that, 'there are some interesting implications to be drawn from the empirical estimates and it would be unduly cautious to ignore them', must itself be treated with considerable caution.[5]

It is not of course possible to assess the precise quantitative importance of this problem since the joint distribution of x and y over occupations is not available. Some indication may, however, be obtained by using the assumption that x and y are jointly lognormally distributed as $\Lambda(\mu_x, \mu_y, \sigma_x^2, \sigma_y^2, \rho)$; where μ and σ^2 are the respective means and variances of the logarithms and ρ is the correlation coefficient.[6] In this case the distribution of x/y is conveniently given by $\Lambda(\mu_x-\mu_y,$

---

[5] Mulvey compares his estimate of 26% with that of Pencavel of 0–10% (see 1976, pp. 425–426), and suggests that there has been a 'significant increase in the impact of unions on relative wages'. In fact the differences are not statistically significantly different, and although Mulvey uses 1973 earnings data a number of the independent variables refer to earlier years.

[6] It may initially seem unusual to specify a lognormal distribution for the distribution of the arithmetic mean wage over a cross-section of occupations, but for an early use see Aitchison and Brown (1957, p. 110). The 'ratio of averages' problem has been examined, in the context of Engel curve analysis, in Creedy (1973).

$\sigma_x^2 + \sigma_y^2 - 2\rho\sigma_x\sigma_y$),[7] and using the fact that the expected value of a variable distributed as $\Lambda(\mu, \sigma^2)$ is equal to $\exp(\mu + \tfrac{1}{2}\sigma^2)$, it can easily be shown that

$$\frac{E(y)}{E(x)} E\left(\frac{x}{y}\right) = \exp(\sigma_y^2 - \rho\sigma_x\sigma_y) \tag{8}$$

Thus the coefficient on t in equation (3) is equal to the average union/non-union differential only when $\rho = \sigma_y/\sigma_x$, which is obviously unlikely to hold. There is therefore a strong *a priori* probability that the usual method will overstate the 'true' average differential. When $\sigma_y > \sigma_x$ the coefficient cannot possibly be the average differential (since this would require $\rho > 1$). When, for example, $\sigma_x = \sigma_y = \sigma$ the 'overstatement' decreases as ρ increases, and increases as σ increases.

III. Variations in Hours and Earnings

There is a further criticism of the approach which arises because of the fact that the hourly rate and the number of hours worked will not in general be independent, and of course trade union bargaining will usually be concerned with both variables.[8] Consider the following framework, where each variable applies to the jth occupation, (but this subscript is dropped for convenience). Let

w_i = weekly earnings of individual i
h_i = weekly hours worked by individual i
λ_i = ratio of overtime to total hours
   $= h_i^o/h_i$ where h_i^o are overtime hours
α = proportional difference between normal and overtime hourly rate
w = hourly rate for normal hours

Then $w_i = wh_i(1 + \alpha\lambda_i)$

and if normal hours are standardised within the occupation at τ

$$w_i = w\{\tau + h_i^o(1 + \alpha)\} \tag{9}$$

so that average earnings are given by

$$\bar{w} = w\{\tau + \bar{h}^o(1 + \alpha)\} \tag{10}$$

The effect on $\bar{w}$ of changes in either w, τ or α will of course be different, and the priorities which unions attach to changes in w, τ or α will vary according to the existing values of these and other variables.[9] Thus a simple comparison of earnings across occupations may give a misleading indication of the effectiveness of unions.

Furthermore, it can be shown that the coefficient of variation of weekly earnings in each occupation, η_w, is given by

$$\eta_w = \eta_h(1 + \beta\tau/\bar{h})^{-1} \tag{11}$$

where η_h is the coefficient of variation of total hours worked in the occupation and

---

[7] See Aitchison and Brown (1957, p. 11).
[8] In this context bargaining over a piecework rate may be regarded as equivalent to bargaining over an hourly rate. Discussion of piecework rates usually involves the 'standard time' for the job.
[9] For fixed $\bar{h}$ it is easily seen that $\partial\bar{w}/\partial\tau = -w\alpha$, $\partial\bar{w}/\partial\alpha = \bar{h}^o w$ and $\partial\bar{w}/\partial w = \tau + \bar{h}^o(1 + \alpha)$.

$\beta = 1/(1+\alpha)$. Equation (11) clearly shows that there may well be a trade-off between the desire to increase average earnings and the desire for greater equality within occupations.[10] For example, a decrease in standard hours τ (with total hours constant) increases both $\bar{w}$ and η_w.

It is also of interest to consider the aggregation of equation (10) over several occupations or groups. It is obvious that the average wage cannot simply be expressed in the same form as (10), but with the variables re-defined in terms of averages over groups. Appropriate covariance terms, such as that between w and $\bar{h}^o$, must be added. For example, in the simplest case where both τ and α are the same for all occupations or groups, aggregation gives

$$E(\bar{w}) = E(w)\{\tau + E(\bar{h}^o)(1+\alpha)\} + (1+\alpha)\,\mathrm{Cov}\,(w, \bar{h}^o) \tag{12}$$

where $\mathrm{Cov}\,(w, \bar{h}^o) = E(w\bar{h}^o) - E(w)E(\bar{h}^o)$ is the covariance (over occupations) between the standard wage and overtime hours. The last term in (12) is, of course, unlikely to be zero. Equation (12) may also be regarded as referring to an aggregate over different groups within an occupation, the groups being distinguished according to the coverage of union negotiated agreements. Using this slightly wider framework, wage comparisons are seen to be significantly more complex than the simple decomposition in equation (1).

Until much more *direct* evidence on union covered and non-union covered earnings becomes available, it is therefore suggested that the results of recent studies should be treated with considerable caution.

University of Durham.

REFERENCES

Aitchison, J. and Brown, J. A. C. (1957), *The Lognormal Distribution*, C.U.P.

Creedy, J. (1973), 'A problem in the estimation of double-log Engel curves', *BULLETIN*.

Layard, R. et. al. (1978), 'The effect of collective bargaining on relative and absolute wages', *British Journal of Industrial Relations*.

Mulvey, C. (1976), 'Collective agreements and relative earnings in U.K. manufacturing industry in 1973', *Economica*.

Mulvey, C. (1977), 'A note on the impact of unionisation on negotiated wages in the manufacturing sector in Kenya', *BULLETIN*.

Mulvey, C. (1978), *The Economic Analysis of Trade Unions*, Martin Robertson.

Pencavel, J. (1974), 'Relative wages and trade unions in the U.K.', *Economica*.

Prais, S. J. and Houthakker, H. S. (1955) *The Analysis of Family Budgets*, C.U.P.

[10] Compare the statements on inequality in Layard et al. (1978, p. 287).

[16]

Trade Unions, Wages and Taxation

JOHN CREEDY and IAN M. McDONALD*

I. REAL WAGE BARGAINING

The recognition that trade unions are more likely to be concerned with the level of post-tax real wages of their members, rather than simply the gross wage, has led to a great deal of debate concerning the use of tax policy to affect the supply side of the economy in addition to the more traditional demand side factors. A prime example is the use of tax cuts in an attempt to reduce trade unions' wage demands and thereby help in the 'battle' against inflation and unemployment. This type of supply-side argument contrasts with those suggesting that tax cuts can have a significant effect on the supply of labour; for discussion of these issues see Dilnot and Kell (1988) and Brown (1988).

It has sometimes been assumed that unions attempt to keep the value of post-tax real wages constant in the face of changes in prices and the tax system. But although this assumption may seem to be intuitively reasonable and quite innocuous, it actually implies a rather special assumption about unions' behaviour and the demand for labour. It is argued here that unions' responses are unlikely to be so simplistic and will depend not only on the precise labour market situation of the unions' members and their preferences, but also on the way in which average and marginal tax rates are affected by any tax policy.

In the last decade a considerable literature, recently surveyed by Oswald (1985) and Ulph and Ulph (1988), has developed analysing the economic behaviour of trade unions. A general feature of virtually all this recent work is the assumption, in some form or another, that unions attempt to maximise some 'objective'. It is often assumed that this objective involves a trade-off or balance between the separate aims of high real wages and low unemployment of members of the union. Other work assumes an alternative

---

* John Creedy is Truby Williams Professor and Reader in Economics, and Ian M. McDonald is a lecturer, both at The University of Melbourne. The authors are grateful to Jim Perkins and Jeff Borland for comments on an earlier versions of this paper.

form of the objective function, in which the interests of the employed members, or 'insiders', dominate decision making. The analysis reported in this paper is based on the first specification of the objective function. The assumption made here that employed members of the union consider the welfare of unemployed members is based on the argument that in a market with some labour turnover, all members of the union face a similar risk of unemployment.[1]

The purpose of this paper is therefore to explore some implications of the existence of a willingness to trade off the two separate aims for unions' responses to various types of tax change. Although a complete analysis involves many technical difficulties, the paper aims to provide a non-technical discussion of the main results. Only basic heuristic arguments will be given and detailed proofs are excluded.[2] Some preliminary but important results concerning basic changes in the tax system are examined in Sections II and III; these concern respectively changes in marginal and average rates of tax, and changes in the progressivity of the system as a whole. Section IV goes on to use these results to examine a shift in the tax mix towards a general consumption tax. Section V examines the further macroeconomic implications, particularly for investment, of a tax policy that is seen as part of a 'deal' between unions and the government in order to control inflation.

First, however, it is necessary to clarify the way in which the process of wage determination is envisaged. One way of modelling the process is to regard the union as behaving monopolistically by simply stating a particular 'wage demand' that is consistent with achieving its objective. The level of employment of the union's members is then determined by the derived demand for labour (whereby employment is set such that the wage is equal to the marginal revenue product of labour). The union is assumed to know the form of the demand curve. Alternatively the process of wage setting could be modelled explicitly as a bargaining process. The union may be envisaged as bargaining over wages, with the firm still having full control over the level of employment.

However, it can be shown that such arrangements will be inefficient, so that it is possible to make at least one party better-off without the other suffering. In general, a range of efficient bargains concerning both the wage and the level of employment can be specified. In each of the bargaining contexts, a unique outcome can however only be determined if a particular equilibrium solution is adopted. A common form is the so-called 'Nash' equilibrium, according to which a weighted geometric mean of the two parties' pay-offs is maximised, where the weights depend on the respective bargaining 'power'. It turns out that the influence on wages of the changes in

---

[1] Preliminary work suggests that very similar results also apply to 'insider dominated' unions.

[2] For further details see Creedy and McDonald (1988a).

taxation examined here are very similar for the different processes of wage determination mentioned above. Surprising as it may seem, it really doesn't matter which type of model is used; that is, the comparative static properties are similar.

In the analysis reported below the real value of unemployment benefits plays an important role. In many countries, unemployment benefits, along with other transfer payments, are included as part of taxable income. But the level of benefits is usually very similar to the value of a tax-free threshold; the idea of making benefits taxable is of course not to recover part of the benefits in tax but to make *all other* sources of income subject to taxation. However, unemployment benefits are subject to consumption taxes, such as Value Added Tax (VAT), once they are spent. For the changes in taxation considered below, it is assumed that the real, post-tax, value of unemployment benefits is kept at a constant level. This assumption is necessary in order to restrict the discussion to a single type of policy. For example, if a change in either income or consumption tax were allowed to change the real value of unemployment benefits then two policies would be involved — a change in taxation plus a change in unemployment benefits.[3]

II. CHANGES IN AVERAGE AND MARGINAL TAX RATES

It is first necessary to develop two basic results that are completely general and on which much of the later analysis depends. The average tax rate (the total tax paid divided by income) and the marginal tax rate (the extra amount of tax paid as a result of an increase in income of one unit) are fundamental measures of any tax system. The way in which these two rates vary with income provides a great deal of information about the tax structure. If the marginal rate exceeds the average rate the tax is described as 'progressive', although the precise degree of progression is more awkward to define. It is useful to consider 'pure' changes in marginal and average rates; that is, changes in one rate while leaving the other rate unchanged. The achievement of such pure changes in any practical tax system will usually require changes in more than one of the tax parameters, but these complications need not be considered at this stage.

Suppose first that only the marginal tax rate facing the members of a union increases. At the initial wage (that is, the wage obtained before the change in the tax rate) there is no alteration in the total tax paid and hence also in the real after-tax wage, since by assumption the average tax rate is unchanged. The higher marginal tax rate reduces the pay-off to the union from an attempt to increase the wage. While the benefit from a higher wage demand

---

[3] When the VAT rate was increased in Britain in 1979, unemployment benefits were in fact increased in order to maintain their real value, allowing for the consequent effect on prices.

has been reduced, the benefit from an increase in employment is unchanged: more union members would be earning at an unchanged average tax rate. As a result the relative advantage of employment gains has increased and the rational union will reduce its wage demand so as to induce a rise in employment. The extra employment is of course achieved only by reducing the value of the gross (or before tax) wage demanded by the union. Such a reduction is less unattractive than otherwise, in view of the higher marginal tax rate. Hence the 'pure' *increase* in the marginal tax rate faced by a union's members leads to a reduction in the wage demands of that union. The precise extent of the reduction will of course depend on the exact nature of the union's preferences, but there is no question of the direction of change involved.

Next consider an increase in the average tax rate facing a union's members, with the tax structure adjusted in order to keep the marginal rate unchanged. This means that, at the initial wage, there is an increase in the total tax paid per member, while the value of an extra dollar in wages is unchanged. An increase in employment is now relatively less attractive, since the after-tax real wage has been reduced relative to unemployment benefits. Hence the union will demand a higher before-tax wage. The resulting additional unemployment will be less unattractive than otherwise. Therefore, the second basic result is that a 'pure' *increase* in the average tax rate faced by a union's members leads to an *increase* in the wage demands of that union. Again, the direction of the change is quite general, although the amount will depend on the exact form of the union's preferences.

It is important to recognise that 'pure' increases in marginal and average tax rates have opposite effects on wage demands. Analyses are thereby often complicated by the need to examine the net effect of any policy which simultaneously changes both rates. For example, suppose that income tax is calculated simply as a proportion of 'taxable income', where the latter is the excess of income above some tax-free threshold. If the proportional rate of tax is reduced and other parameters of the system are left unchanged, then both the marginal and the average tax rates fall. The first effect, from the preceding analysis, tends to raise wage demands while the second effect tends to reduce them; the problem is to work out which effect dominates. In this simple case it is not difficult to show that for practical values of the relevant variables (such as the threshold and the level of unemployment benefits) the average rate effect dominates at all wage levels and so wage demands would be reduced. The following sections will discuss some rather more awkward cases.

III. CHANGES IN PROGRESSIVITY

The previous discussion referred to the tax situation facing the members of a particular union. A change in the tax system that leads to a 'pure' change in the marginal tax rate facing one union will not involve a 'pure' change for another union with a different wage rate and facing a different set of demand conditions. The progressivity of a tax system is usually thought of in terms of the difference between the dispersion (however measured) of the pre- and post-tax distributions of income. A 'pure' change in progressivity, altering the dispersion of after-tax incomes while leaving total tax revenue unchanged, is thus not straightforward to specify. It will depend, among other things, on the measure of progressivity used, depending in turn on the measure of dispersion.

It is, however, possible to consider the following general situation using an intuitive argument. Suppose that it is required to increase the progressivity of the tax system while leaving total revenue from all wage earners constant. The required reduction in the dispersion (however measured) of post-tax income will involve increasing the marginal tax rate facing most wage earners, particularly the high wage groups. But in order to keep total revenue constant it will also be necessary to decrease average tax rates, at least for some groups of wage earners. Now the previous section has show that a pure *increase* in the marginal tax rate and a pure *decrease* in the average tax rate facing a union both lead to the union *reducing* its wage demand, and obtaining an increase in the employment of its members. Thus changes in progressivity lead to changes in average and marginal tax rates that operate in the same direction in influencing the wage demands of unions. The argument suggests that an *increase* in progressivity will lead *all* trade unions to *reduce* their wage demands, irrespective of their wage levels before the change. Conversely, reductions in progressivity lead to increases in the wage demands of all unions. These results do not, however, have the degree of generality attached to those obtained in the previous section, because of the complications arising from the introduction of a complete distribution of wages and the many ways in which progressivity may be measured. Nevertheless detailed analyses show that there is a very strong presumption that the result will hold for practical values of relevant variables.[2]

IV. CHANGES IN THE TAX MIX

The general results obtained in Sections II and III can now be applied to a particular policy question. A number of governments in recent years have, for a variety of reasons, wished to shift away from direct taxes towards a greater reliance on some form of broad-based consumption tax. But there has, perhaps surprisingly, been little analysis of the possible response from trade unions. This section considers the effect on unions' wage demands of various types of revenue-neutral shift from income taxation towards a consumption tax. For ease of exposition, the income tax system will be assumed to have a single marginal rate applied to all wages measured above a threshold. This convenient assumption does not affect the main results.[4] Assume further that the consumption tax is similar to a Value Added Tax system, whereby a single rate is applied to the tax–exclusive price of all goods and services. It will also be supposed that the real level of unemployment benefits is constant in the face of a change in the tax mix; that is, any increase in prices as a result of an increase in the VAT rate leads to an appropriate adjustment of benefits. This kind of adjustment has been carried out in practice; indeed, failure to adjust would involve a quite distinct policy of reducing real benefits.

The change in the tax mix can be brought about in two basic ways, arising from separate use of the two parameters of the income tax system. Suppose first that income tax revenue is reduced by cutting the marginal income tax rate. This involves a loss of revenue that depends, among other things, on the complete distribution of income. For revenue neutrality, the VAT rate must be increased by an appropriate amount. The consumption tax is a proportional tax on all expenditure, whereas income tax is proportional to income measured in excess of the threshold. Because of this difference in bases, the required increase in the VAT rate will be less than the reduction in the income tax rate.[5] The overall (effective) marginal tax rate, from income tax and VAT combined, is therefore lower, irrespective of the level of income. But the increase in the consumption tax rate involves a higher average tax rate for the lower income groups and a lower average rate for the higher incomes. There is of course a particular level of wages for which the average tax rate is unchanged.

This policy clearly has the effect of reducing the progressivity of the tax system (increasing the dispersion of the post-tax distribution of wages). The argument of Section III suggests that this would lead all trade unions to increase their wage demands. Alternatively, this can be seen from the fact that the lower income groups experience a lower marginal rate and a higher average rate, both of which (from Section II) lead to a desire for higher wages. The higher income groups experience changes in average and marginal rates which operate in opposite directions on wage demands. Only for those with very high wages will the average tax rate effect dominate. These wages are so high as to be irrelevant for trade unions in practice. This kind of policy has often been advocated in the belief that lowering the overall marginal tax rate will stimulate the supply of labour. Against this must now be set the argument that the policy is likely to lead to higher wage demands from unions and higher unemployment of unions' members.

A second way of reducing income tax revenue is to raise the tax-free threshold. This has the effect of reducing taxable income for all wage earners

---

[4] A multi-rate tax structure is examined in Creedy (1988).

[5] The analysis of this section ignores savings and the associated complex intertemporal issues.

while leaving the marginal rate unchanged for those above the new threshold. As before, the consumption tax rate must be raised by an amount that depends partly on the nature of the income distribution. This means that everyone (earning more than the threshold) will face a higher overall marginal tax rate. Furthermore, this policy has the effect of increasing progressivity; the lower income groups experience a lower average tax rate than before the change while the higher incomes face a higher average tax rate. In this situation the results of Section III suggests that the revenue neutral increase in progressivity will *reduce* the wage demands of all unions. Again this is reinforced by Section II. The lower income groups experience a higher marginal and a lower average tax rate, both of which lead to a reduction in wage demands in favour of higher employment. The relatively high income groups experience changes in average and marginal rates that pull in opposite directions on their wage demands, but generally the higher marginal rate dominates the average rate effect. Only for the extremely high incomes (for whom the reduction in the threshold has a negligible proportional effect on taxable income) will the average rate effect dominate. Again it is found that such high incomes are likely to be outside the relevant range for unions. Simultaneously raising the threshold and the consumption tax rate will therefore be expected to reduce the wage demands of all unions.[6]

After considering these two types of policy, the question of whether it is possible to combine them in some way naturally arises. Is it possible to shift from direct to indirect tax and simultaneously to reduce the marginal income tax rate in such a way that all unions will reduce their wage demands? The answer is 'yes' if the package includes a rise in the income tax threshold in addition to the reduction in the marginal income tax rate and an increase in the VAT rate. The threshold effect will tend to reduce wage demands while the reduction in the marginal rate of income tax will work in the opposite direction. There seems no *a priori* reason why a combination should not be found in which the former effect dominates sufficiently for wage demands to be reduced, while still allowing the marginal income tax rate to fall sufficiently for the overall (effective) marginal tax rate to fall, after allowing for the required increase in the consumption tax rate.[7] Formal analysis of this type of policy is naturally more complicated, but does support the more heuristic argument. It is indeed possible to change the tax mix in favour of

---

[6] These policy shifts are examined in detail in Creedy and McDonald (1988b).

[7] The overall marginal rate of tax is not simply the sum of the income tax and consumption tax rates. Suppose the income tax rate is 0.30, so that an increase in income of \$1 gives rise to an increase in disposable income of only \$0.70. If all this is consumed it has to be borne in mind that the consumption tax rate is expressed as applying to the tax *exclusive* price of goods. A rate of 0.10 translates into a rate of 0.091 when applied to the tax inclusive price; that is, 0.10/(1 + 0.10). The extra dollar of income thus leads to an increase in the consumption tax paid of 0.70 multiplied by 0.091, or 0.0637. Thus the overall (effective) marginal tax rate is 0.3637, whereas the simple sum of two rates is of course 0.40.

Trade Unions, Wages and Taxation

consumption taxes, lower the overall marginal tax rate *and* reduce the wage demands of unions.[8] An increase in the income tax threshold plays a crucial role in such a policy.

V. A WAGE AND TAX DEAL

Changes in taxation which reduce the wage demands of trade unions will allow employment and output to rise. To achieve such a favourable outcome various governments have tried to strike wage–tax deals with trade union leaders, offering tax cuts in exchange for wage restraint. The economic analyses of trade unions discussed here suggest that for any given reduction in taxation, some types of tax cut will have greater appeal than others to trade union leaders as part of a wage tax deal. In particular, increasing the income tax threshold would be likely to lead to greater wage reductions than if only the income tax rate were reduced.

Even if tax cuts lead, via reduced wage demands, to higher levels of employment, they cannot be recommended without reservation if they crowd out investment spending. Tax cuts will crowd out investment spending if the stimulus they give to aggregate supply is exceeded by the stimulus to aggregate consumption demand. If, on the other hand, the increase in aggregate demand caused by tax cuts is smaller than the increase in aggregate supply then investment need not suffer and there is a strong case for those tax cuts.

The supply-side effect of tax cuts depends on the size of their restraining effect on wage demands and on the size of the output response to a fall in pre-tax wages. The latter depends on the production technology of the economy. Obviously the tax cut policies which have the largest restraining effect on wages will have, for a given technology, the largest supply-side effect. The stimulus to total consumption demand arises from the increase in disposable incomes that results from the tax cuts, and depends on the proportions of any increases in wages and profits that are consumed. Not only do real wages and profits increase, but demand increases because of the fact that fewer people are unemployed.

Detailed analysis shows that raising the income tax threshold has, given reasonable assumptions about the nature of technology, the tax system and the propensities to consume out of wages and profits, a sufficiently strong effect on supply to offset the effect on demand. In comparison with raising the income tax threshold, the case for cutting the marginal rate of income tax is not quite as strong. However, even when the marginal rate of income tax is cut, it would appear likely that investment will not be crowded out.

It is also possible for total tax revenue from income, profits and

---

[8] Ranges of parameter values for which this result holds are given in Creedy and McDonald (1988c).

Fiscal Studies

consumption taxes combined to *increase* as a result of either a reduction in the marginal rate of income tax or an increase in the tax-free threshold. This arises from the expansion in employment, output and hence taxable incomes and profits, combined with the fact that any increase in consumption expenditure will generate more revenue from the 'indirect' consumption tax. But there is nevertheless a range of situations in which tax cuts are likely to increase investment while reducing total tax revenue, after allowing for all the subsequent effects on supply and demand.[9]

The results therefore lead to some optimism about the efficacy of tax cuts, especially where achieved by increasing the threshold level, in reducing inflation and simultaneously increasing employment, output and investment. But it must be recognised that they have been obtained using a model of a closed economy; hence any implications for the balance of payments have been ignored. Further research is needed in order to investigate the robustness of the results.

VI. CONCLUSIONS

This paper has summarised the major results of a number of economic analyses of the effects of specified tax changes on the behaviour of rational trade unions. The basic starting point has been the assumption that trade unions are concerned with the real wages of their members, and are prepared to trade off the joint objectives of high employment and high real wages. The assumption, sometimes used in debate, that unions attempt to keep their real wages constant is a very special case of this more general approach. Unions would in general be expected to examine closely the implications of any changes in the tax system for the average and marginal tax rates confronting their members. It has been seen that 'pure' reductions in average and marginal rates have opposite effects on unions' wage demands. A reduction in the marginal rate of income tax will reduce both the average and the overall marginal rate of tax; in general the 'average rate effect' will dominate so that unions would be expected to reduce wage demands. However, an increase in the tax-free threshold affects only the average tax rate and therefore leads to a larger reduction in wage demands. This potentially useful effect of changes in thresholds on unions' wage demands seems to have been neglected in previous policy debates, and seems worthy of further investigation.

---

[9] A detailed analysis of investment and revenue implications of tax cuts is given in Creedy and McDonald (1989).

Trade Unions, Wages and Taxation

REFERENCES

Brown, C. (1988), 'Will the 1988 income tax cuts either increase work incentives or raise more revenue?' *Fiscal Studies*, vol. 9, no. 4, pp. 93–107.

Dilnot, A. and Kell, M. (1988), 'Top-rate tax cuts and incentives: some empirical evidence' *Fiscal Studies*, vol. 9, no. 4, pp. 70–92.

Creedy, J. (1988), 'Flattening the tax rate structure, changing the tax mix and unions' wage demands' *The University of Melbourne, Department of Economics, Research Paper*, no. 212.

Creedy, J. and McDonald, I.M. (1988a) 'Income tax changes and trade union wage demands' *The University of Melbourne, Department of Economics, Research Paper*, no. 201.

Creedy, J. and McDonald, I.M. (1988b) 'The shift from direct to indirect taxation and trade union wage demands' *The University of Melbourne, Department of Economics Research Paper*, no. 206.

Creedy, J. and McDonald, I.M. (1988c) 'A tax package to reduce the marginal rate of tax and the wage demands of trade unions', *The University of Melbourne, Department of Economics, Research Paper*, no. 215.

Creedy, J. and McDonald, I.M. (1989) 'Tax cuts, wage demands and investment in a unionised economy', *The University of Melbourne, Department of Economics, Research Paper*, no. 220.

Oswald, A.J. (1985) 'The economic theory of trade unions: an introductory survey', *Scandinavian Journal of Economics*, 87, pp. 160–193.

Ulph, A.M. and Ulph, D.T. (1988) 'Union bargaining — a survey of recent work', *University of Southampton, Department of Economics Discussion Paper*.

17

A Tax Package to Reduce the Marginal Rate of Income Tax and the Wage Demands of Trade Unions*

JOHN CREEDY and IAN M. MCDONALD

University of Melbourne,
Parkville, Victoria 3052

To reduce the level of tax evasion, a shift of taxation away from income tax and towards a consumption tax has been proposed in Australia. This paper shows that for such a shift to maintain revenue but not induce trade unions to raise their wage demands, it is necessary that the income tax threshold be increased. Numerical examples of desirable tax packages are given.

I Introduction

Many governments in recent years have been concerned to reduce the marginal rate of income tax. This desire has been motivated partly by the belief that high marginal tax rates have a strong disincentive effect (even though it has been difficult to find empirical support for this view). In addition, it is believed that high levels of tax evasion are stimulated by high marginal tax rates. Governments have attempted to reduce tax rates partly by reducing government expenditure and partly by changing the structure of the tax system. A major structural change involves a shift of taxation away from income tax and towards a general consumption tax. Such a change was achieved in Britain in 1979, and was proposed in Australia in the much debated *Reform of the Australian Tax System* (1985).

This paper is concerned not with individual responses to changes in the tax structure but with the response of trade unions. Previous discussions of the effects of tax changes on unions' behaviour in Australia have assumed simply that unions attempt to maintain a fixed level of post-tax real wages. However, the present analysis assumes rather less simplistic responses by using an explicit

* We are grateful to Jeff Borland and two anonymous referee's of this journal for helpful comments on an earlier draft.

assumption about the unions' objectives, in terms both of wages and employment of their members.

One way of shifting towards a consumption tax simply involves reducing the marginal rate of income tax and simultaneously increasing the rate of consumption tax by an amount sufficient to maintain revenue. It has been shown in Creedy and McDonald (1988) that such a change will increase the wage demands of all trade unions, irrespective of their level of wages before the change in the tax structure. Such a shift would be both inflationary and tend to lower employment. This paper considers a more complicated tax package that simultaneously alters the income tax threshold, the marginal income tax rate and the consumption tax rate. It is shown that the appropriate change in these three parameters will allow the marginal rate of income tax to be reduced whilst revenue is maintained and trade unions are induced to reduce wage demands. The crucial ingredient of this package is an increase in the income tax threshold.

The general framework of analysis is presented in Section II, followed by discussion of the unions' objective and wage demands in Section III. The specification of changes in the tax system which are revenue neutral are examined in Section IV. The wage-reducing tax package is presented in Section V, followed by conclusions and qualifications in Section VI. First, however, the basic tax structure is described in the following subsection.

The Tax Structure

The analysis assumes that the income tax system has a single threshold, a, and a single marginal tax rate, t, applying to all income measured in excess of the threshold. Thus the income tax paid on a wage of w, denoted $t(w)$, is given by:

$$t(w) = 0 \qquad \text{for } w \leqslant a$$
$$= t(w\text{-}a) \qquad \text{for } w > a \qquad (1)$$

Assume that all disposable income is consumed, that the consumption tax involves a fixed proportional rate, v, applied to the tax-exclusive price of all goods, and that the tax is fully shifted to consumers. Then prices may be considered as increasing from the normalized value of unity to $1 + v$. Thus net of tax real income, y, $= y(w)$, is given for $w > a$, by:

$$y = \frac{w - t(w)}{1 + v}$$

$$= \frac{at + (1 - t)\, w}{1 + v} \qquad (2)$$

This paper concentrates on the transformation between y and w given by equation (2).

It should be stressed that the overall marginal tax rate (the total amount of tax paid on an extra dollar of income) is not simply the sum of the income and consumption tax rates. This is because v is applied to the tax-exclusive price of goods and only $\$(1\text{-}t)$ is available to spend of an increase in gross earnings of $\$1$. Hence the overall marginal tax rate is $t + (1\text{-}t)\, v/(1 + v)$ where $v/(1 + v)$ is the rate of consumption tax as applied to the tax-inclusive price of goods. An implication of this is that a decrease in t of one percentage point, matched by an increase in v of more than one percentage point, can still lead to a reduction in the overall marginal tax rate. For example if $v = 0.10$ and $t = 0.30$, the overall marginal rate is $0.3 + (0.7)\,(0.09) = 0.36$. For a constant overall marginal rate it is required that $dv/dt = -(1 + v)/(1\text{-}t)$. While the emphasis of the paper is on designing a package that simultaneoulsy reduces the *income* tax rate and unions' wage demands, the implications for the overall marginal rate are also indicated.

II   A General Framework

The analysis is concerned with the change in the wage demands of a trade union in response to changes in all three parameters of the tax system. Furthermore, the tax changes have to satisfy a basic revenue neutrality requirement. This section describes a general framework of analysis; specific assumptions about the process of wage determination and functional forms will be used to make appropriate substitutions in later sections.

Revenue Neutrality

Total tax revenue per capita, R, can be written as a function of the three tax parameters, a, t and v. It will be seen in Section IV that the nature of the function depends on the characteristics of the distribution of wages of all workers. However, the present discussion is concerned only to provide a framework for allowing the tax parameters to change while keeping total revenue constant. Revenue neutrality requires:

$$dR = R_a\, da + R_v\, dv + R_t\, dt = 0 \qquad (3)$$

where a subscript denotes a corresponding partial derivative, so that $R_a = \partial R/\partial a$, and so on. Rearranging (3) gives:

$$dv = -(R_t\, dt + R_a\, da)/R_v . \qquad (4)$$

Equation (4) shows how the consumption tax rate needs to be changed as a result of changes in the income tax structure, in order to keep total revenue constant. The precise form of the partial derivative will be derived in Section IV below.

Changes in Wage Demands

As with tax revenue, the wage obtained by a trade union can be written as a function of, among other things, the three parameters of the tax schedule. As will be seen in Section III, the precise nature of the function depends on the form of the union's objective function and the wage determination process assumed, but the present discussion concentrates on developing a general approach. When all three tax parameters change, the change in the optimal wage is given by the total differential:

$$dw = \frac{\partial w}{\partial t}\, dt + \frac{\partial w}{\partial a}\, da + \frac{\partial w}{\partial v}\, dv. \qquad (5)$$

From (5) it can be seen that the pre-tax wage rate falls, that is $dw < 0$, if:

$$\frac{\partial w}{\partial a} \, da + \frac{\partial w}{\partial v} \, dv < -\frac{\partial w}{\partial t} \, dt.$$

Substituting for dv from (4) and rearranging, a change in the tax parameters which is revenue neutral and which lowers wage demands must satisfy:

$$da \left[\frac{\partial w}{\partial a} - \frac{R_a}{R_v} \frac{\partial w}{\partial v} \right] < - dt \left[\frac{\partial w}{\partial t} - \frac{R_t}{R_v} \frac{\partial w}{\partial v} \right]. \quad (6)$$

Restricting the analysis to cuts in the marginal rate of income tax, that is, where $dt < 0$, condition (6) can be rewritten as:

$$\frac{(da/a)}{(-dt)} \left[\frac{a\partial w}{\partial a} - \frac{aR_a}{R_v} \frac{\partial w}{\partial v} \right] < \left[\frac{\partial w}{\partial t} - \frac{R_t}{R_v} \frac{\partial w}{\partial v} \right]. \quad (7)$$

From (4), and imposing the restriction that $dt < 0$, revenue neutrality implies the following relation:

$$dv \gtrless 0 \text{ as } \frac{(da/a)}{(-dt)} \frac{_aR_a}{R_v} \lessgtr \frac{R_t}{R_v}. \quad (8)$$

Condition (7) has to be satisfied for the tax shift to lower wage demands whilst maintaining revenue neutrality. Condition (8) determines whether a chosen value of $(da/a)/(-dt)$ implies an increase or a decrease in the rate of consumption tax to maintain revenue neutrality. Although not strictly necessary, it is most convenient to consider, as in (8), proportional changes in the tax threshold. For changes in the tax mix examined in this paper it is of course necessary for dv to be positive. These two conditions will play an important role in Section V.

III The Wage Demand of a Simple Monopoly Union

As mentioned in the introduction, it is assumed that unions are willing to trade employment for wages, and vice versa. Hence the welfare of unemployed members of the union is counted equally with that of employed members in the union's objective function. If n denotes the level of employment, the union is assumed, following McDonald and Solow (1981), to maximize the collective welfare, W, of its m members, where:

$$W = n \{U(y) - D\} + (m - n) \, U(b) \quad (9)$$

and y is post-tax income, D is the disutility of work and b is the level of unemployment benefits. If the opportunity cost of working, x, is defined using $U(x) = U(b) + D$, then (9) can be rewritten as:

$$W = n \{U(y) - U(x)\} + m \, U(b). \quad (10)$$

For the 'simple monopoly union' model, W must be maximized with respect to w and subject to the constraint that employment is on the labour demand curve $n(w)$, with $n'(w) < 0$ and that $n \leq m$. For interior solutions, where $n < m$ and the tangency of the union's indifference curve with the labour demand curve implies positive profits, the first-order condition is obtained by writing W as a function of w and setting $W'(w) = 0$. Hence:

$$W'(w) = n'(w)\{U(y) - U(x)\}$$
$$+ n(w) \, U'(y) \, y'(w) = 0 \quad (11)$$

and (11) can be rearranged to give the condition:

$$\theta = \epsilon \xi \quad (12)$$

where $\theta = -wn'(w)/n$ is minus the wage elasticity of demand for labour, $\epsilon = y \, U'(y)/\{U(y) - U(x)\}$ is the elasticity of the excess of the utility from working over that of the opportunity cost of working, with respect to the post-tax real wage, and $\xi = wy'(w)/y$ is the elasticity of the post-tax wage with respect to the pre-tax wage.

The Risk-Neutral Case

It can be seen that, even where θ is assumed to be constant, the use of the tax function in (2) means that it is not possible to solve the first-order condition (12) explicitly for w except in the special case where the union is risk neutral, that is where $U(y) = y$. For this reason the present paper concentrates on this special case, although further investigation shows that the results are not very sensitive to the degree of relative risk aversion. Appropriate substitution into (12) gives the following expression for the union's optimal wage demand:

$$w = \frac{\{x(1 + v) - at\}}{h(1 - t)} \quad (13)$$

where $h = 1 - 1/\theta$.

Section II has shown that it is necessary to obtain explicit results for the partial differentiation of w with respect to a, v and t. Differentiation of w, from (13) gives:

$$\frac{\partial w}{\partial a} = \frac{-t}{h(1-t)} \tag{14}$$

$$\frac{\partial w}{\partial v} = \frac{x}{h(1-t)} \tag{15}$$

$$\frac{\partial w}{\partial t} = \frac{\{x(1+v)-a)\}}{h(1-t)^2} \tag{16}$$

These three results will be used in Section V to substitute into (7).

Other Models of Trade Union Behaviour

The simple monopoly union model can be criticized on two grounds. First, by assuming the union can set any wage it wishes, too much power may be given to the union. A more general model which allows the degree of union power relative to the firm to vary is the 'right to manage' model of Nickell and Andrews (1983) in which the union and the firm bargain over the wage but the firm, as in the simple monopoly union model, has complete control over employment. With this structure of wage bargaining it is shown in Creedy and McDonald (1989) that the bargained wage is determined by (13) with $h = (\theta - 1)(1 + \gamma) / \{\theta(1 + \gamma) - 1\}$, where γ is the union power parameter giving the power of the union relative to the firm.

The second criticism of the simple monopoly union model is that it yields outcomes for wages and employment which are Pareto sub-optimal. A long literature, starting with Edgeworth (1881), has pointed out that the firm and the union can achieve Pareto efficient outcomes by jointly bargaining over both wages and employment. Creedy and McDonald (1989) show that for efficient bargains the bargained wage is given by the same value of h as for the wage-bargaining case discussed in the previous paragraph. But employment is higher with efficient bargains than with wage bargaining.

The presumption that union's are prepared to trade off wages for employment gains, which underlies the union's objective function (9) and the results for the bargained wage just given for the wage-bargaining model and the efficient bargains model, has also been criticized. Many commentators argue that insiders dominate the union's objective; see Carruth and Oswald (1987), Lindbeck and Snower (1985) and Blanchard and Summers (1986). Assuming the union is dominated by a group of insiders who enjoy a high degree of job security, Creedy and McDonald (1989) show that the bargained wage is given by (13) with $h = (\theta - \gamma - 1)/(\theta - 1)$. Equation (13) and its partial derivatives, (14), (15) and (16), is therefore not a special case but, with the appropriate definitions of h, embraces a wide variety of union models. Hence, the subsequent analysis in the paper, based on (13), has a much wider applicability.

IV Total Tax Revenue

The Wage Distribution and Tax Revenue

An essential restriction on policy packages considered here is that they should be revenue neutral in aggregate, since the government budget constraint concerns total revenue. In view of the nature of the tax system, information is required about the complete distribution function of wages, $F(w)$. The approach taken here is to impose a form of F that is descriptively appropriate; some wage levels will be influenced by unions but the model of Section III is not assumed to apply to every wage. Furthermore, changes are considered which are *ex ante* revenue neutral, so that subsequent effects on unions' wages are not taken into account.

The paper therefore makes no attempt to endogenize either the complete distribution of wages or the complete tax and transfer system. However, it must be acknowledged that a completely general approach would wish to allow for a vast range of possible 'feedbacks'. To allow for such endogeneity presents intractable analytical problems, and some researchers would no doubt wish to use some type of computable general equilibrium model containing a sophisticated treatment of the tax structure. The present approach simply takes the view that it is useful to clarify the details of the processes involved in a more limited model. The structure of the problem can in this way be more clearly understood.

Total per capita revenue from income tax is equal to:

$$t \int_a^t (w-a)\, dF(w) \tag{17}$$

which can be shown to simplify to:

$$t\overline{w}\, G(a) \tag{18}$$

where $G(a) = \{1 - F_1(a)\} - (a/\overline{w})\{1 - F(a)\}$. (19)

The term $F_1(a)$ is equal to $\int_0^a w\,dF(w)/\overline{w}$ and is the 'first moment distribution' of w. When $a = 0$, $G(a) = 1$ and (18) is simply the tax rate multiplied by the average wage, $\overline{w}$. Equations (18) and (19) can be explained intuitively as follows. Only those with earnings above the threshold, a, are subject to taxation; the total earnings (per capita) of this group is equal to the value of average earnings multiplied by the proportion of total earnings obtained by those with $w > a$. The latter proportion is just $1 - F_1(a)$. But this total is not the tax base, since taxable income for each person is measured by income in excess of the threshold. Since the proportion of people who pay tax is equal to $1 - F(a)$, the effect (per capita) of the threshold in reducing the tax base is simply $a\{1 - F(a)\}$.

From (18), the value of disposable income per person is equal to $\overline{w}\{1 - tG(a)\}$. Assuming that all disposable income is consumed, and noting that a tax-exclusive consumption tax rate of v translates to a tax-inclusive rate of $v/(1 + v)$, the total per capita tax revenue from income and consumption taxes, R, is given by:

$$R = \overline{w}[tG(a) + \{1 - tG(a)\}v/(1 + v)]. \quad (20)$$

The result in (20) can then be used to obtain the required partial derivatives R_a, R_t and R_v. These are given by:

$$R_t = \overline{w}G(a)/(1 + v) \quad (21)$$

$$R_v = \overline{w}\{1 - tG(a)\}/(1 + v)^2 \quad (22)$$

$$R_a = -t(1 - F(a))/(1 + v) \quad (23)$$

The latter uses the result that $\partial G(a)/\partial a = -\{1 - F(a)\}/\overline{w}$. Defining τ and ϕ as:

$$\tau = (1 - t)/\{G(a)^{-1} - t\} \quad (24)$$

and $$\phi = (1 - t)\{1 - F(a)\}/\{1 - tG(a)\} \quad (25)$$

then $$\frac{R_t}{R_v} = \frac{(1 + v)\tau}{(1 - t)} \quad (26)$$

$$\frac{R_a}{R_v} = \frac{-\phi t(1 + v)}{\overline{w}(1 - t)} \quad (27)$$

TABLE 1
Values of ϕ and τ

$a/\overline{w}$	t	θ	τ
0.17	0.3	0.93	0.77
	0.4	0.70	0.74
0.5	0.3	0.72	0.41
	0.4	0.66	0.38

Note: These values are based on values of F, F_1 and G for a lognormal distribution of income given in Creedy (1985, p.143). The distribution has a coefficient of variation of 0.5.

and $$\frac{R_t}{R_a} = -\frac{\overline{w}\tau}{\phi t} \quad (28)$$

The results in (26), (27), and (28) can then be used for substituting into the general equations (7) and (8). It will be seen in the next section that, not surprisingly, unequivocal results cannot be stated concerning the effect on wage demands of any type of tax structure change. It will be necessary to use numerical results, so that values of τ and ϕ, for alternative values of a and t, are required. For this purpose it is most convenient to make the reasonable assumption that the distribution function of wages, $F(w)$, follows the well-known lognormal distribution. Hence the logarithms of w follow the normal distribution, and standard numerical routines may be used to evaluate the required integrals. Table 1 gives values of τ and ϕ based on results for the functions $F(\ )$, $F_1(\ )$ and $G(\ )$ given in Creedy (1985), where the distribution has a coefficient of variation of 0.5. These values will be used in the following section.

V The Tax Package

Analytical Results

It is now possible to make appropriate substitutions into the general results derived in Section II. It is worth stressing here that the result stated in equation (7) holds under the assumption that $dt < 0$; that is, the marginal rate of income tax is reduced. Substituting (14), (15), (16), (26) and (27) into (7) yields the following condition for a revenue-neutral shift in the three tax parameters to lower the wage demands of a trade union:

$$\frac{da/a}{-dt} A > B \quad (29)$$

where $A = t[1 - t - \phi(1 + v)(x/\overline{w})]$ (30)

$B = 1 - (1 + v)(1-\tau)(x/\overline{w})/(a/\overline{w})$.   (31)

It is worth stressing that (29) does not depend on the value of h. To determine the direction and size of the changes in the threshold and the marginal tax rate required for a revenue-neutral, wage-reducing tax package, it is necessary to divide both sides of (29) by the term A. However, the effect of this division on the inequality sign depends on whether A is positive. From the definition given in (30):

$$A > 0 \text{ if } (x/\overline{w}) < (1-t)/\phi(1+v) = H. \quad (32)$$

This condition for $A > 0$ is likely to be satisfied. A realistic set of values of $\phi = 0.7$, $t = 0.4$ and $v = 0.15$ gives $H = 0.7453$ and so requires $x/\overline{w} < 0.7453$ for $A > 0$. Reducing t to 0.3 raises ϕ to 0.93 and lowers H to 0.6545. For $t = 0.2$ and $\phi = 0.5$, H is 0.7323. In each case lower values of v give higher values of H. Remembering that x consists of unemployment benefits and the income equivalent of the disutility of work, it is reasonable to suppose that $x/\overline{w}$ is less than 0.65. There is an additional argument suggesting that a reasonable value of $x/\overline{w}$ is less than 0.65. The trade union model implies a relation between x and wages. Suppose there is a union which, by following the simple monopoly union model, happens to set a wage equal to the arithmetic mean wage, $\overline{w}$. Using (13), this embodies a value of $x/\overline{w}$ of

$$x/\overline{w} = [h(1-t) + (a/\overline{w})t]/(1 + v). \quad (33)$$

With $t = 0.4$, $a/\overline{w} = 0.17$, $v = 0.15$, equation (33) gives $x/\overline{w} = 0.4765$ if θ is set at five. In fact, a union setting a wage equal to the average wage would be expected to face a less elastic demand for labour than five (unions facing high elasticities of labour demand would be setting relatively low wages). Hence a value of $x/\overline{w}$ less than 0.65 would appear to be consistent with the trade union model and it is therefore reasonable to restrict attention to cases where $A > 0$. With this restriction, (29) can be rewritten as

$$\frac{da/a}{-dt} > \frac{B}{A}. \quad (34)$$

Numerical Examples

A revenue neutral tax package that reduces the marginal rate of income tax has to satisfy condition (34) if wage demands are to be reduced. To get some idea of how condition (34) might constrain a tax package in practice, values of B/A based on a range of values of $t, v, x/\overline{w}, a/\overline{w}, \tau$ and ϕ are shown in Table 2. To interpret the entries consider the top row, which applies to a marginal income tax rate of 0.4, a consumption tax rate of 0.05, $x/\overline{w} = 0.3$ and $a/\overline{w} = 0.17$. A reduction in the marginal rate of income tax of one cent in the dollar (that is, t is reduced by 0.01) will reduce trade union wage demands if accompanied by a rise in the income tax threshold of *more* than 3.4139 per cent, assuming that the consumption tax is also adjusted so that the overall tax package is revenue neutral. In Australia the income tax threshold is currently \$5099, so an increase of 3.4139 per cent is a dollar increase of \$174.07.

The fourth column in Table 2 suggests that reductions in t would have to be accompanied by a rise in the threshold, a, such that $(da/a)/(-dt) > 3.2940$ for a revenue-neutral tax package to reduce wage demands. The sixth column in Table 2 is based on $a/\overline{w} = 0.5$. On the basis of the current income tax schedule this is an unrealistically high value for $a/\overline{w}$ and is included to show that B/A is fairly insensitive to this parameter and the associated values of τ and ϕ.

The change in v required by the revenue-neutral tax package is given by (13). Substituting (26) and (27) into (13) and setting $(da/a)/(-dt) = B/A$ (which implies $dw = 0$) gives:

$$dv/-dt = (1+v)\{\phi\, t\,(a/\overline{w})(B/A) + \tau\}/(1-t) = J. \quad (35)$$

The reduction in income tax revenue implied by the simultaneous reduction in t and the increase in the threshold, a, requires a rise in v to maintain revenue, so that $dv/-dt$ is positive. Values of J are reported in the fifth and seventh columns of Table 2. In all cases J is greater than unity implying that the required increase in the consumption tax rate exceeds the absolute size of the decrease in the marginal rate of income tax. While the marginal rate of income tax is reduced, the consumption tax is increased and so the implication for the overall marginal tax rate, $m = t + (1-t)\,v/(1+v)$, is not immediately clear. Differentiating m totally with respect to t and v, and substituting for $dv/dt = -J$ from (35), gives

$$dm/dt = 1/(1+v) - (1-t)\,J/(1+v)^2. \quad (36)$$

TABLE 2

Some Numerical Examples

t	v	$x/\overline{w}$	$a/\overline{w} = 0.17$		$a/\overline{w} = 0.5$	
			B/A	J	B/A	J
0.4	0.05	0.3	3.4139	1.5794	3.8855	1.5625
		0.4	2.9220	1.5384	3.7113	1.5223
		0.5	2.1189	1.4715	3.4418	1.4601
0.4	0.15	0.3	3.2940	1.7189	3.8423	1.7004
		0.4	2.6661	1.6616	3.6235	1.6451
		0.5	1.5264	1.5576	3.2540	1.5516
0.3	0.05	0.3	4.6990	1.4893	4.4259	1.3320
		0.4	4.6516	1.4859	4.2287	1.3001
		0.5	4.5405	1.4795	3.9389	1.2531
0.3	0.15	0.3	4.6880	1.6303	4.3763	1.4501
		0.4	4.6246	1.6254	4.1323	1.4068
		0.5	4.4793	1.6140	3.7471	1.3384

Note: The values of ϕ and τ were set according to Table 1.

For the tax package to reduce the overall marginal rate of tax, the reduction in the marginal rate of income tax would have to offset the effect of the increase in the rate of consumption tax, so that $dm/dt > 0$. From (36) the condition for $dm/dt > 0$ is $J < (1+v)/(1-t)$. This condition is satisfied for all the entries in Table 1. So, for the numerical examples considered, the tax package reduces the overall marginal rate of tax.

VI Conclusions

This paper puts forward a revenue-neutral tax package designed to reduce the marginal rate of income tax and the wage demands of trade unions. The crucial ingredients in this package are an increase in the income tax threshold and a rise in the consumption tax rate. The calculations suggest that, as part of the tax package, the threshold would need to be raised by about $200 for every one percentage point reduction in the marginal rate of income tax.

The analysis of this paper suggests that an *increase* in the progressivity of the tax system is a crucial part of a tax package designed to reduce trade union wage demands. This conclusion is diametrically opposed to the flat-tax proposal. Indeed the analysis here shows that a move towards a flat tax, that is a reduction of the threshold, will lead to increase wage demands by trade unions if the amount of tax revenue collected is to be maintained.

In evaluating these results several points should be borne in mind. The analysis is based on a simple schedule of income taxation with a single marginal tax rate above a threshold. It would be of interest to extend the analysis to a multi-step schedule. The concept of *ex ante* revenue-neutrality ignores the feedback from changed wage demands to tax revenue collected. To allow for this feedback would require a theoretical determination of the entire income distribution. Finally, the models of trade union behaviour used in this paper have not been applied empirically to wage setting in Australia, and so their applicability is uncertain. Nevertheless, the properties of these models, especially that, *ceteris paribus*, lower marginal rates of tax raise wage demands whilst higher income tax thresholds lower wage demands, arise in all the major models of trade union behaviour, including those models in which there is, in the wage-setter's objective function, a trade-off between wages and employment and insider-models, in which the wage-setter's objective function is simply to maximize wages with no regard for the employment implications.

One motivation for the analysis of this paper is the possibility that a shift from an income tax to a consumption tax will reduce evasion. By embodying a reduction in the marginal rate of income tax in that shift, the incentive for evasion is reduced. Because little is known about the sensitivity of evasion to these changes in the tax structure the concept of revenue neutrality used in this paper ignores the possibility of increased revenue from less evasion. However, to the extent that evasion is significantly affected, the consumption tax rate would need to increase by rather less than the calculations reported here. This would make it easier to achieve reductions in unions' wage demands while also reducing the overall marginal tax rate (in addition to reducing the marginal income tax rate).

A similar comment applies to the exclusion of unemployment benefits from the definition of revenue-neutrality in this paper. In as far as the tax package allows, due to its wage-reducing property, aggregate employment to be increased unemployment benefit payments may be expected to fall. Revenue net of unemployment benefits would rise. However since little is known about the size of this effect on unemployment benefit payments, it is better not to introduce it in a formal way. If this were taken into account it would be easier to achieve reductions in unions' wage demands while also reducing the marginal rate of tax.

REFERENCES

Blanchard, O.J. and Summers, L.H. (1986), 'Hysteresis and the European Unemployment Problem', in S. Fischer (ed.), *NBER Macroeconmic Annual*, MIT Press, Cambridge.

Carruth, A.A. and Oswald, A.J. (1987), 'On Union Preferences and Labour Market Models: Insiders and Outsiders', *Economic Journal* 97, 431–45.

Commonwealth of Australia (1985), *Reform of the Australian Tax System*, Australian Government Publishing Service, Canberra.

Creedy, J. (1985), *Dynamics of Income Distribution*, Basil Blackwell, Oxford.

——— and McDonald, I.M. (1988), 'Union Wage Responses to a Shift from Direct to Indirect Taxation', *Research Paper Number 206*, Department of Economics, University of Melbourne.

——— and ——— (1989), 'Trade Unions and Taxes: A Synthesis', *Research Paper*, Department of Economics, University of Melbourne.

Edgeworth, F.Y (1881), Mathematical Psychics, Kegan Paul, London.

Lindebeck, A. and Snower, D.J. (1985), 'Explanation of Unemployment', *Oxford Review of Economic Policy* 1, 34–59.

McDonald, I.M. and Solow, R.M. (1981), 'Wage Bargaining and Employment', *American Economic Review* 71(5), 896–908.

Nickell, S.J. and Andrews, M (1983), 'Unions, Real Wages and Employment in Britain 1951–79', *Oxford Economic Papers* 35, 183–206.

18

Flattening the Tax Rate Structure, Changing the Tax Mix and Unions' Wage Demands

John Creedy

University of Melbourne, Australia

In view of the considerable interest during the last decade in the analysis of trade union behaviour, it is surprising that there have been so few discussions of the effects of tax changes on unions' wage demands. The subject was discussed by Oswald (1982, p. 588), who gave sufficient conditions under which a rise in the marginal rate of income tax, applied to income measured above a threshold, would lead to an increase in wage demands. This was followed by Hersoug (1984) who examined the effects of "revenue neutral" changes in progressivity and "progressivity neutral" changes in revenue. He used a simple non-linear tax function which has a constant value of the elasticity of the post-tax wage with respect to the pre-tax wage; this elasticity was also used as a measure of progressivity. Sampson (1986) then considered the effect of a "revenue neutral" shift to indirect taxation in a unionised economy, using an income tax function in which tax is a constant proportion of income measured above a single tax-free threshold and a proportional value added tax (VAT) applied to all expenditure. All the above studies used the model of a "simple monopoly union" in which the union is assumed to specify its wage demand while the firm has complete discretion over the level of employment (so that employment is on the standard labour demand curve); this model is described in, for example, McDonald and Solow (1981).

A serious limitation of the studies by Hersoug (1984) and Sampson (1986) is their specification of what is meant by a "revenue-neutral" tax change. Hersoug assumes that the average tax rate is constant for the single union under consideration, while Sampson assumes that the average rate is constant for some arbitrary wage level (sometimes associated with the "average" wage). Both authors therefore examine only a single union. It is argued, however, that in practice any government will be concerned with total tax revenue derived from all wage levels; it must ensure that changes in the tax structure leave aggregate revenue unchanged. It is important to consider changes in the tax structure quite separately from changes in overall tax revenue, though of course governments may combine both types of policy in a single package.

Changes in progressivity and in aggregate revenue, allowing for a large number of unions and a complete distribution of wages, have been considered in Creedy

The author is very grateful to Ian McDonald for discussions and encouragement in the preparation of this article, and to two referees who provided extremely helpful comments on an earlier draft.

Journal of
Economic
Studies
17,1

6

and McDonald (1988a) for both the constant elasticity tax function used by Hersoug and the simple linear tax function. Progressivity is defined more appropriately in terms of the difference between a measure of dispersion of pre- and post-tax wage distributions. "Pure" increases in aggregate revenue (keeping progressivity constant) and decreases in progressivity (keeping aggregate revenue constant) are both shown to increase the wage demands of *all* trade unions. Shifts from direct to indirect taxation which keep aggregate revenue constant have been examined in Creedy and McDonald (1988b) for simple monopoly unions and for a model in which all unions are assumed to reach a Nash equilibrium in bargaining with firms over both the level of employment and wages. It is shown that an increase in the tax-free threshold, combined with an appropriate rise in the VAT rate, will reduce the wage demands of all unions. However, a reduction in the marginal income tax rate, combined with a revenue neutral rise in the VAT rate, is most likely to lead to an increase in the wage demands of all unions. In view of the effects of the overall progressivity of the tax system of these two types of tax structure change, the results obviously complement those of Creedy and McDonald(1988a).

All the above analyses are, however, limited by the use of simple tax structures using, for example, a single rate of income tax. In practice, the tax systems of most countries use a series of rates; the marginal tax rate takes a number of discrete "jumps" but remains constant within specified bands or thresholds. In the United Kingdom the major shift from direct to indirect taxation, that took place as a result of the 1979 Budget, was brought about by simply eliminating the highest rates of income tax and leaving all other rates unchanged.

The purpose of this article is therefore to extend the previous results by considering a multi-rate tax system that can easily be applied to most countries. The effect on unions' wage demands of eliminating the top marginal rate in such a system, while raising the VAT rate in order to keep aggregate tax revenue constant, is examined in detail. Since the effect is ambiguous only for those previously paying the top marginal rate, it is sufficient for present purposes to deal with just a "two-step" tax function. The basic analytics of the general multi-rate function are however set out in the Appendix. The next section briefly describes the model of union behaviour used and the wage demands resulting from the tax system. The third section then examines the effects on wage demands of the specified change in the tax mix. The complete evaluation of these effects is seen to require the full specification of revenue neutral changes; this is the subject of section four.

Simple Monopoly Unions

The model of union behaviour is taken from the analysis of McDonald and Solow (1981) in which unions are regarded as trading employment for real wages. The union is assumed to maximise the utility function:

$$W = n\{U(y) - D\} + (m-n) \ U(b) \tag{1}$$

where D is the disutility of work and b is the level of unemployment benefits. The union is therefore regarded as maximising the expected utility of each of its identical members. It is convenient to rewrite (1) as:

$$W = n\{U(y) - U(x)\} + mU(b) \tag{2}$$

where $U(x) = U(b) + D$ and x is the opportunity cost of working. The framework is one in which a monopolistic union, all of whose m members have the same wage, w, sets the wage and allows employment, n, to be determined according to the labour demand function, $n = n(w)$.

It might be argued that a more appropriate framework of analysis is one in which unions and firms bargain over both wages and the level of employment. There has been much recent research into the analysis of alternative bargaining processes, surveyed by Oswald (1986) and Ulph and Ulph (1988). The justification for concentrating on the simple monopoly union model here is that the comparative static predictions of the various models are very similar, although they produce different wage and employment levels[1].

7

The Optimal Wage
Utility, W, must be maximised with respect to w, subject to the constraint that $n \leq m$. For interior solutions, the first order condition for a maximum is obtained by writing W as a function of w and setting $W'(w) = 0$. Hence:

$$W'(w) = n'(w) \{U(y) - U(x)\} + n(w) U'(y) y'(w) = 0 \tag{3}$$

where the real post-tax wage is written as $y = y(w)$, the nature of the function depending on the structure of taxation. The first order condition (3) can be rearranged as:

$$\phi = \epsilon\xi \tag{4}$$

where $\phi = - wn'(w)/n$ is minus the wage elasticity of demand for labour, $\epsilon = yu'(y)/\{U(y) - U(x)\}$ is the elasticity of the excess of the utility from working over that of the opportunity cost of working, with respect to the post-tax wage, and $\xi = wy'(w)/y$ is the elasticity of the real post-tax wage with respect to the pre-tax wage.

The Tax Structure
Consider the following income tax structure, where $T(w)$ represents the tax paid on a gross wage of w:

$$
\begin{aligned}
T(w) &= 0 & w &< a \\
&= t_1(w - a_1) & a_1 &\leq w \leq a_2 & (1)\\
&= t_1(a_2 - a_1) + t_2(w - a_2) & w &> a_2 & (2)
\end{aligned}
$$

The system therefore has two thresholds, a_1 and a_2, and two marginal rates, t_1 and t_2; there are two steps in the function. A multi-step function is outlined in the Appendix. Suppose that there is a consumption tax levied at the single rate, v, on the tax exclusive price of all goods. The VAT is assumed to be fully shifted to consumers in the form of an increase in the retail price of all goods. It must also be acknowledged that the analysis of unions is quite "partial" in the sense that they are not assumed to take account of any implied changes in the amount of unemployment benefits that may need to be financed as a result

Journal of
Economic
Studies
17,1

8

of changes in wage demands[2]. If the pre-tax price of each good is normalised
to unity, the post-tax price is $1 + v$ and the real net-of-tax wage, y, is given by:

$$y = \frac{a_1 t_1 + w(1 - t_1)}{1 + v} \qquad\qquad a_1 \leq w \leq a_2 \qquad (5)$$

$$y = \frac{a_2 t_2 - t_1(a_2 - a_1) + w(1 - t_2)}{1 + v}$$

$$= \frac{a_1 t_1 + a_2(t_2 - t_1) + w(1 - t_2)}{1 + v} \qquad w > a_2 \qquad (6)$$

The policy to be considered here involves eliminating the second "step" in
the income tax schedule and simultaneously increasing the consumption tax
rate in order to maintain total revenue at a constant level. This policy involves
making $t_2 = t_1$. It may be added here that the overall (effective) marginal tax
rate for anyone facing a marginal income tax rate of t is not equal to the sum
of t and v but is given by $t + (1 - t)v/(1 + v)$. This is because for an extra
unit of income only $1 - t$ is available for spending, and the tax-exclusive rate
of v must be translated into a tax-inclusive rate of $v/(1 + v)$.

Risk-neutral Unions
It can be shown that substitution of the tax structure in (5) and (6) into the
first order condition (4) gives an explicit solution for the optimal wage only where
the union has a simple linear utility function $U(y) = y$. For this reason the
following discussion is limited to the risk-neutral case. However, this assumption
is not as restrictive as it may initially appear to be. If the members are assumed
to have constant relative risk-aversion, then the wage demand can be solved
numerically for alternative values of the Arrow-Pratt measure of aversion.
Although wage *levels* are different, it is again found that the comparative static
effects of risk aversion are negligible in the present context.
   In view of the "two step" nature of the tax structure, two types of interior
solution need to be considered according to the value of w in relation to the
tax thresholds. Substitution into the first-order condition and rearrangement
gives:

$$w = \frac{\phi}{\phi - 1} \frac{[x(1 + v) - a_1 t_1]}{(1 - t_1)} \qquad \text{for } a_1 \leq w \leq a_2 \quad (7)$$

$$w = \frac{\phi}{\phi - 1} \frac{[x(1 + v) - [a_1 t_1 + a_2(t_2 - t_1)]]}{(1 - t_2)} \qquad \text{for } a_2 < w \quad (8)$$

It can therefore be seen that, in each case, the optimal wage is given by the
pre-tax wage corresponding to a real after-tax wage equal to the opportunity
cost of working, multiplied by a factor that depends on the elasticity of demand
for labour. The situation where $w < a_1$ is not considered explicitly here. Notice

that the minimum wage any union would accept is that wage whose post-tax real value is equal to the opportunity cost of working. Since the latter is largely dominated by unemployment benefits, which are usually lower than the threshold a_1, this case can reasonably be neglected.

Changes in the Tax Mix

Effects on Wage Demands

Suppose that there is a shift towards indirect taxation, achieved by eliminating the second step in the income tax schedule. Define v^* as the VAT rate that gives the same total revenue, in a one-step income tax function, as before the policy change.

In examining the effects of such a change in the tax structure on wage demands it is necessary to consider separately those unions whose wages are between a_1 and a_2, and those whose wages exceed a_2. For the first group the only relevant effect on the tax structure is an increase in the consumption tax rate from v to v^*. From equation (7), which gives the optimum wage in terms of the elasticity of demand for labour and the parameters of the tax system for those with $a_1 \leq w \leq a_2$, it can be seen that $\delta w/\delta v > 0$. Hence those who initially paid income tax at the lower rate t_1 will unequivocally raise their wage demands.

For those with a wage initially above a_2, the new equilibrium wage, w^*, is given, after appropriate substitution into (7), by:

$$w^* = \frac{\phi}{\phi-1} \frac{\{x(1 + v^*) - a_1 t_1\}}{(1 - t_1)} \tag{9}$$

Then the change in the optimal wage is given by

$$w^* - w = \frac{\phi}{\phi-1} \left[\frac{x(1 + v^*) - a_1 t_1}{(1 - t_1)} \right.$$

$$\left. - \frac{x(1 + v) - \{ a_1 t_1 + a_2 (t_2 - t_1) \}}{(1 - t_2)} \right] \tag{10}$$

After much manipulation, this can be rewritten as:

$$w^* - w = \frac{\phi}{(\phi - 1)(1 - t_1)(1 - t_2)} \left[x\{(v^* - v) - (t_2 v^* - t_1 v)\} \right.$$

$$\left. + (t_2 - t_1) \{ a_1 t_1 + a_2(1 - t_1) - x\} \right] \tag{11}$$

Wage demands will increase so long as the term in square brackets in (11) is positive. To consider the necessary condition for this to occur, define θ and ψ as:

$$\theta = \{(v^* - v) - (t_2 v^* - t_1 v)\}/(t_2 - t_1) \tag{12}$$

Journal of
Economic
Studies
17,1

10

$$\psi = a_1 t_1 + a_2(1 - t_1) \tag{13}$$

Notice that ψ is the post-income tax value of a wage equal to a_2. It can then be seen that a necessary condition for wage demands to decrease is that:

$$x > \psi/(1 - \theta) \tag{14}$$

It is therefore necessary to consider the orders of magnitude involved. This requires precise information about the change in the VAT rate needed to achieve revenue neutrality in aggregate, and is examined in the following section.

Revenue Neutral Changes
The purpose of this section is to derive the implications for the consumption tax rate, v, of a policy change involving the elimination of the second step in the income tax function, such that total tax revenue remains unchanged at the initial wage distribution. The imposition of this kind of *ex ante* revenue neutrality is of course standard in the public finance literature.

Allowing for endogenous changes in the distribution raises enormous complexities[3]. In order to examine aggregate revenue it is necessary to specify some distribution of wages for all workers. The approach taken here is to impose an exogenous distribution function $F(w)$: some wage levels may be determined by monopolistic unions of the type considered here while other wages will be determined by quite different processes.

Total Tax Revenue
For the income tax schedule specified in the first section, the tax raised per person, R_t, is given by:

$$R_t = t_1 \int_{a_1}^{a_2} (w - a_1) dF(w) + t_1(a_2 - a_1) \int_{a_2} dF(w)$$

$$+ t_2 \int_{a_2} (w - a_2) dF(w) \tag{15}$$

This expression can be simplified by using the concept of the first moment distribution. The "first incomplete moment distribution" of an essentially positive variable is denoted $F_1(w)$ and is defined as:

$$F_1(w) = \frac{\int^w u \, dF(u)}{\int u \, dF(u)} \tag{16}$$

The denominator of (16) is simply the arithmetic mean (that is, the first moment of w about the origin), denoted $\bar{w}$. Hence $F_1(w)$ represents the proportion of total wages obtained by those below w, who in turn compromise a proportion $F(w)$ of wage earners. The relationship between $F_1(w)$ and $F(w)$ is the familiar Lorenz curve of income distribution. Using (16) it can be seen that in general:

$$\int_a wdF(w) = \bar{w} \{ 1 - F_1(a) \} \tag{17}$$

Using this result it can be found that, after much manipulation, (15) can be reduced to the following convenient expression:

$$R_t = \bar{w}\left[t_1 G(a_1) + (t_2 - t_1) \, G(a_2) \right] \tag{18}$$

where the function $G(\ )$ is defined as:

$$G(a) = \{1 - F_1(a)\} - (a/\bar{w}) \{1 - F(a)\} \tag{19}$$

This type of function plays a fundamental part in the analysis of non-linear tax schedules and tax/transfer models [4]. If the term in square brackets in (18) is denoted Z, then

$$R_t = \bar{w}Z \tag{20}$$

The per capita value of disposable income is thus $\bar{w}(1 - Z)$. Assuming that all disposable income is consumed, and noting that a tax rate of v on the tax-exclusive price translates into a rate of $v/(1 + v)$ on the tax-inclusive price of goods, the per capita revenue raised by the consumption tax, R_v, is therefore:

$$R_v = \frac{v}{1 + v} \, \bar{w} \, (1 - Z) \tag{21}$$

Total per capita tax revenue, R_2, can thus be written as:

$$R_2 = \bar{w} \left\{ Z + \frac{v}{1 + v} (1 - Z) \right\} \tag{22}$$

The subscript on R is used here to indicate that it is the revenue obtained from a system that uses a two-step income tax schedule. It can be seen from (22) that the effective average tax rate is a weighted average of unity and the tax-inclusive consumption tax rate, with weights depending on the two income tax thresholds, the corresponding marginal rates, and the form of the distribution function $F(w)$.

From (18), the per capita income tax raised by an income tax system which has just one threshold and one marginal rate is obtained simply by setting $t_2 = t_1$. It is therefore just $\bar{w}t_1 G(a_1)$. Total per capita revenue from such an income tax and a consumption tax combined, R_1, therefore follows directly from (22) with Z replaced by $t_1 G(a_1)$. Hence:

$$R_1 = \bar{w}\left[t_1 G(a_1) + \frac{v}{1 + v} \{1 - t_1 G(a_1)\} \right] \tag{23}$$

Eliminating the Top Marginal Rate
The above results can then be used to find the consumption tax rate, v^*, that gives the same total revenue in a one-step income tax function as with a two-step function combined with a consumption tax rate of v. Revenue neutrality requires, from (22) and (23):

Journal of
Economic
Studies
17,1

$$Z + \frac{v}{1 + v}(1 - Z) = t_1 \, G(a_1) + \frac{v^*}{1 + v^*}\{1 - t_1 G(a)\} \qquad (24)$$

It is useful to define $\delta = v/(1 + v)$ and $\delta^* = v^*/(1 + v^*)$. After some manipulation, and substituting for Z from (18), it can be found that (24) reduces to:

12

$$\frac{\delta^* - \delta}{1 - \delta} = \frac{(t_2 - t_1) \, G(a_2)}{1 - t_1 G(a_1)} \qquad (25)$$

writing the right hand side of (25) as k, the value of v^* can be obtained from

$$\delta^* = k + \delta(1 - k) \qquad (26)$$

and

$$v^* = \delta^*/(1 - \delta^*) \qquad (27)$$

The effect on a union's wage demands of a revenue neutral change in the tax mix, arising from a flattening of the rate structure, can now be investigated in detail. The following subsection returns to the condition specified in equation (14), using the result in (27).

A Numerical Example
The above analysis of revenue neutral changes applies to any distribution of wages. Investigation of orders of magnitudes requires, however, an explicit assumption about the form of $F(w)$, from which the appropriate values of the function $G(.)$ may be calculated. Suppose that wages are log-normally distributed with mean and coefficient of variation of income of 6,000 and 0.5 respectively [5]. The absolute value of the mean is not important here, since comparisons can be made in terms of wage levels and tax thresholds relative to the mean. The coefficient of variation of 0.5 is an appropriate order of magnitude for Britain. If $a_1 = 2,000$ it can be found that $G(a_1) = 0.7$; and if $a_2 = 8,000$, then $G(8,000) = 0.1$. Suppose that $t_1 = 0.3$, $t_2 = 0.4$ and $v = 0.10$. It can be found, on substituting in (27), that $v^* = 0.1128$. Furthermore, $\psi = 5,400$ and $\theta = -0.022$. Hence from (14) it is seen that wage demands will decrease if x exceeds 5,283, which is 88 per cent of the arithmetic mean wage. This is a rather high value of the opportunity cost of working.

A value for x of 88 per cent of the mean wage can be placed in perspective by considering the associated pre-tax wage. Substituting for x, and the other parameters, into equation (8), a labour demand elasticity of 2 implies an optimal wage that is 2.5 times the arithmetic mean wage. It therefore seems most unlikely that any union's members will have such a high opportunity cost of working. Hence it appears that the policy of flattening the income tax rate structure, accompanied by a revenue neutral increase in the consumption rate tax, is likely to *increase* the wage demands of *all* trade unions. Such a policy would therefore have the effect of increasing inflation and unemployment.

Conclusions

This article has examined the implications for trade unions' wage demands of a change in the tax mix from direct to indirect taxation, achieved by eliminating the top marginal rate of income tax and simultaneously raising the consumption tax rate in order to leave total tax revenue unchanged. Unions were considered to maximise an objective function involving the real after-tax wage and the level of employment of members. It was found that, for reasonable values of the opportunity cost of working relative to the average wage, the policy would be expected to lead to an increase in the wage demands of all unions, thereby producing a once-and-for-all increase in nominal wages and unemployment. The intuition behind this result is as follows.

The workers who were initially not paying the top marginal rate of income tax experience an increase in their average tax rate through the increase in the consumption tax, and therefore increase their wage demands. Those initially paying the high marginal tax rate experience a reduction in their overall effective marginal tax rate which, other things remaining unchanged, would raise wage demands by making wage increases relatively more attractive than employment increases, in terms of the union's objective function. This tendency was found to dominate the wage reducing effect of the decrease in the average tax rate facing that group. These results confirm the general argument that a *decrease* in the progressivity of the tax is likely to lead to an *increase* in the wage demands of all unions.

It must be acknowledged that there is some uncertainty about the wide applicability of the model of trade union behaviour used here. Nevertheless the results would be expected to apply to any situation in which workers were prepared to trade employment for wage increases, and vice versa. The approach could also be used to examine the implications for unions' wage demands of alternative types of policy change involving changes in the parameters of the tax system.

Notes

1. See Ulph and Ulph (1988, p. 11). In fact the conditions derived below also relate precisely to the Nash solution for efficient bargains between the union and firm. It is shown in Creedy and McDonald (1988b), that in the determination of the optimal wage, only the term involving the elasticity of labour demand is affected. This enters in a simple proportional manner, as shown in equations (7) and (8), so that the condition for wages to increase when a tax parameter changes is not affected.

2. In a general equilibrium setting the change in the tax structure may also be allowed to alter the structure of demand and hence prices, but this complication is ignored here. If the demand shift is iso-elastic, then the wage demands are anyway unchanged by a change in (pre-tax) prices; see McDonald and Solow (1981). On the special case of Cobb-Douglas technology, see Ulph and Ulph (1988, p. 13).

3. Thus any attempt to allow for the effects of policy on the wage distribution would require a complete model of the determination of the wage distribution and is outside the scope of this article.

4. On the use of function G( ) in tax/transfer models see Creedy (1985, pp. 131-45).

5. These values apply to a log-normal distribution with mean and variance of the logarithms of wages of 8.5879 and 0.2231 respectively. Values of the function G(.) for such a distribution

Journal of
Economic
Studies
17,1

14

are reported in Creedy (1985, p. 143), from which the following values are taken. Calculation of the G function is made easier in the case of the log-normal distribution by the convenient relationship between F and the first-moment distribution function F_1.

References

Creedy, J. (1985), *Dynamics of Income Distribution*, Basil Blackwell, Oxford.

Creedy, J. and McDonald, I.M. (1988a), "Income Tax Changes and Trade Union Wage Demands", Department of Economics, University of Melbourne, Research Paper Number 206.

Creedy, J. and McDonald, I.M. (1988b), "Union Wage Responses to a Shift from Direct to Indirect Taxation", Department of Economics, University of Melbourne, Research Paper No. 206.

Hersoug, T. (1984), "Union Wage Response to Tax Changes", *Oxford Economic Papers*, Vol. 36, pp. 37-51.

McDonald, I.M. and Solow, R.M. (1981), "Wage Bargaining and Employment", *American Economic Review*, Vol. 71, pp. 896-908.

Oswald, A.J. (1982), "The Microeconomic Theory of the Trade Union", *Economic Journal*, Vol. 92, pp. 576-595.

Oswald, A.J. (1982), "The Economic Theory of Trade Unions: an Introductory Survey", *Scandinavian Journal of Economics*, Vol. 87, pp. 160-93.

Sampson, A.A. (1986), "The Shift to Indirect Taxation in a Unionised Economy", *Bulletin of Economic Research*, Vol. 38, pp. 87-91.

Ulph, A.M. and Ulph, D.T. (1988), "Union Bargaining — A Survey of Recent Work", University of Southampton Department of Economics Discussion Papers.

Appendix
A Multi-step Tax Function

This appendix sets out the basic analytics of a multi-step tax function, and shows how revenue neutral changes in tax rates and thresholds can be specified. For the particular policy examined in the article, the elimination of the top marginal rate, the effects on wage demands were equivocal only for those previously facing the high rate, so that a two-step function was sufficiently complex. The result of this appendix may be used for the analysis of alternative types of tax policy. Let the tax, $T(y)$, paid on an income of y be given by:

$$
\begin{aligned}
T(y) &= 0 & 0 &< y \leq a_1 \\
&= t_1 (y - a_1) & a_1 &< y \leq a_2 \\
&= t_1 (a_2 - a_1) + t_2(y - a_2) & a_2 &< y \leq a_3 \\
&= t_1 (a_2 - a_1) + t_2 (a_3 - a_2) + t_3(y - a_3) & a_3 &< y \leq a_4
\end{aligned}
$$

Thus, in general, the tax paid on income between the Rth and $(R+1)$th thresholds is:

$$
T(y) = \sum_{i=1}^{R-1} t_1 (a_{i+1} - a_i) + t_R(y - a_R) \qquad a_R < y \leq a_{R+1} \tag{A1}
$$

Hence (A1) holds for $R = 2, \ldots, N$. Setting $t_0 = 0$ and $a_{N+1} = \infty$, total revenue per person, T, is given by:

$$
T = \sum_{i=1}^{N} \left\{ t_i \int_{a_i}^{a_{i+1}} (y - a_i) \, dF(y) \right\} + \sum_{i=1}^{N-1} \left\{ t_i (a_{i+1} - a_i) \int_{a_{i+1}}^{\infty} dF(y) \right\}
$$

$$
= \sum_{i=1}^{N} \left\{ t_i \int_{a_i}^{a_{i+1}} y dF(y) \right\} - \sum_{i=1}^{N} \left\{ a_i (t_i - t_{i-1}) \int_{a_i}^{\infty} dF(y) \right\} \tag{A2}
$$

This expression can be simplified by noting that:

$$\int_{d_i}^{\infty} dF(y) = 1 - F(a_i)$$ (A3)

$$\int_{d_i}^{a_{i+1}} y dF(y) = \bar{y} \left\{ F_1(a_{i+1}) - F_1(a_i) \right\}$$ (A4)

where $\bar{y}$ is the arithmetic mean value of income and F_1 is the first moment distribution function given by:

$$F_1(a_i) = \left\{ \int^{a_i} y dF(y) \right\} / \bar{y}$$ (A5)

Appropriate substitution then gives total revenue as:

$$T = \bar{y} \sum_{i=1}^{N} t_i \left\{ F_1(a_{i+1}) - F_1(a_i) \right\} - \sum_{i=1}^{N} a_i (t_i - t_{i-1}) \{1 - F(a_i)\}$$ (A6)

Changes in revenue resulting from a change in any threshold can then be found using:

$$\frac{\delta T}{\delta a_i} = -\bar{y} \, t_i \frac{\delta F_1(a_i)}{\delta a_i} - (t_i - t_{i-1})\{1 - F(a_i)\} + a_i (t_i - t_{i-1}) \frac{\delta F(a_i)}{\delta a_i}$$

$$= -(t_i - t_{i-1}) \{1 - F(a_i)\} - a_i t_{i-1} f(a_i)$$ (A7)

where $f(y)$ is the density function, such that $dF(y) = f(y)dy$.

For example:

$$\frac{\delta T}{\delta a_1} = t_1 \{1 - F(a_1)\}$$ (A8)

Changes in revenue resulting from a change in any marginal income tax rate can also be found using:

$$\frac{\delta T}{\delta t_i} = \bar{y} \left[\left\{ F_1(a_{i+1}) - F_1(a_i) \right\} - (a_i/\bar{y}) \left\{ 1 - F(a_i) \right\} \right]$$ (A9)

where

$$G(a) = \{1 - F(a)\} - (a/\bar{y}) \{1 - F(a)\}$$ (A10)

For example:

$$\frac{\delta T}{\delta t_N} = \bar{y} \, G(a_N)$$ (A11)

The results in (A7) and (A9) can be used to specify alternative types of revenue neutral change in tax parameters.

[19]

Models of Trade Union Behaviour: A Synthesis*

JOHN CREEDY and IAN M. McDONALD

University of Melbourne,
Parkville, Victoria 3052

In this paper, the following four models of wage determination by trade unions, namely simple monopoly, wage-bargaining (or 'right to manage'), efficient bargains and insider-dominated, are placed within a single framework. It is shown that the pattern of wage behaviour is the same in each of the four models. It is also shown that when taxation is introduced the impact on wages of changes in marginal and average rates of tax is similar across the models.

I Introduction

In recent years the analysis of trade union behaviour has been seen as a fertile field for economic research. Surveys include Oswald (1985), Farber (1986), Ulph and Ulph (1990) and Nickell (1990). There has also been much stress on the importance of taxation in the decision-making of individuals, firms and trade unions. The aim of this paper is to offer a synthesis of several models of trade union behaviour and then to show how taxation can be fitted into the synthesis.

The literature on trade unions has emphasized the following four questions. First, do trade unions bargain with firms over wages or over wages and employment? Second, is the allocation of jobs to trade union members determined by a random process or by a seniority-based process? Third, are trade union decisions determined by majority voting or by maximizing the total welfare of all members? The fourth question, related to the third, asks whether trade union decisions are dominated by insiders (especially the employed) or whether the interests of outsiders (especially unemployed members) are taken into account? In this paper, four models of wage determination which capture alternative answers to these four questions are placed within a single framework. It will be seen that the pattern of wage behaviour, in particular the qualitative relation between wages and the exogenous variables, is the same in each of the four models. Furthermore it will be seen that when taxation is introduced the impact on wages of

changes in marginal and average rates of tax is similar across the models. Thus, for wage determination, it does not make much difference whether bargaining is over wages or wages and employment, whether jobs are allocated randomly or by seniority, whether trade union decisions are determined by a median voter or the entire membership, and whether insiders alone or insiders and outsiders determine union decisions.

While the synthesis covers a variety of assumptions made by different writers, there are omissions which should be noted. Assumptions of uncertain demand and asymmetric information about the firm's revenue function are not examined. Given the result shown below, that the position of the revenue function does not have an influence on wages independent of its curvature, the omission of uncertainty is not serious. This paper also ignores bargaining over the size of the capital stock, as for example in Grout (1984), bargaining over hours of work and bargaining situations involving several unions or several firms: see for example Ulph and Ulph (1990). However, from results based on these assumptions it seems unlikely that their inclusion would overturn the relations between wages and the exogenous variables stressed below.

The impact of taxation on trade union wage demands is frequently discussed in public debates over economic policy. However this concentration of interest has not been matched in the literature on the economic analysis of trade unions. Furthermore where the literature does address

346

issues involving the influence of taxation on union wages, a highly restrictive approach in which post-tax real wages are held constant is often adopted. See Nickell (1990), McDonald (1984), Corden and Dixon (1980), Corden (1981) and Pitchford (1981). The present paper derives the relations between union wages and average and marginal rates of tax. Because the analysis synthesizes a variety of different assumptions about union behaviour, the derived relations have a high degree of generality.

The outline of the paper is as follows. Section II presents two alternative specifications of a trade union's objective function. This is followed in Section III by an examination of four basic methods of modelling the wage determination process. The implications of the four models are then compared in Section IV. Comparisons are made for completely general functional forms and for constant elasticity revenue and utility functions. The effects of taxation within each model are examined in Section V. Conclusions are given in Section VI.

II The Union's Objective

The theory of the economic behaviour of a trade union is based on the idea that the union aims to maximize an objective function, usually based on the utility of a group of members. With some exceptions, for example Ashenfelter and Johnson (1969) and Borland (1985), a separate utility function for the leaders of the union is not included. Usually it is assumed that the members have identical utility functions and market opportunities, although in the median voter model of Booth (1984) and Grossman (1983) members are heterogeneous. In the present paper the members of the group are assumed to have identical tastes and market opportunities.

A Trade-off Between Employment and Wages

In McDonald and Solow (1981) the group for whom the union's objective function applies is a pool of labour which generally exceeds those workers currently employed; it includes both employed and unemployed individuals. To specify the union's objective it is useful to follow the proposal of Layard and Nickell (1990) which applies the concepts of bargaining theory in Bishop (1964) and Binmore, Rubinstein and Wolinsky (1986) to the trade union and firm bargain. The union consists of m members. At the time of bargaining, n_0 are employed at the firm. The remaining $(m - n_0)$ are engaged in the best

alternative to working at the firm, from which they receive a utility flow of $\bar{U}$. This alternative allows people to resume work at the firm if a job becomes available for them after a bargain is made. The alternative could be subsisting on unemployment benefits or working in a job which is considered inferior to working in the firm. After bargaining, the wage at the firm is w and the level of employment is n. In view of the partial equilibrium nature of the analysis in this paper, nominal values may be regarded as equivalent to real values. The $(m - n)$ members who fail to gain employment at the firm then turn to alternative activities from which they receive a utility flow of $\bar{U}$. These alternative activities may involve a period on unemployment benefits and then employment in an alternative job. Layard and Nickell (1990) implicitly assume that $\bar{U} = \bar{U}$. Given this framework, the union's utility is, after bargaining:

$$W = n\{U(w) - D\} + (m - n)\bar{U} \quad \text{for } n \le m \quad (1)$$

and $W = m\{U(w) - D\} \quad$ for $n > m$

where D measures the disutility of work and $U(\ )$ is the concave utility function of each member. If bargaining breaks down then there is no employment at the firm and if s represents strike income, the utility level to the union is $\bar{W}$, and is given by:

$$\bar{W} = n_0 U(s) + (m - n_0) \bar{U}. \quad (2)$$

It is useful to define $U(x) = \bar{U} + D$, where x may be called 'layoff pay'; it refers to the income equivalent of not being employed by the firm after the completion of negotiations plus the disutility of work. By subtracting (2) from (1), the net payoff to the union is:

$$W - \bar{W} = n\{U(w) - U(x)\} + m(\bar{U} - \bar{U}) - n_0[\bar{U} - U(s)]. \quad (3)$$

It simplifies the subsequent analysis to assume that $m(\bar{U} - \bar{U}) - n_0(\bar{U} - U(s)) = 0$. This expression is zero under the Layard and Nickell (1990) assumption that $\bar{U} = \bar{U} = U(s)$. However, it is reasonable to suppose that $\bar{U}$, the alternative utility to that gained from union employment in the firm exceeds, after the bargain, $\bar{U}$, the alternative utility to union employment before the bargain is made. Furthermore, $\bar{U}$ probably exceeds $U(s)$, the utility enjoyed when on strike. The pattern $\bar{U} > \bar{U} > U(s)$ is consistent with $m(\bar{U} - \bar{U}) - n_0(\bar{U} - U(s)) = 0$, so the simplifying assumption is not unreasonable. Making this assumption the net payoff to the union becomes simply the first term on the right-hand side of (3), that is, $n\{U(w) - U(x)\}$.

With the objective function given by (1), employment is traded for wages. The marginal rate of substitution between employment and wages, $MRS_{n/w}$, is obtained by total differentiation of $n\{U(w) - U(x)\}$ and is given by:

$$MRS_{n/w} = \frac{-dw}{dn} = \frac{w}{n\epsilon} \qquad (4)$$

where ϵ is the elasticity of the excess utility from work with respect to the wage, defined by:

$$\epsilon = \frac{wU'(w)}{U(w) - U(x)}. \qquad (5)$$

The indifference curves in $\{w,n\}$ space are downward sloping, asymptotic to $w = x$ for $n \leq m$. For $n > m$, the entire labour pool is employed and the union is not prepared to bear any sacrifice in wages in return for higher levels of employment. Consequently for $n > m$ the indifference curves are horizontal. This pattern is shown in the indifference map of a trade union depicted in Figure 1.

An alternative frequently used specification also yields the same type of union trade-off between wages and employment. If a union has identical members who share an equal probability of employment because jobs are allocated at random, a natural objective is the expected utility of each member. If each member has a probability of employment of n/m then the expected utility of any member is the right-hand side of (3) divided by m. Taking m as exogenous to the union, the indifference curves that represent this definition of expected utility have exactly the same shape as the indifference curves discussed above.

Insider-Dominated Unions

A number of authors, especially Oswald (1984), Lindbeck and Snower (1988), Blanchard and Summers (1986) and Carruth and Oswald (1987), have emphasized the idea that the union's objective is based on the utility of the employed 'insiders'. If the group of insiders corresponds to those in employment then, as discussed in McDonald and Solow (1984) and McDonald (1989), there is a 'travelling' kink in the indifference curve; that is, the kink in the indifference map shown in Figure 1 is always at the current level of employment. A problem with this approach is that the travelling kink leads to somewhat irregular patterns of wage behaviour. For example, changes in the demand for labour can have large effects on wages with no effect on employment; but such a pattern is not usually observed.

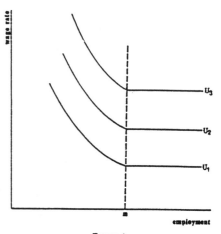

FIGURE 1
The Union's Indifference Map

An alternative objective which does not lead to this problem is based on a sub-group of the employed who face little risk of layoff, rather than all those employed by the firm. This may be called the 'insider-dominated union' in contrast with the above 'insider' model; see McDonald (1991). One situation which will lead to an insider-dominated union is where layoffs are determined by seniority and union wage decisions are made by a median voter; see Oswald (1985) and Farber (1986). The objective for an insider-dominated union is the net gain from working of each of the identical members of the dominant inside group who face no risk of unemployment, that is:

$$W = U(w) - D. \qquad (6)$$

This objective applies for all levels of employment greater than m^d, the size of the dominant inside group. It will be assumed that the bargained outcome yields employment levels greater than m^d. One case for which this assumption is guaranteed to hold is the median voter case with the franchise equal to the level of employment. If negotiations break down, each insider gets utility $U(s)$ and the objective function takes the value $\bar{W} = U(s)$. Thus the payoff to the insider-dominated union is given by:

$$W - \bar{W} = U(w) - D - U(s). \qquad (7)$$

The objective (6) does not trade-off wages against

employment, and so the indifference curves are horizontal lines in $\{w,n\}$ space over $n > m^d$. It will however be seen below that when the objective of the insider-dominated union is placed along with a firm's profit function in a bargaining model, there are strong similarities with the pattern of wage behaviour using the objective (3) in which employment is traded for wages.

In the insider-dominated model, layoff pay, x, is defined by $U(x) = D + U(s)$. This contrasts with the definition used in the first model where the payoff is given by (3), and where the layoff pay depends on market alternatives. This is a simple consequence of the assumption that the dominant insiders face no risk of unemployment. One implication of this is that, for the insider-dominated model, layoff pay may be realistically regarded as being less than the value of the outside option. As Binmore, Rubinstein and Wolinsky (1986) argue, this raises the possibility that the bargained solution will be determined by the outside option. However, it is assumed throughout this paper that the outside option is *not* a binding constraint on the wage outcome. If the outside option were a binding constraint, there would be no role for the union.

III Four Models of Wage Determination

The previous section examined two alternative specifications of the union's objective function. The next stage in the determination of the wage and the employment level requires the specification of the process by which the firm and the union reach agreement. Where the union's objective function involves an explicit trade-off between employment and wages, two basic processes may be distinguished. First, the firm may be assumed to have complete control over the level of employment, so that bargaining takes place only over the wage rate. Such bargains are constrained to be on the labour demand curve. An extreme case of this kind of process occurs when the union has the complete power to set the wage; this is considered separately below in view of its frequent use in the literature. Second, the firm and the union may be assumed to bargain over the joint determination of the wage rate and the level of employment; in the absence of transaction costs such bargains will be Pareto efficient as in the standard analysis of barter.

For the insider-dominated union, where the level of employment does not enter into the union's objective function, there is no reason to distinguish between bargaining over the wage alone and

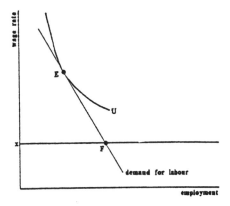

FIGURE 2
The Simple Monopoly Union Model and Wage Bargaining

bargaining over wages and employment. That is because these two bargaining processes yield the same wage and employment outcomes. Control over employment by the employer does not lead to sub-optimal outcomes.

Combining the various assumptions about the union's objective function and the bargaining process yields four models of trade union behaviour. In the *simple monopoly union* model the union has complete control over the wage. In the *wage bargaining* model the union bargains with the firm over the wage, although the firm still has complete control over employment as in the simple monopoly union model. In the *efficient bargains* model the union and the firm bargain over both wages and employment. In the fourth model, the *insider-dominated* model, the union is not prepared to trade wages for employment. These are examined in turn below.

The Simple Monopoly Union

The situation in which the union is powerless to influence the employment level while the firm is powerless to control the wage rate is called the 'simple monopoly union' model. The union sets the wage which enables it to reach the highest indifference curve, subject to the constraint that employment takes place on the labour demand curve. This outcome is shown in Figure 2 as point E.

If the firm's revenue, expressed as a function of employment, n, is written as $R(n)$, then profit maximization requires $w - R'(n) = 0$. The demand curve for labour is defined by $w = R'(n)$, and the simple monopoly union outcome is given by maximization of the Lagrangean, L, given by:

$$L = n\{U(w) - U(x)\} + m\bar{U} + \lambda\{w - R'(n)\}. \quad (8)$$

Setting the partial derivative of L with respect to w equal to zero gives $\lambda = -nU'(w)$, and substituting into $\partial L/\partial n = 0$ gives, with $w = R'(n)$, the result that:

$$\frac{wU'(w)}{U(w) - U(x)} = \frac{-R'(n)}{nR''(n)}. \quad (9)$$

The left-hand side of (9) is the wage elasticity of the net utility from work, ϵ, defined in Section II, while the right-hand side is interpreted as the negative of the wage elasticity of demand for labour, denoted θ. Hence the first-order condition can be rewritten simply as:

$$\epsilon = \theta. \quad (10)$$

Notice that this could be obtained simply by setting the slope of the union's indifference curve, $-w/n\epsilon$, equal to the slope of the labour demand curve, given by $R''(n)$.

Wage Bargaining

The more general case of bargaining over wages while the employer retains unilateral control over employment, has been called the 'right to manage' model by Nickell (1982). In this case, where the wage is jointly determined by the union and the firm through bargaining, a bargaining solution concept is required. The bargaining solution usually used is the asymmetric Nash solution, given by the values of w and n which maximize the weighted geometric mean of the union's and the firm's payoffs. In the case of wage bargaining the Nash solution is subject to the constraint that bargains are on the firm's labour demand curve. The union's payoff has already been considered in Section III above. If the firm's 'threat point' is assumed to be zero profits, the payoff is simply the value of profits, $R(n) - wn$. The Lagrangean for this problem is:

$$L = [n\{U(w) - U(x)\}]^{\phi/(1+\phi)}[R(n) - wn]^{1/(1+\phi)} + \lambda\{w - R'(n)\} \quad (11)$$

The weights $\phi/(1+\phi)$ and $1/(1+\phi)$ reflect the bargaining power of the union and the firm respectively. When $\phi = \infty$, all the bargaining strength is in the hands of the union, and maximizing (11) is equivalent to the simple monopoly union model of (8). Using the interpretation of Binmore, Rubinstein and

Wolinsky (1986, p. 187), ϕ is positively related to the speed of response of the union to the firm's offers and inversely related to the speed of the firm's response to the union's offers. Furthermore, ϕ is inversely related to the union's estimate of the probability that the bargaining process will break down and positively related to the firm's estimate that the bargaining process will break down.

Differentiation of (11) with respect to n, w and λ, setting the resulting partial derivatives equal to zero and rearranging, gives the first-order condition that:

$$\epsilon = \left[\phi\left\{\frac{R(n)}{nR'(n)} - 1\right\}\right]^{-1} + \left[\frac{-R'(n)}{nR''(n)}\right] \quad (12)$$

The second term in (12) is the elasticity θ. The term $nR'(n)/R(n)$ is the ratio of the marginal revenue product to the average revenue product, and is the elasticity of revenue with respect to employment, which will be denoted α. Equation (12) can therefore be rewritten as:

$$\epsilon = \frac{\alpha}{\phi(1-\alpha)} + \theta. \quad (13)$$

Bearing in mind that ϵ is a function of the wage, equation (13) determines the bargained wage. The level of employment is determined by the labour demand function. In terms of Figure 2, the outcome under wage bargaining will lie on the labour demand curve somewhere between E and F. If the union has complete power over wages then $\phi = \infty$, the first term on the right-hand side of (13) is zero and (13) reduces to the simple monopoly union result given by (10). The wage-employment outcome would be at point E in Figure 2. If the union has no power over wages then $\phi = \infty$, the value of the term on the right-hand side of (13) is infinite and, for ϵ to be infinite the wage has to equal x. The wage-employment outcome would be at point F in Figure 2. Intermediate values for union power yield solutions on the labour demand curve between E and F in Figure 2.

Efficient Bargains

When the union and the firm bargain over both the wage rate and the employment level, the bargains are no longer constrained to take place on the labour demand curve. Hence the Nash bargaining solution is given by the unconstrained maximization of:

$$L = [n\{U(w) - U(x)\}]^{\phi/(1+\phi)}[R(n) - wn]^{1/(1+\phi)} \quad (14)$$

Appropriate differentiation and manipulation gives

the first-order conditions as:

$$\epsilon = \frac{w}{w - R'(n)} \qquad (15)$$

$$w = \frac{1}{1+\phi}\left[\frac{\phi R(n)}{n} + R'(n)\right] \qquad (16)$$

Equation (16), which may be called the 'power locus', shows that the wage is equal to a weighted average of the average and marginal revenue products of labour, with weights equal to $\phi/(1+\phi)$ and $1/(1+\phi)$ respectively. Equation (15) defines the contract curve of efficient bargains, which is the locus of points of tangency between the union's indifference curves and the firm's iso-profit curves. This result can be confirmed by equating the slope of an indifference curve, $-w/n\epsilon$, with the slope of the iso-profit curve. The latter is obtained, from total differentiation of $\Pi = R(n) - wn$, as:

$$\frac{dw}{dn} = -\frac{\{w - R'(n)\}}{n} \qquad (17)$$

The efficient bargains model is presented graphically in Figure 3. The iso-profit curves have a slope of zero where they cut through the curve of $R'(n)$. The contract curve of tangencies of the iso-profit curves and the indifference curves is the upward sloping curve from A to B. At A, where, because $w = x$ the indifference curve is horizontal, the contract curve touches the $R'(n)$ curve. At B, where the level of profits is zero, the contract curve ends. The power locus runs from C to D. It can be seen from the equation of the power locus, (16), that for the level of employment at which $R'(n) = R(n)/n$, the power locus goes through the wage and employment levels given by $w = R'(n) = R(n)/n$, whatever the value of the union power parameter. This is point C on the power locus. Because the bargaining solution is assumed to be at $n \leq m$, the power locus ends at point D where $n = m$. For an analysis of outcomes that occur at $n > m$ see Carruth and Oswald (1987).

To derive an expression determining the bargained wage, substitute (16) into the contract curve (15). This gives the resulting first-order condition that:

$$\epsilon = \frac{\phi\frac{R(n)}{nR'(n)} + 1}{\phi\left\{\frac{R(n)}{nR'(n)} - 1\right\}} \qquad (18)$$

Using the definition of α to substitute for

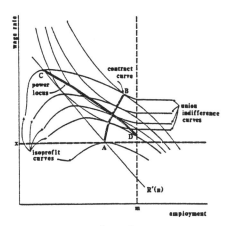

FIGURE 3

The Efficient Bargains Model

$nR'(n)/R(n)$), equation (18) becomes

$$\epsilon = \frac{\phi + \alpha}{\phi(1 - \alpha)} \qquad (19)$$

Notice that the wage elasticity of the demand for labour, θ, does not appear in (19). This is not suprising in view of the fact that efficient bargains for which $m > n$ are not on the labour demand curve. The fact that efficient bargains (with $m > n$) are on the contract curve and require bargaining over wages *and* employment was first stated by Edgeworth (1881) and clarified by Dunlop (1944), although its discovery is often attributed to Leontief (1946).

Insider-Dominated Bargains

The insider-dominated model of trade union behaviour, as explained in Section II, applies to a union which is concerned only with a sub-group of the employed, and corresponds to a situation in which $m < n$. This has been contrasted with the 'insider' model, in which $m = n$ and which produces a 'travelling' kink in the indifference curves at the current level of employment. The Nash solution for insider dominated bargains is therefore given by the values of w and n which maximize:

$$L = [\{U(w) - D - U(s)\}]^{\phi/(1+\phi)}[R(n) - wn]^{1/(1+\phi)} \qquad (20)$$

Appropriate differentiation and rearrangement

gives the first-order conditions as:

$$w = R'(n) \tag{21}$$

$$\text{and} \quad \epsilon = \left[\phi \left\{ \frac{R(n)}{nw} - 1 \right\} \right]^{-1} \tag{22}$$

It should be recognized that ϵ differs slightly from its earlier definition in (5), and is now equal to $wU'(w)/\{U(w) - D - U(s)\}$. Thus for the insider-dominated case, ϵ refers to the elasticity, with respect to the wage, of the excess of utility from working over *utility from being on strike*. As explained in Section II, for the insider-dominated case, x is defined by $U(x) = D + U(s)$. Calling x layoff pay now means the income equivalent of being on strike. For the other three cases ϵ is the elasticity, with respect to the wage, of the excess of utility from working over utility gained from the alternative activities to which workers turn if they fail to gain employment at the firm after the completion of the bargain; that is, $U(x) = D + \bar{U}$.

Equation (21) shows that efficient insider-dominated bargains are on the labour demand curve. The same is true of the 'insider' model, a result which was first stated by Leontief (1946), somewhat elliptically, and Fellner (1949), and later rediscovered by Oswald (1987).

As can be seen from Figure 4, the horizontal indifference curves are tangential with the iso-profit curves where the latter cut the labour demand curve. The contract curve is the segment of the labour demand curve running from A, where the level of profit is zero, to B, where $w = x$. A powerful union can achieve the outcome at A, whilst a powerless union will have to accept the outcome at B (remember that the outside option was assumed earlier not to be a binding constraint). Intermediate values of the union power parameter yield outcomes between A and B on the contract curve in Figure 4.

By substitution of (21) and using the definition of α, (22) can be simplified to:

$$\epsilon = \frac{\alpha}{\phi(1 - \alpha)} \tag{23}$$

Equation (23) shows that the bargained wage is related to the elasticity of the revenue function and the power parameter, the same variables that are important when the union trades employment for wages; compare (23) with equations (19), (13) and (10). This similarity in the results of the models is a basis of the synthesis put forward in this paper.

The similarity between the insider-dominated model and the other three models is in marked

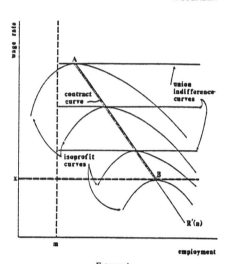

FIGURE 4

The Insider-Dominated Model

contrast to some of the recent literature dealing with 'insider' models. For example, Nickell (1990, p. 418) states that 'the foundation of the insider-outsider model' is that 'wages are inversely related to initial membership'. However, the insider-dominated model of this section has no relation between wages and initial membership. Any such relation is a consequence, not of the general idea that insiders may dominate trade union decision-making, but of the assumption concerning the size of the dominating group of insiders. In the model referred to by Nickell the dominating group of insiders do not have secure employment. This is the underlying reason why, in that model, wages are inversely related to initial membership. On the other hand in the insider-dominated model presented here insiders have secure employment and so the relationship emphasized by Nickell does not hold.

IV The Four Models Compared

General Functional Forms

The previous section derived the equations determining the behaviour of wages and employment for four bargaining models: the simple monopoly union; wage bargaining; efficient bargains and insider-dominated bargains. In the first three models the trade union's objective included both employment and wages while for insider-dominated bargains the trade union was only concerned with the level of wages. Table 1 summarizes the results for the four models. The sixth column, labelled employment, shows that for three models employment is on the marginal revenue product of labour curve. For the simple monopoly union and for the wage-bargaining models this outcome is inefficient; the outcome for efficient bargains lies to the right of the marginal revenue product of labour curve. For insider-dominated bargains, efficient bargains are on the marginal revenue product of labour curve. In that case the union places no value on employment and ≥ o is not prepared to offer a lower wage in return for the employer giving higher employment.

Wages in the four models are determined by equations (10), (13), (19) and (23). These four equations may be written in general form as:

$$\epsilon = \psi \qquad (24)$$

where ϵ takes the value given by the relevant row in column 2 of Table 1 and ψ takes the value given by the relevant row of column 3 in Table 1. For example, for the simple monopoly union the value of ϵ is $wU'(w)/\{U(w) - D - \bar{U}\}$ and the value of ψ is θ.

McDonald and Solow (1981) emphasized that shifts in the demand for labour will not change the bargained wage if α, θ, ϕ and lay off pay remain constant. Instead employment would bear the brunt of changes in demand. This was for the simple monopoly union and efficient bargains cases, but as Table 1 makes clear, this conclusion can be extended to encompass the wage-bargaining model and insider-dominated bargains. However, in making the extension to the insider-dominated model it should be remembered that the definition of layoff pay in that model differs from the other three models. In the insider-dominated model layoff pay is composed of strike-pay and the disutility of work. So for the insider-dominated model it is constancy in $D + U(s)$ that implies, when α and ϕ remain constant, that shifts in the demand for labour will not change the bargained wage.

Changes in the values of α, θ, ϕ and x will change the bargained wage. The bargained wage may be expected to vary negatively with the elasticity of the revenue function, α, and the elasticity of the labour demand curve, θ, and to vary positively with union power, ϕ, and layoff pay x; that would be a 'normal' relationship. It can be seen from Table 1 that in each of the four models, increases in θ and α and decreases in ϕ will raise ψ (if they

influence ψ at all). So for a normal relation between these parameters and the bargained wage the partial derivative of ϵ with respect to w, denoted ϵ_w, has to be negative. Furthermore, for given values of θ, α and ϕ, an increase in x will raise wages if $\epsilon_w < 0$.

Differentiation of (5) and substitution yields

$$\epsilon_w = \frac{U'(w)}{U(w) - U(x)} (1 - r - \epsilon) \qquad (25)$$

where r measures the Arrow-Pratt measure of relative risk aversion, and $r = wU''(w)/U'(w)$. Clearly $r > 1$ is sufficient for the normal relation. So is $r = 0$, since this implies $\epsilon = w/(w - x)$ which is greater than unity. Another sufficient condition for a normal relation is $\psi > 1$ since, in equilibrium, $\epsilon = \psi$. Pursuing this condition, it can be seen from Table 1 that $\theta > 1$ is sufficient for $\psi > 1$ in the simple monopoly union and the wage-bargaining model and $\alpha < 1$ is sufficient for $\psi > 1$ with efficient bargains. From these conditions, there is a strong presumption for a normal relation in the general case. It will be seen below that with a constant elasticity utility function the normal relation between the bargained wage and α, θ, ϕ and x can be proved for all values of r that yield a positive value for the bargained wage.

Further insight into the models can be gained by considering the value of the bargained wage at each of the extreme values of the power parameter, ϕ. At $\phi = 0$, where the union has no power, the value of ψ is infinity for each of the models of wage bargaining, efficient bargains and insider-dominated bargains. This implies an outcome where the wage is equal to x. At the other extreme of an all powerful union, ϕ is infinite. In this case, the wage-bargaining model reverts to the simply monopoly union model, where the union's willingness to increase wages is moderated by the employment losses it would face as it moves up the labour demand curve. By contrast, an insider dominated union places no value on employment losses. For that union an infinite value for ϕ would imply, as long as $\alpha < 1$, a value of ψ of zero and thus an infinite wage demand. This is not realistic, since it is more likely for most firms that there is a finite wage at which profits are zero. At the wage where profits are zero, α is equal to one (as $\alpha = R'(n)n/R(n) = wn/R(n)$, zero profits occur when $wn = R(n)$ and thus when $\alpha = 1$). The combination of $\alpha = 1$ and $\phi = $ infinity makes ψ indeterminate for the insider-dominated bargain, and then the wage is simply the zero profit wage, that is $w = R(n)/n$. For efficient bargains a value

TABLE 1
Determination of Wages and Employment in the Four Models of a Trade Union

Model	Wages Determined by $\epsilon = \psi$				Employment
	ϵ	ψ			
		General case	Constant Elasticity Revenue Function		
			Using α	Using θ	
Simple Monopoly Union	$\dfrac{wU'(w)}{U(w)-U(x)}$ with $U(x)=D+\bar{U}$	θ	$\dfrac{1}{1-\alpha}$	θ	$w=R'(n)$ $n<m$
Wage Bargaining	$\dfrac{wU'(w)}{U(w)-U(x)}$ with $U(x)=D+\bar{U}$	$\dfrac{\alpha}{\phi(1-\alpha)}+\theta$	$\dfrac{\phi+\alpha}{\phi(1-\alpha)}$	$\dfrac{\theta(1+\phi)-1}{\phi}$	$w=R'(n)$ $n<m$
Efficient Bargains	$\dfrac{wU'(w)}{U(w)-U(x)}$ with $U(x)=D+\bar{U}$	$\dfrac{\alpha}{\phi(1-\alpha)}+\dfrac{1}{1-\alpha}$	$\dfrac{\phi+\alpha}{\phi(1-\alpha)}$	$\dfrac{\theta(1+\phi)-1}{\phi}$	$w=\dfrac{1}{1+\theta}\left[\phi\dfrac{R(n)}{n}+R'(n)\right]$ $n<m$
Insider-dominated Bargains	$\dfrac{wU'(w)}{U(w)-U(x)}$ with $U(x)=D+\bar{U}(s)$	$\dfrac{\alpha}{\phi(1-\alpha)}$	$\dfrac{\alpha}{\phi(1-\alpha)}$	$\dfrac{\theta-1}{\phi}$	$w=R'(n)$ $n>m$

of ϕ of infinity implies $\psi = 1/(1-\alpha)$. The expression $1/(1-\alpha)$ is the elasticity of the iso-profit curve of zero profits (taken positively). In the efficient bargains model, an all-powerful union forces the firm to operate along its zero-isoprofit curve. So that is the wage-employment trade-off that the union faces. That is why, in the expression for ψ for efficient bargains, $1/(1-\alpha)$ appears, instead of, in the expression for ψ for wage bargaining, θ.

A Constant Elasticity Revenue Function

Suppose now that the employment elasticity of revenue, α, is constant. This implies that the revenue function is such that $R(n) = kn^\alpha$ where k is a constant. The wage elasticity of demand for labour is equal to $-1/(1-\alpha)$. The negative of this elasticity has already been defined as θ, so that $\theta = 1/(1-\alpha)$, and the first-order conditions in Section III can be expressed either in terms of α or θ. These are shown in the fourth and fifth columns of Table 1. Note that, with a constant α, the wage rate is precisely the same for both

wage bargaining and efficient bargains; in the latter case employment is higher. In Figure 5 the outcome from wage bargaining is at point E and with efficient bargains is at point F. However, one should not make too much of this equivalence. The institutional processes for wage bargaining differ from the institutional processes for efficient bargains. In the latter case, bargaining is over employment as well as wages. Because of this difference in the variables to be bargained over, it is not clear whether 'equal power' in wage bargaining compared with wage and employment bargaining means that the power parameter should have the same value.

A Constant Elasticity Utility Function

Explicit expressions for the wage rate can only be obtained when a particular form for the utility function has been chosen. Consider the constant relative risk-aversion function given by:

$$U(w) = \frac{w^{1-r}}{1-r} \quad r \geq 0 \qquad (26)$$

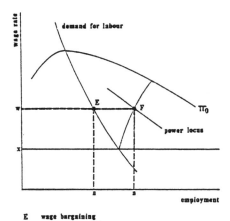

E   **wage bargaining**
F   **efficient bargaining**
Π_0 **zero iso-profit curve**

FIGURE 5

Constant Elasticity Revenue Function

and r measures the degree of relative risk aversion, defined earlier. With this function a useful general expression for the wage can be obtained, given by:

$$w = xh^{-1/(1-r)} \qquad (27)$$

with $h = 1 - (1-r)/\psi$. $\qquad (28)$

In the case of constant relative risk aversion the results in (27) and (28) provide completely general expressions covering the four models of trade union behaviour that can be used to determine the wage rate. It is only necessary to substitute the appropriate value of ψ, taken from Table 1, into (28). For the bargained wage to be positive, h has to be positive. From (28), the condition for $h > 0$ is $r + \psi > 1$, which places a lower limit on $r + \psi$. As $r + \psi$ approaches one from above the bargained wage approaches infinity. Furthermore, given that at the bargained wage $\psi = \epsilon$, it follows that with constant relative risk aversion ϵ_w, as given by (25), is negative if the bargained wage is positive. So with constant relative risk aversion there is a normal relation between the bargained wage and the exogenous variables α, θ, ϕ and x.

The similarity between the models in which the union's objective trades employment for wages, and the insider-dominated union in which the union is only concerned with wages, is remarkable. For the insider-dominated union the wage outcome is the result of a power struggle between the union and the firm. While the union only cares about wages, the firm's profit objective depends on both wages and employment. It is because of this dependence that the insider-dominated model yields similar results to the other models. As explained above, the insider models in McDonald and Solow (1984), Blanchard and Summers (1986), Carruth and Oswald (1987), Lindbeck and Snower (1988) and McDonald (1989) are 'travelling kink' models, and are not easily brought into the framework of this paper.

V The Effects of Taxation

A General Tax Function

There have been relatively few studies of the effects of taxes on unions. Early examples include the brief discussions in Oswald (1982, 1985) and papers by Hersoug (1984) and Sampson (1983). These studies make the assumption either that x is untaxed or that any tax change is accompanied by a policy which ensures that the real after-tax value of x remains unchanged. This approach is appropriate to those situations where x is thought to be dominated by transfer payments. Even if such payments are taxable, it can be argued that it is sensible to concentrate on the single policy of a tax change, rather than combining it with a policy to reduce the real value of transfer payments. For example, when value added tax was significantly increased in the UK in 1979, transfers were simultaneously increased to maintain their real value. Alternatively, it can be argued that there are situations in which x is affected by changes in taxation. Not surprisingly, the implications for wage bargains of tax changes are sensitive to the assumption made about x; for a detailed treatment, see Pemberton (1991).

In general any tax structure can be represented by a relationship between post-tax income, y, and the pre-tax wage, w, so that:

$$y = y(w) \qquad (29)$$

It is useful to introduce the concept of the elasticity of the post-tax wage with respect to the pre-tax wage, denoted ξ where:

$$\xi = \frac{wy'(w)}{y} \qquad (30)$$

The advantage of the synthesis presented here is that with taxation, the first-order condition determining the bargained wage can be written as a simple modification of the general form given in equation (24). It can be expressed as:

$$\epsilon\xi = \psi \tag{31}$$

where ϵ has to be redefined in terms of y rather than w, so that it is now $yU'(y)/\{U(y) - U(x)\}$, and the appropriate value of ψ is taken from Table 1. Thus all four models are covered by (31), irrespective of whether or not taxes are assumed to affect x.

The impact on bargained wages of changes in the tax structure can be examined using comparative static analysis based on the first-order condition in (31). Suppose that τ is one (unspecified) parameter of the tax function and that x does not depend on τ; there may be other parameters but the following considers the general comparative static effect of a change in any parameter. Equation (31) gives rise to a solution for w given by w^*, where $w^* = w^*(x, \tau)$. Substitution into (31) gives the identity:

$$\epsilon(w^*(x, \tau), x, \tau)\, \xi(w^*(x, \tau), \tau) = \psi(w^*(x, \tau)) \tag{32}$$

where ϵ, ξ and ψ are written as functions of w^* and the exogenous variables x and τ. Differentiating (32) with respect to the tax parameter and rearranging gives:

$$w_\tau^*(\epsilon_{w^*}\xi + \epsilon\xi_{w^*} - \psi_{w^*}) = -(\epsilon_\tau\xi + \epsilon\xi_\tau) \tag{33}$$

where $w_\tau^* = dw^*/d\tau$ and so on. The term in brackets on the left-hand side of (33) is strictly negative if the second-order condition is satisfied, so that the sign of $dw^*/d\tau$ is given by the sign of the term in brackets on the right-hand side of (33). From the definition of ϵ given above, it can be seen that $\epsilon_\tau = \epsilon_y y_\tau$. The analysis in Section IV yielded a strong presumption that ϵ_w is negative. In the present context this carries over, suggesting that $\epsilon_y < 0$. This leaves the signs of y_τ and ξ_τ to be determined.

Further progress can be made by considering certain types of tax function. The most simple tax function is proportional, by which $y = (1-t)w$ with t being both the average and the marginal tax rate. With this tax function, $\tau = t$, ξ is equal to one, $\xi_t = 0$ and $y_t = -w$. Substituting these expressions into (33), it can be concluded that:

$$\text{sign}(w_t^*) = \text{sign}(-\epsilon_y w) = \text{positive}. \tag{34}$$

Thus an increase in the average and marginal tax rate will increase wage demands.

A simple progressive tax function is the linear function with a tax-free threshold, a, whereby $y = w-(w-a)t$. This function is the one-step version of the income tax scales in general use. With this

function, $\tau = a$ or t, $y_a = t$,
$$\xi_a = -\xi^2(1/w)\,(t/(1-t)) < 0 \text{ and so:}$$

$$\text{sign}(w_a^*) = \text{sign}(\epsilon_y t\xi + \epsilon\xi_a) = \text{negative}. \tag{35}$$

By (35) a decrease in a, which represents an increase in the average rate of tax holding the marginal rate constant, will increase the trade union's wage demand. However, the effect on wages of increasing the marginal rate of tax is not clear. With the linear progressive function, $y_t = (w-a) < 0$, assuming that the wage exceeds the threshold a, and $\xi_t = -\xi\,(a/w)\,(1-t)^{-2} < 0$, and so:

$$\text{sign}(w_t^*) = \text{sign}(-\epsilon_y(w-a)\xi - \epsilon\xi^2(a/w)\,(1-t)^{-2}) \tag{36}$$

which is ambiguous.

Finally, consider the constant elasticity function, by which $y = \mu w^\beta$ with $\mu > 0$ and $0 < \beta < 1$. This function seems to have been first used by Edgeworth (1925), and has been used in the analysis of trade union wage determination by Hersoug (1984) and Creedy and McDonald (1990). The main attractions of this function concern the neat analytic results that can be derived from it, as is so often the case with constant elasticity functional forms. The parameter β may be regarded as a measure of the progressivity of the function. Under this convention a decrease in μ represents an increase in the average rate of tax, holding progressivity constant. The derivatives of y and ξ are $y_\mu = w^\beta > 0$, $y_\beta = y\log(w)$, $\xi_\mu = 0$ and $\xi_\beta = 1$. Using these derivatives, gives:

$$\text{sign } w_\mu^* = \text{sign}(\epsilon_y w^\beta\beta) = \text{negative} \tag{37}$$

implying that an increase in the average rate of tax will increase wages. For changes in the elasticity of the tax function,

$$\text{sign } w_\beta^* = \text{sign}(\epsilon_y\beta\log(w) + \epsilon) \tag{38}$$

which is ambiguous.

For each of the three tax functions considered, a change in the average rate of tax increases the trade union wage. However, for the two tax functions which can allow for a progressive tax structure, the impact on trade union wages of a change in the marginal rate of tax is ambiguous. The effect of a change in the tax structure will therefore typically require the precise specification of the utility function.

It is often required to examine changes in a tax structure, such as a change in marginal tax rates, which are in some sense 'revenue neutral'. One reason is that the imposition of revenue neutrality allows a clearer comparison of alternative tax rates and structures. Furthermore revenue neutrality can remove income effects and allow the analyst to concentrate on the impact of substitution effects. Hersoug (1984) and Sampson (1983) have interpreted revenue neutrality to mean an unchanged average tax rate for the particular union under consideration. Suppose that $y = y(w, t, a)$ where t and a are two tax parameters such that $y_t < 0$ and $y_a > 0$, and t is the marginal tax rate; the linear schedule considered earlier is a special case of such a tax function in which $a = 0$. A change in t which leaves the average tax rate unchanged leads to a change in the bargained wage given by:

$$\frac{dw^*}{dt} + k\left(\frac{dw^*}{da}\right) \qquad (39)$$

where $k = da/dt$, calculated under the assumption that the average rate, $(w-y)/w$, remains constant. As t is increased it is necessary to raise the other parameter, a, in order to keep the average rate constant. An alternative approach may require not simply that the average tax rate facing a group of workers remains fixed but that the total tax revenue of all workers in the economy remains constant, thereby complicating the expression for k. For a non-technical discussion of a variety of tax changes which impose aggregate revenue neutrality, see Creedy and McDonald (1989). In general, under various specifications of revenue neutrality, increases in marginal rates of tax decrease trade union wages. However, Pemberton (1991) has shown that this result may be modified if x depends on the tax structure.

The Constant Elasticity Utility Function and the Linear Progressive Tax Function

It has been suggested above that clear results concerning the direction of wage changes in response to tax changes usually require the utility function to be specified. This subsection briefly combines the constant elasticity utility function with the linear progressive function, considered earlier. For this case the bargained wage can no longer be solved explicitly, as it could be in the case without tax shown in (27), but is the solution to the non-linear equation:

$$w(1-t)h + at - y^r x^{1-r} = 0, \qquad (40)$$

where $h = 1-(1-r)/\psi$. In the special case where the tax is proportional, that is if $a = 0$, then (40) can be solved explicitly for w, which is equal to the right-hand side of (27) divided by $(1-t)$.

The earlier analysis has already proved that $dw/da < 0$. But the sign of dw/dt is ambiguous.

However, the case of $r = 0$, that is of risk-neutrality, yields a condition for $dw/dt > 0$, which is easy to interpret. Furthermore, the use of numerical methods of solving (40) for cases with $r > 0$ reveals a very close similarity with the risk-neutral case, so that the risk-neutral case is a good guide to the more complicated cases where $r > 0$. A microcomputer program to examine these alternatives can be obtained from the authors.

With $r = 0$, equation (40) reduces to the following expression:

$$w = \frac{(x-at)\psi}{(1-t)(\psi-1)} \qquad (41)$$

from which:

$$\frac{dw}{dt} = \frac{x-a}{(x-at)(1-t)} > 0 \text{ if } x > a \qquad (41)$$

Hence $dw/dt > 0$ if $x > a$. If, as is realistic, x is greater than the threshold, a, then the bargained wage is increased by an increase in the marginal rate of tax.

Employment Effects of Tax Changes

In three of the four wage determination processes summarized in Table 1, employment occurs on the demand curve for labour. Hence the employment effects of tax changes are easily obtained in the partial equilibrium context in which the firm's revenue function is assumed to remain unaffected by the wage tax. For efficient bargains (with $n < m$) the tax change will cause the contract curve to shift, while leaving the power locus unchanged. This is because the power locus is obtained by differentiating the Nash maximand (the product of the pay offs) with respect to employment, and the introduction of taxation has no influence on this relationship. Hence employment will in this case expand or contract along a fixed power locus.

Consider the special case where the employment elasticity of revenue is constant. Appropriate substitution of $R(n)$ and $R'(n)$ into the power locus given by (17), and rearrangement to make n the subject of the resulting equation, gives:

$$n = bw^{-1/(1-\alpha)} \qquad (42)$$

with $b = \{k(\alpha+\phi)/(1+\phi)\}^{1/(1-\alpha)}$.

This result shows that the wage elasticity of employment along the power locus is precisely the same as that along the demand curve. Hence any given change in wages, induced by tax change, will have the same employment effect in all models.

VI Conclusion

In analyzing the economic behaviour of trade unions, writers have tended to contrast the basic assumptions of alternative models. One contrast is between bargaining over wages and bargaining over both wages and employment. The latter assumption leads to efficient bargains. Another contrast is between a union's objective based on wages and employment and a union's objective based on wages alone. The latter assumption captures the notion of insider power. All these alternative assumptions are covered by the four models of trade union behaviour examined in this paper. The synthesis put forward here shows that these four models are sufficiently similar to be fitted into a general framework. In each model, the bargained wage is inversely related to the elasticity of the firm's revenue function and/or the elasticity of the labour demand function, the elasticity of the union member's utility function and the marginal rate of tax on workers and positively related to the opportunity cost of labour, the power parameter of the trade union and the average rate of tax on workers. Furthermore shifts in the demand for labour have their major effect on employment and little or no effect on wages, as emphasized in McDonald and Solow (1981). This behaviour is consistent with the results of empirical studies on the cyclical pattern of real wages, which show little correlation between real wages and recent employment. Kennan (1988) provides a recent study of six OECD countries and Ackland and Borland (1990) provide a recent study of the Australian pattern.

The one qualification to the similarity of wage behaviour between the four models is that layoff pay has a different definition for the insider-dominated models than for the other three models. For the insider-dominated model layoff pay is the income equivalent of strike pay plus the disutility of work. For the other three models layoff pay is the income equivalent of not being employed by the firm *after* the completion of negotiations plus the disutility of work. In this latter definition, layoff pay is more sensitive to market opportunities, through their influence on alternative employment prospects, than in the definition derived from the insider-dominated model.

The emphasis in this paper has been on the behaviour of wages. The similarity in this behaviour for the four models of trade unions holds even although in one model outcomes are not on the labour demand curve. As Edgeworth (1881) pointed out a long time ago, if a union places a positive value on additional employment then efficient bargains lie to the right of the labour demand curve. The major contribution of the modern literature on the economics of trade unions has been to elucidate the nature of wage behaviour.

REFERENCES

Ackland, R. and Borland, J.I. (1990), 'Real Wages over the Business Cycle in Australia', University of Melbourne, mimeo.

Ashenfelter, O. and Johnson, G.E. (1969), 'Bargaining Theory, Trade Unions and Industrial Strike Activity', *American Economic Review* 59(1), 35–49.

Binmore, K., Rubinstein, A. and Wolinsky, A. (1986), 'The Nash Bargaining Solution in Economic Modelling', *Rand Journal of Economics* 17(2), 176–88.

Bishop, R. (1964), 'A Zeuthen-Hicks Theory of Bargaining', *Econometrica* XXXII, 410–17.

Blanchard, O.J. and Summers, L.H. (1986), 'Hysteresis and the European Unemployment Problem' in S. Fischer (ed.), *NBER Macroeconomics Annual* (MIT press, Cambridge, Massachusetts).

Booth, A. (1984), 'A Public Choice Model of Trade Union Behaviour and Membership', *Economic Journal* 94, 883–98.

Borland, J.I. (1985), 'The Economic Analysis of Trade Unions', Master of Arts Thesis, University of Melbourne.

Carruth, A.A. and Oswald, A.J. (1987), 'On Union Preferences and Labour Market Models: Insiders and Outsiders', *Economic Journal* 97, 431–45.

Corden, W.M. (1981), 'Taxation, Real Wage Rigidity and Employment', *Economic Journal* 91, 309–30.

—— and Dixon, P.B. (1980), 'A Tax-Wage Bargain in Australia: Is a Free Lunch Possible?', *Economic Record* 56(154), 209–21.

Creedy, J. and McDonald, I.M. (1989), 'Trade Unions Wages and Taxation,' *Fiscal Studies* 10, 3, 50–9.

—— and —— (1990), 'Income Tax Changes and Trade Union Wage Demands', University of Melbourne, mimeo.

Dunlop, J.T. (1944), *Wage Determination Under Trade Unions*, Macmillan, New York.

Edgeworth, F.Y. (1881), *Mathematical Psychics*, Kegan Paul, London.

—— (1925), *Papers Relating to Political Economy*, 3 vols, Macmillan, London.

Farber, H.S. (1986), 'The Analysis of Union Behaviour', in O.C. Ashenfelter and R. Layard (eds), *Handbook of Labor Economics*, Volume 2, North-Holland, Amsterdam, 1039–89.

Fellner, W. (1949), *Competition Among The Few*, Alfred Knopf, New York.

Grossman, G. (1983), 'Union Wages, Seniority and Unemployment', *American Economic Review* 73, 277–90.

Grout, P.A. (1984), 'Investment and Wages in the

Absence of Legally Binding Labour Contracts: A Nash Bargaining Approach', *Econometrica* 52, 449–60.

Hersoug, T. (1984), 'Union Wage Responses to Tax Changes', *Oxford Economic Papers* 36, 37–51.

Kennan, J. (1988), 'Equilibrium Interpretations of Employment and Real Wage Fluctuations', *NBER Macroeconomics Annual* 3, MIT press, Cambridge, Massachusetts.

Layard, R. and Nickell, S. (1990), 'Is Unemployment Lower if Unions Bargain over Employment', *Quarterly Journal of Economics*, CV (3), 773–87.

Leontief, W. (1946), 'The Pure Theory of the Guaranteed Annual Wage Contract,' *Journal of Political Economy* 56, 76–9.

Lindbeck, A. and Snower, D.J. (1988), 'Cooperation, Harassment, and Involuntary Unemployment: An Insider-Outsider Approach', *American Economic Review* 78(1), 167–88.

McDonald, I.M. (1991), 'Insiders and Trade Union Wage Bargaining', Manchester School of *Economic and Social Studies* (forthcoming).

—— (1989), 'The Wage Demands of a Selfish, Plant-Specific Trade Union', *Oxford Economic Papers* 41, 506–27.

—— (1984), 'Anti-Stagflationary Tax Cuts and the Problem of Investment', *Economic Record* 60(170), 284–93.

—— and Solow, R.M. (1981), 'Wage Bargaining and Employment', *American Economic Review* 71, 891–908.

—— and Solow R.M. (1984), 'Union Wage Policies:

Reply', *American Economic Review* 74(4), 759–61.

Nickell, S. (1982), 'A Bargaining Model of the Phillips Curve', Centre of Labour Economics Discussion Paper No. 130, *London School of Economics*.

—— (1990), 'Unemployment: A Survey', *Economic Journal* 100, 391–439.

Oswald, A.J. (1982), 'The Microeconomic Theory of the Trade Union', *Economic Journal* 92, 576–95.

—— (1984), 'On Union Preferences and Labour Market Models: Neglected Corners', Institute for International Economic Studies Paper 296, University of Stockholm.

—— (1985), 'The Economic Theory of Trade Unions: An Introductory Survey', *The Scandinavian Journal of Economics* 87(2), 160–93.

Oswald, A.J. (1987), 'Efficient Contracts are on the Labour Demand Curve: Theory and Facts', Discussion Paper No. 284, Centre of Labour Economics, London School of Economics.

Pemberton, J. (1991), *Taxation and wage bargaining*, University of Reading.

Pitchford, J.D. (1981), 'Taxation, Real Wage Rigidity and Employment: The Flexible Price Case', *Economic Journal* 91, 716–20.

Sampson, A.A. (1983), 'Employment Policy in a Model with a Rational Trade Union', *Economic Journal* 93, 297–311.

Ulph, A. and Ulph D. (1990), 'Union Bargaining: A Survey of Recent Work' in D. Sapsford and Z. Tzannatos (eds), *Current Issues in Labour Economics*, Macmillan, Basingstoke, UK, 86–125.

[20]

Bulletin of Economic Research 44:3, 1992, 0307-3378 $2.00

UNION WAGE RESPONSES TO A SHIFT FROM DIRECT TO INDIRECT TAXATION*

John Creedy and Ian M. McDonald

I. INTRODUCTION

This paper examines the implications for trade union wage demands of a shift away from income tax towards a commodity tax such as Value Added Tax (VAT). This subject warrants detailed analysis in view of the shift towards indirect taxation by most of the major industrialized countries and the widely held view that unions are concerned with real after-tax earnings rather than gross wages. A basic analysis of a union's objective in the presence of taxes is described in Section II. A specification of revenue neutrality is given in Section III. Section IV examines the effect of different types of change in the tax structure on the wage demands of monopolistic unions which set the wage rate and allow the level of unemployment to be determined by the demand for labour. Section V then examines the implications of tax changes for efficient bargains in which the agreed wage is given by the Nash solution.

Several authors have investigated the impact of income taxation on union wages using the simple monopoly union model. Oswald (1982) uses a linear negative income tax, while Sampson (1983) models a lump-sum

*We are grateful to Jeff Borland and the referees for helpful comments on an earlier draft of this paper, and participants in seminars at Canberra, Melbourne and Monash.

tax.[1] Hersoug (1984) considers the impact on wage demands of changes in tax rates that are revenue neutral, and changes that retain the degree of progressivity. A shift from income tax to value added tax has been analysed by Sampson (1986), whose specification of a progressive income tax and a proportional value added tax is used here. The major difference from Hersoug and Sampson is the definition of revenue neutrality. For them, revenue neutrality is based on the tax revenue received from the workers of an arbitrary firm. In the present paper revenue neutrality is based on *aggregate* tax revenue, so that the entire distribution of wages needs to be considered. It is more realistic to suppose that the government is concerned with aggregate revenue, not simply the revenue from the workers of one firm. Sampson's conclusion is that the tax shift will increase wage demands for those workers whose wages are initially less than a crucial amount. But where this crucial amount would be set by the restriction of aggregate revenue neutrality cannot be determined from Sampson's analysis. This leaves open the question of whether the tax shift would increase the wages of many workers or of only a few workers.

The definition of aggregate revenue neutrality used here holds revenue constant at the original level and distribution of wages in the economy. This is called *ex ante* revenue neutrality; Sampson's analysis is also based on *ex ante* revenue neutral concept. The weakness of this assumption is that it ignores the effects on revenue of the changes in wages induced by the tax shift. However, to require aggregate revenue to remain constant after all the effects of a tax shift have worked through to all the wages in the economy would necessitate a theory to determine the level of every wage. As argued in Section III, there is no satisfactory theory to determine all wage levels. This theoretical vacuum makes the concept of *ex post* revenue neutrality impossible to apply.

In addition to the tax shift analysed in Sampson (1986), which involved a reduction in the marginal rate of income tax, the present paper analyses another type of shift which involves an increase in the threshold level of income. The analysis is also extended to incorporate the efficient bargains model as well as the simple monopoly union model and shows that the two models of the union yield very similar results.[2] In both models the objective function includes the interests of the unemployed. Some authors have argued that the unemployed have no weight in the objective function of union; see for example Oswald (1985), Blanchard and Summers (1986), and Lindbeck and Snower (1988). Such a possibility is not considered

[1] Oswald (1982, p. 588) gives *sufficient* conditions for an increase in the marginal tax rate to increase wage demands.

[2] This contrasts with the analysis of the tax-based incomes policy of Layard (1982) and Chatterji (1986, p. 351), who concludes that in an efficient bargains model the effect of such a policy would be 'exactly the opposite' of its effect in a simple monopoly union model. Hence it would be wrong to assume that insights gained from analysing the tax-based incomes policy of Layard can be carried over to the analysis of income taxes and value added taxes.

here. However, further work has shown that the impact of taxation on wages in a model with an insider-dominated union yields very similar results to the conventional case; see Creedy and McDonald (1991). In view of this, extending the analysis of the tax shifts in this paper to the case of an insider-dominated union would not be expected to yield radically different conclusions.

II. TAXATION AND UNIONS' WAGE-EMPLOYMENT PREFERENCES

The Tax Structure

The analysis uses a tax schedule in which incomes above a threshold, a, are taxed at a constant rate, t. If w is the gross wage, then the income tax paid, $T(w)$, is given by:

$$
\begin{aligned}
T(w) &= 0 & \text{for } w \leq a \\
&= t(w-a) & \text{for } w > a
\end{aligned}
\tag{1}
$$

Value Added Tax is a constant proportion, v, of the tax-exclusive price of goods, which is normalized to unity. Hence the market price of output is $1+v$ and for $w > a$ the real wage, $y = y(w)$, is given by:

$$
y = \frac{w - t(w-a)}{1+v}
\tag{2}
$$

A shift from direct to indirect taxation may be achieved by reducing t while raising v, or by increasing the threshold, a, while raising v. Both types of change are examined below. The first policy reduces progressivity while the second policy increases progressivity.

A Union's Objective

The framework of analysis is one in which there are many trade unions, differing in, for example, the size of membership and demand conditions faced. But each union has the same basic objective and follows the same kind of wage determination procedure, based on the model in McDonald and Solow (1981). Consider a trade union whose objective is to maximize the collective welfare, W, of its m members. For a level of employment of n workers, W is defined by:

$$
W = n\{U(y) - D\} + (m - n) U(b)
\tag{3}
$$

where D is the disutility of work and b is the real, post-tax value of unemployment benefits. It is assumed that b remains constant in real terms, so that the unemployment benefit is automatically adjusted for any increase in VAT. If this assumption is not made and instead a tax change is allowed to change the post-tax value of unemployment benefits, then, in effect, two policy changes are being considered — a change in policy on taxation and a change in policy on unemployment benefits.

It is useful to rewrite the objective function (3) using the opportunity cost of working, x, defined by $U(x) = D + U(b)$. Thus:

$$W = n\{U(y) - U(x)\} + mU(b) \tag{4}$$

For $n < m$, the indifference curves are convex to the origin, but become horizontal at the pre-tax wage, $\{x(1 + v) - at\}/(1 - t)$, which equates y with x, when $n \geq m$. The analysis in Sections IV and V assumes the solution to each trade union's maximization problems occurs at a level of employment less than m.[3]

III. REVENUE NEUTRAL TAX CHANGES

The tax shifts are constrained to be *ex ante* revenue neutral in aggregate. This assumption is not ideal because it is likely that the tax shift will change some wage and employment levels. However, *ex post* neutrality is virtually impossible to impose because it would require the specification of a theory which determines all wages in the economy. At present there is no consensus on a theory of wage determination, and to assume that all wages are determined by the trade union bargaining model would be unrealistic.[4]

The purpose of this section is to specify combinations of t, a and v for which aggregate tax revenue is constant, for a given distribution of wages. Let $F(w)$ represent the distribution function of wages; thus F, is the proportion of individuals with wages $\leq w$. The total revenue from income tax, per employed person, R_t, is given by:

$$R_t = t \int_a^\infty (w - a) \, dF(w) \tag{5}$$

If $\bar{w}$ denotes the average wage and $F_1(a)$ denotes the proportion of total wages earned by those with $w \leq a$, this can be simplified to:

$$R_t = t\bar{w}G(a) \tag{6}$$

[3] The case where $n > m$ corresponds to the insider-dominated union analysed in Creedy and McDonald (1991) which, as pointed out above, suggests that the insider-dominated case would yield the same results as the more conventional case analysed in this paper.

[4] For any group of workers, if employment is on the labour demand curve, it can be shown that the sum of income tax and VAT moves in the opposite direction from the wage change if the elasticity of labour demand exceeds $[1 - at/\{w(t + v)\}]^{-1}$. But of course w is endogenous and depends on the method of wage determination and the demand elasticity itself.

with

$$G(a) = \{1 - F_1(a)\} - (a/\bar{w})\{1 - F(a)\} \tag{7}$$

In general the value of $G(a)$ is less than or equal to one and increases with the dispersion of wages.[5]

Using (6), the per capita after-income-tax income is $\bar{w}\{1 - tG(a)\}$, and assuming that this is all spent, total revenue from income tax and VAT combined per capita, R, is given by:

$$R = \bar{w}[tG(a) + \{v/(1+v)\}\{1 - tG(a)\}] \tag{8}$$

Notice that $v/(1+v)$ is the tax *inclusive* rate of VAT. Then using:

$$\frac{\partial R}{\partial t} = \bar{w}G(a)/(1+v) \text{ and } \frac{\partial R}{\partial v} = \bar{w}\{1 - tG(a)\}/(1+v)^2 \tag{9}$$

it can be seen that, for $dR = 0$:

$$dt/dv = -\{(1-t)/(1+v)\}\,\tau \tag{10}$$

where $0 < \tau = (1-t)\{G(a)^{-1} - t\}^{-1} < 1$, and τ increases with the dispersion of wages.[6] In order to examine changes in the threshold, it is necessary to use the result that:

$$\partial G(a)/\partial a = -\{1 - F(a)\}/\bar{w}$$

hence

$$\partial R/\partial a = -t\{1 - F(a)\}/(1+v) \tag{11}$$

and, for $dR = 0$:

$$\frac{da}{dv} = \frac{\bar{w}(1-t)}{\phi t(1+v)} \tag{12}$$

where $0 < \phi = (1-t)\{1 - F(a)\}/\{1 - tG(a)\} < 1$. When $a = 0$, $\phi = 1$, and if a is positive but less than $\bar{w}$, ϕ is positive but less than one.

IV. THE WAGE RESPONSE OF SIMPLE MONOPOLY UNIONS

A simple monopoly union sets a wage to maximize (3), subject to the employer responding with a level of employment that maximizes profits.

---

[5] If a is zero then $F(a)$ and $F_1(a)$ are both zero and $G(a)$ is equal to one; income tax is proportional and the total receipts from income tax are equal to $t\bar{w}$. With a positive but less than $\bar{w}$, $G(a)$ is positive but less than one. With perfect equality of wages, that is each individual earns $\bar{w}$, $F(a) = 0$ and $G(a) = 1 - a/\bar{w}$. If there is sufficient dispersion of wages for $F(a) > 0$ then $0 < F_1(a) < F(a)(a/\bar{w})$ and so $G(a)$ is greater than $1 - a/\bar{w}$.

[6] A tax change using (10) that is revenue-neutral in aggregate will also be revenue-neutral for a particular wage level, say w^*. It can be shown that $w^* = \bar{w}\{1 - F(a) + (\bar{w}/a)F_1(a)\}^{-1}$ and will generally be below the mean. Those below w^* are made worse-off, *ex ante*, by the change.

Writing $n = n(w)$ as the labour demand function, interior solutions are given by the first order condition:

$$W'(w) = n'(w)\{U(y) - U(x)\} + nU'(y) y'(w) = 0 \tag{13}$$

This can be rewritten as:

$$\theta = \varepsilon \zeta \tag{14}$$

where

$$\theta = -(w/n) n'(w)$$
$$\zeta = (w/y) y'(w)$$

and

$$\varepsilon = [y/\{U(y) - U(x)\}] \{\partial\{U(y) - U(x)\}/\partial y\} = yU'(y)/\{U(y) - U(x)\}$$

The term θ is (minus) the elasticity of the demand for labour with respect to the pre-tax wage, and ζ is the elasticity of the post-tax real wage with respect to the pre-tax wage. The term ε is the elasticity of the difference between the utility of y and the utility from not working, with respect to the net-of-tax real wage. With no taxes, (14) reduces to $\theta = \varepsilon$, which is the condition given in McDonald and Solow (1982, p. 899).

Reducing the Marginal Rate of Income Tax

The first tax shift to be considered is a reduction in t accompanied by an increase in v. For the shift to be revenue neutral these changes have to satisfy (10). The effect on the wage demand is given by:

$$\frac{dw}{dt} = \frac{\partial w}{\partial t} + \frac{\partial w}{\partial v} \frac{dv}{dt} \tag{15}$$

where $\partial w/\partial t$ and $\partial w/\partial v$ are calculated using (14) and dv/dt is taken from (10). For presentation purposes, results are given for the special case where workers are risk-neutral and the labour demand curve has a constant elasticity. For risk neutrality, $U(y) = y$, and assuming the labour demand curve has constant elasticity implies $n = \bar{n}w^{-\theta}$ with $\theta > 1$. Then (14) gives:

$$w = \frac{x(1 + v) - at}{h(1 - t)} \tag{16}$$

where $h = (\theta - 1)/\theta$. Allowing for risk aversion significantly complicates the analysis. Thus if $U(y) = y^{1-r}/(1 - r)$, appropriate substitution into the first order condition gives:

$$at + w(1 - t) h - y^r x^{1-r}(1 + v) = 0 \tag{17}$$

with $h = 1 - (1 - r)/\theta$. This can only be solved for w using numerical methods. Further treatment of the risk averse case is thus given in the Appendix, where it is shown that allowing for risk aversion makes very little difference to the results.

Equation (16) can be used to obtain the partial derivatives $\partial w/\partial t$ and $\partial w/\partial v$, which, combined with (10) can be substituted into (15). The impact on the wage demands of a trade union of a reduction in the marginal rate of income tax offset by an increase in the VAT rate which is *ex ante* revenue neutral is:

$$\frac{dw}{dt} = \{x(1+v)(1-\tau) - a\}/\{h(1-t)^2\} \tag{18}$$

For the shift in tax to *reduce* wage demands, the necessary and sufficient condition is thus:

$$x/a > \{(1+v)(1-\tau)\}^{-1} \tag{19}$$

Hence a shift in tax will reduce the wage demands of those unions whose ratio of the opportunity cost of working to the income tax threshold is greater than a critical amount that depends on v and τ. The latter depends, as shown in Section III, on the income tax parameters and the form of the distribution of wages. Some illustrative calculations are reported in Table 1, where the conditions are given in terms of $x/\bar{w}$ and $a/\bar{w}$ in the sixth

TABLE 1
Critical Values of $x/\bar{w}$

$a/\bar{w}$	t	τ	ϕ	v	Minimum $x/\bar{w}$ for $dw/dt > 0$	Maximum $x/\bar{w}$ for $dw/da < 0$
1/6	0.2	0.79	0.95	0.05	0.77	0.80
				0.15	0.70	0.73
	0.3	0.77	0.93	0.05	0.70	0.72
				0.15	0.64	0.65
	0.4	0.74	0.70	0.05	0.62	0.82
				0.15	0.57	0.75
1/2	0.2	0.44	0.78	0.05	0.85	0.98
				0.15	0.78	0.89
	0.3	0.41	0.72	0.05	0.81	0.93
				0.15	0.74	0.85
	0.4	0.38	0.66	0.05	0.77	0.87
				0.15	0.70	0.79

column. The values of τ are shown in the third column of Table 1 and are calculated from a lognormal distribution with a coefficient of variation of 0.5, which is a suitable value in the present context.[7]

The unions whose demands are reduced by a tax shift which reduces t and raises v will have a value of $x/\bar{w}$ that exceeds the critical value reported in the sixth column. Low values of t generate high critical values. At the higher values of t, the critical values of $x/\bar{w}$ reported in Table 1 are lower but are still relatively high; there are few if any unions who have a value of $x/\bar{w}$ higher than 0.6 to 0.7. These calculations suggest that all trade union wage demands would tend to increase following this type of tax shift.

Raising the Income Tax Threshold

Increasing the threshold, a, accompanied by an increase in v given by equation (12), will be *ex ante* revenue neutral. The impact of this shift on trade union wage demands is:

$$\frac{dw}{da} = \frac{\partial w}{\partial a} + \frac{\partial w}{\partial v}\frac{dv}{da} \tag{20}$$

The condition for wage demands to be reduced is thus:

$$x/\bar{w} < (1-t)/\{\phi(1+v)\} \tag{22}$$

Values of the right-hand side of (22) are reported in the seventh column of Table 1; these are critical maxima. For wage demands to be reduced by a shift which increases a and v, $x/\bar{w}$ has to be *less* than the critical value shown. These critical values are lower for higher income tax rates and higher VAT rates. In general they are large, suggesting that a shift involving an increase in the threshold will reduce all unions' wage demands.

V. THE WAGE RESPONSE WITH EFFICIENT BARGAINS

This paper has so far concentrated on the simple monopoly union model. The present section examines efficient bargains in a framework in which each union deals with a single firm. In general there is of course a range of indeterminacy along the contract curve; the bargaining solution adopted is the symmetric Nash solution, as in McDonald and Solow (1981, p. 905).

---

[7] When a is one sixth of the average wage, $G(a)$ is approximately 0.83; if a is one half of the average wage, then $G(a)$ is approximately 0.50.

The Nash Solution

With the objective function in (4), the worst situation is one where all the union's members are unemployed. Hence the threat point is $mU(b)$ and the union's payoff is $n\{U(y) - U(x)\}$. If the threat point of the firm corresponds to zero profit, its payoff is $\pi = R(n) - wn$, where $R(n)$ denotes total revenue. The Nash solution is given by the values of w and in which maximize the product of the two payoffs, L, where:

$$L = n\{U(y) - U(x)\}\{R(n) - wn\} \tag{23}$$

The first-order conditions for a maximum give:

$$\partial L/\partial w = nU'(y)\,y'(w)\,\pi - n^2\{U(y) - U(x)\} = 0 \tag{24}$$

$$\partial L/\partial n = \{U(y) - U(x)\}\,\pi + n\{U(y) - U(x)\}\{R'(n) - w\} = 0 \tag{25}$$

Substituting the constant relative risk-aversion utility function, the constant elasticity revenue function, $R(n) = kn^{(\theta - 1)/\theta}$, with $\theta > 1$, and the linear tax structure, into (24) and (25) gives the union's wage demand as the root of:

$$at + w(1 - t)\,h - y^r x^{1-r}(1 + v) = 0 \tag{26}$$

where $h = 1 - (1 - r)/(2\theta - 1)$.

Changing the Tax Structure

The only difference between (26) and (17) is the definition of h, which is independent of the endogenous variables and the parameters of the tax system. Because of this very convenient property, the conditions for a tax shift to reduce wage demands derived for the simple monopoly union case with risk aversion can be easily reinterpreted for the case of efficient bargains. With a linear utility function, the condition with efficient bargains is precisely the same as (19), which is independent of h and so is the same for the two cases.

For an increase in a accompanied by an increase in v, the conditions derived in the simple monopoly union case carry over, with the simple redefinition of h, to the case of efficient bargains. With a linear utility function the condition on $x/\bar{w}$ for $dw/da = 0$ is precisely the same for the simple monopoly union case and for efficient bargains; so the values in the seventh column of Table 1 apply to both cases.

VII.   CONCLUSION

This paper has derived conditions for a revenue-neutral shift from direct to indirect taxes to reduce the wage demands of a trade union. Two types of tax shift were considered; one in which a higher VAT rate was offset by a lower marginal rate of income tax, and a second in which a higher VAT rate was offset by a higher threshold level of income. Two versions of the standard economic model of a trade union were used — the simple monopoly union and the Nash solution to efficient bargains.

It appears from the numerical examples that the tax shift involving an increase in the threshold income level is likely to reduce wage demands. However shifting taxes by reducing the marginal rate of income tax would be likely to increase wage demands. For a union trading wages for employment, the marginal rate of tax is a tax on wage increases. Reducing the marginal rate of tax therefore encourages wage increases. However, a number of governments in recent years have wished to reduce marginal income tax rates as part of a shift towards indirect taxation. This paper suggests that, for the types of union examined, such a *ceterus paribus* policy is likely to lead to a once-and-for-all increase in the wages of union members and reduce their level of employment.

The policy chosen by any government will of course depend on its broad objectives and many other factors not examined here. For example, a major argument for shifting to indirect taxes is to reduce income tax evasion. To allow for a reduction in evasion in the analysis of this paper, revenue-neutrality could be modified to revenue-reducing. This would reduce the stringency of the conditions. Of course improving the equity of the tax system by reducing evasion may properly be considered an end in itself.

The University of Melbourne   *Revised March 1990,*
                                            revision accepted June 1991

APPENDIX: ALLOWING FOR RISK AVERSION

Risk aversion can be incorporated by replacing the linear utility function with a constant elasticity utility function, that is with $U(y) = y^{1-r}/(1-r)$ and $r \geq 0$. Substituting into (14) along with the linear tax structure, and the constant elasticity labour demand function yields:

$$at + w(1-t)h - y^r x^{1-r}(1+v) = \Theta = 0, \tag{A1}$$

where $h = 1 - (1-r)/\theta$.

It is required to find critical values of $x/\bar{w}$ for which $dw/dt = 0$, for each type of tax shift. For an increase in v combined with a decrease in t, substitute into (15) with dv/dt taken from (10), $\partial w/\partial t = -(\partial\Theta/\partial t)/(\partial\Theta/\partial w)$ and $\partial w/\partial v = -(\partial\Theta/\partial v)/(\partial\Theta/\partial w)$. This yields an awkward expression for $\partial w/\partial t$, from which the term (x/y) can be eliminated using (A1). The values of w/a, given the parameters, for which $dw/dt = 0$ can then be obtained

UNION WAGE RESPONSES   231

TABLE A1

Values of $x/\bar{w}$ for which $dw/dt = 0$ (higher values of $x/\bar{w}$ yield $dw/dt > 0$)
$t = 0.3, v = 0.15$

			Values of r			
θ	$a/\bar{w}$		0	0.5	2	10
1	0.17	SMU	*	0.49	0.49	0.55
		EB	*	0.49	0.49	0.55
	0.5	SMU	*	0.58	0.58	0.64
		EB	*	0.58	0.58	0.64
2	0.17	SMU	0.64	0.61	0.58	0.58
		EB	0.64	0.63	0.61	0.60
	0.5	SMU	0.74	0.70	0.67	0.67
		EB	0.74	0.72	0.70	0.69
5	0.17	SMU	0.64	0.64	0.63	0.62
		EB	0.64	0.64	0.64	0.63
	0.5	SMU	0.74	0.73	0.72	0.71
		EB	0.74	0.74	0.73	0.72

Note: The combination of $r = 0$ and $\theta = 1$ yields a wage demand of infinity.

using non-linear numerical methods, and then the corresponding value of x/a can be obtained from the first order condition (A1). Finally, the critical value of $x/\bar{w} = (x/a)(a/\bar{w})$ for $dw/dt = 0$ is obtained. Examples are reported in Table A1, where the rows with the entry SMU in the fourth column refer to the simple monopoly union. Reading across each row, the tendency for the critical value to fall with higher values of r is apparent. However for $\theta = 2$ or 5, this tendency is slight. Indeed the impact of changing the value of r is so small that the case of a linear utility function serves as a good summary value. It is also found that a similar pattern emerges with different values of t and v.

For the second type of tax shift, in which both a and t are increased, the impact on the wage demand can be calculated by substituting into (20), where $\partial w/\partial a = -(\partial \Theta/\partial a)/(\partial \Theta/\partial w)$ and $\partial w/\partial v = -(\partial \Theta/\partial v)/(\partial \Theta/\partial w)$, with dv/da taken from (12). Following a similar numerical procedure to that described for the previous policy, it is possible to calculate critical values of $x/\bar{w}$ for $dw/da = 0$. Calculations following the lines of Table A1 produce comparable results, again showing that the linear utility function provides a good guide.

Comparing the two columns of critical values in Table A1, the maximum value of $x/\bar{w}$ for $dw/dt > 0$ is always less than the maximum value of $x/\bar{w}$ for $dw/da < 0$. This property is also apparent from comparing Table A1 with Table A2. The zones of values of $x/\bar{w}$ for which a tax shift will reduce w overlap. Thus, for the parameter values used it is possible to find a type of tax shift that can reduce wage demands.

It has been seen, by comparing (17) or (A1) and (26), that the efficient bargains case is similar to that of monopoly unions. The condition for a revenue-neutral shift from direct to indirect taxes, made by reducing t and raising v, to reduce wages is therefore calculated in precisely the same way as described above, but with h set to its value for efficient bargains. Calculation are reported in Table A1, in the rows with the entry EB in the fifth column. There is little difference between the two cases when $r > 0$ and, as seen above, no difference when $r = 0$. Comparable results were obtained for the policy of increasing the tax-free threshold while increasing v. Again the EB and SMU cases are similar.

REFERENCES

Aitchison, J. A. and Brown, J. A. C. (1957). *The Lognormal Distribution.* Cambridge University Press, Cambridge.

Blanchard, O. and Summers, L. (1986). 'Hysteresis and the European Unemployment Problem', In *NBER Macroeconomics Annual*, Vol. 1, MIT Press, Cambridge, MA.

Chatterji, M. (1986). 'Unions, Employment and the Inflation Tax', *Economic Journal*, Vol. 96, pp. 342–51.

Creedy, J. (1985). *Dynamics of Income Distribution.* Basil Blackwell, Oxford.

Creedy, J. and McDonald, I. M. (1991). 'Models of Trade Union Behaviour: A Synthesis', *Economic Record*, Vol. 67, pp. 346–359.

Edgeworth, F. Y. (1881). *Mathematical Psychics.* Kegan Paul, London.

Hersoug, T. (1984). 'Union Wage Response to Tax Changes', *Oxford Economic Papers*, Vol. 36, pp. 37–51.

Layard, M. (1982). 'Is Incomes Policy the Answer to Unemployment?', *Economica*, Vol. 49, pp. 219–39.

Lindbeck, A. and Snower, D. J. (1988). *The Insider–Outsider Theory of Employment and Unemployment.* MIT Press, Cambridge, MA.

McDonald, I. M. and Solow, R. M. (1981). 'Wage Bargaining and Employment', *American Economic Review*, Vol. 71, pp. 896–908.

Oswald, A. J. (1982). 'The Microeconomic Theory of the Trade Union', *Economic Journal*, Vol.92, pp. 576–95.

Oswald, A. A. (1985). 'The Economic Theory of Trade Unions: An Introductory Survey', *Scandinavian Journal of Economics*, Vol. 87, No. 2, pp. 160–93.

Sampson, A. A. (1983). 'Employment Policy in a Rational Trade Union', *Economic Journal*, Vol. 93, pp. 297–311.

Sampson, A. A. (1986). 'The Shift to Indirect Taxation in a Unionized Economy', *Bulletin of Economic Research*, Vol. 38, pp. 87–91.

[21]

INCOME TAX CHANGES AND TRADE UNION WAGE DEMANDS*

JOHN CREEDY and IAN M. McDONALD

University of Melbourne

I. INTRODUCTION

This paper examines the effect on unions' wage demands of two types of policy. The first changes tax revenue while keeping progressivity constant; the second policy changes the degree of progressivity of the tax structure while keeping total revenue constant. Progressivity is measured in terms of the relative dispersion of the distribution of post-tax wages. These types of policy were examined by Hersoug (1984), using a two-parameter tax function first suggested by Edgeworth (1925, ii, p.249). However, a linear function with a threshold level of income and a constant marginal rate is more realistic and has parameters which are more readily interpreted. This paper uses both types of tax function, the Edgeworth tax function in Section II and the progressive linear tax function in Section III.

Hersoug (1984, p.43) derived a condition which was necessary but not sufficient for a progressivity-constant reduction in tax revenue to reduce wage demands. The present paper shows that, under either of the two tax functions, a progressivity constant reduction in revenue will definitely reduce wage demands in the simple monopoly union model. The major point of departure from Hersoug is in the definition of revenue neutrality used to analyse the second policy. For Hersoug, revenue neutrality is based on the tax paid by a group of workers belonging to a single bargaining unit. In the present paper revenue neutrality is based on the aggregate tax revenue from all workers.

A problem with Hersoug's approach is that it is difficult to interpret his results. His conclusion is that the reduction in progressivity will increase wage demands for those workers for whom, at the initial wage, tax revenue is constant. But where in the income distribution these workers would be if the policy were revenue neutral in aggregate cannot be determined from Hersoug's analysis. This leaves open the question of whether a revenue neutral reduction in progressivity would increase the wages of many or of only a few workers. By using a complete distribution of income, progressivity is defined in terms of the difference between the relative dispersion of the pre- and post-tax distributions, contrasting with Hersoug's definition, which is based on the tax schedule.

The definition of aggregate revenue neutrality used in the present paper holds revenue constant at the original level and distribution of wages in the economy; it is an *ex ante* concept.

* We are grateful to a referee for comments in an earlier draft of this paper.

47

Hersoug's analysis is also based on an *ex ante* concept. The weakness of assuming *ex ante* revenue neutrality is that it ignores the effects on revenue of the changes in wages and employment induced by the change in tax rates. This issue is examined further in Section II, and some comments on the implications for *ex post* revenue neutrality are made in Section IV.

The following subsections present the basic model of union behaviour to be used throughout the paper.

A Simple Monopoly Union

The framework is one in which a union, all of whose m members have the same wage, w, sets the wage and allows the employer to determine employment by the labour demand function. This is the 'simple monopoly union' model described by McDonald and Solow (1981), and is used only to simplify the exposition. The analysis of 'efficient bargains' produces very similar results, but is more cumbersome. Furthermore, if the union is assumed to be dominated by a group of insiders then, again, a similar response to taxation can arise. The similarities of these various models of trade union behaviour are brought out in Creedy and McDonald (1991). The union chooses the wage to maximise the utility function:

$$W = n\{U(y) - D\} + (m - n)U(b) \tag{1}$$

where $n = n(w)$ is the labour demand function, D is the disutility of work, b is the level of unemployment benefits, and y is the post-tax wage. The latter may be written as $y = y(w)$ where the function $y(w)$ depends on the structure of income taxation. Throughout the paper it is assumed that b remains constant in real terms. If unemployment benefits are taxed then holding b constant requires an adjustment to unemployment benefits when tax rates are changed. The alternative approach, under which a tax change is allowed to change the post-tax value of unemployment benefits, would mix two policy changes — changes in taxation and unemployment benefits.

Defining $U(x) = U(b) + D$, where x is the opportunity cost of working, rewrite (1) as:

$$W = n\{U(y) - U(x)\} + mU(b) \tag{2}$$

Utility, W, is maximised with respect to w and n, subject to the constraint that $n < m$. The following analysis concentrates on interior solutions, for which the first-order condition for a maximum is obtained by writing W as a function of w and setting $\partial W(w)/\partial w = W'(w) = 0$. Hence:

$$W'(w) = n'(w)\{U(y) - U(x)\} + n(w)U'(y)y'(w) = 0 \tag{3}$$

If $\theta = -wn'(w)/n$ is the absolute value of the wage elasticity of demand for labour, $\epsilon = yU'(y)/\{U(y) - U(x)\}$ is the elasticity of the excess of the utility from working over that of the opportunity cost of working with respect to the post-tax wage, and $\xi = wy'(w)/y$ is the elasticity of the post-tax wage with respect to the pre-tax wage, (3) can be rearranged to give the condition:

$$\theta = \epsilon\xi \tag{4}$$

This first-order condition can be solved for w, given assumptions about the form of each of the functions, y and U. Differences between unions in their attitude towards risk, and particularly the labour demand function faced, generate variations in wages among unions although they all face the same tax function.

Changes in Average and Marginal Tax Rates

It is useful to consider the slope, s, of an indifference curve for variations in w and n. This is given by:

$$s = \frac{-\{U(y) - U(x)\}}{nU'(y)y'(w)}$$

Insight into the way in which tax changes affect any union's wage demand can be obtained by examining the way in which the slope, s, changes. If the indifference curve becomes less steep, the optimal wage demand will increase. This is illustrated in Figure 1. The effect on s of a change in taxation can be decomposed into a change in the average tax rate which leave the marginal rate unaffected and a change in the marginal rate which leave the average rate unaffected. The average rate is $1 - y/w$, so the first effect is:

$$\partial s/\partial(1 - y/w) = -w\partial s/\partial y = w(1 + r/\epsilon)/ny'(w) > 0$$

where r is the Arrow-Pratt measure of relative risk aversion given by $r = -yU''(y)/U'(y)$. Since s is negative, an increase in s will make indifference curves flatter and increase wage demands. This is not surprising because an increase in the average rate of tax will reduce the advantage of working relative to not working. The marginal tax rate is $1 - y'(w)$, so the second effect is:

$$\partial s/\partial\{1 - y'(w)\} = -\partial s/\partial y'(w) = s/y'(w) < 0$$

Hence an increase in the marginal tax rate, holding the average rate constant, increases the slope of the indifference curve and reduces the wage demand. The post-tax pay-off from wage increases is reduced, so that employment increases are more attractive. Changes in average and marginal rates therefore move a union's wage demand in opposite directions. It is useful to bear this point in mind because changes in the parameters of specified tax functions can change both average and marginal rates at the same time.

II. A Constant Elasticity Tax Function

Consider the tax function used by Hersoug (1984), given by:

$$y = \alpha w^\beta \qquad\qquad \alpha, \beta > 0, \beta < 1 \qquad\qquad (5)$$

This function was used by Edgeworth (1925), who pointed out that (5) holds for $w > \alpha^{1/(1-\beta)}$, otherwise the tax becomes negative. The elasticity of the post-tax wage with respect to the pre-tax wage, ξ, takes the constant value β, which Hersoug uses as the measure of progressivity. This is the well-known measure of 'residual progression', whose properties in the context of a fixed pre-tax income distribution have been extensively examined by Jacobsson (1976).

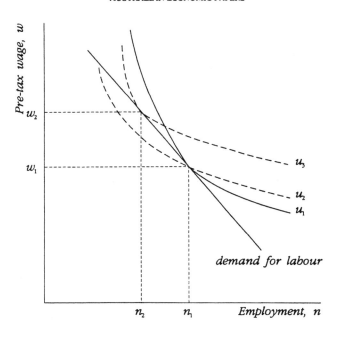

FIGURE 1

The Simple Monopoly Union

Jacobsson showed that an increase in ξ shifts the Lorenz curve of post-tax income inwards. The effect of changing tax revenue, while maintaining progressivity constant, can be examined in terms of changes in α alone. Changes in β affect revenue as well as progressivity and so have a more complicated effect.

Progressivity and Revenue Neutrality

In planning a change in the progressivity of the taxation system, policy makers are concerned about the implications for aggregate revenue, so the change in progressivity analysed in this paper is constrained to be *ex ante* revenue neutral in aggregate. Using *ex ante* revenue neutrality is less than ideal because it is likely that the tax shift will change some wage levels. However, the application of *ex post* revenue neutrality would require the specification of a theory which determines all wages in the economy and the way in which changes in taxes affect all those wages. To assume that all wages are determined by the trade union model would be unrealistic, while taking a mixture of theories would appear arbitrary. An analysis using *ex post* revenue neutrality based on a mixture of theories would be of little use, even if tractable results could be obtained. The basis would be so complex that it would be extremely difficult to unravel the influence of the various constituent theories and to form a clear idea of the major forces that generated the results. Hence, this paper is based on the concept of *ex ante* aggregate revenue neutrality. However, in Section IV some comment is made on the possible implications of the tax shift for revenue *ex post*.

The relationship between pre and post-tax wages for the tax function in (5) are most easily investigated using the assumption that pre-tax wages are lognormally distributed, which is a reasonable approximation to reality. Then wages, w, not all of which are determined by union bargaining, are distributed as $\Lambda(w|\mu, \sigma^2)$, where μ and σ^2 are respectively the mean and variance of the logarithms of wages. A property of the lognormal distribution (see Aitchison and Brown, 1957, p.11) is that

$$y = \alpha w^\beta \text{ is } \Lambda(y|\log\alpha + \beta\mu, \beta^2\sigma^2) \tag{6}$$

Hence the variance of the logarithms of y is $\beta^2 \sigma^2$ and is affected only by the parameter β of the tax function; this is not surprising in view of Jacobsson's (1976) result and the fact that Lorenz curves of the two-parameter lognormal distribution do not cross. In the remaining analysis an increase in the variance of the logarithms of y will be interpreted as a decrease in the progressivity of the system.

In view of the fact that changes in β also affect tax revenue, it is necessary to consider combinations of changes in α and β that leave revenue unchanged. Using the assumption of lognormality, the arithmetic mean wage, $\bar{w}$, is given by:

$$\bar{w} = \exp(\mu + \sigma^2/2) \tag{7}$$

Tax revenue per person, R, is $\bar{w} - \bar{y}$, and combining (6) and (7) it is found that:

$$\bar{y} = \exp(\log\alpha + \beta\mu + \beta^2\sigma^2/2) \tag{8}$$

Hence total differentiation gives:

$$dR = -(\bar{y}/\alpha)d\alpha - \bar{y}(\mu + \beta\sigma^2)d\beta \tag{9}$$

Combinations of changes in α and β that leave total revenue unchanged are given by

$$d\alpha/d\beta = -\alpha(\mu + \beta\sigma^2). \tag{10}$$

This result is used below when considering revenue neutral changes in progressivity. But first consider the effect of progressivity neutral changes in revenue.

Changes in Tax Revenue

Differentiating (3), with respect to α gives:

$$\frac{\partial W'}{\partial\alpha} = n'(w)U'(y)w^\beta + n(w)\alpha\beta w^{\beta-1}U''(y)w^\beta + n(w)U'(y)\beta w^{\beta-1}$$

$$= n(w)U'(y)w^{\beta-1}\{\theta + \beta(r-1)\} \tag{11}$$

The effect on the wage is given by $\partial w/\partial\alpha = -\{\partial W''(w)/\partial\alpha\}/\{\partial W'(w)/\partial w\}$, so if the second order condition $W''(w) < 0$ holds, an increase in α reduces wage demands if the term in curly brackets in (11) is positive; that is, if:

$$r > 1 - \theta/\beta \tag{12}$$

and because $\theta > \beta$ by the first order condition (4) with $\xi = \beta$ this will hold. Hence a cut in tax revenue (an increase in α) that keeps the degree of progressivity constant will lead to a reduction in the wage demands of all unions, irrespective of the wage of their members.

Changes in Progressivity

First differentiate (3) with respect to β, giving:

$$\frac{\partial W'}{\partial \beta} = -n(w)U'(y)\alpha w^{\beta-1}\log w\{\theta + r\beta - (1+\beta\log w)/\log w\} \tag{13}$$

Using the fact that $\partial w/\partial \beta = -(\partial W'/\partial \beta)/W''$, and $W'' < 0$, an increase in β (a reduction in progressivity) will reduce wage demands if the term in curly brackets in (13) is positive. The increase in β reduces the average tax rate, so an *ex ante* revenue neutral reduction in progressivity is achieved by combining an increase in β with a reduction in α, as given by equation (10). The total effect on wages is equal to:

$$\frac{dw}{d\beta} = \frac{\partial w}{\partial \beta} + \frac{\partial w}{\partial \alpha}\frac{d\alpha}{d\beta} \tag{14}$$

Substitution and rearranging terms gives:

$$\frac{dw}{d\beta} = \frac{n(w)U'(y)\alpha w^{\beta-1}}{W''(w)}[\{\theta+\beta(r-1)\}\{\log\frac{w}{M}-\beta\sigma^2\}-1] \tag{15}$$

where $M = \exp(\mu)$ is the median pre-tax wage. Hence a 'pure' reduction in progressivity reduces wages for those unions for whom:

$$\log(w/M) > \beta\sigma^2 + \{\theta+\beta(r-1)\}^{-1} \tag{16}$$

which specifies the wage demand by the workers of a particular union in relation to the median value. This condition will not necessarily be met for all trade unions, unlike the condition for a cut in revenue to reduce wage demands.

A Special Case

The examination of condition (16) is simplified if it is assumed that the elasticity of labour demand is constant and that the utility function displays constant relative risk aversion, so that $U(y) = y^{1-r}/(1-r)$. The first-order condition $\theta = \epsilon\xi$ can be solved explicitly for the optimal wage, w, giving:

$$w = \left(\frac{x}{\alpha}\right)^{1/\beta}\left(\frac{\theta(1-r)-\beta}{\theta(1-r)}\right)^{1/\beta(r-1)} \tag{17}$$

Substituting for w in (16) gives:

$$x > (\alpha M^\beta)\left\{\frac{\theta(1-r)-\beta}{\theta(1-r)}\right\}^{1/(1-r)}\exp\left\{\beta^2\sigma^2+\frac{\beta}{\theta-\beta(r-1)}\right\} \tag{18}$$

The first term on the right hand side of (18), αM^β, is the after-tax value of the median wage. Hence a reduction in progressivity reduces wage demands for those unions whose members have an opportunity cost of working that exceeds the post-tax median wage by a proportion that depends on β, r, θ and σ^2. These results, using aggregate revenue neutrality, therefore provide a simple criterion which has a clear interpretation. The value of the opportunity cost, x, along with θ and r, will of course vary between unions. Suppose that β and σ^2 are 0.95 and 0.2 respectively, and consider a union with $\theta = 2$ and $r = 2$. Substitution into (18) shows that $x/\alpha M^\beta$ must exceed 1.12, otherwise a reduction in progressivity will raise the wage demand of the union. Without further information about the empirical orders of magnitude, particularly concerning the opportunity costs of various unions' members, it is not possible to make a priori predictions about the general effect of a change in progressivity.

III. A LINEAR TAX FUNCTION

A function with parameters that are easier to interpret than the parameters of the constant elasticity tax function is the frequently used linear function given, for $w > a$, by:

$$y = a + (1 - t)(w - a)$$
$$= at + (1 - t)w \tag{19}$$

Here a is the threshold below which no tax is paid and t is the constant marginal tax rate. An increase in tax revenue can be brought about by either increasing t or reducing a, or both. But these policies will influence the progressivity of the system. Hence for a progressivity-neutral change it is necessary to examine combinations of changes in parameters a and t.

Progressivity and Revenue Neutrality

Unlike the tax function of Section II, no simple transformation between the pre- and post-tax distributions is available for the linear tax function. However, concentrating on those above the threshold, a, the coefficients of variation of the distribution of y and w, denoted η_y and η_w respectively are related by:

$$\eta_y = \eta_w \left\{ 1 + \frac{at}{\bar{w}(1-t)} \right\}^{-1} \tag{20}$$

where $\bar{w}$ refers to the arithmetic mean wage of those liable to pay tax. Hence, $\partial \eta_y / \partial a$ and $\partial \eta_y / \partial t$ are both negative, so increases in t and a *reduce* the relative dispersion of y and thus *increase* progressivity[1] Combinations of a and t which are progressivity neutral are given by:

$$\frac{da}{dt} = \frac{-a}{t(1-t)} \tag{21}$$

An increase in t increases tax revenue and at the same time increases progressivity. In order to maintain progressivity constant it is therefore necessary to reduce the threshold, a, according

---

[1] If the complete distribution, rather than just those above the threshold, are considered, it can be shown that for very high values of a, further increases which are revenue neutral actually increase the dispersion of net income (for a fixed pre-tax distribution).

to (21); such a reduction also has the effect of increasing revenue, working in the same direction as t.

Total tax revenue per person is given by $\bar{w} - \bar{y} = (\bar{w} - a)t$. Combinations of a and t that are *ex ante* revenue neutral in aggregate are therefore given by:

$$\frac{da}{dt} = \frac{\bar{w} - a}{t} \tag{22}$$

Consider increasing the progressivity of the system by raising t, which also has the effect of increasing revenue. From (22) this can be matched with an increase in the threshold that maintains revenue at its initial level. The increase in the threshold reinforces the increase in progressivity, so there is no ambiguity in examining revenue neutral changes that alter the progressivity of the system. These policies are examined below.

Changes in Tax Revenue

To calculate the effect on any trade union's wage demand of progressivity neutral changes in tax revenue, calculate $y'(w)$ from (19), substitute the result into (3), and then, as in Section II, take partial derivatives. This yields:

$$\frac{\partial W'}{\partial a} = -n(w)U'(y)t\left\{\frac{\theta}{w} + \frac{(1-t)r}{y}\right\} \tag{23}$$

and since $\partial w/\partial a = -(\partial W'/\partial a W'')$ and $W'' < 0$ an increase in the threshold reduces wage demands of all unions, irrespective of their wage. Furthermore:

$$\frac{\partial W'}{\partial t} = n(w)U'(y)\left[\theta(1-\frac{a}{w}) + \frac{r}{y}(1-t)(w-a) - 1\right] \tag{24}$$

so that an increase in t raises wage demands if the term in square brackets in (24) is positive.

An increase in revenue that keeps η_y constant is thus examined by combining (23) and (24) with the condition (21). After some manipulation:

$$\frac{dw}{dt} = \frac{-n(w)U'(y)}{W''(w)}\left[\theta\left\{1 + \frac{a}{w}\left(\frac{w}{1-t}\right) - 1\right\} + \frac{rw}{y}\left\{1 - t\left(1 - \frac{a}{w}\right)\right\} - 1\right] \tag{25}$$

which is positive. Precisely the same condition is also obtained when examining progressivity neutral changes in a. Thus a cut in tax revenue, however obtained, with constant progressivity reduces the wages demands of all unions.

Changes in Progressivity

Changes in progressivity that are *ex ante* revenue neutral can be examined using (23) and (24), combined with the revenue neutrality condition (22). It can be shown that:

$$\frac{dw}{dt} = \frac{-n(w)U'(y)}{W''(w)}\left[\left(1 - \frac{\bar{w}}{w}\right)\left\{\theta + \frac{r(1-t)w}{y}\right\} - 1\right] \tag{26}$$

A revenue neutral increase in t increases wage demands for any union for whom the term in square brackets in (26) is positive. From the simple monopoly union model, a union's wage is determined by other parameters such as the elasticity of labour demand and the opportunity cost of working. Further interpretation of (26) therefore requires substitution of the endogenous wage.

Some Special Cases

Suppose first that a union has a linear utility function, for which $r = 0$, and faces a constant elasticity of labour demand. Solve $\theta = \epsilon \xi$ for the pre-tax wage, giving:

$$w = \frac{\theta(x - at)}{(\theta - 1)(1 - t)} \tag{27}$$

Substituting for $r = 0$ in (26) gives the condition that a revenue neutral increase in t *reduces* wages demands for those unions for whom:

$$w < \bar{w}\theta/(\theta - 1) \tag{28}$$

Using (27) to substitute for w in (28), gives:

$$x < at + \bar{w}(1 - t) \tag{29}$$

This states that the opportunity cost of working must be less than the after-tax value of the arithmetic mean wage, $\bar{w}$, of those with $w > a$, for a revenue neutral increase in t (an increase in progressivity) to reduce the wage demand of the union. This condition is slightly simpler than the corresponding result of Section II, but again depends on the value of the opportunity cost of working.

With a constant relative risk aversion utility function and a constant elasticity labour demand function, (26) becomes

$$\frac{dw}{dt} = \frac{h - (\bar{w}/w) + [\{\bar{w}/w - 1\}r(x/y)^{1 - r}]}{w(1 - t)\{h - r(x/y)^{1 - r}\}} \tag{30}$$

where $h = 1 - (1 - r)/\theta$. To evaluate (30), w must be determined from the first-order condition, (3), which becomes:

$$(a/w)t + (1 - t)h - (x/y)^{1 - r}(y/w) = 0 \tag{31}$$

Using (30) and (31), critical values of x/a for which $dw/dt = 0$ can be calculated for values of r, θ, $a/\bar{w}$ and t. This procedure is not as straightforward as using condition (18), because (31) can only be solved numerically using iterative procedures. For example consider the values of $\bar{w}/a = 3$ and $\theta = r = 2$. Calculations show that if x/a is less than 2.17 then $dw/dt < 0$; that is an increase in progressivity, arising from a revenue neutral increase in t, will reduce the wage demand of this particular union. With $\bar{w}/a = 3$, x/a will be less than 2.17 if $\bar{w}/x$ is greater than 1.39. These calculations are not very sensitive to r. As with the Edgeworth tax function, without further information about the empirical orders of magnitude of x, a

priori predictions about the effects of progressive changes do not seem warranted. If opportunity costs are relatively low, an increase in progressivity is likely to reduce wage demands.

IV. *Ex Ante* Revenue Neutrality and *Ex Post* Revenue

It has been suggested above that the analysis of what happens to total revenue, *ex post*, would require a complete model that is capable of determining all wages and employment levels in the economy. This is clearly beyond the scope of the present paper. However, this section discusses in general terms the situation in which the above results would be robust.

Suppose an increase in progressivity reduces the wage demands of a group of workers. This will have the effect of increasing the level of employment of the group; the extent of this depends on the elasticity of labour demand for that group. It is therefore possible for the wage bill, and the tax paid, of this group to increase if the elasticity of labour demand is sufficiently high. For a linear progressive tax, the revenue from a group of n workers, each with wage w, is given by $t(w-a)n(w)$. Differentiation with respect to w shows that the tax revenue moves in the opposite direction to the wage if $\theta > 1/(1-a/w)$. What happens to aggregate revenue is more complex. For aggregate revenue to increase it is required that a sufficient amount of extra tax revenue is collected from those groups which face more elastic labour demands, in order to compensate for any loss of revenue from other groups. If this were to result, then to maintain *ex post* revenue neutrality would require an adjustment to tax rates to reduce revenue.

The policy can be consistently carried out so long as there is no aggregate 'Laffer effect'; that is, so long as the reduction in taxes does not lead to an increase in revenue. It has been suggested that wages which are influenced by trade union bargaining are likely to fall when their average tax rate is reduced. For those groups, the tax revenue will fall so long as the elasticity of labour demand is *below* some critical value. It is important to realise that the condition under which a change in progressivity will lead to a group paying more tax is not the same as the condition under which a reduction in the average tax rate leads to an increase in total revenue. Indeed, the former elasticity can be shown to be less than the latter, so that there is a range of values over which the results of this paper are quite robust.

V. Conclusions

This paper has examined the wage responses of trade unions to changes in income taxation. Both 'progressivity constant' changes in revenue and 'revenue neutral' changes in progressivity were considered. For revenue neutrality, *aggregate* revenue was held constant, whereas previous analyses of tax changes and union wage demands have considered changes that are revenue neutral for only one specified wage level. The present approach provides more conclusive results that are easier to interpret.

Two tax functions were used. The first is a non-linear function with a constant elasticity of the post-tax wage with respect to the pre-tax wage. The second is a simple but more realistic linear function with a single threshold and marginal tax rate. In both cases it was seen that an increase in total revenue, keeping progressivity constant, raises the wage demands of all monopolistic trade unions. Increases in progressivity, with total revenue held constant, do not give unequivocal results, although a simple criterion was established in which the opportunity cost of working of a union's members plays a crucial role. This condition is much easier to interpret than that produced by Hersoug. It would therefore be of much interest to obtain empirical estimates of the opportunity cost for a variety of unions. Although the simple monopoly union model of wage determination has been presented, the cases of wage bargaining, efficient bargaining and insider-dominated unions have very similar comparative static properties. The results may, however, be less robust with respect to the assumption that real benefits while unemployed remain constant[2] It is suggested that the approach provides a useful basis for the inclusion of trade unions into the wider analysis of issues in public finance.

REFERENCES

Aitchison, A.B. and Brown, J.A.C. (1975), *The Lognormal Distribution* (Cambridge: Cambridge University Press).

Creedy, J. and McDonald, I.M. (1991), "Trade unions and taxes: A Synthesis", *Economic Record*, vol. 67, no. 196.

Edgeworth, F.Y. (1925), *Papers Relating to Political Economy* (London: Macmillan).

Hersoug, T. (1984), "Union wage responses to tax changes", *Oxford Economic Papers*, vol. 36.

Jacobsson, U (1976), "On the measurement of the degree of progression", *Journal of Public Economics*, vol. 5.

McDonald, I.M. and Solow, R.M. (1981), "Wage bargaining and employment", *American Economic Review*, vol. 71.

Pemberton, J. (1992), "Taxation and Wage Bargaining", *Economic Record*, forthcoming.

---

[2] For an analysis for this aspect see Pemberton (1992).

Economic Analysis & Policy   Vol.23 No.2, September 1993   **123**

CAN TAX CUTS INCREASE INVESTMENT IN A UNIONISED ECONOMY?*

John Creedy and Ian McDonald
University of Melbourne
Parkville Victoria 3052

This paper derives conditions for tax cuts to stimulate output without crowding out investment. In the model the level of output is constrained by an aggregate supply constraint. This constraint is based on the real wage demands of an insider-dominated trade union seeking to maximize its objective function. It is found that, in the model, tax cuts have a powerful supply-side effect and, for reasonable values of the parameters, will not force a crowding-out of investment. Of the tax cuts considered, raising the income tax threshold has a larger supply side effect than reducing the marginal tax rate.

I. INTRODUCTION

The idea of using tax cuts to moderate the wage demands of trade unions was put forward several times in the 1970s and 1980s. Faxén (1982) has called such a policy 'tax bribery'. However, a policy of tax cuts runs the risk of forcing a reduction in investment spending and thereby reducing future levels of consumption. For example, Weale *et al.* (1989, pp.14-5) have argued that "[I]t becomes all too easy, even with the most inflationary cost-push wage-setting institutions, to combine full employment with uninflated prices by means of lax fiscal policy ... Full employment is achieved by living on capital (eating up the seed corn or "selling the family silver") with adverse longer-term results". This risk is the motivation for this paper. If tax cuts can expand output without forcing a reduction in investment then they can be recommended. If, instead, they force a reduction in investment, then the economy is "living on capital" and the case for tax cuts is weakened.

The complexity arises because a tax cut has both a demand and a supply effect. In the early 1980s several papers showed how employment subsidies have both a demand and a supply effect; see Layard and Nickell (1980), Oswald (1979) and Sampson (1983). Those papers did not consider, however, the implications of their analysis for aggregate investment. Another literature concentrates on the effects on investment of trade union responses to a

---

*   This paper was presented in seminars at the Australian National University and the Universities of Melbourne, Monash, Tasmania and Western Australia. We are grateful to participants at these seminars for their comments.

reduction in personal income tax; see Corden and Dixon (1980), Corden (1981), Pitchford (1981), McDonald (1984) and, for a more elementary exposition, McDonald (1992, Chapter 14). However, these analyses did not use a model of trade union behaviour and assumed instead that real post-tax wages are held constant. The present paper has the advantage of examining investment while using a maximising model of the union.

The analysis is set up in a way which allows investment to be treated as a residual. The model assumes monetary policy is set at whatever level is necessary to ensure that the actual level of investment is equal to the residually-determined level. The precise setting of monetary policy would depend on the nature of the mechanism that determines investment, but the paper does not analyse this precise setting of monetary policy. It is simply assumed that the monetary authority can adjust the monetary base to induce a level of investment equal to the residually-determined level. The important point is that it is impossible for monetary policy to induce a level of investment in excess of the residually-determined level; the resources would not be available. The analysis concentrates on the largest of the possible outcomes for investment.

The effect of a tax change on investment cannot be predicted from qualitative analysis alone. The supply-side effect of the reduction in wage demands, resulting from the tax cut, will lead to an increase in employment and hence aggregate output. The demand-side effect is that aggregate demand will increase as a result of the increase in disposable incomes. If the increase in aggregate supply is large relative to the increase in aggregate demand, then investment will not be crowded out. The size of the supply-side effect depends on the product of three elasticities: the elasticity of output with respect to employment, the elasticity of employment with respect to wages, and the elasticity of wages with respect to taxation. The larger any of these elasticities the greater is the supply-side effect. The demand-side effect is influenced by the distribution of income between wages and profits and the pattern of consumer demand. A complete analysis therefore involves many elements. The present treatment is highly aggregative and abstracts from a number of complicating factors in order to clarify the essential features of the process.

The nature of the tax system and the way in which unions may respond to tax changes are examined in Section II. The model includes taxes on incomes and profits in addition to a consumption tax. The debate has been largely restricted to the case of a reduction in the marginal rate of income tax, but the present paper shows that a richer variety of policies can usefully be considered. In particular, it will be seen that raising the income tax threshold has a stronger supply-side effect than cutting the marginal rate of tax. Aggregate supply and demand are considered in Section III. Section IV solves the model and provides the substantive results of the paper. The effect on total tax revenue is then examined in Section V. First, however, it is useful to consider the basic analytics of tax cuts in terms of the simple IS-LM model.

1.1 The simple macroeconomics of tax cuts

FIGURE 1

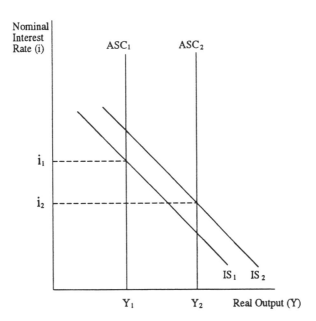

In Figure 1 two IS curves and two aggregate supply constraints are shown. The aggregate supply constraints show the maximum level of output firms are prepared to supply given the wage demands of trade unions. Suppose that initially the aggregate supply constraint is ASC_1 and the IS curve is IS_1, with the intersection at the point (i_1, Y_1). Assuming the LM curve passes through this point, the economy achieves output Y_1; to avoid cluttering the figure, the LM curve is not shown.

Suppose that taxation is cut in some way, leading to an increase in aggregate demand and a rightward shift in the IS curve to IS_2. If the tax cut also reduces the wage rate, then the aggregate supply constraint will also shift to the right as a result of the increased demand for labour; suppose that it shifts to ASC_2. With an appropriate monetary policy, the equilibrium point (i_2, Y_2) could be attained without causing excess demand and an upward pressure on the rate of inflation. The figure illustrates a situation in which the equilibrium level of output has increased and the equilibrium rate of interest has decreased, implying a higher level of investment. Thus Figure 1 shows a case where the cut in taxation does not crowd out investment, but instead allows investment to be increased. The condition required for the tax cut to increase investment is that the rightward shift in the aggregate supply constraint must exceed the rightward shift in the IS curve. The shift in the IS curve is lower, the lower is the marginal propensity to consume, while the shift in the supply constraint is larger, the larger are the three elasticities mentioned earlier. The remainder of the paper derives the precise conditions for such a favourable result to occur.

2.   THE TAX STRUCTURE AND WAGE DEMANDS

2.1 The tax structure

The model contains three types of tax; income tax, sales tax and profits tax. Let w and a respectively denote the pre-tax real wage and the tax threshold. The wage or income tax is imposed at a single marginal rate, t, on wages measured above the threshold; hence the tax paid per person is equal to $t(w - a)$. The analysis abstracts from the problems raised by the taxation of interest income arising from past savings. Any other approach would involve allowance for the workers' saving behaviour and for the possibility of owning shares in firms. This would significantly complicate the union's decision-making problem.

It is assumed that profits are taxed at a constant proportional rate, τ. The specification avoids the difficulty arising from a situation in which profits are taxed once at source and then again when, after being distributed, they are counted as the taxable income of individuals. The dichotomy between wage income and profits will be continued in Section III when consumption behaviour is examined, and in the following subsection.

A consumption tax is applied at the proportional rate, v, to the tax-exclusive price of goods. The tax-exclusive rate of v translates to a tax-inclusive rate of $v/(1 + v)$. The tax-exclusive price is normalised to unity, so that if the consumption tax is fully shifted to consumers, the price of output becomes $1 + v$. The union's wage demand depends on the relation between the post-tax real wage, y, and the pre-tax real wage, w. A pre-tax real wage of w is judged by the union to yield an after-tax income for its members of y, where:

$$y = \frac{at + w(1 - t)}{1 + v} \tag{1}$$

2.2 The insider-dominated union

The economy is assumed to consist of many identical firms, at each of which wages are determined by bargaining between a union and the firm. The union is dominated by a group of insiders, each member of which is risk-neutral, enjoys secure employment and seeks to maximize the post-tax real wage, y; see McDonald (1991). The assumption of risk-neutrality is not important for comparative statics, as shown in Creedy and McDonald (1991). If negotiations

Economic Analysis & Policy   Vol.23 No.2, September 1993   **127**

break-down and the union strikes, each member enjoys an alternative income of x.

The union is assumed not to include the firm's investment programme in its bargaining. Some papers, see Grout (1984) and Ulph and Ulph (1990), have shown, using partial equilibrium analysis of a single firm, that if the union cannot commit itself to a bargain made before the capital stock is installed then the firm will, given the market rate of interest, choose a capital stock that is less than the optimal level. By contrast the analysis of investment in this paper is at the macroeconomic level; the market rate of interest is endogenous and will be assumed to adjust, by the appropriate monetary policy, to induce the level of investment determined by the analysis. If the union were assumed to be able to commit itself to a bargain then the effect on the analysis would be to change the equilibrium rate of interest rather than the conditions derived for a tax cut not to crowd out investment.

The firm wishes to maximize profits, $R(n) - wn$, where $R(n)$ is the concave revenue function and n is employment at the firm. The outcome of bargaining is the wage and employment combination which maximizes:

$$[y-x]^{\phi/(1+\phi)} [R(n) - wn]^{1/(1+\phi)} \tag{2}$$

where ϕ measures the power of the union, and may take values between zero and infinity.

Choosing w and n to maximize (2) and using (1) to define y, gives a bargained wage:

$$w = \frac{x(1 + v) - at}{h(1 - t)} \tag{3}$$

where h depends on the union's power parameter ϕ and the elasticity of output with respect to employment, α, and is given by:

$$h = 1 + \phi \ (1\text{-}1/\alpha). \tag{4}$$

Given that $\alpha < 1$, it follows that $h < 1$. As can be seen from (3), as h approaches zero the wage becomes infinitely large, so that for sensible results h must be greater than zero. This constraint jointly places an upper limit on ϕ and a lower limit on α.

2.3 Tax changes and wage demands

Suppose the government decides to 'give' a particular absolute amount to each employed person in the form of a cut in personal income tax, based on the wage ruling before the policy change. This reduction may be achieved by reducing the marginal rate of income tax, t, or by raising the tax-free threshold,

a. For example, a cut in tax of $1 per person can be achieved by reducing the marginal rate by an absolute amount $1/(w-a)$ or by increasing the threshold by $1/t$. Differentiating (3) with respect to t and a respectively gives:

$$\frac{\partial w}{\partial t} = \frac{hw-a}{h(1-t)} \text{ and } \frac{\partial w}{\partial a} = \frac{-t}{h(1-t)} \tag{5}$$

Thus, an increase in the threshold that cuts tax per person by the same amount as a one percentage point reduction in t will reduce the wage demand by $(w-a)/\{h(1-t)\}$. This exceeds the reduction in the wage demand that would occur as a result of a one percentage point reduction in t, so it is necessary to consider separately the effects of reducing t and raising a.

Convert (5) into an elasticity, so that:

$$\zeta = \frac{t}{w}\frac{\partial w}{\partial t} = \frac{t}{1-t}\left(1 - \frac{a}{hw}\right) \tag{6}$$

As mentioned in the introduction, this elasticity is one component of the change in aggregate supply resulting from the change in t.

If instead of maximising the objective function (2) the union aims simply to keep y constant as t changes, then the elasticity of wages with respect to the marginal rate of income tax is given by:

$$\zeta = \frac{t}{1-t}\left(1 - \frac{a}{w}\right) \tag{7}$$

The only difference between (6) and (7) is the term h, which from (4) depends on α and ϕ. As α approaches 1 or ϕ approaches zero, h approaches unity and there is no difference between (6) and (7). Thus the previous literature is equivalent to the union model if either a = 0 (income tax is directly proportional) or if the demand for labour is perfectly elastic or if the union has no power.

A crucial assumption in considering the effect of tax changes is that the alternative income, x, is not affected by the tax change and is independent of the wage rate. For the insider-dominated unions examined here, McDonald (forthcoming) has argued that this assumption is reasonable. However, it is harder to justify for the other union models in which the unemployed (that is outsiders) receive an equal weighting with the employed insiders in the union's objective function.

3. AGGREGATE SUPPLY AND DEMAND

3.1 Aggregate supply

Assume that the value of α is constant, so that the good is produced under conditions described by the following aggregate Cobb-Douglas production function, for a given input of capital:

$$Y = AN^{\alpha} \tag{8}$$

where Y is the real (tax-exclusive) value of output and N is the aggregate level of employment. In insider-dominated bargains, each of the identical firms sets employment such that the wage equals the marginal revenue product of labour and so the aggregate level of employment is determined by:

$$N = (w/\alpha A)^{1/(\alpha-1)} \tag{9}$$

Substituting for N, from (9), into the production function (8) gives the aggregate supply in terms of the real wage as:

$$Y = A(w/\alpha A)^{\alpha/(\alpha-1)} \tag{10}$$

Furthermore, substituting the value of w determined by the insider-dominated bargains, given by (3), gives the aggregate supply constraint, as:

$$Y = A \left[\frac{x(1+v) - at}{\alpha Ah(1-t)} \right]^{\alpha/(\alpha-1)} \tag{11}$$

3.2 Aggregate demand

Consumption, like output, is measured in terms of its real tax-exclusive value. The approach allows for the possibility that the propensity to save from wage income differs from that of profits, but in each case consumption is proportional to real disposable income. If the marginal propensity to consume is γ, aggregate consumption from wage income is γNy.

Although unions are not directly concerned with unemployment, it is necessary to allow for unemployment in determining aggregate demand and tax revenue. If M is the total labour supply, and b the tax-exclusive level of unemployment benefits, then the aggregate value of benefits is b(M-N). It is reasonable to assume that all this income is spent on consumption goods.

In the insider-dominated union model, wage and employment outcomes are on the labour demand curve. Given these outcomes, price-taking firms and the Cobb-Douglas production function, the share of wages in aggregate output is

Vol.23 No.2, September 1993

equal to the elasticity of output with respect to labour input, α. Then real after-tax profits, π, are given by

$$\pi = Y(1 - \tau)(1 - \alpha)/(1 + v) \tag{12}$$

If the marginal and average propensity to consume out of profits is β, total consumption demand, C, is

$$C = \gamma Ny + \beta\pi + b(M-N) \tag{13}$$

Using $\alpha = wN/Y$ and equations (3), (4) and (12), (13) can be written as:

$$C = cY + bM \tag{14}$$

where $c = \dfrac{\alpha(1-t)}{1+v} \left\{ \gamma + \dfrac{h(\gamma at - b(1+v))}{x(1+v) - at} \right\} + \dfrac{\beta(1-\alpha)(1-\tau)}{(1+v)}$ $\tag{15}$

If the consumption functions contained constant terms, they would simply be added to (14) and would drop out when differentiating with respect to the tax parameters. Thus the assumption of proportionality does not affect the results of the paper.

4. TAX CHANGES AND INVESTMENT

4.1 The determination of investment

In equilibrium aggregate demand is equal to aggregate supply given by (11). Aggregate demand is C+I+G, with consumption determined by (14). If government spending is exogenous, this leaves the level of investment as a residual as discussed in the introduction; it is equal to the output remaining after consumption and government demand have been met. By combining (11) and (14) with the condition that aggregate demand is equal to aggregate supply, investment is given by

$$I = (1-c)Y - bM - G \tag{16}$$

As already suggested, this really determines the maximum level of investment. A contractionary monetary policy could reduce investment below the level given by (16), in which case output would be demand-determined because the aggregate supply constraint would not be binding. An expansionary monetary policy cannot increase investment above the level given by (16); any attempt to increase investment above this level will lead to inflation.

The effect on the maximum level of investment of a change in any of the tax parameters can be determined by the appropriate differentiation of (16).

This is the focus of the analysis in the remainder of the paper. The simplest tax parameter to deal with is the rate of profits tax, τ. Since aggregate supply is not affected by τ, but a reduction in the tax rate will stimulate demand, a cut in τ will necessarily lead to a reduction in investment. The extra demand for consumption can only be met by reducing the amount of the good that is devoted to investment. This result is confirmed from (16), since

$$\frac{\partial I}{\partial \tau} = \frac{(1-\alpha)\beta Y}{(1+v)} > 0 \tag{17}$$

Differentiation of (16) with respect to the other tax parameters is rather awkward so, as a preliminary exercise, the following subsection focusses on a special case.

4.2 A special case

Consider a special case in which income tax is proportional to income, so that $a = 0$; the income tax and profits tax rates are equal, so that $t = \tau$; and the average propensity to consume out of wages is equal to the average propensity to consume out of profits, so that $\gamma = \beta$. This is a useful reference point as these assumptions have usually been made in the earlier literature. Then (16) becomes:

$$I = (1-\tilde{c})Y - bM - G \tag{18}$$

$$\text{with } \tilde{c} = \frac{(1-t)}{(1+v)} \{\gamma - \alpha hb/x\} \tag{19}$$

Differentiation of (18) with respect to t yields, after some manipulation:

$$\frac{\partial I}{\partial t} = \frac{\tilde{c}-\alpha}{(1-t)(1-\alpha)} Y \tag{20}$$

A cut in the rate of income tax increases investment if the numerator on the right hand side of (20) is negative. This reduces to the following:

$$\frac{\partial I}{\partial t} < 0 \text{ if } \alpha > \frac{b\phi+\gamma x}{b(1+\phi)+(1+v)x/(1-t)} \tag{21}$$

This condition may be interpreted in terms of a minimum value of α and a maximum value of the response of consumption to a rise in pre-tax income. A high α implies a large response of aggregate supply to a tax cut, which reduces the pressure on resources available for investment following a tax cut. A small propensity to consume and large values of the income tax rate and the consumption tax rate imply a small increase in aggregate demand following a tax cut which, again, reduces the pressure on resources.

If (18) is differentiated with respect to the consumption tax rate, v, it can be found that precisely the same condition as that given in (21) also holds. This arises because when the threshold, a, is zero, both the income tax and the consumption tax are directly proportional. Furthermore, the simple assumption that the union seeks only to maintain the real value of the after-tax wage, makes no difference in this special case. The basic reason for this is given in Section II, where the elasticity, ζ, in formulae (6) and (7) was seen to be identical when a = 0.

Suppose now that the threshold is still zero, but that $t \neq \tau$ and $\gamma \neq \beta$. Substitution into (15) and (16) and differentiation with respect to t yields the result that a cut in the marginal rate of income tax increases investment if:

$$\alpha\,\beta(1-\tau) - \frac{\phi b(1-t)}{x\alpha} > (1-t)\,\gamma + (1-\tau)\beta - \frac{b(1+\phi)(1-t)}{x} - (1+v) \qquad (22)$$

Changing t now only influences demand through its effect on disposable wage income. In the previous case where $t=\tau$, changing t changed the rate of tax from both profits and wages. Because of this difference (22) does not reduce to (21) simply by substitution of $t=\tau$ and $\gamma=\beta$.

4.3 The general case

Returning to the general case, differentiation of (16) with respect to t yields, after some manipulation:

$$\frac{\partial I}{\partial t} = Y\left[\frac{\alpha h\{\gamma at-b(1+v)\}}{(1+v)\{x(1+v)-at\}} + \frac{\alpha\,\gamma}{1+v} - \frac{\alpha(1-t)ha(x\gamma-b)}{\{x(1+v)-at\}^2} - \frac{\alpha(1-c)\{x(1+v)-a\}}{(1-\alpha)(1-t)\{x(1+v)-at\}}\right]$$

$$(23)$$

For the tax cut to increase investment, the term in square brackets in (23) must be negative. In view of the awkwardness of this expression it is useful to examine some orders of magnitude involved.

A realistic value for the propensity to consume out of disposable labour income, γ, is 0.8. Because of the retention of profits by corporations, the propensity to consume out of post-tax profits, β, is much less; a value of 0.4 seems reasonable. A realistic value of b/a, is 1, so that a suitable value of x/a is 2. For ϕ, the union power parameter, the value of 0.5 was chosen. With ϕ equal to 0.5, the insider-dominated union model gives a reasonable value for the bargained wage, given reasonable values of the other parameters (using equation (3)). The critical value that α has to exceed for a cut in t to stimulate investment is inversely related to the three tax rates, t, τ and v. For example if v is 0.05 and t and τ are 0.125 then α has to exceed 0.4017 for $\partial I/\partial t < 0$.

Raising both t and τ to 0.2 reduces the critical minimum value of α to 0.3655. If the consumption tax rate v is raised to 0.1, then with t = τ = 0.2, the critical minimum value of α is 0.3438. The higher are the rates of tax, the smaller the demand effect of a tax cut and so the smaller the supply effect needs to be to allow an increase in investment. The condition on α is sensitive to x/a. Reducing unemployment benefits or raising the income tax threshold tends to raise the critical minimum value of α. For example, with t = τ = 0.2 and v = 0.05, setting b/a = 0.5 and x/a = 1 yields a critical minimum value of α of 0.7128.

The impact on the aggregate level of investment of a cut in the consumption tax rate can be determined by differentiating (16) with respect to v. This operation yields:

$$\frac{\partial I}{\partial v} = Y\left[\frac{\beta(1-\alpha)(1-\tau)}{(1+v)^2} + \frac{\alpha(1-t)h\{\gamma at - b(1+v)\}}{(1+v)^2\{x(1+v)-at\}} + \frac{\alpha(1-t)\gamma}{(1+v)^2} - \frac{\alpha(1-t)hat(b-\gamma x)}{(1+v)\{x(1+v)-at\}^2} - \frac{\alpha(1-c)x}{(1-\alpha)\{x(1+v)-at\}}\right]$$

(24)

Numerical analysis of (24) reveals that the critical minimum value that α must exceed for a cut in the consumption tax rate to allow investment to increase is fairly insensitive to the parameters of the tax system. With γ = 0.8, β = 0.4, b/a = 1, x/a = 2, t = τ = 0.125, v = 0.05 and φ = 0.5 the critical minimum value of α is 0.4101. Raising t and τ to 0.2 reduces α, as expected, but only to 0.3742. With t = τ = 0.2, a value of 0.1 for v reduces α to 0.3603. And reducing b/a to 0.5 and x/a to 1 yields a critical minimum value of α of 0.3541 (with t = τ = 0.2 and v = 0.05). In considering these values it should be borne in mind that the elasticity, α, also directly affects the distributive shares. Hence in practice the share of wages is higher than the critical minimum values obtained.

Finally for increases in the income tax threshold differentiate (16) with respect to a. This yields:

$$\frac{\partial I}{\partial a} = tY\left[\frac{\alpha(1-c)}{(1-\alpha)\{x(1+v)-at\}} - \frac{\alpha h(1-t)(x\gamma-b)}{\{x(1+v)-at\}^2}\right]$$

(25)

For each set of values used in the previous two cases, the expression in square brackets in (25) is positive for all values of α between zero and one. So for the reasonable values of the parameters assumed here, an increase in the income tax threshold always allows an increase in the aggregate level of investment.

An increase in the income tax threshold is more likely to allow an increase in the aggregate level of investment than would a reduction in the marginal rate of income tax or the rate of consumption tax because it has a greater effect on the bargained wage. The greater wage effect is a result of the differential impact on the bargained wage of changes in the average rate of tax compared with changes in the marginal rate of tax. As explained in Creedy and McDonald (1992, p.49), a reduction in the average rate of tax holding the marginal rate of tax constant, will, by making employment more attractive, reduce the bargained wage whilst a reduction in the marginal rate of tax holding the average rate of tax constant will, by making wage increases more attractive, increase the bargained wage. An increase in the income tax threshold reduces the average rate of tax but not the marginal rate whilst a decrease in t or v is a decrease in both the average rate of tax and the marginal rate of tax. Thus a decrease in t or v leads to two offsetting influences on the wage. The net downward effect on the bargained wage is small, and may even increase the bargained wage. A smaller reduction in the bargained wage implies a smaller increase in the level of aggregate supply and so less likelihood that investment may be allowed to increase.

5. TOTAL TAX REVENUE

5.1 Total net revenue

The total revenue raised from wages is the sum of income tax and the consumption tax, and is:

$$N\{t(w-a) + v\gamma y\}. \tag{26}$$

Revenue from profits is the sum of the profits tax and the tax on consumption out of profits and is:

$$\tau(Y - wN) + v\beta\pi \tag{27}$$

Appropriate substitution into (26) and (27), with much manipulation, gives total revenue from wages and profits, R, as:

$$R = Y\left[\frac{\alpha t(1+v) + \alpha v\gamma(1-t) + v\beta(1-\alpha)(1-\tau)}{(1+v)} + \frac{at\alpha h(1-t)}{x(1+v)-at}\left(\frac{v\gamma-(1+v)}{1+v}\right) + \tau(1-\alpha)\right] \tag{28}$$

The term in square brackets may thus be regarded as the overall proportional tax rate. To calculate the net revenue, unemployment benefits should be deducted from (28), remembering that benefits have been defined exclusive of taxation. Hence it is not necessary to allow for the consumption tax revenue arising from the expenditure of benefits. As (M-N) people receive unemployment benefits of b then net revenue, R_n, is

$$R_n = R - b(M - N) \tag{29}$$

Economic Analysis & Policy   Vol.23 No.2, September 1993   **135**

5.2 The special case

Consider again the special case obtained by assuming $a = 0$, $\gamma = \beta$ and $t = \tau$. Then net revenue is

$$R_n = Y\{t + v\gamma(1\text{-}t)/(1 + v)\} - b(M - N) \tag{30}$$

The term in curly brackets has a straightforward interpretation. It is the sum of the income tax rate and the effective consumption tax rate. The effective consumption tax rate is quite different from v because, for each dollar earned, only $\gamma(1 - t)$ is spent and the consumption tax rate applied to the tax inclusive price of goods is $v/(1 + v)$.

Assuming that Y is determined by the aggregate supply constraint, the impact on net revenue of a cut in the marginal rate of income tax is given by the derivative of (30). It is:

$$\frac{\partial R_n}{\partial t} = Y\left[1 - \frac{1}{(1-\alpha)}\left(\frac{v\gamma}{1+v} + \frac{\alpha t}{1-t}\right)\right] + b\frac{\partial N}{\partial t} \tag{31}$$

A sufficient condition for net revenue to increase with a cut in the tax rate is that the term in the square brackets must be negative. A **sufficient** condition for this to hold is $t > (1 - \alpha)$. So if t is greater than $(1 - \alpha)$ there is a 'Laffer' effect, whereby decreases in tax rates increase net tax revenue and *vice versa*.

The **necessary** condition for tax cuts to increase revenue can be derived from (31) by using (3) and (9) to determine $\partial N/\partial t$. Some manipulation yields:

$$\frac{\partial R_n}{\partial t} = Y\left[1 - \frac{1}{(1-\alpha)}\left(\frac{v\gamma}{(1+v)} + \frac{\alpha t}{(1-t)} + \frac{\alpha h(b/x)}{(1+v)}\right)\right] \tag{32}$$

If the term in square brackets is negative then tax cuts raise revenue.

A policy of cuts in **rates** of tax that simultaneously raises investment and net revenue, while also reducing inflation, is of course unequivocally favourable. However, suppose there is a conflict such that tax cuts will raise investment but reduce net revenue? It is certainly possible for such a conflict to arise. For example, for the set of values $\gamma = 0.8$, $\beta = 0.4$, $t = 0.125$, $v = 0.05$, $\alpha = 0.6$, $\phi = 0.5$ and $x/b = 2$, a cut in t will increase investment, from condition (23), and will reduce net revenue, by equation (32). In the event of a conflict between investment and net revenue it is necessary to consider explicitly the costs of increasing the debt in relation to the benefits of higher investment. This is outside the scope of the present paper.

6. CONCLUSIONS

This paper has examined a model in which tax cuts may have a powerful supply side effect. Indeed for reasonable values of the parameters the supply side effect is larger than the stimulus, given by the tax cuts, to aggregate demand, so that tax cuts would not force a crowding-out of investment. It was found that a policy of tax cuts is more likely to be effective in reducing wage demands and increasing investment if the tax cuts are achieved by raising the threshold, rather than by reducing the marginal rate of income tax or the rate of consumption tax. Thus, of the two ways of reducing taxes, the policy that increases the progressivity of the tax system has a greater supply side effect than a policy that reduces progressivity. This contrasts with the emphasis placed on the marginal rate of income tax in policy debates.

The analysis has used a highly aggregative approach, and it would be useful to extend the model in several ways. In particular, it would be of interest to extend the treatment to that of an open economy, rather than the closed economy considered here. In an open economy, to protect the future level of consumption the sum of the level of investment and the current account surplus (that is, national saving) has to be protected. One would expect that an extension of the analysis to an open economy, in which national saving is treated as a residual in the way developed here for the treatment of investment, would yield similar results. It would be useful to consider alternative forms of the production function, although this would considerably complicate the analysis. Finally, it should be noted that the supply-side effects examined here differ significantly from those relating to the labour supply incentive effects of taxation which have received considerably more emphasis in the literature.

REFERENCES

Corden, W.M. (1981), "Taxation, Real Wage Rigidity and Employment", *Economic Journal*, 91(2), pp.309-330.

Corden, W.M. and P.B. Dixon (1980), "A Tax-Wage Bargain in Australia: Is a Free Lunch Possible?", *Economic Record*, 56(154), pp.209-21.

Creedy, J. and I.M. McDonald (1991), "Models of Trade Union Behaviour: A Synthesis", *Economic Record*, 67, pp.346-359.

Creedy, J. and I.M. McDonald (1992), "Income Tax Changes and Trade Union Wage Demands", *Australian Economic Papers*, June, pp.47-57.

Faxén, K.-O. (1982), *Incomes Policy and Centralized Wage Formation,* Swedish Employers' Confederation (SAAF), Stockholm.

Grout, P.A. (1984), "Investment and Wages in the Absence of Legally Binding Labour Contracts: A Nash Bargaining Approach", *Econometrica*, 52, pp.449-60.

Layard, P.R.G. and S. Nickell (1980), "The Case for Subsidizing Extra Jobs", *Economic Journal,* 90, pp.51-73.

McDonald, I.M. (1984), "Anti-Stagflationary Tax Cuts and the Problem of Investment", *Economic Record,* 60(170), pp.284-93.

McDonald, I.M. (1991), "Insiders and Trade Union Wage Bargaining", Manchester School of Economic and Social Studies, LIX, pp. 395-407.

McDonald, I.M. (1992), *Macroeconomics,* Jacaranda-Wiley, Brisbane.

McDonald, I.M. (forthcoming), "Models of the Range of Equilibria" in R. Cross (ed.), *The Natural Rate Hypothesis Twenty-Five Years On,* Cambridge University Press, Cambridge.

Oswald, A.J. (1979), "Wages, Employment and Inflation in a Unionised Economy", mimeo.

Pitchford, J.D. (1981), "Taxation, Real Wage Rigidity and Employment: The Flexible Price Case", *Economic Journal,* 91, pp.716-20.

Sampson, A.A. (1983), "Employment Policy in a Model with a Rational Trade Union", *Economic Journal,* 93, pp.297-311.

Ulph, A. and D. Ulph (1990) "Union Bargaining: A Survey of Recent Work", in D. Sapsford and Z. Tzannatos (eds.), *Current Issues in Labour Economics,* Macmillan, Basingstoke, pp.86-125.

Weale, M., A. Blake, N. Christodoulakis, J. Meade and D. Vines (1989), *Macroeconomic Policy: Inflation, Wealth and the Exchange Rate,* Unwin Hyman, London.

Name index

Abraham, K.G. 154, 191
Ackland, R. 260
Addison, J.T. 183
Aitchison, A.B. 278
Akerlof, G. 148-9, 186
Alexander, A.J. 117, 154, 181, 190
Alvarado, J. 71
Andrews, M. 232
Ashenfelter, O. 249
Ashton, D. 188
Atkinson, A.B. 43
Atkinson, M.E. 87
Azariadis, C. 186

Baily, M. 186
Bartlett, M.S. 48
Becker, G.S. 112, 186
Bevan 43
Binmore, K. 249, 251-2
Bishop, R. 249
Blanchard, O.J. 250, 257, 263
Blandy, R.J. 139, 154, 157, 182
Blaug, M. 112
Booth, A. 249
Borjas, G.J. 112-13, 162, 167, 172, 174
Borland, J.I. 249, 260
Bourlakis, C.A.B. 188
Bray, M. 189
Brown, C. 219
Brown, J.A.C. 278
Brown, W. 182

Carmichael, H.L. 153
Carruth, A.A. 232, 250, 253, 257
Chatterjee, M. 263
Cheshire 20
Coase, R.H. 146
Cole, R.E. 115, 164-5, 191
Coleman, J.S. 25
Corcoran, M.E. 198
Corden, W.M. 249, 286
Courant, R. 30
Creedy, J. 20, 71, 87, 95, 103, 107, 126,
    155-6, 191, 196, 229, 232-3,
    237-8, 245, 258-9, 264-5, 275,
    288, 295
Cripps, T.F. 29, 48
Crockett, G.V. 155-7, 167, 182, 190

Daniel, W.W. 35
Deaton, D. 157, 182
Dex, S. 198
Dickens, W. 189
Dilnot, A. 219
Dixon, P.B. 249, 286
Doeringer, P.B. 113, 124, 138, 142-4,
    150-51, 153, 155, 164, 179, 181,
    188-9
Doob, J.L. 25
Dunlop, J.T. 142, 253

Edgeworth, F.Y. 232, 253, 260, 274, 276,
    282
Edwards, R. 152, 189
England, P. 181, 192

Farber, H.S. 250
Farkas, G. 181, 192
Faxén, K.O. 285
Fellner, W. 254
Felmlee, D. 202
Flemming, J.S. 43
Fligstein, N.D. 197
Freeman, R. 139

George, K. 182-3
Gordon, D. 186, 189
Granovetter, M. 185, 187
Greenhalgh, C.A. 215
Gregory, R.G. 191
Grossman, G. 249
Grout, P.A. 248, 289

Harris, J.E. 146-7
Hart, R.A. 3
Haskyns, M.D. 188
Henman, B. 127, 129-30
Hersoug, T. 237-8, 257-9, 263, 274-6
Hicks, J.R. 4
Hill, M.S. 197
Hudies, P.M. 201
Hunter, L.C. 114, 142, 164

Jack, A.B. 4
Jacobsson, U. 276-8
Jacoby, S. 181, 185, 187, 192
Jaques, E. 129, 197